The Moguls and the Dictators

The Moguls and the Dictators

Hollywood and the Coming of World War II

DAVID WELKY

The Johns Hopkins University Press

Baltimore

© 2008 The Johns Hopkins University Press
All rights reserved. Published 2008
Printed in the United States of America on acid-free paper
9 8 7 6 5 4 3 2 1

The Johns Hopkins University Press
2715 North Charles Street
Baltimore, Maryland 21218-4363
www.press.jhu.edu

Library of Congress Cataloging-in-Publication Data

Welky, David.
    The moguls and the dictators : Hollywood and the coming of World War II / David Welky.
        p. cm.
    Includes bibliographical references.
    ISBN-13: 978-0-8018-9044-4 (hbk. : alk. paper)
    ISBN-10: 0-8018-9044-6 (hbk. : alk. paper)
    1. World War, 1939–1945—Motion pictures and the war.   2. Motion pictures—Political
aspects—United States.   3. Politics in motion pictures.   I. Title.
    D743.23.W45 2008
    940.53'114—dc22   2008007847

A catalog record for this book is available from the British Library.

*Special discounts are available for bulk purchases of this book. For more information,
please contact Special Sales at 410-516-6936 or specialsales@press.jhu.edu.*

The Johns Hopkins University Press uses environmentally friendly book materials, including
recycled text paper that is composed of at least 30 percent post-consumer waste, whenever
possible. All of our book papers are acid-free, and our jackets and covers are printed on
paper with recycled content.

To MLB and RWB,
for teaching me who Tyrone Power is,
and
to JRW,
because one day I'll teach him

"If right thy words
I scan," replied that shade magnanimous,
"Thy soul is by vile fear assail'd, which oft
So overcasts a man, that he recoils
From noblest resolution, like a beast
At some false semblance in the twilight gloom."
—Dante, *Inferno,* Canto II

Hollywood may be full of phonies, mediocrities,
dictators and good men who have lost their way,
but there is something that draws you there that
you should not be ashamed of.
—Budd Schulberg, *What Makes Sammy Run?*

CONTENTS

ACKNOWLEDGMENTS

I USED TO LAUGH at the impossibly long scroll of names that follows a motion picture. "Nobody cares who catered the production," I insisted. Electricians, best boys, grips, boom operators, animal trainers— so much clutter, so much wasted screen time. Writing this book has changed my perspective. Although movies certainly have their headliners, I now accept that everyone listed in the credits contributed something unique to the final product. Similarly, many people shaped this book even though their names do not appear on the cover—or above the title, to continue the movie analogy. Their input aided me immeasurably throughout the research, writing, and editing process. My credit roll is far shorter than a typical feature film's—short enough that perhaps viewers will read to the end, a courtesy we rarely extend to the unfortunate foley artists and prop masters who populate the final few seconds of celluloid.

Archivists are the unsung heroes of a historian's life, and this project enabled me to work with some of the best. The staff of the National Archives' College Park facility deserves thanks from all of us for making the raw materials of our nation's history available to the public. More specifically, I thank that marvelous crew for steering me through the voluminous records of the Departments of Commerce, Justice, and State. Archivists at the Library of Congress and the Wisconsin State Historical Society library in Madison also treated me well. I am further indebted to Jim "Short" Buss, who perused the Wendell Willkie Papers at Indiana University's Lilly Library for me.

The Franklin D. Roosevelt Presidential Library in Hyde Park, New York, is a treasure. Designed by Roosevelt himself, the building complements the area's wonderful views of the Hudson River Valley, and the quality of its personnel is exemplary. Mark Renovitch and Alycia Vivona expertly shepherded me through the library's collections. The since-retired Dennis Bilger showed off his decades of experience at the Harry S. Truman Presidential Library in Independence, Missouri.

Anyone researching the history of Hollywood will eventually end up in Los Angeles, which boasts an array of excellent archives open to those willing to brave the city's traffic. Barbara Hall provided good advice and good humor at the Margaret Herrick Library in Beverly Hills. Randi Hokett at the Warner Bros. Archives kindly ignored my terrible cold and then went out of her way to mail me a copy of her work on the Warner brothers' crusade against Nazism. The staffs at UCLA's Department of Special Collections and at the university's Arts Library Special Collections showed off their extensive script holdings and oral histories. I am convinced that the study of American film history would collapse should Ned Comstock of USC's Cinematic Arts Library ever retire. I count myself among his many, many admirers.

The University of Central Arkansas supported this project with a University Research Council grant that funded most of my travel expenses. UCA's Department of History awarded me reassign time to assist my research and writing. Lisa Jernigan and the rest of UCA's interlibrary loan staff efficiently filled my numerous requests.

Research trips can get lonely in the long hours after an archive closes. Fortunately, a number of friends, some old and some new, brightened my time away from home. Bill Stephens delivered an outstanding tour of Hollywood landmarks that included up-close-and-personal views of the studios (and studio security). Chris and Karen Elzey fed a hungry traveler and took time from their busy schedules to reintroduce me to Washington, D.C. Jack Pointer and the Loayza family enlivened my stay in Madison. Also in Madison, Peter Miskell graciously demonstrated the dangers of consuming too many cheese curds after a dinner of buffalo wings.

Gregory Black, Lorien Foote, Elliott Gorn, Aram Goudsouzian, Noel Murray, Randy Roberts, and Mike Schaefer read part or all of the manuscript. I appreciate their helpful comments and suggestions. I owe an extra debt of gratitude to Randy Roberts for telling me about the Frank McNaughton papers. Thanks also to Bob Brugger, Linda Forlifer, Josh Tong, and everyone else at the Johns Hopkins University Press, as well as to Joe Abbott for his magnificent copyediting.

My family has been incredibly supportive through this entire process. My wife, Ali, stoically endured too many solitary evenings and too many one-sided conversations about obscure films. She also had the good grace not to smirk whenever I claimed to be watching a movie "for work." Our son, Jude, put up with daddy's absences, banged on the keyboard in daddy's room, and generally reminded daddy that movies aren't everything. My mother and stepfather, Mari Lou and Richard Bokern, deserve special mention for introducing me to Hollywood's Golden Age. Sometime around 1983 they took me to a screening of *Jesse James,* the first "old movie" I remember seeing, at the St. Louis Public Library. Viewing conditions were primitive—a room full of straight-backed chairs, a projector, and a screen on the wall—but something in that Technicolor extravaganza caught me and never let go. Life has since improved for fans of Hollywood's yesteryear. Today, anyone interested in a classic picture can usually find it on videocassette, DVD, or Turner Classic Movies. One thing, however, has not changed: I still chuckle whenever I imagine newspaper editor Rufus Cobb exhorting readers to seek out Jesse James's enemies and "shoot . . . them . . . down . . . like . . . dogs." Thanks, you two. This is all your fault.

The Moguls and the Dictators

Introduction

❧ ❧ ❧

IN DECEMBER 1933, fifteen years after the guns of the Great War fell silent, screenwriter Samuel Ornitz sent MGM producer David O. Selznick a treatment for a movie entitled "The Second World War." The story tracked the relationship of a father and son through a vaguely defined conflict set in the indeterminate future. Selznick loved the proposal. He envisioned a big-budget production starring Lionel Barrymore and Franchot Tone. The producer took Ornitz's work to MGM's president, Nicholas Schenck, who nixed the proposal. Schenck insisted that moviegoers would not pay to watch a movie about the next war when the last one remained so fresh in their minds. Selznick mentioned the proposal several times over the following months but failed to budge Schenck. "I'm afraid the Second World War idea is out," he lamented to Ornitz in 1935, "even though, as you know, I have felt for years that the subject, itself, has magnificent potentialities."[1]

The protracted discussion between Ornitz, Selznick, and Schenck reveals the various and often conflicting priorities motivating Hollywood. At the time an outspoken peace advocate, Ornitz hoped to expose audiences to the horrors of war. A gifted producer, Selznick wanted to oversee an important film that brought MGM both profits and prestige. As the head of a large corporation who was ultimately accountable to stockholders, Schenck approached "The Second World War" with a single thought: will this movie make money?

Negotiations between ideology, the desire for respectability, and financial responsibility were hardly unique to "The Second World War," and similar negotiations continue in present-day Hollywood. Rarely, however, has the precise balancing of these goals been so significant and meaningful as during the mid-1930s and early 1940s. These years saw a wave of overseas militarism that forced Americans to reevaluate their role in the world. As German and Italian armies marched across Europe and Japan consumed territory in Asia, actors, screenwriters, directors, and producers contemplated how—and whether—they and their industry should respond to totalitarianism. Many ideologues advocated a strong denunciation of fascism. Not only was it the right thing to do, they contended, but it would also solidify Hollywood's position as the world's preeminent cultural institution by spotlighting film's ability to shape public policy. Others disagreed with equal fervor, claiming that motion pictures should avoid hot-button issues that might destroy the popular goodwill Hollywood had worked so hard to accumulate and, more immediately, might imperil its financial stability by disaffecting moviegoers who disagreed with a film's perspective.

The film industry initially shied away from politicized statements about the dictators or the threat they posed to democratic governments. Moviemakers never liked Hitler, but neither did they want to actively oppose him. Their ambivalence is particularly poignant because most studio executives and many of their underlings were Jewish, a fact that both encouraged and discouraged their willingness to criticize the Nazis. Hollywood Jews lamented the fate of European Jews yet worried that voicing concern would unleash a wave of anti-Semitism at home. Their reticence began to fade in 1936, when studio employees—mostly actors and screenwriters—started criticizing totalitarianism and promoting democracy. Japan's 1937 invasion of China, which marked the opening of World War II in Asia, had little effect on the debate over the proper American response to autocracy. Germany's 1939 blitzkrieg of Poland and the onset of war in Europe, however, added immediacy to the conversation. Tentatively at first, then with growing if never-complete confidence, members of the picture industry joined the crusade against totalitarianism. This book seeks to explain how and why Hollywood shifted from public apathy regarding fascism and the threat of war to publicly condemning the dictators and calling for the United States to oppose them.

Many have argued that movie folk shunned war-related issues prior to December 7, 1941. Interventionist director Garson Kanin bluntly expressed his frustration in late November 1941, mere days before Pearl Harbor. "The producers, instead of producing too many pictures which might have propaganda, have in reality done nothing in the interest of national defense," he told a gathering of the National Board of Review. Producer Jesse L. Lasky Jr. concurred. "Patriotism hung like a dusty long rifle above the hearth," he noted in his memoirs. "We were always expert at closing our eyes and ears to reality, near or far." The journalist Otto Friedrich shared this interpretation. "So Hollywood began going to war," he wrote of the post–Pearl Harbor film business in *City of Nets*. Friedrich implies that prewar Hollywood ambled through the political wilderness, naively whistling in the dark while the world erupted in flames around it.[2]

Although no pre–Pearl Harbor movie called openly for the United States to enter the Asian or European conflict, Hollywood actually played an integral role in preparing the country for war. Representatives of the film industry raised awareness of fascism and renewed faith in democracy through personal appearances and radio broadcasts. Motion pictures laid out the issues at stake, offered hostile portraits of totalitarianism, disseminated President Franklin Roosevelt's hemispheric defense strategies, promoted his pro-British agenda, and familiarized audiences with the idea of participating in a crusade to spread American values around the world.

Historians have taken important strides toward correcting misleading impressions of the industry's work. They have, however, described Hollywood's response to war and the pre–Pearl Harbor war's impact on Hollywood in only fragmentary form. No one has connected these pieces into a comprehensive study. Authors have adequately explained Warner Bros.' battle against the Nazis.[3] The outstanding studies of wartime Hollywood briefly examine prewar affairs but understandably flatten out the era's rich debates, failing to fully explore movie folks' motivations to either act or forestall action. This elision, in turn, conceals the continuities and dislocations between the immediate prewar era and subsequent years.[4] Surveys of 1930s and early 1940s Hollywood focus either on the business of making and selling motion pictures or on the content of motion pictures themselves.[5] Neither approach adequately merges the picture industry's two major elements—its onscreen side and its corporate side—into a complete narrative of the war-related issues that divided Hollywood during these tumultuous years.

An awareness of Hollywood's actions during the late 1930s and early 1940s is essential to comprehending Americans' perceptions of the war, the dictators, and themselves as they moved into a post–Pearl Harbor reality. Hollywood mattered in this era, perhaps more than at any time before or since. Films had the "power to shape the social, moral, and cultural values of today—and of tomorrow," noted the industry insider Alexander Markey. The ideas movies promoted gained immediate cultural currency. Hollywood profoundly influenced the worldview of a generation possessing far fewer connections to the outside world than exist today. "We really have two educational systems in America," observed a 1937 *Christian Century* article, "the public school system and the movies."[6]

Hollywood, at least the Hollywood audiences saw onscreen, was a relative latecomer to antifascism. The first explicitly anti-Nazi picture, *Confessions of a Nazi Spy,* appeared in 1939, long after other mass-culture outlets had begun to question Hitlerism, Italian Fascism, and Japanese militarism. Hollywood did not fully commit to overt antifascism—which is not to say interventionism—until mid-1940. Major studios thrived on a steady stream of optimistic, noncontroversial films. Moving them in new directions was an excruciatingly slow process, akin to turning around an aircraft carrier. The people whom historian Michael Denning identifies as members of the "Cultural Front"—liberal craftsmen and intellectuals, often immigrants or children of immigrants—took the lead in plunging Hollywood into political activism. Screenwriters, actors, and directors charted the film capital's new course years before movie moguls—producers and other major executives—got around to confirming the order.[7]

Although its antifascist perspective paralleled broader trends in mass culture, the motion picture's entry into deliberations over the United States' role in World War II aroused an enormous amount of attention. Hollywood became a flashpoint in the bitter dispute between interventionist and isolationist groups, the center of a national debate about the role of mass culture in a democracy, the position of Jews and other ethnic groups in American life, and the meaning of Americanism. The September 1941 U.S. Senate investigation of alleged Hollywood war propaganda marked the culmination of this conversation and, in the end, reinforced the movie business's standing as the nation's most important culture-making industry.

It is impossible to quantify Hollywood's influence on American thought, to say that a certain number of people changed or reconfirmed their positions because of this movie or that speech. That Hollywood had an impact, however, is undeniable. Americans never yearned for a fight. Polls taken in 1936 showed large majorities favoring the abolition of weapon sales for private profit and supporting a national referendum in advance of any congressional vote for war. A survey taken just before Hitler's September 1939 invasion of Poland revealed that three-quarters of Americans believed their country could avoid playing an active role in a general European conflict. When asked four weeks after the blitzkrieg on Poland, 95 percent opposed declaring war on Germany.[8]

The public eventually came to view the war's outcome as crucial to the United States' long-term well-being. More than two-thirds of respondents to a late-1940 poll believed the nation's safety depended on a British victory over the dictators. A similar proportion considered it more important to defeat Germany than to remain neutral. A majority of those polled in late November 1941 thought war with Japan was imminent. Americans still opposed war, yet grew more comfortable with it, and saw a particular result as essential to their interests. Hollywood bears some responsibility for the shift in perspective.[9]

Hollywood, however, could hardly assume exclusive credit for these movements in public opinion. The Roosevelt administration's aggressive defense policies and vocal antifascism certainly contributed, as did a prodemocracy campaign spanning the mass-culture spectrum. Hitler's bold thrusts across Europe aroused fear of global domination and convinced millions that their future depended on the Nazis' downfall. But we should not minimize the movie community's role in preparing America to fight. Although they never spoke with a single voice, industry members illuminated war-related issues more vividly than any political speech or newspaper story. Hollywood generally promoted internationalism and a hemispheric defense system. It backed a pro-British foreign policy that manifested itself in lend-lease, the Destroyers-for-Bases deal, and the widely held belief that the United States must help Great Britain defeat Germany. It ridiculed the Nazis, depicted the horrors of Hitlerism, and warned that the dictator had designs on the United States. It encouraged audiences to cherish their heritage, to identify with a common national identity, and to spread democracy and freedom around the globe. It introduced tens of millions of movie fans to the military, humanizing what was for most an unfamiliar institution and acquainting audiences with the idea of joining the armed forces. Finally, it seconded President Roosevelt's calls for a stronger national defense and a renewed commitment to defending American principles and interests.

It is easy to imagine Hollywood as confident and secure during these years. American films accounted for 80 percent of the world's screen time. Domestic attendance stood at record levels; 80 million Americans visited movie theaters every week. The studio system churned out some of the most critically lauded movies ever made. *Citizen Kane, Fantasia, Gone with the Wind, The Grapes of Wrath, Mr. Smith Goes to Washington, Stagecoach,* and *The Wizard of Oz* all appeared within this brief moment. Such outward success, however, masked deep insecurities over the industry's direction. The wars in Asia and, especially, Europe endangered Hollywood's economic well-being, jeopardized its warm relationship with the federal government, altered audience tastes, and undermined the fractious movie community's fragile sense of trade unity.[10]

As totalitarianism expanded its reach, many critics, moviegoers, and government officials worried that studios might embark on a cycle of hate-filled, hyperpatriotic pictures. Others lamented movie producers' apparent lack of interest in putting the war, particularly the war in Europe, onscreen. These conflicting voices caught studios on the horns of a dilemma. "If Hollywood produces a picture dealing with the war, it is accused of 'war-mongering,'" wrote Leo C. Rosten in 1941. "If Hollywood doesn't, it is accused of feeding pap to the public and putting profit above the national welfare." The struggle to satisfy competing impulses—seeking relevance through current-events pictures versus making money with safe entertainment—did much to govern the film community's conduct during these years.[11]

Today Americans are accustomed to Hollywood's involvement in political causes. Sean Penn, Tim Robbins, Susan Sarandon, and other stars regularly speak out about war and other sensitive subjects. Their comments rarely elicit much comment. Although right-wing critics still assail "Hanoi Jane" Fonda decades after the Vietnam War, most people no longer ask whether actors have the right to an opinion or express outrage when an actor's position does not align with their own. Celebrities are *supposed* to have opinions now. The world salutes rock singer Bono's devotion to Africa and Angelina Jolie's appeals on behalf of war refugees. It criticizes Michael Jordan and Tiger Woods for refusing to address African American issues.

This notion of celebrities as advocates for controversial issues did not really exist in the early 1930s, at least not in Hollywood. Movie stars were supposed to make movies and live glamorous lives. Producers were supposed to run their companies in the best interests of their shareholders. Screenwriters were supposed to write and otherwise remain silent. Challenging these conceptions took courage. In publicly opposing totalitarianism, writers, directors, actors, and producers defied widely held understandings of Hollywood's purpose. Politicians, civic groups, and even many within the industry believed movies should merely fulfill the public's desire for entertainment. For them, education did not mix with enlightenment.

Critics of Hollywood activism often cited the industry's actions during the Great War as evidence of the dangers of propagandizing. Major studios had promoted Woodrow Wilson's drive for 100 percent Americanism and endorsed his assertion that the war would make the world safe for democracy. Charlie Chaplin, Douglas Fairbanks Sr., and Mary Pickford sold Liberty Bonds. Producers issued such memorable propaganda efforts as *To Hell with the Kaiser* (1918) and *The Beast of Berlin* (1918). These pictures demonized Germans as militaristic baby killers, defilers of pure womanhood, and brutish louts who thirsted to spread autocracy around the globe. As Nicholas Schenck reminded Ornitz and Selznick, most Depression-era Americans saw the Great War as a tragic mistake. Hollywood's patriotic contributions to that conflict were embarrassing twenty years later. Industry leaders disassociated themselves from the warmongering of 1918, and such caution tempered their willingness to denounce the dictators.

✿ ✿ ✿

While largely adhering to a chronological narrative, this book traces four main themes, each crucial to understanding Hollywood's contributions to anti-isolationism and its shift from viewing dictatorial nations primarily as markets to seeing them as dangerous adversaries. The first of these themes is Hollywood's standing with the federal government. Movie moguls and their employees had strong ties to the Roosevelt administration. Many in the film community revered the president and wanted to further his international agenda. Roosevelt accepted the industry's backing. At the same time, his economic agenda put Hollywood in the crosshairs of the Justice Department's campaign to stamp out monopolies. The department's 1938 antitrust suit against major studios threatened Hollywood's fiscal foundations. Rather than focusing on the law, however, the case became inextricably bound up in overseas affairs. Government lawyers eventually consented to a benevolent settlement that left the studio system largely intact, a decision based largely on Roosevelt's desire to keep Hollywood's propaganda power on his side.

The second major theme is the war's impact on Hollywood's relationship with foreign markets. American studios relied on overseas theaters for around half of their total earnings. The conflict devastated overseas revenues. Ultranationalistic regimes in Germany, Italy, and Japan slapped crippling, profit-killing regulations on American pictures. More moderate governments in Great Britain and Latin America also imposed stringent financial guidelines in the hopes of strengthening their own economies, reducing the United States' cultural influence, or winning favor from Axis nations. Axis conquests of Belgium, France, the Netherlands, and other countries put those markets beyond Hollywood's reach, further diminishing foreign income.

The loss of European revenues forced studios to shore up their remaining markets. Hollywood bolstered ties to its most important foreign outlet, Great Britain, while seeking closer bonds with Latin American nations. American films incorporated subjects and characters moviemakers believed would win favor with overseas audiences. Studios constantly modified their onscreen appeals to these regions, fine-tuning their releases in response to evolving global conditions. At the same time, Hollywood advanced Roosevelt's efforts to link the United States, Latin America, and Great Britain into an unbreakable antifascist alliance. Movie moguls had many reasons for acting as they did, some practical and some noble. They wanted to make money, stay in the Roosevelt administration's good graces, and spread what they saw as American ideals during a time of international peril.

A third prominent theme is the development of antifascist voices and organizations within the film community. Liberal screenwriters, actors, directors, and producers created the industry's first avowedly anti-Hitler voice, the Hollywood Anti-Nazi League (HANL), in 1936. HANL and other groups elevated Hollywood's political consciousness over the next few years, forcing studio personnel to confront their feelings about totalitarianism. Prominent Axis-bashers, including Melvyn Douglas, Douglas Fairbanks Jr., and Edward G. Robinson, raised public awareness of the threat dictatorship posed to the United States. Their activism outraged everyone who wanted movie stars to focus on entertainment rather than politicking. Hollywood antifascism also exposed the industry's vulnerabilities, opening moviemakers to attacks from anti-interventionists, anti-Semites, and anticommunists who believed that Hollywood leftists hoped to lure the United States into another overseas conflict.

Fourth, and finally, a complete appreciation of the American film business's reaction to fascism demands an examination of the movies it released during the mid-1930s and early 1940s. In these films we see overt expressions of studios' beliefs, values, and priorities. Much of Hollywood's antifascism occurred outside of the public eye. Nevertheless, most Americans, as well as moviegoers elsewhere, experienced Hollywood primarily through their local theater. Studio executives based production schedules on a series of decisions. They balanced the ideological goals of screenwriters, directors, actors, and producers with the need to draw audiences and achieve financial objectives—although these two sets of interests were not always mutually exclusive. Motion pictures did not follow a straight path from political apathy to antifascism and prodemocracy. Studios continuously recalibrated their pictures' subject matter, zigging and zagging in their efforts to anticipate audience tastes. It took time to determine whether viewers would tolerate military-themed pictures, anti-Nazi pictures, prodemocracy pictures, or boisterously patriotic pictures.

Audience interest was not the only factor influencing Hollywood's output. Studios operated under a self-imposed censorship system that limited their ability to tackle contemporary topics. Will Hays, the powerful president of the Motion Picture Producers and Distributors of America (MPPDA), took the lead in imposing an industry-wide production code in 1934 by appointing a former publicity man, Joseph Breen, to head a new MPPDA subagency, the Production Code Administration (PCA). MPPDA members, which included all of the major studios, could not distribute movies without the PCA's seal of approval. Studios therefore consulted the agency at every stage of the filmmaking process. Joseph

Breen, not the editor, the director, or the producer, approved the final cut. The Production Code profoundly affected Hollywood's approach to events in Europe and Asia. Its regulations forbade scenes of "low, disgusting, [and] unpleasant" topics. Its "National Feelings" clause required studios to offer "consideration and respectful treatment" to "the just rights, history, and feelings of any nation." In Breen's eyes, even despicable regimes deserved consideration and respect. The code's restrictions on depictions of violence made it difficult to produce an honest movie about war. Strong-minded producers, directors, and actors often clashed with Breen, who doggedly opposed the insertion of war-related issues into a medium he believed should be used primarily for entertainment purposes.[12]

In exploring these four themes, this account of the film industry's swing from studied indifference toward the menace of totalitarianism to open antifascism and, to an extent, interventionism is a multilayered narrative that travels along several tracks. Lines connect two primary hubs in the United States: Hollywood and Washington, D.C. Other lines radiate from those stations to link seats of power around the world— New York City, Berlin, London, Rome, Tokyo. Still other spurs run south, terminating in such places as Buenos Aires, Lima, and Mexico City. Decisions made on four continents, choices made by both the world's most powerful men and the most impoverished theatergoer, affected the film industry's actions in the years before Pearl Harbor. This story follows intersecting yet independent plotlines set against the first years of the most violent period of conflict in human history. It touches on foreign policy, domestic politics, religion, economics, business ideologies, military affairs, and courtroom drama.

Studio-era Hollywood typically simplified tangled plots, stripping away anything that interfered with its preferred, linear narrative structure. To do likewise in this case would remove critical pillars of a tale with many intertwined elements. This may not be Hollywood's kind of story, but it is nevertheless to Hollywood that we must go first.

CHAPTER ONE

A Wonderful Place

~ ~ ~

Hollywood is a wonderful place." The title of *Life*'s 1937 examination of the film community summed up Americans' vision of a town that played an enormous role in their lives. Hollywood was more than a moviemaking center. It was a magical city, Oz on the West Coast. "To the youth and beauty of the nation," *Life* gushed, "Hollywood is an unparalleled Land of Opportunity. To foreigners it is America's tourist attraction No. 1. To the shopgirl in Keokuk, the peasant in Siberia and the coolie in Singapore, it is a place more real and familiar than the great cities of the world."[1]

In a sense Hollywood was one of the world's great cities. Its output affected how people dressed, looked, thought, and spoke. Movies offered advice for living, strategies for coping with hard times, and frameworks for understanding domestic and international issues. This cultural center was also a media center. The movie capital generated more news stories than any other city in the United States except Washington, D.C., and New York. Even the Vatican stationed a correspondent there. Efficient studio publicity machines groomed Hollywood personalities into familiar yet ultimately unknowable icons, larger-than-life heroes and heroines who were both ubiquitous and untouchable. Americans followed their favorite stars through feature films, the daily paper, radio shows, fan magazines, and newsreels.[2]

The public envisioned Hollywood as "a sort of Venice without canals, full of glittering conveyances, dazzling maidens, and men like gods." The film community included both dazzling maidens and men of godlike appearance. The rest of Hollywood's image was a myth, or at least a glamorized version of reality. "Hollywood," as most thought of it, was no more real than Shangri-La or Xanadu. Movie studios were businesses above all else. Employing almost three hundred thousand people and representing a $2 billion investment, they existed to make money. Most film executives viewed the celluloid dreams they sold as products, not artistic statements. Hollywood was "an assembly-line operation," one screenwriter remembered. The studio system operated "very much like a sausage factory."[3]

Hollywood was, of course, a real place, a section of Los Angeles between the old central city to its southeast and the rising communities of Culver City and Beverly Hills to its west. It was a center for film folk but not as most movie fans envisioned. Hollywood proper was more of a social than a commercial hub. The two-mile-long district surrounding Hollywood Boulevard and the next major street to the south, Sunset Boulevard, teemed with gathering places for actors, directors, and screenwriters. The famous Brown Derby restaurant, located at the corner of Hollywood and Vine, marked the zone's eastern terminus. Musso & Frank Grill, Stanley Rose's Bookstore, and Pickwick Bookshop were all easy strolls to the west. Beyond them stood Sid Grauman's magnificent Chinese Theatre. Popular eatery Villa Nova and the Trocadero Café marked the western edge of Hollywood's communal scene. Hotels of varying quality dotted this stretch. The run-down Pa-Va-Sed served as home to struggling screenwriter Nathanael West, best known for his Hollywood novel *The Day of the Locust*. Sometime-screenwriter F. Scott Fitzgerald lived down the road in the fabulous Garden of Allah hotel and apartment complex. From his rooms he gathered material for his own Hollywood novel, *The Last Tycoon,* while doing largely uncredited rewrite work and drinking his way to premature death.

Hollywood was not a place so much as an idea, a blanket term used both then and now. It would take a trip of some twenty miles, as the crow flies, to visit all the major movie companies, which arranged themselves in a clockwise arc, with Hollywood Boulevard serving more as an equator than a focal point. Universal, the oldest major, lay a few miles north of Hollywood at about twelve o'clock. Off to the northeast in Burbank, Warner Bros. stood just shy of one o'clock. Coming down the hills and crossing Sunset Boulevard, one found Columbia, Paramount, and RKO bunched near three o'clock. Located in Culver City, at about seven on the dial, Metro-Goldwyn-Mayer (MGM) was the southernmost studio. A few miles to the northwest at eight o'clock, Twentieth Century–Fox marked the end of the arc. The growing town of Beverly Hills lay like a high-class demilitarized zone between it and Universal at the top of the dial.

Half of "Hollywood" remained unseen even after this trip. Much of the industry's power resided in the studios' New York City offices. More than geographical distance separated the two centers, however. East Coast officials procured crucial loans from investment capitalists and focused on ensuring that studio accountants wrote in black ink rather than red. West Coast executives shot movies and fought to extract money from corporate headquarters. New York branches complained that Los Angeles spent extravagantly. Los Angeles branches complained that New York denied them needed funds. Constant quarreling fed familial and corporate discord. Harry Warner ruled Warner Bros. in New York, his despised brother Jack in Burbank. Harry Cohn monitored Columbia's productions in Hollywood while *his* despised brother Jack ran its New York bureau. MGM's Louis B. Mayer referred to Nick Schenck, his New York–based boss, as "Nick Skunk."[4]

A similar split, although one with less animosity, marked the Motion Picture Producers and Distributors of America (MPPDA), the industry's powerful trade organization. The MPPDA represented major studios' political and economic interests in Washington, D.C., and acted as Hollywood's voice with civic, social, and educational groups interested in cinematic affairs. Former Republican functionary Will Hays oversaw the MPPDA's public-relations duties from his New York facilities. He left Joseph Breen in Los Angeles to run the MPPDA's censorship agency, the Production Code Administration (PCA).

Carved from a former orange grove, Hollywood remained in the 1930s a remote outpost on the literal edge of civilization. It was, one screenwriter declared, "a warm Siberia." Savvy real-estate developers still acquired huge parcels of land for a song. Los Angeles newspapers carried little international news. National magazines reached the city days after delivery on the East Coast. Radio stations did not carry some national programs. Unlike the densely packed northeast, Los Angeles was far from other large urban areas. San Diego, more than a hundred miles to the south, had fewer than 150,000 residents. Visits to New York required either a long, expensive train ride on the Super Chief or a string of short flights.[5]

Geographical isolation contributed to a sense of psychological isolation. With 1.2 million residents in 1930, Los Angeles was a large, rapidly growing metropolis. Some 80 percent of its people, however, came from beyond California's borders. A feeling of rootlessness pervaded the city. Everyone was from somewhere else. Many yearned for a sense of belonging. A spirit of transience caused some to seek kinship in religious cults or fringe political movements. Others found meaning in the minutiae of their filmmaking colleagues' everyday lives. "Hollywood was a village," David Niven remembered, "and the studios were the families. Everyone knew everyone else's business, weaknesses, kinky leanings, and good points."[6]

Los Angeles was practically a one-industry town. "As far as I know," laughed actor George Arliss, "nothing is ever made here except moving pictures. Everything has been brought in from some other part of the United States, even the trees." Kit Sargent—the cynical screenwriter from Budd Schulberg's Hollywood exposé *What Makes Sammy Run?*— captured the film community's insular nature. "One of the things which distinguished the old Brown Derby on Wilshire was the way guests at one end of the room could hear distinctly every word being said at the other, because of the trick acoustics of the dome-shaped ceiling," she recalled. "It always seemed as if all Hollywood must be covered by one of those Derby ceilings too." Movie folk discussed studio politics, last night's premiere, whose screenplays were in production, who was cheating on whom, who was on the way up, who was on the way down, and who was washed up. Political or social issues rarely surfaced at dinner parties. Immediate surroundings held the community's focus. As *Life* stated, "the people of Hollywood live in a goldfish bowl, ever conscious that the world is staring at them. But they do not talk about the outside world."[7]

Petty squabbles pervaded Hollywood. Edward G. Robinson likened the industry to the Holy Roman Empire. Hollywood consisted of only eight principalities—Columbia, MGM, Paramount, RKO, Twentieth Century–Fox, United Artists, Universal, and Warner Bros.—as opposed to the hundreds in the fractious old empire. In both cases, however, "feudal lord[s] in battle with each other and yet bound together by their common interest" dominated each entity. Studio heads who had clawed their way to the top zealously defended their positions like the nouveau riche they were. Most of them were Jews of eastern European descent whose outsider status made them sensitive to insults and protective of their place in Hollywood's hierarchy. Minor disputes escalated into feuds that dragged on long after the combatants had forgotten the reason for their original disagreement.[8]

Movie moguls viewed the outside world through selfish eyes and vague political philosophies. They embodied the rags-to-riches dream and expected others to do the same. Hollywood executives instinctively embraced the Republican Party during the 1920s. They admired Warren Harding's and Calvin Coolidge's individualist rhetoric and hands-off approach to business. As representatives of a new and sometimes-controversial industry, big producers recognized the wisdom of aligning with those in power. Even so, they generally had only a rudimentary understanding of civics. Relationships with public officials were like trophies; possessing them became signs of social acceptance. Movie bosses generally left governmental affairs in MPPDA president Will Hays's capable hands, limiting their political awareness to federal censorship of films, amusement taxes, and other immediately relevant issues. The exception was MGM's Louis B. Mayer, a deeply conservative man whose attachment to the Republican Party transcended economic interest. Unlike other studio executives, who rarely considered such matters, he saw the GOP as the guarantor of order and social stability. He played a small role in Coolidge's 1924 campaign and plotted electoral strategy with Herbert Hoover in 1928. Hoover may have offered him the ambassadorship to Turkey in recognition of his labors.[9]

Such cultivation paid off, as the movie business had plenty of friends in 1920s-era Washington. Convinced that foreign acceptance of Hollywood fare opened the door to other American products, the Commerce Department provided studios with information on worldwide business conditions and promoted free access for American movies in overseas markets. The State Department backed Hollywood in negotiations with foreign governments and applied pressure whenever hostile leaders threatened the industry with discriminatory legislation.[10]

The Great Depression jarred Hollywood's political moorings. The financial meltdown crushed a business already reeling from the astronomical expense of converting to sound production. Weekly attendance plummeted from 110 million in 1930 to 60 million in 1932.[11] Executives slashed ticket prices in an unsuccessful effort to bring back crowds. Of the eight major studios, only MGM and Columbia turned a profit every year of the 1930s. Declining profits devastated stock prices. Shares in

Fox Film Corporation plunged from a 1928 peak of 119 5/8 to a 1933 low of 3/4. RKO's stock sagged from 51 1/2 to 1 over that same period. RKO and Paramount went into receivership. Fox submitted to a merger with upstart Twentieth Century Pictures in 1935.[12]

Louis B. Mayer held to the Republican ticket in 1932. He stage-managed pro-Hoover demonstrations at the party's listless Chicago convention, served as chairman of the Republican State Central Committee, and rounded up celebrities such as Wallace Beery and Ethel Barrymore to shill for the president's reelection. Other studio heads either kept silent or switched allegiances. Their desertion of the Republican Party did not result from an ideological epiphany or a newfound concern for the down-trodden, however. They hoped the Democratic presidential candidate, New York governor Franklin Roosevelt, could restore favorable eco-nomic conditions and lift the country out of chaos. Warner Bros. execu-tive and former Coolidge adherent Harry Warner led the charge to the Roosevelt standard. He wired the governor an offer of support during the Democratic convention, then bludgeoned his younger brother Jack into backing the nominee. Jack hesitated to throw his money behind the challenger but persuaded Jesse Lasky, Winfield Sheehan, Merian C. Cooper, and other Hollywood executives to work for the campaign. Jack also helped organize an enormous pro-FDR rally at the Los Angeles Coliseum. He later claimed that 175,000 people piled into the stadium to cheer the candidate and see the stars he summoned to the event.[13]

Roosevelt's election delighted most studio bosses. Darryl F. Zanuck, a registered Republican and future head of Twentieth Century–Fox, said the new president "spoke my language." The always garrulous Jack Warner recounted his 1933 fishing trip with FDR to anyone willing to listen. Roosevelt took him into his confidence, he said, pumped him for infor-mation about Hollywood, and offered him an ambassadorship. Warner was another in a long line of people who saw more in the new president's charm and ambiguous promises than was really there. Universal's Carl Laemmle told FDR that his newsreel department would project "any message you may care to deliver." Will Hays also tried to make a good first impression. He delayed the release of *Gabriel over the White House* (1933), MGM's controversial drama about a president who assumes dic-tatorial powers, until the administration approved it. The MPPDA head's fawning correspondence kept the White House mailroom humming for years to come. His missives—which almost inevitably contained requests for help on some film-related issue—jammed a file presidential secretaries labeled "Boy Scout."[14]

Roosevelt's charisma wooed Hollywood. His policies clinched the deal. Although studio heads had an even slighter grip on economic theory than the president, their account books told them his programs worked. Hollywood rose on the New Deal's tide. *Film Daily Year Book* reported that 1933 "no doubt marked the turning point of the motion picture business from the downward trend of the depression years to the road back to economic stability and prosperity." Profits jumped as the economy improved. Loew's, MGM's parent company, saw its income swell from $4 million in 1933 to almost $7.5 million in 1934. Universal went from a $1 million loss to a $238,000 profit during the same period.[15]

Moviemakers saw no reason to oppose the popular president, who carefully preserved the cozy Washington-Hollywood relationship that existed under his Republican predecessors. Even Mayer nodded toward the New Deal, informing one Roosevelt confidant that MGM "had been used better by this Administration than by the Republicans." Mayer was most likely dissembling, but he reinforced his approval with a series of sycophantic letters that displayed an almost desperate desire to win FDR's favor. More concretely, the erstwhile Hoover operative stayed clear of Republican Alf Landon's 1936 bid for the White House.[16]

Roosevelt had long adored movies. He wrote a screenplay about the life of John Paul Jones while recovering from polio in 1923. Famous Players–Lasky unfortunately lost the manuscript. FDR remained a fan through his presidential years. Several times a week, he joined the first lady, houseguests, White House ushers, butlers, and maids for informal viewings in a second-floor room next to his study. Roosevelt also tucked a tiny screening room under a staircase in his Hyde Park estate. He preferred Disney cartoons, newsreels, and light comedies, which he frequently interrupted with wisecracks.[17]

The new administration boasted numerous links to the film industry. Presidential secretaries Stephen Early and Marvin McIntyre had backgrounds in newsreels. Securities and Exchange Commission head Joseph Kennedy was a former producer. The president's son James joined Goldwyn Studios in 1940. John Boettiger, who became Roosevelt's son-in-law in 1935, formerly worked for Hays in the MPPDA. Hays hired publicity man Gabe Yorke at the request of Postmaster General (and politico extraordinaire) Jim Farley. Frank Walker, executive secretary of the President's Executive Council and Farley's successor as postmaster general, once managed movie theaters.[18]

For all his admiration of Hollywood productions, the president understood that movie executives wanted his ear and craved his approval. He accordingly dished out small favors while keeping producers at arm's length. Roosevelt knew a phone call, a personal note, or an autographed photo made them happy, like dogs that get scratched behind the ears. FDR kept them close but never so close as to owe them any favors. This basic hierarchy remained intact even as the administration's relationship with major studios intensified during the late 1930s and early 1940s. Roosevelt almost always parried movie executives' pleas for an overt alliance, listening to what Hollywood had to say but rarely consenting to requests for assistance or access. It became increasingly clear as the 1930s wore on that Hollywood and Washington needed each other. Although their association was symbiotic, Roosevelt kept the reins firmly in his hands. His leadership, and that of his administration, proved crucial as the film community navigated the most profound overseas crisis of its relatively brief history.

✿ ✿ ✿

Roosevelt's election and initiation of the New Deal coincided with portentous overseas events. Adolf Hitler became Germany's chancellor in January 1933, several weeks before FDR took the oath of office. Hitler soon joined Benito Mussolini, who seized control of Italy in 1922, in the ranks of nationalistic, right-wing dictators. Hitler's ascension did not trouble Hollywood decision makers already accustomed to accommodating dictators who boosted their bottom lines. Moviemakers had done business with the Fascists for years. Many executives admired Mussolini for stifling Italian communists and bringing stability to his country. MGM's Louis B. Mayer modeled his office after Il Duce's. Mayer's visitors tiptoed across sixty feet of white carpet before reaching a massive, semicircular white desk that the five-foot-three-inch-tall executive placed on a pedestal to keep guests below his eye level. A giant window framed Mayer with a panoramic view of his kingdom. A large globe in front of the desk and an American flag over Mayer's right shoulder completed the producer's imperial image.[19]

Columbia's Harry Cohn went even further. Besides appropriating Mussolini's decorating tastes, he also presented him to American movie audiences. Released at the nadir of the Great Depression, the seventy-four-minute film *Mussolini Speaks!* (1933) interspersed footage from a 1931 speech with newsreel scenes of Il Duce's achievements. Declaring its subject "the answer to America's needs," Columbia billed the pseudodocumentary "the wonder picture of today's wonder man." Cohn's movie earned him an audience with Mussolini in the summer of 1933 and an autographed photograph to top off his homage of an office.[20]

Hollywood's affinity for Mussolini echoed official American policy. The conservative Republican administrations of the 1920s saw Fascism as the only movement capable of maintaining order in postwar Italy. A stable Italy, in turn, offered economic opportunities for American businessmen. Richard Child, the American ambassador to Italy, who later ghostwrote Mussolini's autobiography, declared Il Duce a "magnetic character" and extended best wishes for his "fine young revolution." Subsequent American officials viewed Mussolini as a moderate who desired peace and restrained his party's more unruly elements. Most dismissed his fiery rhetoric as posturing designed to energize constituents. Franklin Roosevelt maintained warm relations with Mussolini until Italy declared war on France and Great Britain in 1940.[21]

Neither Washington nor Hollywood perceived Italy as a problem so long as it respected the United States' economic interests. The Fascists set off no alarms until 1933, the year of Roosevelt's inauguration. Mussolini understood the propaganda power of film and sought to grow his country's movie industry. He dispatched Luigi Freddi, a leading Fascist who soon became Italy's Director General of Film, on a tour of Hollywood. Freddi returned with a list of ways the government could aid Italian cinema. His proposals bore fruit that fall, when the Fascists required that all movies sold in Italy be dubbed in Italy, an obligation that added to American studios' production costs and gave Italians valuable filmmaking experience. The government also compelled Italian exhibitors to show at least one Italian film for every three new productions they screened and placed a twenty-five-thousand-lire (approximately $1,250) tax on each dubbed feature. Proceeds from the levy funded prizes for outstanding Italian productions. In essence, the Fascists forced Hollywood to subsidize its own competition. Protests from the MPPDA's top foreign affairs troubleshooter, Frederick Herron, from MPPDA chief European representative Harold Smith, and from Ambassador Breckinridge Long failed to dissuade the Italians.[22]

Profits from the dubbing tax—some 5 million lire by April 1935—began dribbling into the Italian treasury. Hollywood could do little to stop the flow. In an age of rising patriotism and economic nationalism, Italy was not the only country to introduce quotas and discriminatory taxes. Abandoning Italy in retaliation for its new laws would mark the first step down a treacherous slope. Herron and other MPPDA officials peppered the State Department with complaints but avoided any provocative actions. Additional meetings between American and Italian diplomats led to no breakthroughs.[23]

The industry was similarly willing to appease Hitler. With more theaters than any other European country, Germany was a potentially lucrative market for American films. The German government, however, took steps to limit Hollywood's access years before Hitler took office. An effort to promote domestic production, the 1925 *Kontingent* law required theater owners to show one German film for every foreign film they screened. Hollywood's share of the market tumbled. Paramount and other studios considered closing their Berlin offices as the number of American films released in Germany plunged from 205 in 1928 to 59 in 1932. Many film men hoped Hitler's new government would implement a pro-American movie policy. Cooperation might persuade the Nazis to ease *Kontingent* quotas on foreign pictures. Will Hays and Frederick Herron discouraged an independent producer from shooting a hostile biopic of the Führer entitled *The Mad Dog of Europe* after Nazi diplomats complained to the MPPDA and the State Department. Prominent American Jews, who feared reprisals against German Jews, also intervened against the production. Both Columbia and Warners recut films in response to complaints from Nazi censors before distributing them overseas.[24]

Hollywood was not alone in giving the Nazis the benefit of the doubt. Few Americans viewed Hitler's rise to power as the first step toward war and the Holocaust. Many interpreted his electoral success as an inevitable product of the harsh Treaty of Versailles, which devastated Germany's military and economic strength after its loss in the Great War. Others saw Hitler as a strong—and welcome—anticommunist leader. His anti-Semitism disgusted some, but the horrific consequences of that ideology lay far in the future. Most observers saw Hitler as a passing phenomenon. "If he finds that what he believes ought to be done cannot be accomplished," *Commonweal* remarked, "he will resign." Washington hoped to maintain access to the German market. American businessmen, including film executives, adopted a wait-and-see approach.[25]

Hollywood's forbearance quickly waned. Germany's haphazard censoring of American films irritated Hays and Herron, who thought the Nazis should give more credit to the MPPDA's work on their behalf. Hitler's anti-Semitism appalled nearly everyone in Hollywood once it assumed tangible form. Nazi bureaucrats ordered German studios to fire Jews soon after Hitler assumed power. Even Christianized Jews had to go. "It is not religion but race that is decisive," the Nazis decreed. The edict touched off an exodus that ultimately benefited American cinema. Albert Basserman, William Dieterle, Fritz Lang, Peter Lorre, Luise Rainer, Max Steiner, Billy Wilder, and many others left for California. Their arrival infused Hollywood with a wealth of new talent while draining the German film industry of skilled actors, directors, and writers. United Artists producer Sam Goldwyn urged his peers to hire the expatriates. "We are undermanned," he declared. Gifted German refugees might give Hollywood an edge in the fiercely competitive global film market. "In a way," the *Variety* writer Wolfe Kaufman argued, "maybe show business ought to be grateful to Hitler."[26]

Germany's cinematic anti-Semitism had just begun. Having cleansed domestic studios of Jews, in April 1933 the Nazis ordered American film companies to expel Jews from their German branches. Hollywood persuaded the Nazis to grant some exceptions and stalled for time by requesting clarification as to exactly who qualified as a Jew. Officials ruled that people with some non-Jewish blood could keep their jobs for the time being. The Americans otherwise offered little resistance. Warners sputtered about closing its German facilities but did not. Reluctant to lose the market, studio executives quietly transferred Jewish employees to other locations.[27]

Hitler placed Reich Minister for Propaganda Joseph Goebbels in charge of "all areas involving intellectual influence on the nation" two months later. The former journalist and bank clerk's fiefdom encompassed the press, radio, art, music, theater, and motion pictures. Insisting that Germans must learn "to think uniformly, to react uniformly, and to place themselves body and soul at the disposal of the government," Goebbels planned to use the screen to propagate Nazi principles. He admired the quality of American pictures—even those he publicly disparaged—but his quest for ideological purity made life difficult for foreign producers, whose films rarely won the government's unqualified approval.

Hitler's expanding control over the German film industry paralyzed American studio heads. Germany's murky censorship laws made it impossible for Hollywood to tailor pictures to the market. The flow of celluloid into the country slowed to a trickle. Studios laid off German sales representatives. Theaters in Berlin reran old movies to fill screen time. The Americans hoped the dearth of new features would force the Nazis to ease their restrictive policies, but Germany refused to back down. Censorship instead became stricter and more arbitrary. Nazi functionaries asked Hollywood to remove offensive material from prints distributed anywhere in Europe, not just in Germany. They also required studios to certify that Jewish emigrants—a classification the Nazis left deliberately vague—had not worked on films sold in Germany. Nazi diplomats pestered the State Department to suppress pictures they found insulting. Germany barred MGM's *The Prizefighter and the Lady* (1934) after a successful two-week run in Berlin. Its star, Jewish boxer Max Baer, claimed the action resulted from his ten-round demolition of Max Schmeling in Yankee Stadium the previous year. Ironically, MGM donated the proceeds from the Berlin opening of *The Prizefighter and the Lady* to the Nazi Winter Relief Fund.[28]

Germany's actions left studios on tenuous economic ground. Warner Bros. pulled out in July 1934, citing its inability to make money under German censorship laws. MGM, Paramount, and Twentieth Century–Fox maintained their Berlin offices in the hopes that economic conditions would improve. To this point, Hollywood had taken almost no tangible or public steps to oppose Hitler's regime. Improved access to the market remained the industry's top priority in Germany.[29]

Similar economic concerns guided Hollywood's dealings with Italy. The first months of Nazi rule coincided with the high-water mark of pro-Fascist sentiment in the United States. American businessmen admired Mussolini's proclivity for action. The Fascists maintained production rates and wages while much of the world wallowed in depression. "Other nations falter or reel hysterically in search of unity," observed *Fortune* magazine in July 1934, while "Italy is calm and united under the emblem of common strength and effort which is Fascism."[30]

This positive outlook changed as Italy prepared for its 1935 incursion into Ethiopia. Although the Fascists' military buildup inspired little concern within the business community, their fiscal maneuvers aroused fears of trade-killing autarky. Italy limited exports of lire to strengthen its economy in anticipation of war. Hollywood still sold movies to Italy, but it grew harder to send profits home. Italian banks held around 75 million lire ($3,750,000) in frozen studio funds by late 1936. The debt would have been greater except that, after Ethiopia fell in May, Italy allowed studios to use some blocked funds to purchase and export certain Italian goods to the United States, a concession that further lined Italy's pockets.[31]

As an unprovoked conflict marked by widespread killing of civilians (Mussolini's son Vittorio bragged about bombing undefended villages), the Italo-Ethiopian War outraged many, including some American businessmen. Even so, Italian atrocities did not discourage Hollywood from seeking closer ties with the Fascists. Some moviemakers saw the war as an economic plus. Producers reasoned that the League of Nations' invasion-inspired embargo on Italy would increase that nation's dependence on American films. In fact, imports of American films remained relatively stable through the mid-1930s, averaging around 160 a year. Moviemakers were not alone in trying to capitalize on the crisis. Despite Roosevelt's calls for an unofficial boycott of Italy, American exports of oil, copper, iron, and steel skyrocketed in the weeks following Mussolini's invasion of Ethiopia. Roosevelt deplored the trade but did little to stop it for fear of outraging advocates of strict neutrality.[32]

Walter Wanger was among those in Hollywood who saw financial opportunities in Fascism. In the spring of 1936 the producer of the Marx Brothers' first film, *The Cocoanuts* (1929), and *Gabriel over the White House* hatched a plan, in corroboration with United Artists' Italian representative Mario Luporini, to establish a production unit in Rome. The scheme offered tremendous profit potential. The Italians were building Cinecitta, an enormous moviemaking complex on the outskirts of the capital. Space at the new facility would rent for about one-third the cost of other European studios, and Italian theaters would grant favorable treatment to pictures shot there. The Fascists wanted Americans to shoot in Italy, and Luporini wanted United Artists to get in first. Lacking established Italian divisions, other majors would have to either buy United Artists' films or ask the company to produce on their behalf.[33]

Like many in the State Department, the politically astute Wanger believed the United States needed to appease Il Duce to ensure his independence from Hitler. He therefore saw his mission not only as "a chance to root American films in a foreign nation" but also as "a way of establishing friendship for Americanism in Italy." With such support, Wanger believed, Mussolini could force Hitler to stop persecuting Jews and cement his reputation as "the greatest man in the entire world."[34]

Wanger sailed with his wife to Rome in May, just days after Italy concluded its victory in Ethiopia, to discuss his plan with Minister of Popular Culture Dino Alfieri, Director General for Film Luigi Freddi, Cinecitta head Carlo Roncoroni, and other officials. Wanger's tours of Cinecitta and his conversations with Italian exhibitors convinced him of the venture's viability. The Italians were in a generous mood, assuring Wanger that he could freely export profits and promising to waive taxes for his American cast and crew members. The Fascists saw these as worthwhile concessions, as Wanger's presence at Cinecitta would give them both international prestige and a stronger understanding of American cinematic techniques, knowledge they could then use to raise their own film profile.[35]

Wanger incorporated the Societa Anonima Italiana Cinematografica (SAIC) on June 24, 1936. Luporini crowed that the deal gave United Artists "prominence and the first position amongst American companies here for all time." Mussolini granted Wanger a twenty-minute audience to cap off the day. The dictator enthusiastically endorsed SAIC and asked the producer to promote Italy when he returned to the States. After sailing back to New York, Wanger announced the SAIC deal in a press conference at his Waldorf Towers suite. Reporters jotted notes as the producer praised Mussolini. "He's marvelous!" he exclaimed. "Marvelous! Plain! Simple! Sympathetic! Marvelous man! Knows everything! No poverty, no beggars. No kids on the street. All in uniform. New buildings. New roads. Terrific! The people clean, healthy, polite." Wanger, who had a financial stake in pleasing the Italians, sent newspaper reports of his remarks to Fascist officials. "Please note how much publicity I got for Fascism, which, as you know, has been considered a terrible thing in this country," he wrote Luporini.[36]

Wanger's assessment of Fascism's declining reputation in the United States was perceptive. Although the Italian-American press remained almost unanimously pro-Mussolini, mainstream public opinion turned decidedly negative after the Italo-Ethiopian War. Hostile analyses of Italy, including Columbia University historian Michael Florinsky's *Fascism and National Socialism* (1936), became more common. Fascism's bureaucratic and regulatory thickets seemed increasingly impenetrable to industrialists. In their eyes, ever-tightening restraints on business blurred the line between Mussolini-style corporatism and communism. American capitalists still wanted to work in Italy. Those who thought about the morality of dealing with Fascists talked of changing the nature of the regime from the inside. They must stay engaged or else lose leverage over Mussolini.[37]

The Italian market remained profitable. By the summer of 1936 the situation in Germany was nearly intolerable. Hitler's recent remilitarization of the Rhineland elicited few comments in Hollywood. Germany's tightening censorship, however, inspired outrage. Nazi bureaucrats regularly rejected MGM, Paramount, and Twentieth Century–Fox films without offering clear explanations of how to correct the problems. German officials shuttled studio representatives from office to office in "a campaign of delay and evasion." Such uncertainty made it almost impossible to plan future releases. Companies retitled, dubbed, and scheduled pictures for German distribution only to have them shut out at the last moment.[38]

Studio heads were frustrated yet reluctant to surrender their investments. The Roosevelt administration also wanted them to stay in Germany. A Hollywood walkout might derail broader German-American relations and cause the Nazis to seek revenge against other American industries still operating within their borders. Washington also feared that, should Hollywood abandon Germany and therefore free itself from threats of retaliation, villainous Nazis would soon become a stock tool in the arsenal of studio screenwriters needing onscreen bad guys. Such depictions would further outrage Hitler's minions and inspire more attacks on American business. The Commerce Department saw no way to improve the situation but urged studios to hang on. The State Department unsuccessfully sought a rapprochement between Germany and the industry.

The quarreling parties settled into a period of stalemate that neither Washington, Hollywood, nor Berlin found particularly satisfying.[39]

The Jewish issue was the white elephant in the room. Hollywood leaders made hardly a peep when the 1935 Nuremberg Laws disenfranchised Jews and outlawed marriages between Jews and gentiles. Their silence reflected a deep psychological conflict within the film community. As Neal Gabler has observed, most studio moguls were Jews of central or eastern European descent who desperately wanted to win respect from mainstream American society. Their religion marked them as outsiders even though most had abandoned the faith by the time they entered the movie business. Louis B. Mayer, for one, quoted Hebrew prayers and dotted his speech with Yiddish phrases but rarely went to temple. It is of at least symbolic significance that Mayer and several other studio chiefs married Jewish girls when they were young but then dumped them for gentiles after establishing their empires.[40]

Warner Bros.' *The Jazz Singer* (1927) embodied the contradictory forces buffeting Jewish movie magnates. Jakie Rabinowitz, a cantor's son, leaves his tradition-bound family, changes his name to Jack Robin, and masters the most American form of music, yet he cannot escape the call of the past. He finally succumbs to his father's pleas, the lure of his heritage, and sings the Kol Nidre as the old man dies. The late cantor's spirit fills Jack as he pursues his jazz career. He remains spiritually trapped between two worlds—Jewish and American—but manages in true Hollywood style to reconcile his conflict. The closing scene shows Jack belting out "Mammy" as his beloved mother beams from the front row of a packed theater. He is Jewish. He is American. He is happy.[41]

The moguls never truly emulated Jakie Rabinowitz's achievement. Although Harry Warner and a few others retained their religion, they minimized public awareness of their background. Studio bosses had an unspoken agreement to avoid emphasizing Jewishness or Jewish material in films. Hollywood Jews feared that denouncing Nazi persecution would increase anti-Semitism at home and further endanger European Jews, including their own relatives. They were not alone in sidestepping the Jewish issue. The American Jewish Committee, for example, insisted that calls for an economic boycott of Germany would "provide the pretext for further excesses against the Jews in Germany" and "lead to a general retaliation against Jewish business." Those same concerns colored the simultaneous debate over whether the United States should send a squad to the 1936 Berlin Olympics.[42]

A rash of pro-Nazi activities in Los Angeles forced movie folk to acknowledge the anti-Semitism issue, even if they could not agree on what to do about it. Studio executives wavered when two German sympathizers working for the *Los Angeles Times* slipped an anti-Jewish pamphlet into the newspaper's pages. MGM's whiz-kid producer Irving Thalberg advised a policy of silence. "Hitler would eventually disappear," he told them. "The Jews would remain." Some wanted to take at least symbolic action. Mendel Silberberg, a lapsed Jew and the most powerful lawyer in Hollywood, organized the Community Committee in 1934. Counting Harry Cohn, Jack Warner, and RKO producer Pandro Berman among its members, the committee monitored pro-Nazi activities and pressured area media leaders to keep such groups as the pro-Nazi German-American Bund away from public notice. Silberberg's committee pursued a largely negative agenda. Rather than publicize the evils of Nazism, its members hoped merely to prevent its ideas from gaining popularity.[43]

The moguls' timidity reflected their struggles to acculturate and an awareness of anti-Semitism's prevalence in America. Schools, country clubs, and social organizations discriminated against Jews. The 382-person American Olympic team that competed in Berlin included only two Jews—sprinters Sam Stoller and Marty Glickman—neither of whom actually participated in the competition. Groucho Marx joked about America's persistent anti-Semitism. After a Los Angeles swimming club denied his daughter admission, he informed its members that she was only half Jewish. "How about if she only goes in up to her waist?" he asked. Studio executives, whose livelihoods depended on appealing to domestic and international audiences, could not laugh off prejudice. Protesting the status of Jews in the United States and the world might lead to a loss of public favor or retaliation from aggrieved governments.[44]

✺ ✺ ✺

MGM's difficulties with *It Can't Happen Here* crystallized both the problems facing Hollywood at mid-decade and the industry's timidity. Louis B. Mayer paid $50,000 in late 1935 for the rights to Sinclair Lewis's novel about a charismatic president who leads a fascist revolution. With Lionel Barrymore set to star, name recognition alone seemed to guarantee substantial profits. Mayer's studio hit a roadblock when it sent the script to Joseph Breen. The Production Code Administration chief found few violations of Hollywood's censorship rules but worried about the film's potential effect on the industry. Germany would certainly bar any adaptation of Lewis's depiction of "the Hitlerization of the United States." England and France would likely do the same. In fact, Breen argued, MGM might end up getting all its films banned overseas. He also warned that *It Can't Happen Here* could alienate American audiences reluctant to engage contentious issues, especially in the movie theater.[45]

Breen leaned on Mayer to kill the production and asked Will Hays to apply further pressure. MGM persisted, seeking to protect its investment. Breen eventually granted the PCA's stamp of approval even though he thought the story was "enormously dangerous." It was so "inflammatory," he warned Mayer, "and so filled with dangerous material that *only the greatest possible care* will save it from being rejected on all sides." Mayer understood Breen's not-so-subtle subtext. Citing cost concerns, he canceled the production in February 1936. Hays denied any role in Mayer's decision. Screenwriter Sidney Howard agreed that the so-called czar of Hollywood did not personally kill the project. "He just talked the producers out of making it," Howard said.[46]

Sinclair Lewis fumed over the industry's faintheartedness, telling the *New York Times* that Hays's power rivaled Hitler's and Mussolini's. "A fantastic exhibition of folly and cowardice," the novelist huffed. Nazi and Fascist propaganda films mocked democracy, Lewis complained, yet America would not respond with propaganda of its own. German and Italian officials fueled Lewis's anger by voicing approval of MGM's actions.[47]

The propaganda question—what it was and whether it was appropriate for commercial motion pictures—was starting to percolate in Hollywood. The term *propaganda* lacked the negative connotation it carries today; Hitlerism is largely responsible for that baggage. Propaganda could be a good thing, as former ambassador to Germany James W. Gerard told the Motion Picture Club of New York a few months before the *It Can't Happen Here* imbroglio. "The motion picture is one of the most powerful instruments of propaganda in the world," he said. "When you hear talk of sharing wealth and destroying capitalism, bring your propaganda guns to bear." Film's power to persuade left others wary that Hollywood might use its influence to promote dangerous agendas. To them, movies should offer only good, clean fun. As one anonymous letter writer to the *New York Times* explained in early 1937, "those who go to [theaters] for entertainment have a right to expect that advantage will not be taken of their presence to compel them to listen to political propaganda, whether they like it or not."[48]

Hollywood was the world's most powerful creator of mass culture. It was also afraid that using its power to disseminate politically charged messages—even prodemocracy messages—would harm its financial and cultural status. Joseph Breen's concerns about *It Can't Happen Here* were, in a way, absurd. Lewis's book sold well, and the government-financed Federal Theatre Project had already turned it into a successful stage show. Hollywood, however, faced different issues than did authors and playwrights. Studios appealed to mass, diverse audiences at home and abroad. Their enormous expenses left them highly vulnerable to retaliation. As the face of American culture overseas, movies had to maintain a positive worldview to ensure worldwide acceptance and governmental backing. Film executives hesitated to explore political material because they believed audiences wanted escapist pictures. Sam Goldwyn most famously expressed this sentiment when he said that messages were best delivered via Western Union.

MGM's motto, *Ars Gratia Artis* ("art for the sake of art"), looked good surrounding Leo the Lion's roaring visage, but it had serious shortcomings as a business model. Mayer would have had a hard time maneuvering *It Can't Happen Here* past Hays and Breen, who monitored the gates of Hollywood like Cerberus watching Hades. "The question of public order, of public good, of avoiding the inflammatory, the prejudicial or the subversive," Hays wrote a month after MGM pulled the plug on *It Can't Happen Here*, "is a problem of social responsibility everlastingly imposed upon those who would produce, distribute and exhibit pictures." Commercialization and self-regulation brought many benefits to the major studios. Courage and daring were not among them.[49]

Breen's and Hays's insistence that the majors avoid political conflicts—and Mayer's willingness to go along with them—mirrored the wishes of the Roosevelt administration and the American people. Few Americans perceived Hitler as a menace to their security. After the horrific and disillusioning experience of the Great War, the country was content to leave Europe to its own battles. President Roosevelt set official policy toward the possibility of conflict in August 1935 when he signed the Neutrality Act, which prohibited the United States from selling arms to warring nations. A second Neutrality Act, passed in February 1936, strengthened trade restrictions and barred loans to belligerents. Even though American companies made big profits during the Italo-Ethiopian War, it was clear that discretion was the order of the day.[50]

CHAPTER TWO

Fires at Home, Fires Abroad

"Y OU CANNOT POSSIBLY IMAGINE the absolute barrenness of souls out here," screenwriter Herbert Biberman lamented in a 1935 letter to his mother. As Biberman's missive suggests, at mid-decade it was still possible to depict Hollywood as an apolitical wonderland packed with innocents who dove down rabbit holes whenever social, economic, or military issues interrupted their single-minded focus on moviemaking. Despite the tumult around them, film folk, argued screenwriter Morrie Ryskind, maintained a "colossal ignorance of current political happenings."[1]

In fact, although most executives avoided commenting on contemporary events, their employees were starting to speak out even as Biberman made his complaint. Rising political activism in Hollywood stemmed from a number of events. The New Deal opened eyes to the possibilities of reform, as did Upton Sinclair's 1934 California gubernatorial run. The novelist's End Poverty in California (EPIC) program rejected the profit system and called for the state to transfer idle land and factories to unemployed residents. Studio heads mobilized in opposition, threatening to move to Florida if Sinclair won and intimidating employees who supported his campaign. Executives forced their staffs to donate a day's pay to Republican candidate Frank Merriam's war chest. MGM produced a series of bogus newsreels linking Sinclair to a motley array of hoboes, communists, and immigrants. Sinclair's loss revealed the industry's political clout. It also embittered many Hollywood progressives and spurred the development of organizations capable of countering the moguls' ham-fisted conservatism.[2]

The first visible signs of unrest came from the blue-collar studio workers who led a mid-decade charge toward unionization. In 1933 unionized electricians and carpenters rejected a Depression-inspired, producer-sponsored plan to slice studio employees' salaries in half. Producers caved under their pressure, exempting everyone earning less than fifty dollars a week from the cut. The craftsmen's resistance illustrated the power of collective bargaining and inspired imitators. Screenwriters laid the foundation for the Screen Writers' Guild (SWG) soon after. The Screen Actors' Guild (SAG) began coalescing several months later. The Screen Directors' Guild (SDG) followed in 1936.

The Hollywood unions took years to win full recognition, largely because of intense opposition from producers. "I'm not going to coerce or threaten," Jack Warner once fumed, "but any son-of-a-bitch who is a member of the S.W.G.—he's out of a job." Even many union members harbored antilabor leanings. Director Victor Fleming interrupted a 1937 SDG meeting to voice his opinion on the sit-down strikes currently shaking Detroit auto plants. "If I were running Ford or GM or Chrysler," he told his colleagues, "I'd get a lot of guys with machine-guns, poke them in through the windows, and mow the bastards down." The long process of organization nevertheless provided valuable experience in coordinating mass campaigns and introduced Hollywood to the idea of fighting for principles beyond script assignments and character interpretations.[3]

One year after writing his despairing note, Herbert Biberman reported that "the democratic forces are beginning to stand up to be counted." Hollywood communists, including Biberman, were crucial to this awakening. Only about three hundred hard-core communists worked in Hollywood, most of them screenwriters who migrated from New York City. Party discipline was almost nonexistent and outlets for communist messages hard to find. Studios monitored communist organizations and knew who donated to leftist causes. Producers scrutinized films for red propaganda. That they rarely, if ever, found any testifies to either their vigilance or their paranoia. Communists' influence nevertheless exceeded their numbers. Party members had a toehold in Hollywood by 1935, when the introduction of Popular Frontism pushed them to unite liberals of all stripes by focusing on social issues rather than Marxist dogma. The party acted as a conduit for social-democratic activity, inculcating idealistic liberals with the language of protest and channeling them into various political causes.[4]

The spread of European totalitarianism gave the film community's budding political awareness a focus. Organized Hollywood anti-Nazism emerged in the spring of 1936, when twelve hundred people, including James Cagney, Francis Lederer, Groucho Marx, Dudley Nichols, and Basil Rathbone, piled into the Tutor-style Hollywood Women's Club auditorium for a reading of Irwin Shaw's "Bury the Dead." Voiced by Fredric March and his wife, Florence Eldridge, the play imagined six victims of a Great War–era frontal assault who refuse to be buried. Their wives, mothers, and sweethearts beg the corpses to lie peacefully in their graves. The soldiers refuse to submit until humankind promises never to repeat the horrors they witnessed in the trenches. After the performance the crowd heatedly discussed domestic issues, fascism, the Ethiopian conflict, and the possibility of a European war. Screenwriter Donald Ogden Stewart, who chaired the event, urged attendees to study social, political, economic, and racial problems. "The movies aren't good enough," he told the crowd, "and this Hollywood happiness isn't good enough in the face of the misery that there is in the world today." His words found a receptive if timid response. "I am against the war—I know it's insane," one audience member commented, "but what can I do about it?"[5]

Stewart did not have an answer but continued to sound alarm bells. Soon after organizing the "Bury the Dead" reading, the writer staged a party for Prince Hubertus von Lowenstein, an exiled German Catholic touring the United States to drum up anti-Nazism. The $100-a-plate event drew such luminaries as Sam Goldwyn, Mary Pickford, Irving Thalberg, Norma Shearer, and Walter Wanger and represented one more step toward open involvement in the anti-Nazi cause.[6]

Stewart was one of the film community's preeminent communists. A graduate of Yale University, noted Broadway playwright, and veteran of the famed Algonquin Round Table, Stewart exhibited little interest in current events when he came to Hollywood in 1930. His political awakening came four years later, while he was writing a play in London. He wanted one of his minor characters to be a communist. Knowing little about the doctrine, he began doing research and got hooked. Stewart confirmed his new faith soon after returning to the United States. As he walked past some carpenters on an MGM soundstage, he experienced "a happy warm feeling of satisfaction that I was now their brother." It seems unlikely that the carpenters felt the same about one of MGM's best-paid writers. Stewart, however, threw himself into the cause. He fought to legitimate the SWG, which he had ignored prior to his political epiphany, and became one of Hollywood's most outspoken anti-Nazis.[7]

An almost pathological organizer, Stewart helped create the film community's most important antifascist association, the Hollywood Anti-Nazi League (HANL). Stewart, Dorothy Parker, Fritz Lang, Herbert Biberman, Fredric March, and a few others launched HANL with a June 1936 banquet at the Wilshire Ebell Theatre, a lushly decorated hall a few miles south of Hollywood's social hub. Stewart implored the three hundred attendees to "organize to fight the Nazi invasion before Americans lose their constitutional liberties." His call seemed shrill and premature. Hitler had just remilitarized the Rhineland, a blatant violation of the Treaty of Versailles, but to this point the Nazis had only invaded their own territory. Stewart's warning nevertheless garnered a positive reaction. Following his lead, the new group set up shop at 6912 Hollywood Boulevard, conveniently located between Grauman's Chinese Theatre and two popular watering holes for screenwriters, Stanley Rose's Bookstore and Musso & Frank Grill.[8]

The Hollywood Anti-Nazi League drew movie folk who disliked Hitler but had no outlet for their dissent. Melvyn Douglas, for example, had a "dinner table interest in politics" until he visited Germany in 1936. His first direct exposure to Nazism stunned him. The newly politicized actor's search for like-minded people led him to HANL. He signed up, as did several thousand others. Members included radicals like Donald Stewart and Herbert Biberman; New Deal liberals like Eddie Cantor, Ernst Lubitsch, Paul Muni, Dudley Nichols, and Gloria Stuart; and conservatives like screenwriter Rupert Hughes. Some producers joined, including Sam Goldwyn, Carl Laemmle, Irving Thalberg, David O. Selznick, Walter Wanger, and Jack Warner.[9]

Whatever their private beliefs, most executives still hoped for the best in Germany. It was the industry's second tier—its creative talent—that forced Hollywood's hand. With little input from studio heads and no guidance from Will Hays, the alleged face of the movie capital, HANL put Hollywood in the vanguard of American public opinion. It was the first prominent anti-Hitler association not explicitly linked to American Jews. The Hollywood Anti-Nazi League served as the focal point for the industry's anti-Nazism over the next three years. It united the Hollywood émigré community with transplanted New York progressives. Under its influence, area bookstores, salons, and parties became political debating societies. The league, however, was never a tightly run outfit. Stewart and the big-money writers and actors who appeared on the group's letterhead left day-to-day operations to a cadre of anonymous communists. Only a few true believers participated in business meetings, which often occurred in bars rather than the Hollywood Boulevard office.[10]

A massive gathering on October 21, 1936, at the Shrine Auditorium served as HANL's coming-out party. League officials claimed that eight thousand people jammed the Moorish-style hall northeast of the University of Southern California campus. Irving Berlin, Dorothy Parker, and actress Gale Sondergaard were among the honored guests onstage. Writers Philip Dunne, B. P. Schulberg, and Jo Swerling sat in the audience, as did Fritz Lang, Mervyn LeRoy, Gloria Stuart, Walter Wanger, the Gershwin brothers, and other luminaries. After singing the national anthem, the crowd settled in for three hours of anti-Nazi speeches. Los Angeles mayor Frank Shaw attacked local hate groups. Dr. L. M. Birkhead of Kansas City gave a slideshow presentation on 119 domestic organizations "devoted to the establishment of Nazism in this country." In an impassioned oration Eddie Cantor alleged that Nazi agents tried to prevent him from coming. He, like the other speakers, challenged Americans to resist fascism and stand up for democracy.[11]

HANL followed up the Shrine meeting with events throughout Los Angeles and California that brought publicity, new members, and money. Its contributions to the European underground and refugee aid organizations raised awareness of war issues. Special divisions recruited women and young people. In true Popular Front style, members established a Labor Commission in a largely fruitless effort to develop HANL's ties to unions. Launched in October 1936, the league's weekly *Hollywood Anti-Nazi News* assaulted Hitlerites while promoting democracy, minority rights, unionization, religious tolerance, and cultural freedom. Radio offered another outlet for the league's message. In early 1937 the group launched two programs on Warner Bros.–owned KFWB. Donald Stewart and Herbert Biberman scripted most of the broadcasts, which alerted listeners to the dangers of American Nazi sympathizers, the devastating effect Nazism had on the German people, and the menace Hitler posed to world peace. Stewart and Biberman leavened the heavy drama with installments of *The Haddocks Abroad,* a serial comedy about a family of innocent but down-to-earth Americans who encounter Nazism's deficiencies as they travel through Germany.[12]

The Hollywood Anti-Nazi League celebrated its first anniversary with a blowout at the Ambassador Hotel on August 5, 1937. It was the organization's high-water mark. Biberman and Stewart joined other league regulars—Lang, LeRoy, Sondergaard, and Stuart—and more casual members, such as F. Scott Fitzgerald, Chico Marx, Loretta Young, Harry Warner, and MGM executives Joseph Mankiewicz and Harry Rapf, for an evening of fun and anti-Nazism. Stewart introduced comic actor Jimmy Durante as the founder and president of the "Anti-Nosey League." After enjoying the Benny Goodman Quartet, attendees danced to a set of ballads and swing tunes from MGM's fifteen-year-old songbird, Judy Garland.[13]

Goodman's clarinet and Garland's voice temporarily drowned out the discord surrounding the league. Detractors branded the group a communist front, a charge HANL denounced as a "Nazi trap" but did little to refute. Some opponents feared that the rise of Hollywood anti-Nazism might incite America to militarism or even war. The movie community would struggle with this issue for years, striving to balance the economic benefits of domestic and worldwide goodwill with the patriotic desire to protect the United States from hostile ideologies. HANL's pacifist, prodemocratic platform placed it within Hollywood's—and America's—mainstream even as its contention that "peace and the growth of Nazism are incompatible" forced movie folk onto unfamiliar and uncomfortable ground.[14]

Talk of war and peace was not just academic by the summer of 1937. Fighting between Japan and China resumed in July after several years of relative calm. Most Americans found the Spanish Civil War, which began a month after HANL's formation, far more alarming. The clash between the Loyalists and Francisco Franco's Nationalists put Americans in an awkward position. With Franco drawing support from the Italians and Germans and the Loyalists receiving aid from the Soviets, many saw the conflict as a death match between fascism and communism. Taking a side implied favoring one undemocratic ideology or the other. Some chose anyway. The Catholic press and the Catholic Church endorsed Franco's crusade to exterminate godless communism. Interpreting the war as the start of democracy's last stand, many intellectuals made the Loyalists a cause célèbre. A few thousand Americans volunteered for the Abraham Lincoln Brigade and other Loyalist units. Roosevelt ducked the issue by imposing an embargo on both sides. The president underscored his determination to keep the country out of European conflicts during a speech at Chautauqua. "I hate war," he declared. "I have spent unnumbered hours, I shall pass unnumbered hours, thinking and planning how war may be kept from this Nation."[15]

Already enflamed by Sinclair Lewis's EPIC campaign, unionization battles, and the swelling anti-Nazi movement, Hollywood threw its weight behind the Loyalists. The usual suspects—including Melvyn Douglas, Fredric March, Paul Muni, Dorothy Parker, and Donald Stewart—formed the Motion Picture Artists Committee to Aid Republican Spain (MPAC), a fund-raising group that eventually swelled to more than fifteen thousand members. As in HANL, stars served primarily as window dressing, leaving much of the work to anonymous Popular Fronters. Stewart added to his heavy workload by creating the Anti-Franco League and, along with other MPAC founders, opening a Hollywood branch of the Joint Anti-Fascist Refugee Committee. Franchot Tone, Joan Crawford, Luise Rainer, and Gale Sondergaard joined the North American Committee for Loyalist Spain. In addition to donating ambulances, food, medicine, and clothing, the movie community raised about $1 million for the Loyalists over the course of the conflict.[16]

Although Hollywood activists sincerely opposed Franco's right-wing movement, a hint of make-believe pervaded their burst of political consciousness. In early 1937 French author and Loyalist volunteer André Malraux shilled for the Loyalist cause in Los Angeles. After giving a fiery speech to a Hollywood-heavy crowd at the Shrine Auditorium, Malraux raised his hand in a clenched-fist communist salute. Thousands of well-housed, well-clad, well-nourished film folk responded in kind. The theater of the moment meant as much as the message. The same was true at some level for other antifascist meetings. Hollywood loved pageantry and stars. Mass rallies and cocktail parties with big-name guest speakers provided both.[17]

The film industry's burgeoning offscreen activism did not immediately affect its onscreen voice. Writers and actors were keen to discuss the Spanish Civil War, but producers had little interest in putting it on the screen. Few films addressed the conflict, none in any clear or meaningful way. Paramount's *The Last Train from Madrid* (1937) left viewers wondering whether the people on the train were Nationalists or Loyalists. The studio sold the film as a nonpartisan melodrama punctuated with "thrilling battle sequences." Twentieth Century–Fox's *Love under Fire* (1937) began as a pro-Nationalist melodrama about stolen jewels. After several rewrites and a run-in with studio chief Darryl F. Zanuck's blue pencil, it became a forgettable romance that happened to take place in Spain. Zanuck removed the original screenplay's references to "Loyalists" and "Royalists," along with any trace of a political subtext.[18]

The Spanish Civil War was too hot to touch. Pennsylvania's governor, George Earle, condemned the pro-Loyalist documentary *Spain in Flames* (1937), which contained dialogue by Ernest Hemingway, John Dos Passos, and Archibald MacLeish, as "pure communist propaganda." The state's Board of Censors banned it, as did Ohio's. Fearing government interference in their affairs, executives saw no reason to provoke antagonism with war-related films. Tightening censorship abroad, moreover, made it unlikely that such movies could be released in foreign countries.[19]

Most producers wanted to focus on pure entertainment. Andy Hardy pictures, light comedies, and romantic dramas turned profits while keeping the industry clear of political difficulties. But rumblings of change echoed around Hollywood. Walter Wanger, for one, was kicking around the idea of tackling the Spanish Civil War head-on. Before that project reached fruition, however, Hollywood's most rebellious major studio entered the emerging fray between totalitarianism and democracy.[20]

❧ ❧ ❧

The old joke that anyone in politics who wants a friend should buy a dog applied equally well to Hollywood in the 1930s. "It was an age of the buccaneers," recalled MGM producer Dore Schary. The moguls battled their way to the top and intended to stay there. They ran over anyone standing in their way without remorse. If the movie business had a conscience, it took the form of Harry Warner. Although hardly a pushover, the eldest of the Warner brothers was among the first to recognize the long-term danger of Nazism and took the lead in dragging his studio into the fight against it.[21]

Warner's upbringing conditioned him to sympathize with oppressed minorities. He was born in Krasnashiltz, Poland, in 1881, the only one of the four Warner brothers who went into show business born in the Old World. His parents, Benjamin and Pearl, were devout Jews who worshipped in secret to avoid official retribution. Benjamin told his eldest son harrowing tales of studying Jewish texts in a stable while a lookout watched for police. The Warners emigrated to Baltimore in 1883. At Benjamin's urging, Harry held to traditional ways in his new environs. He learned Hebrew, studied the Talmud, and sprinkled his speech with proverbs. He grew to be a level-headed man who rarely raised his voice, believed in hard work, and lived an unimpeachably moral life. Screenwriter W. R. Burnett called him "the biggest bore who's ever lived in the history of the world."[22]

Warner was of slight build, with a swarthy complexion and thinning hair combed straight back from his high forehead. His eyes were piercing yet distracted. In photographs he looks not at the camera so much as through it, grudgingly offering a thin-lipped smile that conveys determination rather than good humor. Harry was a serious man, a shrewd businessman who fought for everything he had. Though a chronic worrier, his pugnacity served him well during the film business's rough-and-tumble early days.

It was actually Sam, the sixth of Benjamin and Pearl's twelve children, who pushed his siblings into the movies. A former carnival barker and ice-cream salesman, Sam convinced the family to pool $1,000 to buy a movie projector. The brothers pitched a tent in their yard in Youngstown, Ohio, and started screening *The Great Train Robbery* (1903). They invested the profits in a nickelodeon in New Castle, Pennsylvania. Realizing there was more money in distribution than exhibition, Harry convinced his brothers to open the Pittsburgh-based Duquesne Film Exchange in 1907. Harry relocated the clan to California after the so-called trust wars shut down Duquesne and many other small companies for violating Thomas Edison's movie patents. Sam, Albert, and Jack Warner opened a new film exchange out west. Harry moved on to New York to oversee the endeavor's finances.[23]

The brothers' fortunes turned again in 1917 when they purchased screen rights to former ambassador to Germany James W. Gerard's autobiography, *My Four Years in Germany*. America's entrance into the

World War pushed the book onto best-seller lists, paving the way for the Warners' first big hit. Their 1918 film version stressed Gerard's anti-German theme, showing vicious Huns murdering without reason, abusing prisoners, and initiating the Russian Revolution. Like many of the brothers' later pictures, it was a flag-waving call for democracy and a powerful if not hysterical condemnation of dictatorship. The picture's smashing success convinced the Warners to open a small production studio in Los Angeles.[24]

Harry did not understand the art of moviemaking but appreciated the income it generated. Equally important, he saw the studio as a way to keep his siblings together while solidifying his position as head Warner. He especially wanted to monitor his unruly youngest brother, Jack. The two were innately, almost exquisitely, mismatched. Jack played Groucho Marx to Harry's Margaret Dumont, or would have were he half as funny as he imagined himself. Jack was a born showman, indifferent to religion and education and devoted to self-aggrandizement. He rebelled from a young age, quitting school in the fourth grade to run with a band of street urchins. A talent for singing fulfilled his need to be the center of attention. He appeared with some local acts around Youngstown before embarking on a brief vaudeville tour. On his return he helped his brothers by entertaining theater patrons between movies. Jack and Sam took charge of the Los Angeles side of the family business following the success of *My Four Years in Germany.* Jack eventually emerged as the main power on the West Coast. Sam's death in 1927 consolidated his control over studio operations.[25]

Unlike his puritanical older brother, Jack favored tacky sports jackets and smoked obscenely large cigars. He adored the glamour of Hollywood life. His sexual ethics were far from pristine. His goofy, toothy grin was as welcoming as Harry's tight smile was suspicious. A stream of vulgar jokes poured from his mouth. John Huston recalled a "funny, childlike candor to the man," noting that "words seemed to escape from him unthinkingly." When Jack saw Madame Chiang Kai-shek at a banquet, he exclaimed, "Holy cow. I forgot to pick up my laundry!" His favorite expression was "uneasy lies the head that wears the toilet seat." Jack Benny said Warner would "rather tell a bad joke than make a good movie." Benny was not far off. Warner generally read one-page synopses rather than full scripts. He spent most days presiding over lunches in the executive dining room, strutting about the studio lot like a peacock, and ordering people around.[26]

Jack's comic stylings masked a cruel streak. He kept promises only so long as they served his needs. He could be a petty tyrant, the kind of man who fenced in the writers' building at his studio to prevent staffers from sneaking out early. On one occasion, legend has it, he overheard a guard singing a Verdi aria in a voice that far surpassed his own.

"Which would you rather be," Jack asked, "a singer or our gateman?"
"Oh, a singer," replied the hapless employee.
"You're fired," Warner shot back.

Writer Wilson Mizner compared working for the Warners with making love to a porcupine: "It's a hundred pricks against one."[27]

Warner Bros. limped through the early 1920s until its *Rin Tin Tin* features finally brought some financial stability. Jack called the dog his "mortgage lifter." The series' scripts came from a promising screenwriter named Darryl F. Zanuck, who became Warners' head of production and witness to some of Jack's most repulsive acts. Milton Sperling, an office boy who later became a producer, once stumbled on Zanuck in Jack's bathroom. "Warner was sitting on the toilet," he remembered, "taking a crap and pressing, and then I heard the plop, and Zanuck, who was talking to him, pulled the chain and continued talking."[28]

Warner Bros.' defining moment came when it released *The Jazz Singer* (1927) and ushered in the talking-picture era. The brothers' enhanced status, however, did little to erase their underdog spirit. Although similar to most movie moguls in biographical terms, the Warners believed they were "neither in Hollywood nor of it." Jack and Harry hated outsiders even more than they hated each other—and their most famous battle featured a lead pipe–wielding Harry shouting, "I'll kill you, you son-of-a-bitch!" as he chased his brother around the lot. Their mistrust of power drew them to projects featuring social outcasts—gangsters, factory workers, miners, chorus girls—scuffling their way to legitimacy and acceptance. Though Zanuck helped set the tone for Warner films, Harry's shadow loomed over the studio. Whereas Jack was indifferent to current events, Harry came to see movies as tools for spreading morality, tolerance, and democracy. His violent dislike of oppression shone through in such searing productions as *The Public Enemy* (1931),

I Am a Fugitive from a Chain Gang (1932), and *Wild Boys of the Road* (1933).[29]

Harry's first taste of Hitlerism came when he visited Berlin in 1932 to close a deal to buy UFA, Warner Bros.' German distributor. Although Hitler was not yet in power, the anti-Semitic slogans plastered on walls and the Brownshirts stalking the streets shocked Harry, who cancelled the deal. Warners announced plans for an anti-Nazi film within weeks of Hitler's election as chancellor. No such picture appeared, but "Bosko's Picture Show," a Looney Tunes short from September 1933 that mocked a lederhosen-wearing lout bearing a strong resemblance to the dictator, conveyed the studio's position.[30]

Jack's annual European vacations exposed him to Hitlerism. Those trips, along with his brother's harassment, eventually convinced him to join Harry's crusade, although he never matched his sibling's antifascist fervor. The Warners backed the United Jewish Appeal and raised money to resettle German refugees in Palestine. Harry assigned staffers to locate homes and jobs for European expatriates. Such passion sometimes estranged him from other studio moguls—his final break with Louis B. Mayer came after Harry accused Mayer of skimping on contributions to the Jewish Welfare Drive. The Jewish issue drove Jack and Harry to focus their altruism on Germany. The brothers showed little interest in Japan's expansion in the Pacific or the Spanish Civil War, which Jack simplistically interpreted as a fight to kill communism.[31]

It was only logical that the Warners would eventually carry their crusade to the silver screen. Indeed, the studio began slipping antifascism into feature-length films at mid-decade. Political and economic realities hampered the vigor of their campaign. The Neutrality Act, Joseph Breen's Production Code Administration, and public opinion discouraged filmmakers from saying anything too courageous or divisive. The Warners instead attacked Hitlerism through metaphor, crafting productions that conveyed their point without overtly commenting on contemporary conditions.

The Story of Louis Pasteur (1936) was Warner Bros.' most oblique anti-Nazi parable. The first in a series of biographical pictures, or biopics, starring Paul Muni, *The Story of Louis Pasteur* frames the famous doctor's life as a struggle between ignorance and enlightenment. It closes with an incongruous scene of the aged doctor urging a crowd of well-wishers to keep the flame of knowledge burning. Do not let "the sadness of certain hours that creep over nations" overwhelm you, he advised his admirers. His statement could easily be interpreted as a swipe at Germany. Jack Warner, on the other hand, completely missed the film's subtext. He thought *The Story of Louis Pasteur* was "the story of a milkman."[32]

Black Legion (1937) made its point more directly. The Black Legion was a real organization, centered in the Midwest, whose anti-Jewish, anticommunist, anti-Catholic, antiblack, and anti-immigrant members saw themselves as protectors of white Protestantism and traditional morality. Several legionnaires stood trial for murder in 1936. The resulting publicity provided story material and fueled interest in a movie about the group. Warners hoped to capitalize on this interest but battled the PCA over the script. Breen found the studio's treatment too angry for his tastes. Warners tempered the film's message, appeasing Breen by focusing on the legion's economic appeal to blue-collar workers rather than its racial and religious prejudices. Even after editing, it remained the sharpest cinematic attack on domestic fascism to date.[33]

Black Legion centers on Frank Taylor (Humphrey Bogart), a factory worker who dreams of rising to the top. The company dashes his aspirations when it promotes a young "greaseball" named Joe Dombrowski (Henry Brandon) over him. An angry Frank accepts a coworker's invitation to a Black Legion meeting. Frank nods in agreement as speakers attack "rotten, ungrateful foreigners," giving him a scapegoat for his problems and a reason for joining the legion. Frank starts packing a pistol—the firearm makes the pathetic loser feel like a big man. Burning down the Dombrowskis' store drives the family out of town and gets Frank the foreman's job he coveted. Other violent crimes follow as the legion enforces its narrow vision of true Americanism. The police finally dismantle the group, arresting Frank in the process. His trial turns into a primer on American liberty. The judge—staring into the camera to ensure the audience understands he is also speaking to them—lectures Frank on the meaning of freedom, the importance of tolerance, and the danger of extralegal organizations, then sentences him to life in prison.

A solid success at the box office, *Black Legion* offered a compelling look at right-wing fringe outfits. It harshly critiqued the insecure, small-minded bullies who filled their ranks. Critics saw it as a "stinging indictment of false patriotism, race hatred and bigotry." They were less willing to view the movie within an international context. Reviewers ignored *Black Legion*'s obvious if implicit criticism of Nazism, instead seeing the film as merely another example of Warners' socially conscious filmmaking.[34]

They Won't Forget (1937), another cinematic denunciation of prejudice, appeared several months later. In it, Warners rehashed the 1915 Leo Frank case, in which a mob lynched the manager of a Marietta, Georgia, pencil factory convicted of murdering a twelve-year-old employee named Mary Phagan. The screen version concerns Robert Hale (Edward Norris), a small-town teacher accused of killing one of his students. A judge condemns Hale to death on the flimsiest of evidence. The governor later reduces his sentence to life in prison, a leniency that outrages his alleged victim's brothers, who lynch the poor man in retaliation.

While containing some gutsy scenes that plead for tolerance, decry mob rule, and lament the death of the rule of law, *They Won't Forget* also exposed the injustice of lynching without uttering the word *lynching*. Director Mervyn LeRoy claimed that "any sociopolitical message it may have had was purely a byproduct of its story." More revealing was the picture's unwillingness to address the anti-Semitism at the heart of the real Leo Frank case. Frank's religion helped turn public opinion against him—a crowd outside the courthouse chanted "Hang the Jew" during the trial. Honoring Hollywood's tradition of maintaining public silence on Judaism, *They Won't Forget* skirted the issue completely.[35]

Major studios showed little interest in breaking down this self-imposed wall of silence, as Warners' *The Life of Emile Zola* (1937) further demonstrated. While sidestepping anti-Semitism, the film revealed the psychological impact of Hitler's policies on the refugees crowding the film capital. Hollywood's émigré community played a crucial role in bringing the French novelist to the screen. Two central European exiles, Heinz Herald and Geza Erczeg, crafted the picture's initial outline. Their treatment centered on Zola's defense of Captain Alfred Dreyfus, a Jewish artillery officer whom French military officials exiled to Devil's Island in 1894 on a spurious charge of leaking secrets to German diplomats. Director William Dieterle, a German refugee, completed the task of molding Dreyfus's champion into a universalized symbol of liberty. Originally titled *The Truth Is on the March,* the film tracks Zola's fanatical devotion to uncovering the grimy reality of everyday life.[36]

Zola's (Paul Muni) zeal for uncovering social ills has waned by the time of Dreyfus's banishment. The once-great writer is a fat, rich, and complacent shadow of his former self. Mrs. Dreyfus (Gale Sondergaard) rouses Zola from his languor, begging him to rediscover his love for truth by taking up her husband's case. His investigation persuades him that the tribunal's decision was "a supreme slap at all truth, all justice." He hammers away at the military and popular opinion, all the time insisting that "truth is on the march and nothing will stop it." French authorities finally pardon Dreyfus in the last days of Zola's life.[37] His release is a testament to the author's willingness to sacrifice for freedom and his refusal to "applaud the lies of fanatical intolerance."

After filming Paul Muni's speech about the ennobling power of the truth, Dieterle exclaimed to the crew, "You see, he is speaking to the Fascists!" Dieterle's outburst stunned Gale Sondergaard. " 'Fascism' was a word you never mentioned," she said. "You didn't, that was a bad word." Reviewers shared her awe. *Christian Century*'s Bernard Clausen said the film "purged" audiences "of some of their own unworthiness." Even Joseph Breen thought it was a "magnificent picture." The movie racked up more than $1 million in profits and captured the Academy Award for Best Picture.[38]

Like *They Won't Forget, The Life of Emile Zola* sidestepped the Jewish issue. Although anti-Semitism lay at the heart of the Dreyfus affair, it plays no role in the movie. This omission resulted from the moguls' long-standing aversion to the subject and, to a lesser extent, from PCA censorship. Breen toned down early versions of the script. Scenes of angry crowds burning copies of Zola's *J'Accuse* especially concerned him. Such images, he warned, recalled "recent activities in Germany, as regards the books authored, or published by, Jews." No one ever says the word *Jew* in the film. The only reference to Dreyfus's religion is a quick shot of a finger pointing at "Jew" on a personnel form. Many reviewers lamented Warners' suppression of this crucial element. Their criticisms probably drew more attention to anti-Semitism than the use of *Jew* in the movie would have. Even with this gaping thematic hole, Warners' call for truth was a dangerous message. Germany, Italy, Peru, and other countries banned *The Life of Emile Zola.*[39]

They Won't Forget, Black Legion, and *The Life of Emile Zola* are all above-average pictures. Jack and Harry Warner's implied anti-Nazi films, however, constituted a mere handful of around three hundred features their studio shot between 1933 and 1938, and their personal involvement in them was minimal. Even this small contribution to the antifascist cause surpassed what other studios offered. Warner Bros.' competitors refused to dip a toe into these dangerous waters. Hollywood would not and could not engage the emerging menace so long as the industry remained bound by self-censorship and the need to maintain foreign and domestic goodwill. By the time of *Zola*'s fall 1937 release, however, the situation appeared to be changing.

ↄ ↄ ↄ

Frequent moviegoers may have sensed a subtle change in the content of movies during 1937. *They Won't Forget* and *The Life of Emile Zola* joined *The Story of Louis Pasteur* in articulating a prodemocracy, projustice, protolerance message that echoed growing fears for the fate of free governments in Europe. Not coincidentally, the slowly shifting onscreen reality paralleled a time of overseas troubles for major studios. Although most Americans remained unaware of Hollywood's behind-the-scenes dealings, the movie capital found itself increasingly engaged with hostile foreign parties.

The good feelings Walter Wanger encouraged for Italy evaporated when the Fascists imposed new film guidelines in October 1936, the same month in which Mussolini formed the Axis alliance with Hitler and the Hollywood Anti-Nazi League held its Shrine Auditorium gathering. The regulations restricted imports of films to forty-eight per year and capped exports of profits. Foreign movie companies sent about 50 million lire ($2,500,000) out of Italy in 1935. Under the new system, Hollywood could return only 8 million lire in profits to the United States. Studios had to invest earnings above that amount in the Italian film industry. As they had with their 1933 dubbing tax, the Fascists wanted American companies to subsidize a competitor. Economic nationalism had imperiled Hollywood's dominance of the Italian market.[40]

Italy's unexpected actions outraged Hollywood. Will Hays asked Secretary of State Cordell Hull to address the issue and dispatched MPPDA attorney Charles C. Pettijohn to Rome to synchronize the industry's movements with the embassy. Pettijohn, Ambassador William Phillips, and Commerce Department representatives spent months trying to convince the Italians that their harsh film decrees might derail broader Italian-American trade talks. Hollywood cut off shipments to Italy to lend additional pressure. Some studios were reluctant to anger the Fascists; it took everything Hays had to hold the boycott together. But not even the embargo moved the Italians.[41]

Disregarding the stalemate, Wanger proceeded with plans to shoot at Cinecitta studio. Members of his production unit took Italian lessons while Hollywood fought to reopen the market. Wanger nurtured ties with the Fascist inner circle and promoted Italy in the United States, knowing full well that Americans' impressions of Mussolini affected his own public image. He told Minister of Popular Culture Dino Alfieri in the midst of the crisis that "anything I can do to further an Italo-American alliance, will indeed be a pleasure." Wanger also viewed Hollywood's departure from Italy, which left the market wide open for his venture, as an excellent financial opportunity. His ongoing courtship of Fascists reflected Americans' differing perceptions of the two Axis nations. He saw no inconsistency in wooing Italy even as he enrolled in the Hollywood Anti-Nazi League.[42]

American studio bosses played their strongest card in late 1936 by dispatching Hays to Italy. Armed with a State Department endorsement that granted his mission quasi-official status, the MPPDA chief stepped off the *Conte di Savoia*'s gangplank and into Naples on November 14. He met MPPDA European representative Harold Smith and United Artists' Italian representative Mario Luporini at the dock, then toured Pompeii and Cinecitta before journeying to Rome for an audience with Pope Pius XI, a longtime acquaintance of Joseph Breen. The pontiff commended Hays for improving the moral content of motion pictures and enjoined him to remain vigilant against the threat of communist propaganda polluting the screen. With the formalities out of the way, Hays settled in to break the film stalemate. Ambassador Phillips gave him an office in the American Embassy and arranged meetings with Italian officials, who, Hays soon discovered, were not in an accommodating mood. The Fascists wanted to link their dispute with Hollywood to larger Italian-American trade issues. They refused to modify their film laws unless the United States slashed tariffs on Italian goods.[43]

Hays needed to detach cinematic matters from general commercial concerns. He determined the best way to achieve this was to go straight to the top. Hays cabled Roosevelt to ask whether the president would arrange for him to meet with Mussolini. FDR communicated Hays's request to Mussolini, who agreed to see the movie czar. Their meeting started poorly, as Il Duce's lavish office and dominating presence momentarily threw Hays on the defensive. Quickly regaining his poise, Hays flattered his host by marveling at the dictator's achievements and then eased into an amiable discussion of their differences. The smooth-talking Hays shamelessly stoked the dictator's vanity. Italy will be a great film-making nation one day, he said. Its movies will inspire audiences around the world. Restrictive cinematic policies therefore acted against the country's long-term interests. Other nations would surely respond in kind, Hays argued, sealing their borders to Italian productions at the very moment when Fascist filmmakers were poised to capture a healthy slice of the global market. Having grabbed Il Duce's interest, Hays suggested boosting the new export quota from 8 million lire per year to 40 million. Mussolini seemed convinced. He grabbed a phone on his desk and called his son-in-law, Minister of Press and Propaganda Galeazzo Ciano. After a brief conversation, Il Duce informed Hays that he would eliminate the forty-eight-film quota and hike the export limit to 24 million lire a year. Hays agreed. Just like that, the deal was done.[44]

Formalized in late December, the final settlement allowed American studios to export only 20 million lire (about $1 million) but did not compel them to invest blocked funds in Italian film production. They could import up to 250 features a year—a largely symbolic number, as they generally sent around 160. It was not an ideal arrangement. Italian exhibitors still had to show at least one domestic film for every three foreign releases. The dubbing tax of thirty thousand lire per feature and the requirement that Hollywood studios dub movies in Italy remained. But the agreement gave the studios enough; they could earn a profit. Breathing a sigh of relief, producers praised Hays's diplomacy and lifted their boycott.[45]

With the Hays agreement in place and Wanger set to shoot a Technicolor version of *Arabian Nights* once Cinecitta opened, Italo-American film relations appeared to be on solid footing. Cinematic détente, however, proved illusory, as Italy's anti-Hollywood sentiments reemerged in the spring of 1937. Cinecitta's completion convinced Italians that their pictures could equal Hollywood's in quality. American market dominance galled Fascists who strove for national self-sufficiency. Italian producers demanded government protection from American competition. Rumors of a new crackdown swirled through Hollywood and Washington. The MPPDA heard reports that the Fascists planned to jump the dubbing tax from thirty thousand lire to one hundred thousand lire per film, an amount "so high that it seems ridiculous to even think of it."[46]

Ridiculous or not, the rumors were true. Italy boosted its dubbing tax from 30,000 lire ($1,500) to between 50,000 ($2,500) and 110,000 lire ($5,500) per feature, depending on a movie's earnings, in April 1937. Hollywood cried foul even though the tax hike did not violate the Hays-Mussolini agreement. Hays blasted Italy's latest move as a violation of "all international trade practices." He believed the Fascists wanted to drive American films from their country altogether. Mussolini compounded the trade's anger in June when he replaced Italy's 3:1 foreign/domestic film quota with a more punitive 2:1 ratio.[47]

Italian Fascists simultaneously narrowed their definition of an acceptable cinematic import. Hollywood was accustomed to adjusting films to suit national tastes and censorship requirements. Great Britain objected to scenes showing cruelty to animals, Japan cut lengthy kisses, and Latin American nations barred criticisms of the military. Producers altered scripts accordingly before shooting began. Italy's censorship, in contrast, was unpredictable. Its ban on *The Life of Emile Zola* made at least some sense. Its denunciation of *The Charge of the Light Brigade* and *Lives of a Bengal Lancer* as "British propaganda" held slight merit. No one could adequately explain why its censors deemed *Romeo and Juliet* and the Marx Brothers' *A Night at the Opera* inappropriate. Italy's mercurial moves left the studios in perpetual uncertainty, never knowing whether its censors would accept or reject a film.[48]

MGM experienced the worst of the censorship battles. Still smarting from the *It Can't Happen Here* fiasco, the studio embarked on another odyssey in late 1936 when it paid dramatist Robert Sherwood $125,000 for the rights to *Idiot's Delight*. The Broadway smash featured the husband-and-wife team of Alfred Lunt and Lynn Fontaine as international travelers trapped in a hotel when Italy launches a surprise attack on France. Joseph Breen's opinion that "a picture based on this play would be banned widely abroad, and might even cause reprisals against the American company distributing it" scared off other studios interested in purchasing the play. As expected, the Italian Embassy filed an objection with the MPPDA after reading reports that MGM was casting the film.[49]

The Hays Office thought the Italians were overreacting, yet believed Hollywood should concede. "It is their country," MPPDA foreign manager Frederick Herron advised Breen, "and they have, of course, a perfect right to say what shall be brought in." Breen asked the Italian consul in Los Angeles, Roberto Caracciolo, for an opinion. The consul said MGM must rename the play and render the film completely "inoffensive to Italians."[50]

MGM refused to change the name. *Idiot's Delight* was a valuable title, and it was clear that the studio could salvage little more than the title from the original production. MGM producer Hunt Stromberg promised the film would be a love story, not an antiwar piece, that never identified the countries involved. "I would like to assure you most sincerely," he told Breen, "that since we ourselves think of Italy only in terms of highest respect and friendliness, we would find our task as producers of this picture most unhappy if we did any single thing, in the final analysis, to injure or offend the executives or people of that nation." Stromberg granted Caracciolo final script approval and agreed to preview the completed picture for representatives of the Italian government. Rather than sign or reject the deal, the Italians bided their time and kept MGM in limbo. The spring of 1937 passed without a resolution.[51]

Those same months saw a further deterioration in Hollywood's crumbling relationship with the Nazis. Germany imported about one hundred American features a year, around thirty of which survived the Propaganda Ministry's censors to actually appear onscreen. Some moviemakers believed Nazi bureaucrats intentionally cleared second-rate productions as a way of undercutting Hollywood's appeal in Germany. Only MGM, Paramount, and Twentieth Century–Fox still braved the market by 1937. Other majors remained willing to work with the Nazis if the financial prospects were right. Universal president J. Cheever Cowdin visited Berlin in early 1937 to request relaxed censorship on his studio's movies. His main selling point, which the Nazis rejected, was that Jews no longer ran Universal now that its board had expelled Carl Laemmle, the studio's founder.[52]

Joseph Goebbels, who already determined which foreign movies showed on German screens, completed the Nazi takeover of the domestic film industry when he bought out the last independent German studios in March 1937. "Everything that smells of the celluloid is tagged, filed and neatly pigeonholed," *Variety* lamented. The Germans now censored and reviewed movies according to ideological content, not quality. One Propaganda Ministry official explained that "if a work of art and its presentation contain a National Socialist idea we favor it. If the opposite is the case, we have not only the right but the duty to be against it." That attitude did not bode well for American studios. Whatever a "National Socialist idea" was—and the Nazis saw no need to clarify their rhetoric—Hollywood executives suspected their pictures did not disseminate it. Worse, the Germans bullied Austria into reducing imports of American films. When taken in combination with the growing problems in Italy, the continent was becoming a more hostile place.[53]

The simmering tensions between Italy and Hollywood boiled over that fall. Vittorio Mussolini arrived in New York in September 1937, just months after HANL's anniversary bash and soon after the *Idiot's Delight* negotiations ground to a standstill. Il Duce's son came to the United States seeking Hollywood crews to produce movies at Cinecitta. He already had a partner in Hal Roach, a noted producer of slapstick comedies, with whom he had formed a company called RAM (Roach and Mussolini) in early 1937. The two planned to make films primarily for the continental market but also inked an American distribution deal with MGM. Mussolini hoped his trip would fortify relations with Hollywood and attract technical personnel to RAM.[54]

The mission got off to a promising start. The MPPDA attorney Charles C. Pettijohn, who happened to be on board the *Rex* with Mussolini, found him "a fine, quiet, modest young man." The mood soured when the ship docked in New York. City officials feared for Mussolini's safety. A government tugboat ferried him to an undisclosed location far from the protesters gathered at the pier. After a whirlwind city tour and a ride to the top of the Empire State Building (accompanied by thirteen carloads of police officers, Secret Service agents, and Italian consulate officials), Mussolini holed up in the Ritz Tower Hotel. He flew with Roach to Hollywood a few days later. Their trip unfortunately coincided with Benito Mussolini's arrival in Munich to consult with Hitler. Il Duce met with German film stars as his son kibitzed with their American counterparts.[55]

Mussolini's West Coast visit went poorly. The Hollywood Anti-Nazi League rallied liberals with an anti-Mussolini campaign in industry trade journals. The organization's protests made life difficult for the "Fascist princeling," who went into seclusion at Roach's Beverly Hills estate. Police kept him under constant guard. Roach hoped a party celebrating Vittorio's twenty-first birthday would mend the widening rift between his business partner and Hollywood activists. Invitees found themselves in a tough spot. They did not want to insult Italians by staying home, but neither did they want to be associated with Mussolini's son. Roach's fete was an awkward, sparsely attended affair. Not even the gaily decorated cake, topped with a Fascist soldier and a model of the *Rex,* could save it. Roach absorbed considerable abuse from HANL, unaffiliated liberals, and everyone who wanted Hollywood to stay out of politics. Antifascist members of the Screen Actors Guild, led by Fredric March, James Cagney, and Luise Rainer, picketed outside his studio.[56]

RAM was going nowhere. Antifascist protests wounded the venture, but the company's inability to interest bankers finished it off. American financiers worried about Italy's currency restrictions and feared that Il Duce would meddle in the company's affairs. "In the end," *Variety* concluded, "it became obvious that there would be no money in making pictures in Rome for anybody in Hollywood." Stymied, Mussolini departed Hollywood a week earlier than planned. After a brief stop at the White House (appeasement still lived), he went home.[57]

It was getting harder to do business with the Fascists. Even Walter Wanger started to get cold feet. His assurance that Italian production plans were "more alive than ever" seemed sincere, however. The producer's contracts with Henry Fonda, Madeline Carroll, Sylvia Sidney, and Joan Bennett allowed him to send the actors to Italy. Tay Garnett and King Vidor wanted to direct at Cinecitta. Wanger arranged a warm welcome for Joseph Breen when the PCA head vacationed in Italy in 1938. But the producer struggled to find the right project, the right cast and crew, and the right financing. The Italians were getting fed up with Wanger's delays, and Wanger was getting fed up with the Italians.[58]

Although less pressing than Hollywood's European troubles, problems were also arising in Asia. Japan was Hollywood's most important Asian market, screening some two hundred features a year and generating around $1 million in annual profits. Japan was insignificant compared to large European nations but nevertheless a reliable income producer whose people loved American films. That comfortable relationship changed in 1937. Japan's invasion of China unleashed a nationalistic outpouring that weakened the popularity of foreign pictures. Its officials hoped to wean audiences from Hollywood and refocus them on domestic releases. Achieving this goal would encourage patriotism while addressing a trade deficit of $200 million a year.[59]

Japan struck at its competitors in September 1937, the same month Vittorio Mussolini arrived in Hollywood. In an unexpected move, the government forbid the importation of motion pictures and other luxuries. Hollywood executives who rarely contemplated Japan now found themselves desperately fighting to reenter the market. "No development ever has proved as serious to foreign film activity in Japan as has this blockade by the Finance Ministry," one observer wrote. Neither studio heads nor their allies in Washington saw much chance of lifting the ban. Japan is "virtually lost," the Commerce Department warned.[60]

MPPDA negotiators spent months talking with Japan's Finance Ministry. The two sides finally brokered a deal in the summer of 1938 that returned Hollywood pictures to the market. Japan agreed to import around 250 American-made features a year and deposit $800,000 of Hollywood's profits in the Yokohama Specie Bank's San Francisco branch, where it would remain for three years, interest free, before studios could touch it.[61] Profits above $800,000 remained frozen in Japan. It was the best arrangement the majors could hope for. Studio bosses were happy to be back in Japan's nearly eighteen hundred theaters but feared the dispute represented the beginning, not the end, of their troubles with the islands. "Ultra-nationalistic entities" might seek additional repressive measures—quotas, limitations on imports, or tougher censorship—at any moment.[62]

❧ ❧ ❧

A tide of antidictatorship was rising around the film community at the end of 1937. Warner Bros. subtly jabbed at the Nazis. Major studios and the MPPDA were tiring of the Axis nations' financial chicanery. Actors and studio workers were vocalizing their anti-Nazism. War raged in Spain, Japan's armies rolled through China, Italy had wrapped up its invasion of Ethiopia, and Germany was preparing for its *Anschluss* with Austria. The Roosevelt administration was also getting antsy. FDR told a Chicago audience in October 1937 that "peace-loving nations" should "quarantine" regimes contributing to the rise of "world lawlessness."[63]

Americans did not want war. A palpable sense of relief swept the country when Japan defused international tensions by apologizing for its December 1937 bombing of the USS *Panay*. Even so, foreign affairs were clearly assuming greater importance in both America's political capital and its entertainment capital. After years of hesitation and negotiation, people were choosing sides.

CHAPTER THREE

Fingers in the Dike

W ITH INTERNATIONAL TRAVEL a rarity and television in its extreme infancy, The March of Time's "Inside Nazi Germany—1938"
gave most American moviegoers their first extended look at Hitler's
empire. RKO, the distributor of The March of Time series, publicized
its sixteen-minute-long January release by promising hair-raising tales
about the dangers photographer Julien Bryan risked to smuggle twenty
thousand feet of film out of Germany and by assuring audiences that the
newsreel unveiled juicy details about the regime's inner workings.[1]

RKO's hype far exceeded the short's reality. Most of "Inside Nazi Germany" was so innocuous it could have come from official sources. German
civilians looked happy and healthy. Army drills felt more like pageantry
than militarism. Scenes of Hitler and other top Nazis conveyed little sense
of menace. The March of Time supplemented Bryan's pedestrian images
of everyday life with stagy reenactments of military training and concentration camps shot in New York. Even Nazi sympathizer Fritz Kuhn's
address to the German-American Bund felt phony. "Inside Nazi Germany" did little to suggest the repression gripping Germany, including,
for example, only one brief image of an anti-Semitic sign.[2]

Spoken with his trademark clipped cadence and booming voice, West-
brook Van Voorhis's narration offered a different story, tagging the mild
scenes onscreen as dramatic evidence of Nazi misrule. His closing counsel typified the soundtrack. "Nazi Germany faces her destiny with one of
the great war machines in history," Van Voorhis exclaimed, "and the
inevitable destiny of the great war machines of the past has been to
destroy the peace of the world, its people, and the governments of their
time. TIME MARCHES ON!"

Around 25 million Americans saw "Inside Nazi Germany." None of
them seemed to agree about what it meant. Opening night at Broadway's

Embassy Newsreel Theatre brought a mix of boos, cheers, raised fists, "Heil Hitlers," and "Heil Roosevelts." German consuls in San Francisco and Buffalo lodged protests against it. Chicago's board of censors banned it. New York City rabbi Stephen Wise praised it. Producer David O. Selznick called it "one of the greatest and most important reels in the history of pictures." *New Republic* dubbed it "an editorial for democracy and against suppression, militant nationalism and shoving people around." Harry Warner disagreed. Insisting that "the effect and appeal of a motion picture is to the eye primarily," the president of the company that popularized talking films barred "Inside Nazi Germany" and its "pro-Nazi propaganda" from his studio's 460 theaters.[3]

Newsreel content intrigued Warner, who believed that onscreen depictions of Hitler or his armies, no matter how tame, encouraged support for Nazism. In 1936 he decided that his theaters would no longer show newsreels that glorified the Nazis. He put trusted lieutenant Harold Rodner in charge of enforcing his vague edict. Rodner interpreted Warner's mandate broadly, judging fifty-seven reels inappropriate in 1936 alone. Warner personally banished footage of German boxer Max Schmeling's demolition of heavyweight Joe Louis from his theaters that year. Rodner monitored newsreels throughout the late 1930s. With Harry's backing, he pressured other studios' executives to downplay or eliminate footage from Germany but could not coordinate newsreel makers behind a single policy. Fox Movietone, MGM News of the Day, Paramount News, RKO-Pathé, and Universal Newsreel played a game of tit-for-tat, refusing to cut scenes of Nazis unless their rivals did so first.[4]

Hollywood's unwillingness to lay down arms in the battle for American eyeballs made Hitler a prominent character on the country's movie screens. His presence weighed heavily on Warner. "I am sick and tired of telling everybody else what to do," he complained in a memo that revealed more about his character than he intended. "They have as much at stake with their own life as we have. Therefore I have made up my mind to forget it and let them do as they please." Harry Warner was good at many things. Forgetting and letting his peers do as they pleased when a righteous cause was at hand were not among them.[5]

As one of the first cinematic shots across Hitler's bow, "Inside Nazi Germany" forced Hollywood to consider whether overtly discussing the Nazis—as opposed to dealing with fascism through parables, as in *The*

Story of Louis Pasteur and *The Life of Emile Zola*—fell within its purview as an entertainment medium. *Motion Picture Herald* publisher and Joseph Breen confidant Martin Quigley, for one, thought the newsreel exceeded its bounds. "We hold that the motion picture theatre is and should remain devoted to the mission of providing entertainment," Quigley decreed. "Controversial political material" had no place on American screens, even in newsreels.[6]

The argument that movies, even newsreels, should provide happy escapism strongly influenced Hollywood's approach toward the dictators. Quigley's pure-entertainment ethos made good business sense. Most producers agreed when *Saturday Review of Literature* writer Ben Ray Redman argued that "it is impossible to say anything without offending somebody." Moviegoers wanted to be amused, not informed, the theory went. Darryl F. Zanuck held that "the surest way to fail in screen drama is to attempt to preach to your public."[7]

Zanuck's maxim applied to overseas theatergoers as well as domestic ones. Studios took about half their total revenues from foreign markets and had little interest in risking governmental sanctions by taking sides on contentious issues. The film community knew it was being watched. Los Angeles was an important consular post, filled with sharp-eyed diplomats. Rumors of a project that negatively depicted their homeland nearly guaranteed an angry call to Joseph Breen, Will Hays, or the State Department.[8]

Hollywood's dominance of mass entertainment made it a target for critics who feared the motion picture's power. "What chance has the average citizen to protect himself?" wondered Margaret Farrand Thorp, author of the 1939 *America at the Movies*. "He walks down Main Street in the evening not as a free agent, simply as a puppet at the mercy of . . . the movies." Cinema's unique relationship with viewers made the medium dangerous. Audiences sat in the dark as oversized images transfixed them like victims of a skilled hypnotist. They stared at onscreen giants whose seductive voices poured into the ears and into the subconscious, subtly guiding the viewer's thoughts and actions. Or so detractors argued.[9]

Fear of government censorship left producers staring at their ceilings at night. Several states maintained censorship boards, and the federal government was theoretically capable of censoring Hollywood. The Supreme Court's *Mutual Film Corp. v. Industrial Commission of Ohio*

(1915) decision denied the industry free speech protections on the grounds that movies were organs for profit rather than opinion. The Court claimed that states needed protection from the possibility that corporations might use movies "for evil." "There are some things that should not have pictorial representation in public places and to all audiences," Justice Joseph McKenna observed.[10]

While the federal government was unlikely to inject itself into determining film content, other groups tried to accomplish this indirectly by attacking Hollywood's distribution system. Studios typically forced theater owners to purchase pictures in groups of thirty-five or more, a system known as block booking. Exhibitors chose their season's slate blindly, selecting from brief, written summaries of movies that were often still in preproduction. Block booking and blind selling gave studios a guaranteed market; theaters bought lesser films as a prerequisite for getting the upcoming Clark Gable or Shirley Temple feature. Civic and religious organizations claimed that these practices prevented exhibitors from tailoring choices to local values, which were presumably superior to Hollywood's values. *Christian Century* called block booking and blind selling "the very foundations of the morally and socially destructive policies of the Hollywood magnates." Senator Smith Brookhart (R-Iowa) repeatedly introduced a bill to abolish block booking. Congressman Samuel Pettengill (D-Indiana) and Senator Matthew Neely (D-West Virginia) took up the anti-block-booking cause after Brookhart left the Senate in 1933.[11]

Anti-block-booking crusades not only struck at Hollywood's distribution structure but also provided nagging reminders that the government was watching and could act if the film capital displeased it. Executives had heard rumors that the Justice Department was preparing an antitrust suit against major studios well before "Inside Nazi Germany" appeared. With two branches of government considering action and reformers poised to pounce on transgressors, now was not the time to stir the pot with message films. Pure, wholesome entertainment was the order of the day.

Hollywood's creative element despised producers' thematic conservatism. Screenwriter Jo Swerling complained that "there is practically nothing you can say in a picture. . . . You've got to lay off politics altogether. No race problems. Miscegenation is out. Nix on war. Stay away from social conditions. Steer clear of labor problems. Eschew the class conflict. Soft pedal on sex. Avoid religion. In short, lay off life."[12]

While Swerling's complaint was true in a way, Hollywood could not "lay off life." It could, however, present a particular kind of life. Despite their cries of pure entertainment, moviemakers were in fact propagandists who sold an idea called "Americanism." Motion pictures denied what Will Hays called "the alleged failures of our ideals, our policies, our efforts and our system" that emerged during the Depression. With a few inevitable exceptions, they celebrated individualism, pragmatism, and free enterprise. Hollywood concealed class divisions and promoted nationalism. Movies presented luxurious, mannered lives. Their reality wore tuxedoes and cocktail dresses and partied in champagne-drenched clubs. Although all studios disseminated this vision to some extent, actor Edward G. Robinson thought MGM embraced it most tightly. According to him, Louis B. Mayer "believed movies should be an escape from the ugliness of the world and should contain no messages except that love and fieldstone houses and gorgeous women and manly men were, in sum, God's true purpose."[13]

This was a pretty big message for an industry that supposedly eschewed messages. The "entertainment/propaganda" debate that set so many pens scratching and so many tongues wagging was a sham. American moviemakers portrayed themselves as mere entertainers but were actually as ideological as Joseph Goebbels. Most producers understood propaganda as totalitarian, government-sponsored, ominous. To them, a film with an all-American message was not a "message film." In some hazy way, movie moguls believed Americanism was right and propaganda was wrong. Their thinking rarely took them beyond this Manichean duality.

The banner of pure entertainment burnished Hollywood's credentials as a respectable cultural institution. It separated movies from European "isms" and shielded studios from censorship and government regulation. The Production Code's restrictions shoved American movies into an ideological box but served Hollywood's financial interests nicely by demanding sunny pictures that circumvented difficult subjects and offended no one. The industry had its blind spots, as major studios routinely caricatured Hispanics, African Americans, and non-Western ethnicities in productions Joseph Breen blithely approved. The PCA head was less forgiving when movies disparaged Western Europeans. Armed with this unequal sense of who needed protection, Breen had an almost Pavlovian response to scripts that touched on European totalitarianism. Any prospective producers of such films could safely assume that they would receive a letter from Breen citing the Production Code's insistence that studios respect "the just rights, history, and feelings of any nation" within days of submitting their treatment. The PCA's shadow loomed large over writers, directors, and producers who sought to address international issues. And moviemakers knew that Breen did not stand alone in the fight against current-events pictures, for he almost always strode into battle with support from his boss, MPPDA president Will Hays.

✿ ✿ ✿

To call Will Hays "jug-eared" is almost redundant. Writers always referred to him as jug-eared. The juxtaposition of description and name occurred so frequently a reader could imagine the movie czar's mother dubbing the newborn in her arms "Jug-Eared William Harrison Hays." Hays indeed had magnificent ears. Flaring from his head at perfect forty-five degree angles, they were the only part of him that assumed heroic proportions and therefore were the feature that chroniclers seized on. His ears thrust out from his small, lean frame like two kites straining against their strings. Flanking a thin nose and languid blue eyes, they resembled nothing so much as a Valentine's Day heart bisected and affixed to either side of his head. The "jug-eared" moniker described Hays's nature as well as his appearance. He heard everything. He spent a lifetime cultivating a global network of contacts that poured information into those magnificent ears. Political titans, religious figures, and masters of industry all spoke into the jug ears of Will Hays.[14]

Producer Jesse Lasky Jr. said Hays "looked like Uncle Sam, minus the beard." Hays would have liked that image, as he saw himself as the embodiment of small-town, American virtues. He idealized his birthplace of Sullivan, Indiana, as a bucolic hamlet of tree-lined streets and comfortable homes. His father, a well-connected attorney, raised him with the upstanding morality and Republican politics that Hays forever associated with right-thinking Americanism. Will neither smoked nor drank. He wrapped his youth around community picnics, lemonade stands, the Presbyterian Church, a pony named Daisy, and political conservatism. He listed his "deepest personal convictions" as "faith in God, in folks, in the nation, and in the Republican Party." One of his first memories was of meeting Republican presidential candidate James Blaine during the 1884 campaign. Will's father took him to St. Louis in 1896 to witness William McKinley's nomination.[15]

Hays was an average student at Wabash College. He was, however, an extraordinary joiner—Babbitt personified, a Solid Citizen in a dark suit, a devotee to the faith that business is next to godliness. He was an elder in the Presbyterian Church and a member of the Elks, the Knights of Pythias, the Kiwanians, the Masons, the Moose, Phi Delta Theta, and the Rotarians. He became a Republican precinct chairman in 1900, the year he joined his father's law firm. The Republicans' laissez-faire economics and frequent invocations of Horatio Alger's rags-to-riches mantra meshed with the lessons his father taught him.[16]

Although bright and articulate, Hays never amounted to much as a lawyer, in part because so many other things distracted him. He taught Sunday school, remained active in fraternal organizations, and expanded his political activities. At twenty-five he became chairman of the Sullivan County Republicans. The party elevated him to the state chairmanship ten years later. Hays used his position to improve grassroots organization, win good publicity, and heal the party establishment's rift with Teddy Roosevelt's Bull Moose faction. His network of Indiana Republicans included several future MPPDA staffers, including publicity man Fred Beetson, foreign manager Frederick Herron, and general counsel Charles C. Pettijohn.[17]

Indiana repudiated its 1912 vote for Democrat Woodrow Wilson by going Republican in 1916. Hays's managerial and oratorical talents contributed to the switch. Party leaders elected him head of the Republican National Committee in acknowledgment of his achievement. His fundraising work during Warren Harding's successful 1920 presidential run introduced him to many important Hollywood players. Operating through Pettijohn, who did legal work for an exhibitors' association, Hays persuaded studio executives to flood screens with positive newsreel footage of the probusiness Republican. Hays's abilities so impressed Fox Studio head William Fox that he offered the politico a position in his company. Hays politely declined. Film was an unfamiliar field and, besides, his friend Harding wanted him to serve as postmaster general.

Hays excelled in the post, streamlining the 326,000-person agency while overseeing efforts to humanize the mail service and improve its image.[18]

Hollywood called again in December 1921. Studio heads needed a savior, and fast. Unimpressed by Hollywood's repeated promises to clean up motion picture content, several states and scores of cities passed censorship laws. Cries for regulation swelled when moon-faced comedian Fatty Arbuckle stood trial for allegedly raping a showgirl in a San Francisco hotel. Although a jury acquitted Arbuckle, the incident ruined his career and inspired a rash of stories about moral turpitude in the film community. This bad publicity, along with a harsh recession and competition from radio, devastated profits. With their finances in disarray and talk of federal intervention in the air, movie moguls dove for cover. They needed someone with unimpeachable morals, extensive political ties, and a gift for public relations to save the industry. Will Hays fit the bill perfectly.[19]

Producer Lewis Selznick, who met Hays during the 1920 campaign, headed a committee that visited the postmaster general's suite at the Wardman Park Hotel in Washington, D.C. Hays was in poor shape, having recently been injured in a train wreck, but listened to their pitch. Selznick presented a petition asking him to assume the presidency of the Motion Picture Producers and Distributors of America and a $100,000 salary. Hays asked for time. He returned to Sullivan for the holidays, pondered his options, and accepted the job a few weeks later.

His stated reason for leaving the government is revealing. He often told the story of watching his six-year-old son playing with two friends (or sometimes with a cousin; the tale evolved over the years) in cowboy costumes they received for Christmas. Rather than taking the names of Wild West heroes, the kids argued about who got to play characters from the latest William S. Hart oater (or, in other versions, who was William S. Hart and who was Douglas Fairbanks). Hays studied their play. "A new vision of the motion pictures came to me," he wrote in his autobiography. "I saw them not only from the viewpoint of men who had millions of dollars invested in them but from the viewpoint of the fathers and mothers of America who have millions of children invested in them." His son's antics may not have been Hays's sole motivation for switching careers. A 1928 Senate investigation revealed that he accepted improper gifts during Harding's nomination campaign. Though hardly the worst offense committed by a Harding appointee, he may have wanted to get out while the getting was good.[20]

Hays immediately proved his value to movie executives, in the process installing himself as a crucial cog in the industry's machinery. During his first months in office the unflappable bureaucrat navigated studios through the fallout from a sex/murder/drug scandal involving director William Desmond Taylor, headed off efforts by Latin American governments to ban Hollywood films, and killed censorship bills in thirty-two state legislatures.[21]

Such accomplishments lifted the mood of immediate crisis, but Hays had little time to enjoy his victories. His job brought enormous pressures. Hays spent twelve-hour workdays promoting the industry, smoothing out misunderstandings, and lobbying against harmful legislation. He met daily with studio executives, government officials, representatives from public organizations, lawyers, and theater managers. Anyone with a problem related to movies turned to him. Producers complained about censorship. Religious groups complained about the lack of censorship. School groups protested when films depicted comic stutterers. Glassblowers opposed the prevalence of canned beer onscreen. Cab companies objected to films showing taxis used as getaway vehicles. The National Billiard Association grumbled that Hollywood stereotyped pool halls as immoral places. Hays dealt with all of them.[22]

His tact, discretion, and cool-headedness proved key to his success. He only raised his high-pitched, gently twangy voice when discussing the evils of government interference with motion pictures. Then his volume rose from a whisper to a roar, and his face turned red under his graying hair as he banged his fist on the table. Self-censorship and self-regulation constituted the lifeblood of his political philosophy. To surrender them was to abandon the core tenets of American business.

Hays asserted in his memoirs that he "abandoned politics officially" when he resigned as postmaster general, but he added a qualification: "I remained a staunch Republican," he wrote, "and I still played the game of politics, not behind the scenes—because I make no secrecy of my actions—but unofficially." He certainly stayed involved in politics. Newspaperman Roy Howard noted in 1938 that Hays "probably carries as much weight in Washington today as any man out of office and not actually functioning as a professional politician." His claim to always act openly was less truthful. Hays looked like a man with no secrets but actually loved intrigue. He littered his correspondence with enigmatic references to "XYZ" affairs—matters too sensitive to discuss in writing. He sent ciphered telegrams and maintained an extensive code book for delicate subjects, particularly those involving foreign governments. He code-named the American ambassador to England "WHEEL." Warner Bros. was "GOOSE." Hays, with perhaps a hint of conceit, was "TONIC." In 1937 he hired Count Enrico Galeazzi, a close adviser to the future Pope Pius XII, Cardinal Eugenio Pacelli, to act as his spy in Italy. Count Galeazzi, who had arranged Hays's 1936 meeting with Pius XI, provided inside information on leading Fascists over the next several years. Hays's desire for secrecy extended to domestic politics. As the 1938 midterm elections neared, for example, he engaged a covert agent of sorts to investigate the nation's political mood. Known only as "P.D.T.," Hays's man reported on hot-button local issues from around the country and suggested ways for Republicans to capitalize on them.[23]

Although Hays maintained a cordial relationship with Roosevelt, his contempt for the New Deal lingered close to the surface. Its meddling with business affairs struck him as antithetical to American traditions. His personal opposition did not dissuade him, however, from asking the State Department, Commerce Departments, and FDR to protect Hollywood's interests. Hays's vision of government resembled Herbert Hoover's. Both wanted Washington to cooperate with business, helping it to succeed without getting in its way.[24]

The MPPDA president was more consistent in his attitude toward movies. Hays often referred to motion pictures as a "Cause," and he meant it. His image of the silver screen bordered on childish wonder. "I like motion pictures for the happiness they spread, for the beauty they distribute, for the inspiration they bring, and for the relief they give from all the burdens of humanity today," he told a group of exhibitors. He genuinely wanted Hollywood to uplift, to be "the entertainment of the people." He saw movies as "the product of the American spirit—vision, initiative, enterprise and progress," and he urged the film community to acknowledge its ideological debt by promoting "Americanism." To him, that demanded the movies celebrate democracy, hard work, and individual effort. Americanism, as Hays saw it, could not be propaganda, for propaganda was the bane of "pure entertainment," and pure entertainment meant promoting Americanism.[25]

Such projects as *Black Legion, The Life of Emile Zola,* and "Inside Nazi Germany" indicated that some moviemakers were expanding their definition of "Americanism" to include "antifascism." Hays articulated no clear response to this reinterpretation of one of his core doctrines. His abhorrence of totalitarianism collided with his desire to avoid controversies that could hurt revenues. He walked a fine line, hailing socially relevant films as evidence of Hollywood's artistic maturity while disingenuously claiming that those movies "shout no message, point no moral or teach no lesson." They were "splendid entertainment, not propaganda."[26]

Will Hays's narrow shoulders bore a heavy burden in the summer of 1938. Congress debated anti-block-booking bills, critics hurled charges of propaganda, and a few moviemakers explored subjects that threatened to arouse more disapprobation. Hays saw himself as one of the few men capable of holding back the deluge. It was at this pressure-filled moment that an even more dangerous problem fell on his already-crowded desk.

✿ ✿ ✿

The "principal evil" in the movie industry, a department of justice investigator told Assistant Attorney General Robert Jackson in the fall of 1937, is "the control and monopolization of exhibition by the major companies . . . coupled with their own production of the great part of the finer motion pictures." To restore competitive balance, the government should force "the complete severance and separation of the production and distribution branches of the industry from the exhibition branch." Separation—or divorcement—of theaters from production studios would upend Hollywood's financial structure. Five of the majors—Warner Bros., MGM, Paramount, RKO, and Twentieth Century–Fox—owned around one-sixth of the movie houses in the United States. More specifically, they owned most big, first-run theaters, particularly those in large cities. Their control of key theaters ensured audiences for their pictures and shut independent upstarts out of the most profitable outlets. Big studios could dominate the production and distribution of movies so long as they kept their theaters.[27]

Assistant Attorney General Thurman Arnold imperiled this lucrative, self-contained system by filing a 118-page petition with the United States District Court in New York City on July 20, 1938. His brief accused Hollywood of "monopolizing, attempting to monopolize, combining and conspiring with each other to monopolize, and contracting, combining, and conspiring to restrain interstate trade and commerce in the production, distribution, and exhibition of motion pictures." Arnold's suit condemned such "harsh, onerous, and unfair" practices as block booking, blind selling, requiring independent theater owners to buy shorts and newsreels in order to get desirable features, and pooling creative talent to keep it out of independent producers' hands. Arnold particularly objected to studio ownership of the best theaters. "Free, open, and untrammeled competition in the motion picture industry is impossible," he concluded, so long as unaffiliated exhibitors had to compete against affiliated, or studio-owned, movie houses.[28]

"The motion picture industry is on trial for its life," worried one Columbia studio lawyer. His comment was not hyperbole; Arnold's action challenged the majors' fundamental economic structure. The antitrust case grew into one of Hollywood's most pressing problems in an era that brought more headaches than New Year's Day. Although Europe was at peace when Arnold filed suit, the antitrust matter eventually played a significant role in determining Hollywood's response to World War II. Legal affairs became inextricably entwined with the war, with the unexpected consequence of binding Hollywood more tightly to Washington before the two sides resolved their dispute.[29]

The movie business had seen three efforts at monopolization. The Thomas Edison–led Motion Picture Patents Company, also known as the Trust, collapsed in 1915 after independents—some of whom went on to build the majors—successfully sued under the Sherman Antitrust Act. Adolph Zukor's Paramount nearly established complete dominance over the industry in the 1920s. Fox did the same when it came within an eyelash of swallowing MGM in 1931. Big studios settled into an uneasy peace after Fox's bid for mastery, coexisting under MPPDA supervision and upholding a gentlemen's agreement to center their theater holdings in different regions of the United States. Loews/MGM focused on New York, Paramount on New England and the South, Fox on the West Coast, and Warners on Pennsylvania and New Jersey.[30]

Gossip about a possible federal antitrust suit began flying around studio offices in 1935. A 1936 case filed against Warners' theater-buying in St. Louis fueled the fears. Justice Department officials were indeed snooping around Hollywood after receiving dozens of complaints from independent exhibitors. Will Hays promised to "cooperate unqualifiedly" with investigators but then did his best to slow the flow of information from studios to the government. Hays also asked independents to register grievances with his office rather than the Justice Department. His stalling tactics backfired, as they further convinced Washington lawmen that Hollywood was up to no good.[31]

The movie probe gained momentum in 1938. Although Roosevelt did not directly order the lawsuit, it stemmed in part from his new emphasis on an antimonopoly agenda. Influenced by old-line Progressives and his own Wilsonian impulses, FDR believed that breaking up big business could restore free enterprise and spark economic recovery. He accordingly strengthened enforcement of antitrust laws and created the Temporary National Economic Committee (TNEC) to investigate monopoly in the United States.[32]

Roosevelt's appointment of Thurman Arnold to head the Justice Department's Antitrust Division provided another spark. Raised in Laramie, Wyoming, and educated at Princeton University and Harvard Law School, Arnold had long advocated a more forceful application of the Sherman Act. He gained a measure of renown for *The Symbols of Government* (1936) and *The Folklore of Capitalism* (1937), which he published while on the Yale Law School faculty. His friends knew him as an original thinker with a biting sense of humor. His enemies saw him as disjointed and sarcastic. Both views had merit. On first glance Arnold appeared almost grandfatherly. His double chin, pipe, and slightly unkempt mustache gave him a deceptively soft facade. His slicked-back dark hair emphasized his oval-shaped face. One look at his eyes, however, indicated the hard man underneath. They were inquiring, skeptical, somehow dismissive or even contemptuous of those around him. They were the eyes of a man who was comfortable with himself and confident of his actions.[33]

Arnold started consulting for the government in 1933 and built his reputation as Roosevelt prepared his antimonopoly campaign. Arnold's friend Assistant Attorney General Robert Jackson saw him as an up-and-comer. "We certainly need lots of help," Jackson told him in late 1937. "There is nothing I would like better, if you have any jobs at which I can be of assistance," Arnold replied. Roosevelt elevated Jackson to United States solicitor general in March 1938 and nominated Arnold as his replacement.[34]

Arnold energized the Antitrust Division. He increased its staff of lawyers from forty-eight to more than three hundred. During his five-year tenure the bureau launched more than two hundred investigations and brought ninety-three antitrust suits—more than it had filed in its previous history—against industries ranging from oil to shoes to tobacco. Arnold was a pragmatist, not a wild-eyed idealist. Generally he hoped to force businesses to accept consent decrees that corrected antitrust violations without resorting to long, expensive trials.[35]

The new assistant attorney general knew Hollywood, having represented the Screen Writers Guild during its mid-decade struggle for recognition. After familiarizing himself with the ongoing movie inquiry, Arnold was ready to move forward by early summer 1938. Hays and the producers lobbied for another chance to solve their own problems, but to no avail. Hollywood made a last-ditch attempt to stop the suit on June 25, when Hays led some of the industry's most important people into the Oval Office for a twenty-minute conference with Roosevelt. Barney Balaban (Paramount), Nate Blumberg (Universal), Harry Cohn (Columbia), Sidney Kent (Twentieth Century–Fox), George Schaefer (United Artists), Nick Schenck (MGM/Loews), Leo Spitz (RKO), and Albert Warner (Warner Bros.) trooped into FDR's office. Hays informed Roosevelt that he was putting Sidney Kent in charge of a blue-ribbon panel charged with addressing Arnold's concerns. This was "an honest effort to seek a solution of our trade problems," Kent told the president, and the administration should reward their sincerity by delaying the suit. Kent's committee planned to discuss block booking and other distribution issues. Divorcement of theaters was not on its agenda. Roosevelt remained noncommittal, offering pleasantries without directly addressing the movie men's entreaties.[36]

Hays assumed a pleasant face for the press afterward, sidestepping discussion of the conference's true purpose in favor of bland platitudes. Reading from handwritten notes on a yellow legal pad, he told reporters that the group had discussed "general conditions and the steps of industrial activity by producers and distributors." He followed this vague statement with a carrot for the administration. "These are times that call for increased cooperative endeavor not only within industry but between industry and government," he said. Hays's intention was clear. Hollywood would help Roosevelt if Roosevelt helped Hollywood.[37]

The president understood the quid pro quo. He let Hays form his commission but, while giving movie men the impression he was on their side, did nothing to stop Arnold's work. Kent's panel did not impress Arnold. The Justice Department concluded that only divorcement could rectify Hollywood's transgressions, and the committee was not talking about divorcement. Arnold filed his grievance as planned a few weeks after the Washington meeting. Hays optimistically portrayed the suit as an opportunity rather than a threat. "If the present action . . . clarifies the law applicable to the complex business operations of the motion picture industry," he told reporters before boarding a train for Hollywood, "it should promote the further progress of the screen."[38]

Hollywood's rhetoric hardened as studio leaders grasped the magnitude of Arnold's action. Producers would negotiate any subject except divorcement. Hays painted the industry as a victim of overzealous bureaucrats and cast its plight in terms of great American ideals. "It is hard to see why an alien philosophy of statism . . . should have gained credence here," he observed. Movies were the all-American business, the offspring of democracy, and the bearer of pure entertainment. To oppose Hollywood was to oppose America, to violate the sacred traditions handed down by the Founding Fathers. In Hays's mind this was not just an antitrust suit; it was a battle between free enterprise and government domination. Or, to view it in the context of contemporary events, it was part of a larger struggle between democracy and totalitarianism.[39]

The two sides settled in. Government prosecutors built their case for divorcement while Kent's team tried to draft an industry code of conduct that satisfied the Justice Department without surrendering the majors' theaters. Lawyers did not discuss a consent decree until September, when the teams assembled in the posh Georgetown home of war hero and prominent attorney William "Wild Bill" Donovan. Talks proceeded through dinner and deep into the night. Not surprisingly, divorcement was the primary sticking point. While maintaining a friendly, casual atmosphere, Justice Department representatives refused to budge. The meeting broke up in the wee hours of the morning, and lawyers straggled home no closer to a consent decree than they had been before dinner.[40]

CHAPTER FOUR

Misfires

C LEAN UP THE STUFF about Spain. . . . The guy that wrote it was a
Red and he's got all the Spanish officers with ants in their pants. Fix
up that." Pat Hobby, F. Scott Fitzgerald's fictional screenwriter from a
series of short stories, had his marching orders.[1]

Hobby's mandate reflected Hollywood executives' suspicion of anything smelling of politics, especially communist politics. Along with the
Production Code's apolitical guidelines, fears of alienating audiences or
foreign governments kept the political genie safely bottled through the
Italo-Ethiopian War, the remilitarization of the Rhineland, the first
months of the Spanish Civil War, and the second Japanese invasion of
China. This blackout began to lighten with the political Warner Bros.
films of 1936 and 1937 and "Inside Nazi Germany." The June 1938 appearance of independent producer Walter Wanger's *Blockade* shone a
bright light on it, pushing the screen in directions that horrified purists
like Will Hays and Joseph Breen. *Blockade* demonstrated both Hollywood's new boldness and its old timidity. Appearing alongside Thurman Arnold's courtroom assault on Hollywood's financial backbone,
the picture ignited a national dialogue on war and peace and the screen's
role in depicting them. It also suffered from an insurmountable flaw: the
need to appease viewers and censors by cleaning up "the stuff about
Spain."

Blockade's whole is considerably less than the sum of its scenes, some
of which are remarkably intense. It is a film without a center. Wanger's
inability to settle on a title symbolized his struggle to define what the
picture would be about. It went through names like Mae West went
through men. The producer discarded "The Love of Jeanne Ney" in favor of "Castles in Spain" and then dumped that for "The Adventuress,"
"The River Is Blue," "The Rising Tide," and, finally, "Blockade." It was

a romance, a war drama, a spy flick, a red-blooded comedy, an ode to the pastoral life, and an homage to pacifism—a lot to ask of eighty-four minutes of celluloid.

Wanger's determination to make the picture contrasted with the indecision that marred the final product. His long dalliance with Mussolini aside, he was a passionate antifascist who saw Hitler leading Germany into another world war and viewed Spain as a tune-up to that impending conflict. "Wanger understood the significance of the people's struggle in Spain," screenwriter John Howard Lawson wrote, "and believed it was a public service to tell the truth about it."[2]

Walter Feuchtwanger was always confident of his own significance. About the only thing this son of German immigrants shared with such major producers as Louis B. Mayer, Adolph Zukor, and Jack Warner was his lapsed Judaism. Born into a cultured, well-to-do San Francisco family, he reveled in arts, theater, and literature. He vacationed in Europe as a child and spoke fluent French and Italian. With his center-parted and slicked-back hair, articulate speech, and spotless suits, he looked every bit the educated elitist. He attended Dartmouth, although he did not graduate, and closely followed current events and scholarly debates. He was so well read that some colleagues thought him a fraud, suspecting that his refined image concealed a vulgar lowbrow—which he was at times, especially with women.[3]

The stage, not the classroom, held his interest in college. He elevated the Dartmouth dramatic club's profile with a series of cutting-edge productions and then set out to make his fortune on Broadway. The world war interrupted his dreams but shaped his future. He used family connections to wrangle a second lieutenant's commission in the Army Signal Corps, hoping eventually to go into aerial intelligence. By all accounts he was one of the worst pilots in military history. The army instead sent him to Rome in 1918 to work for the Committee on Public Information (CPI), the American government's wartime news and propaganda agency. He enjoyed Italy, which no doubt influenced his decision to forge ties with Mussolini. More important, his time in the CPI exposed him to the power of motion pictures. Wanger credited a CPI-made film promoting U.S.-Italian friendship with lifting morale and keeping Italy in the war. He served as an aide to the American delegation at the Versailles peace talks before heading home to renew his theater career.[4]

Wanger could not recapture his earlier success. After a string of flops he refocused his attention from the boards to the screen. Jesse Lasky made him general manager of production for Famous Players–Lasky (later Paramount) in 1920. The blossoming movie business accommodated Wanger's desire to create innovative, socially relevant art. The new executive experimented with Technicolor, widescreen, and 3-D, always searching for ways to distinguish Famous Players' productions from those of its competitors. Never afraid to buck the system, especially when it brought him attention, he imported Russian director Sergei Eisenstein to adapt Theodore Dreiser's epic novel *An American Tragedy*. Wanger also signed such distinctive performers as the Marx Brothers, Tallulah Bankhead, Maurice Chevalier, Claudette Colbert, and Fredric March. Except for a three-year sojourn in Great Britain, he remained with Paramount until the company cut him loose amid falling revenues in 1931.[5]

Wanger bounced around Hollywood for several years, making stops at Columbia and MGM before entering independent production in 1934. He now had the freedom he always desired, a chance to make daring films without a studio bearing down on him. Wanger hardly enjoyed complete autonomy, of course. He still needed money, a major studio (United Artists) to distribute his pictures, and the PCA's approval for every project. His gift for publicity nevertheless made his projects appear special even when they fit into Hollywood's ideological mainstream. "He had courage without being a courageous man," explained screenwriter Robert Sodenberg.[6]

Wanger excelled at organization, fund-raising, and signing talented subordinates but had little sense of story construction or character development. Trusting his hired hands to do their jobs, the producer remained distant from scripting, shooting, and editing. "My experience with Wanger was that he wasn't really much interested in what was on the pages, as long as they came back" on time, recalled screenwriter Maurice Rapf. This did not mean he lacked ideals. Wanger believed motion pictures could be a force for world peace because they introduced different nationalities to each other. Working from this premise, in early 1936 he set his sights on making a movie that benefited humanity by illustrating the horrors of war. He went into *Blockade* hoping to make an important picture. If the film also added to his fame, all the better.[7]

In early 1937 the producer paired Lewis Milestone, a talented screen-writer who had also directed *All Quiet on the Western Front* (1930) and *The Front Page* (1931), with radical playwright Clifford Odets, best known for his prounion drama *Waiting for Lefty* (1935), to adapt *The Love of Jeanne Ney* for the screen. Ilya Ehrenburg's novel focused on a Bolshevik who flees Russia for Paris after her lover murders her treason-ous uncle. Wanger wanted Milestone and Odets to transform the book into a story about Spanish exiles who return from Paris to fight for their homeland.[8]

Wanger thrived on publicity, so hiring two liberals to write a screen-play that defied Hollywood's taboo on the Spanish Civil War was hardly out of character. It was the kind of bold idea that made him one of the industry's few successful independents. His almost primal urge to distin-guish himself made him a premier self-promoter in a town crowded with inflated personalities. *Blockade* served the producer's ideological, eco-nomic, and egoistic needs. It enabled him to articulate his views on Eu-ropean affairs while generating media attention that drew moviegoers. *Blockade*'s controversial subject ensured that it was one of those rare pictures whose significance transcended the screen.

Wanger, Milestone, and Odets carefully navigated the PCA's boundar-ies. Breen made only minor deletions when early drafts reached his office in 1937. The censor, for example, advised Wanger to make sure a statue of a nude nymph was not "too pointedly nude." The script was not exces-sively violent or explicitly sexual. Even so, Breen sensed that *Blockade* raised issues that transcended the code's specific strictures but never-theless fell within his jurisdiction. As with *It Can't Happen Here,* Breen wondered whether *Blockade* should be made at all. "There is consider-able difference in opinion in Europe at the present time regarding the Spanish Civil War," he told Wanger. Some European nations would likely ban the film regardless of its specific content. But Breen did not wield absolute power. He could no more kill a film about the Spanish Civil War than he could one about the Revolutionary War or any other war so long as it met code requirements. He advised Wanger to consult United Artists' foreign department before proceeding and recommended that he dodge overseas censors by not identifying either side in the conflict.[9]

Although *Blockade* had Breen's reluctant go-ahead, repeated delays threatened to shelve the production. Odets was bored with the work and wanted out. Wanger bickered with Milestone about casting. The producer's Cinecitta venture distracted him, as did United Artists' persistent requests that he disavow his recent decision to withdraw his pictures from Germany. The studio still saw chances for profit there. Wanger restarted *Blockade* in the summer of 1937, luring radical screenwriter John Howard Lawson from his Long Island retreat and putting him to work revising the Milestone-Odets treatment. Lawson disliked their draft. He wanted to author "a real documentary about the Spanish struggle." Taking inspiration from a 1937 incident in Bilbao, a Loyalist city suffering under a Franco-imposed blockade, the screenwriter shifted the scenario from Paris to Spain and centered its action in a starving town waiting for a supply ship.[10]

Lawson wrote at a deliberate pace. The Breen Office did not review the new *Blockade* until early 1938. While finding few direct code violations, Breen again asked Wanger to avoid taking positions on foreign happenings. He must not identify either Nationalists or Loyalists with incriminating uniforms, insignia, or place-names, and must remain rigorously neutral. "Your picture is certain to run into considerable difficulty in Europe and South America if there is any indication in the telling of your story, that you are 'taking sides' in the present unfortunate Spanish Civil War," Breen warned. Still predicting disaster, he granted a PCA seal of approval in May.[11]

Lawson later claimed that *Blockade* suffered from censorship imposed by Washington. Rumors circulated on the picture's release that the Hays Office had interfered with the production. Neither charge bears up under scrutiny. Whatever damage Hays and Breen inflicted occurred during the preshoot vetting process. There is no evidence of meddling once cameras rolled. Breen even tried to help Wanger—and to demonstrate the merit of the PCA's objections—by previewing *Blockade* for European diplomats to give the producer a chance to anticipate foreign censor boards. Resenting Breen's meddling, Wanger refused to change a frame.[12]

If Wanger should be commended for making a well-intentioned film, he should not escape criticism for his stubbornness. He could have made an antiwar film that denounced atrocities against civilians without even mentioning Spain. As is, Spain is merely a prop in *Blockade*. The only concrete evidence of the film's setting is a card in the first scene titled, "Spain, Spring 1936." This itself is disingenuous, or at least sloppy, as the

Spanish Civil War did not begin until that summer. As Bernard Dick has pointed out, Castelmare, the scene of the action, is not a Spanish name, and there is nothing particularly Spanish about the peasant-turned-warrior Marco (Henry Fonda). Wanger's desire to gain publicity through topicality resulted in a frustrating mishmash. Revelatory moments coexist with narrative somersaults designed to keep the viewer from having any sense of what is going on.[13]

United Artists' publicity campaign added to the confusion. One press release called *Blockade* "a story that might be laid, with equal success, in India or Mexico or the United States." The studio ran away from relevance, instead promising audiences "vivid adventure," "tense, unforgettable drama," and a "powerful love story." The film's ads mentioned the war solely to emphasize *Blockade*'s neutrality. Even Wanger sounded uncertain of his picture's point. "If it was propaganda for peace," he told a CBS radio interviewer, "I am very proud." The *London Daily Mail* expressed the film's central weakness more bluntly. "I am not very sure what Walter Wanger tried to do when he made *Blockade*," its reviewer wrote.[14]

Blockade opens with a *Good Earth*–style paean to the land. Marco reveres the soil. He cradles it in his hands, drawing its scent as if it were a bouquet of flowers. The mountains surrounding him, the pond where he swims, and his flock of sheep make him content. "This belongs to us," he tells his friend Luis (Leo Carrillo), "and nothing can take it from us." The first tremor comes when the beautiful Norma (Madeleine Carroll) asks for a lift into Castelmare after running her car off the road to avoid hitting a cow. Marco and Luis tow the car to town behind a team of oxen. Simple-hearted Marco falls in love with Norma along the way. She is everything he is not—worldly, well-traveled, and well-educated. What he does not know is that she is also a spy, although for whom she is spying is never made clear.

Marco's idyll takes a second hit when war comes to his valley. The approaching soldiers—from some unnamed army—drag him into a larger cause for the first time in his life. He takes up arms and inspires his fellow peasants to defend their land. Ideology is irrelevant; the farmers do not preach socialism, anarchy, or fascism. They fight to save their ancestral homes, a cause understandable to Americans of all political leanings. Marco's defense of Castelmare earns him the rank of lieutenant (the same rank Wanger held) in whatever army is fighting the one that ruined his home.

The film meanders from here. Norma gets embroiled in a plot to sink a blockade runner attempting to resupply the starving residents of Castelmare. Marco's task is to ensure the ship gets through. The two eventually find themselves on the same side. Norma defects when she sees the hungry children who will die if her mission succeeds, her basic humanity overcoming her devotion to a particular ideological cause. She surrenders to Marco and then tries to rescue the city by sabotaging her own assignment.

While serving as *Blockade*'s male and female leads, Marco and Norma were ancillary to what Lawson and Wanger hoped to accomplish. The people themselves, those anonymous proletarians caught in the cruelty of modern war, were *Blockade*'s real stars. Their shattered lives form the movie's emotional heart. *Blockade*'s Spaniards are gentle, kindhearted, and deeply religious. They huddle in churches to pray for relief from their sufferings. A shrine to the Virgin Mary glows with votive candles, the light from their flames forming a desperate plea for God's intervention. Lawson's script ignored the fact that Loyalists shuttered houses of worship in areas they controlled. Showing the death of religious freedom would complicate the film's morality and undermine sympathy for the anti-Francoists the writer was straining to depict.[15]

Fresh off a solid job on *The Life of Emile Zola,* director William Dieterle created compassion without descending into pity. *Motion Picture Herald* called *Blockade* "a convincing triumph of directorial talent over story material." Some sequences retain their emotional power today. A woman cradles her dead baby on the steps of a church. Another sits on top of the rubble that buried her family. A camera pans a line of doomed civilians, their faces etched with sorrow as an enemy submarine sinks the rescue ship. "Why did they do that?" asks a little girl watching from a window. "We must have been very naughty," her sister replies. But all is not lost. The children will not perish. With Norma's assistance, Marco tricks his adversaries into torpedoing an abandoned hulk. The real supply ship, laden with food and clothing, follows close behind. Marco's commandant rewards the hero and the redeemed Norma with a lengthy leave so that they may find peace.[16]

The weary peasant, however, knows this hope is illusory. "Peace?" he asks. "Where can you find it? Our country's been turned into a battlefield! There's no safety for old people and children! Women can't keep their families safe in their houses. They can't be safe in their own fields! Churches, schools, hospitals are targets! It's not war. War's between soldiers!" He turns to the camera, imploring the audience to heed his words. "It's murder, murder of innocent people. There's no sense to it! The world can stop it! Where's the conscience of the world?" Marco's violation of the cinematic fourth wall is a graceless but effective approach, like driving a nail with a sledgehammer. Dieterle had used the same technique when Emile Zola tells the court that his "principal aim has been to fight for truth." While the result is uplifting in *The Life of Emile Zola*, in *Blockade* it transforms a happy ending into a depressing plea for involvement in a foreign war.

Wanger recognized the problems with his film. "All the way down the line it just misses," he told publicity director Johnny Johnston. He knew he had a tough sell on his hands. *Blockade* was a downbeat movie about a conflict few wanted to discuss. It was a war flick without exciting battle scenes, a spy drama without panache. Wanger saved *Blockade* by daring opposing sides to weigh in on an invented controversy. Johnston composed a bogus telegram claiming that Franco's spies had infiltrated United Artists' British office in an effort to destroy prints of the picture. Wanger forwarded the fraudulent document to Secretary of State Cordell Hull. "I have been subjected to criticism and scrutiny in European circles because I have made a film title[d] 'Blockade' dealing with the present war in Spain," he complained. It was a shameless ploy, and it worked. Reporters picked up the story, making *Blockade* the hot topic of the day. Not wanting to stumble into a real international incident, Wanger backpedaled when the State Department requested additional information. "I am happy to say that the difficulties . . . regarding *Blockade* did not become as serious as we supposed they would," he replied.[17]

Veiled as it was, Wanger's implicit criticism of Franco angered Catholic groups. Their ferocious response to *Blockade* unwittingly gave the production the publicity he needed to sell tickets. The Knights of Columbus blasted it as "historically false and intellectually dishonest . . . Leftist propaganda." Picketers marched outside the movie's Radio City

Music Hall premiere, assailing patrons with chants of "war propaganda." Similar protests cropped up in Louisiana, Michigan, Nebraska, Ohio, New York, and elsewhere. Kansas City's Holy Name Society denounced the picture. The Boston city council voted to ban it. Mayor Maurice Tobin overruled the decision only after the ACLU threatened to sue.[18]

Wanger could not believe his good fortune. He played his manufactured firestorm to the hilt, transforming his well-meant movie into a circus act. He persuaded the National Peace Conference to give him an award the day after *Blockade*'s opening and served as the featured speaker at a Motion Picture Artists Committee rally called to protest the protests. The producer cast himself as a lonely patriot battling narrow thinking. "Not only do we meekly take intimidation from abroad," he thundered, "but we jump obediently when almost anybody in this country says 'Frog!'" Wanger stressed *Blockade*'s neutrality in a bid to defuse charges of propaganda and heighten his own martyrdom. "This picture carefully avoided entering into the political problems of the present Spanish conflict," he explained to a meeting of the Associated Film Audiences. "I only hoped it would make Americans realize how fortunate they are to be Americans . . . compared to the poor Spaniards."[19]

Wanger's brashest move was attempting to involve Roosevelt in the discussion. He sent the president a lengthy telegram ten days after *Blockade* opened. Surely intended for publication, the missive cast the producer as an advocate of "American ideals and principles of freedom and liberty" under fire from an antidemocratic minority. *Blockade,* Wanger argued, merely reiterated comments Roosevelt had made about the immorality of bombing civilians. "As an American citizen I certainly demand freedom of expression and a right to fight for better things," he insisted. He closed by asking the president to encourage Hollywood to make more pro-American films. Roosevelt ignored the telegram, which aimed more for attention than action anyway.[20]

Blockade was too clunky and preachy to be a box-office success or an effective "message" film. *Hollywood Now,* the Hollywood Anti-Nazi League's organ, saw "great force and effectiveness" in it. *New Republic*'s Otis Ferguson derided it as "a deadly numb level of shameless hokum." Most notices fell somewhere in between, giving *Blockade* a sort of collective critical shrug that reflected its mediocrity. *Blockade* was a missed opportunity that could have done so much more with its timely topic if not for the code and the fear of alienating viewers and censors.[21]

Despite the film's flaws, a few perceptive observers saw *Blockade* as the beginning of a new cinematic trend. "Courage, even in the smallest degree, is so unusual in Hollywood," marveled Frank Nugent of the *New York Times*. Perhaps, *Time* speculated, Wanger's tentative production might "jolt other producers' self-imposed silence on controversial subjects." Hollywood stood at an ideological crossroads. The industry's future direction rested to no small degree on *Blockade*'s success or failure. A profitable run opened the door to a cycle of international stories. Poor returns suggested a retreat from current-events pictures. Studio executives did not like what they saw. Despite Wanger's publicity bonanza, *Blockade* earned less than $650,000 against total costs of $812,406. Censor boards across Europe and South America rejected it. Moderate audience interest in the United States failed to compensate for the shortfall overseas. *Blockade* merely argued that murdering civilians was wrong, yet it aroused considerable wrath. A movie about concentration camps, fascism, or anti-Semitism might unleash much worse.[22]

Some still hoped that Wanger's movie represented a beginning rather than an end. *Blockade* moved the entertainment-vs.-propaganda debate to Hollywood's front burner. Many, and not just radical screenwriters and HANL ideologues, thought the industry should assert a more aggressive pro-Americanism and antifascism. "We believe," wrote *Boxoffice* editor Maurice Kann, "that motion pictures can, and should, have a great deal more to them than escapist subjects, as necessary as they may be; that motion pictures have inherent in their very concept sustenance and comfort for democracy which sorely needs both."[23]

Wanger's failed experiment propelled the producer into the upper echelon of Hollywood's growing band of agitators for cinematic relevancy. He urged the Hays Office to fight industry critics and chided moviemakers for shunning divisive themes. Much of this was posturing designed to spur sluggish ticket sales, but as was often the case in Hollywood, Wanger's actions blended economic and ideological concerns. His interest in socially relevant films was as genuine as his interest in putting his company into the black. He continued his crusade to use movies as ideological weapons over the next few years, demonstrating a fervent commitment to the cause of democracy that eventually made him one of the industry's leading spokesmen.[24]

○ ○ ○

Walter Wanger's protests of neutrality aside, Italian Fascists recognized *Blockade* as a slap at their ally, Franco, and stiffened their opposition to the American's plans to shoot at Cinecitta. In the end, however, Wanger's Italian production deal collapsed from financial rather than philosophical concerns. His reliance on an opium-trader-turned-venture-capitalist proved unwise; agents could not locate suitable replacement investors when that shady character bailed out. Bereft of funds, Wanger liquidated SAIC, his Italian production company, in August 1938, two months after *Blockade*'s release. After years of false starts, he was almost relieved that the deal collapsed.[25]

Wanger's Italian difficulties paralleled the industry's. As SAIC ground to its unsatisfying conclusion, MGM faced renewed difficulties with *Idiot's Delight,* which had lain dormant since the studio granted Italian consul Roberto Caracciolo script approval rights in the summer of 1937. MGM finally submitted a revised screenplay to the PCA in May 1938 and geared up for shooting. Breen thought the writers had masterfully blurred the play's antiwar message. "The whole question is so splendidly and so convincingly handled," he wrote Louis B. Mayer, "that it would be, indeed, a difficult thing to support any thesis, or philosophy, which is contrary to the splendid spirit set forth in this magnificent play." As promised, Breen forwarded the script to Consul Caracciolo's office to ensure it contained "no possible offense to the Italian government or people." He passed another copy around during his two-month vacation in Italy. The new draft named no countries, yet Caracciolo complained that it gave him "reason to believe that some of its principal scenes" took place in Italy. Additional tinkering pacified the consul but failed to mollify higher-ups in the Italian government, leaving MGM and Breen baffled about how to make everyone happy.[26]

Finally released in early 1939, *Idiot's Delight* was a wretched bastardization of a Pulitzer Prize–winning play. Its stars, Clark Gable and Norma Shearer, never look quite sure whether they are in a comedy or a tragedy. They seem confused about who is fighting and what the fight is about. The rest of the cast, who speak a borderless mélange of Italian, French, Spanish, and German, do little to solve the mystery. Besides criticizing arms dealers and speaking sympathetically of peace—two sure crowd pleasers—the picture is essentially toothless. MGM excised playwright Robert Sherwood's cutting denunciations of Fascism, shearing the immediacy from the movie's antiwar message. Audiences did not embrace the film. Neither did critics. *Newsweek* mocked its "Alpine never-never land in celluloid." *Time* complained that "Hollywood not only has no courage but is not concerned with having any."[27]

After all the fuss and revision, *Idiot's Delight* never showed in Mussolini's Italy. Undeterred by increasing discord with Hollywood, Italy intensified its campaign for cinematic autarky while MGM shot the film. In July 1938 Italian producers adopted a five-year plan to eliminate foreign pictures from its screens. Censors again tightened the screws, banning movies projecting "false and unfavorable impressions of Italians." Fascists simultaneously stepped up official anti-Semitism. Prominent officials publicly mocked financier Bernard Baruch and other American Jews. More concretely, the Fascist Grand Council adopted the *Carta Della Razza,* which prohibited marriages between Christians and Jews and expelled foreign-born Jews. Italy also raised its anti-Roosevelt rhetoric. References to the president as "Delano," a homophone of the Italian *dell'ano* (of the anus) became common. These moves demoralized American studio executives, who felt the cost of doing business with Rome was reaching "the danger point."[28]

Mussolini's men took Hollywood past the danger point that fall. A few weeks before the Munich Conference guaranteed European peace at the expense of the Czechoslovakian Sudetenland, Italy issued a decree creating the Ente Nazionale Industrie Cinematografiche (ENIC), a government-operated monopoly established to purchase and distribute foreign pictures. As of January 1, 1939, American studios had to sell films to ENIC for Italian distribution rather than distribute through their own networks. Sales to ENIC would generate around $1 million a year for Hollywood, about what some individual studios earned under current laws. The proposal prompted an unprecedented mobilization of the movie community. ENIC struck at the heart of the free-enterprise system. Caving in to it would invite similar attacks from other nationalistic governments. Executives gathered at MPPDA headquarters in New York to coordinate their response. Studios' foreign managers did the same in Paris. Will Hays hustled to Washington to brief Secretary of State Hull, who opened negotiations to modify the decree.[29]

Italian newspapers intensified their anti-Hollywood rhetoric in the wake of the ENIC announcement, laughably asserting that the arrogant Americans refused to adjust their products to suit Italian needs. Economic nationalists decried even the limited exports of cash allowed under the existing arrangement. ENIC would keep lire in Italy, enabling film officials to further subsidize homegrown studios. Such talk suggested the improbability of reaching an acceptable compromise. Confident that their cause was just, the Italians refused to budge. After years of appeasement, Italians could not imagine the eight major studios abandoning their market when there was money yet to be made.[30]

Doubts of Hollywood's doggedness proved false. The foreign managers forged unanimity by appealing to their companies' long-term economic interests. Robert Schless of Warner Bros. told his peers that his studio would shutter its Italian office on December 31. He urged them to do the same. This was about more than Italy, Schless insisted. It was a "world film fight." American movies would be on the retreat around the globe should they surrender to Rome. Schless convinced studios with Italian distribution offices—MGM, Twentieth Century–Fox, and Paramount—to close their operations at the end of the year. He promised legal support to United Artists, RKO, Columbia, and Universal, which distributed through Italian companies, if the Italians sued them for canceling contracts. The New York offices accepted the foreign representatives' recommendations. One monopoly—the eight major studios— battled another—the Fascist Party—to determine who would go further to defend its financial self-interests.[31]

Italy blinked when the studios boycotted in 1936. This time both sides were too entrenched to give in. Italy refused to drop ENIC, and Hollywood refused to participate in a system that whittled its profits to almost nothing. Major studios imposed their embargo on the last day of 1938. As Will Hays remarked, they had "no choice." Both sides treated Hollywood's departure as a victory. Vittorio Mussolini, sounding equal parts Nazi and Fascist, expressed satisfaction that "American films, produced in that Hebrew Communist center which is Hollywood, are not to enter Italy." Walter Wanger told a February 1939 luncheon gathering that he was glad Hollywood left Italy. "We had to distort our productions to conform with their tribal taboos," he explained. Wanger's talk put a positive spin on the last several years, ignoring the fact that moviemakers often worked with dictatorial regimes, so long as cooperation enhanced their bottom line.[32]

Such bluster concealed quiet, ongoing negotiations. Italy wanted to achieve self-sufficiency but was incapable of producing enough movies to satisfy its citizens. It sent out feelers through 1939 and 1940, hinting at its willingness to negotiate a new agreement. Italian diplomats met frequently with Hays and other industry leaders. Although Rome's duplicity and unpredictability frustrated him, Ambassador Phillips kept his embassy involved in the discussions. Hollywood executives believed their return to Italy was simply a matter of getting the right deal. Hollywood's experience paralleled America's. Franklin Roosevelt largely gave up on appeasing Italy in early 1939 but worked for peace until the Fascists declared war on Britain and France in June 1940. As with Roosevelt, the right deal never came for the film capital. Although Italo-American parleys continued until Italy joined the conflict, the majors were finished with the Fascists, and Hollywood looked to cultivate new markets to make up for the loss.[33]

CHAPTER FIVE

New Directions

M ESS THAT IT WAS, *Blockade* represented Hollywood's tentative first step into a dangerous world trapped between irreconcilable political ideologies. The movie's inability to draw crowds despite its hot-button subject matter dissuaded other producers from following Walter Wanger into Spain. The film capital nevertheless explored new directions in the summer of 1938, establishing genres that would prove crucial when Europe fell into general war. Mainstays of the war years, the pro-British film, promilitary film, and combat film grew increasingly familiar to late 1930s moviegoers. At this point economic factors, not ideological concerns, were largely responsible for the development of these cycles.

"It's the English-speaking race against the world!" declared one early-twentieth-century music-hall tune. The United States' special relationship with Great Britain is deeply entrenched in the American psyche. The two nations share a language and possess overlapping cultures. Alexander Hamilton had taken Britain's industrializing economy as a model for his own fledgling republic. Readers in the United States knew Shakespeare, Kipling, and Sherlock Holmes as thoroughly as did their British counterparts. The Magna Carta and British legal thinkers like Coke and Blackstone had provided a basis for the Founding Fathers' political theories. At the same time, stereotyped images of tyrannical George III and the bloodthirsty redcoats remained ingrained in the American mythology. Many viewed Britain's rigid class system and sprawling global empire as antithetical to American values. Millions of Irish Americans and German Americans despised the English. The experience of World War I still stung for many U.S. citizens. Many assumed that a massive British propaganda campaign had duped the United States into joining the Allies. Britain's failure to repay its war debts added to Americans' resentment.[1]

Hollywood had its own reasons for blending Anglophilia with Anglophobia. The British Empire had long been an important market for American films. It grew even more crucial when the Nazis and Fascists began sealing off swaths of territory in the late 1930s. As the continental market dried up, moviemakers concerned for the future of democratic values and American security became unabashed supporters of British interests. Such anxieties never overshadowed their devotion to the bottom line, however. Hollywood remained willing to take tough financial stances against the island nation. Ideology sometimes dovetailed with economics, as helping Britain resist trade-killing totalitarianism improved major studios' long-term financial prospects. At other times, however, the desire to aid Britain would run counter to Hollywood's desire to make money. American interests spent years seeking an appropriate balance between these motivations.

The British shared Hollywood's ambivalence. They loved American movies, which accounted for around 95 percent of films shown on the empire's screens, but resented Hollywood's enormous influence. Movies featuring violent, stupid, decadent, or lazy white people undermined their stature in Britain's largely nonwhite colonies. Imported pictures caused an exodus of money overseas, replaced Anglo traditions with American customs, and diluted notions of British greatness. "We want to show our ideals and our life as it is and not American ideals and American life as portrayed by American films," complained one frustrated member of Parliament.[2]

Great Britain could not compete on a level playing field with Hollywood. American studios had bigger stars and a massive domestic market that sustained lavish productions the poorly funded British studios could not equal. Anglo filmmakers therefore joined nationalistic politicians in asking Parliament to tilt the table in their favor. Their demands bore fruit with the 1927 Cinematograph Films Act. Passed after intense debate and over the Hays Office's objections, the Films Act required that at least 5 percent of footage shown on British screens, and 7.5 percent of films more than three thousand feet long (roughly forty-five minutes), be made in Britain. Both quota numbers increased in subsequent years, reaching 20 percent in 1936.[3]

Parliament aimed to increase the number, not the quality, of British pictures. That good films might outperform bad films seems not to have crossed MPs' minds. Most of them agreed with Lord Newton of the House of Lords. "If our people are content to witness perpetual rubbish," he said in 1925, "let it, at any rate, be English rubbish in preference to American rubbish." The Films Act guaranteed screenings of any British-made picture. The result was a wave of "quota quickies," cheap movies designed to fill time rather than display excellence. Studios like MGM and Warner Bros. contributed to the genre, renting space in British facilities and churning out quota quickies to bank time for their more prestigious American-made productions. The Films Act, moreover, failed to spur the British moviemaking industry, which still suffered from a lack of technical expertise and a relatively small domestic market. Only about a dozen British films turned a profit in the United States by the mid-1930s. American studios at least partly financed most of these, including Alexander Korda's blockbuster *The Private Life of Henry VIII* (1933).[4]

Hollywood executives opposed British tinkering with free enterprise. They wanted the quota dropped. Or, as they phrased it, they wanted American movies in Britain treated the same as British movies were in America. Considering Hollywood's massive advantages over its Anglo counterparts, achieving this cinematic Open Door Policy meant certain victory for the majors. Pressing too hard, however, might anger Parliament into passing more punitive laws. Great Britain accounted for about 30 percent of Hollywood's foreign take, sending over $30 million to the majors in 1936. Losing this revenue through economic blundering or rash diplomacy was unthinkable. Studios had to entice the market, not bludgeon it.[5]

Cognizant of Britain's importance, Hollywood produced with that market in mind. Studios anticipated British censors by cutting depictions of insanity and cruelty to animals. The majors also respected England's ban on cinematic portrayals of Christ, an edict that made it nearly impossible for Cecil B. DeMille to show *The King of Kings* (1927) there. They deleted anything ridiculing British social life or the monarchy and avoided scenes that questioned the politics of empire, steering clear of fights between light- and dark-skinned characters, mixed-race romances, and sophisticated Asians or Indians.[6]

Hollywood began tailoring its output even more specifically to the British Empire in the mid-1930s. Paramount's *The Lives of a Bengal*

Lancer (1935) initiated a pro-British cycle of pictures. Directed by Henry Hathaway, who usually oversaw westerns, the Gary Cooper vehicle is essentially an oater with an accent. Anglo defenders of a lonely outpost in India substitute for the cavalry. Fanatical Muslim rebels, depicted as primitive barbarians who communicate in whoops, stand in for Native Americans. Packed with star power, romantic locations, and exciting action scenes, *The Lives of a Bengal Lancer* was a worldwide hit that earned admiring reviews on both sides of the Atlantic. *Canadian Magazine* critic Laura Elston said the film did "more to glorify British traditions than the British would dare to do for themselves."[7]

Seeking to emulate Paramount's success, Warner Bros. modeled *The Charge of the Light Brigade* (1936) on *The Lives of a Bengal Lancer*. Director Michael Curtiz's thrilling spectacle of elephants, emirs, and epic battles commemorated British actions during the Crimean War. Warners staffers coached Errol Flynn, Olivia de Havilland, and David Niven to speak "the Queen's English." The Hungarian-born Curtiz spoke awful English—he gave his infamous order to "bring on the empty horses" during the shoot—yet made the California foothills feel like India. In his hands Tennyson's ode to a military disaster became an homage to British stoicism, sacrifice, and patriotism. British soldiers launch their climactic assault after vicious Suristanis massacre innocent residents of an Indian village. Their outrage at the senseless slaughter fuels their willingness to attack with inferior numbers, transforming the colonizers into sympathetic underdogs. Even though the charge fails, the movie manipulates it into a long-term triumph. British officials characterize the charge as "a magnificent blunder" that turned momentum in the war, ensuring an English victory in the larger campaign. Although in tatters, the Union Jack stands upright, flapping in the breeze, as the music rises and the screen fades to black.[8]

Time's reviewer wondered "why the U.S. film industry can wave the British flag even more effectively than its own." The answer was economics. While a pro-American spectacle might have limited international appeal, these action-packed extravaganzas attracted both American and British audiences, earning big takes at home as well as in Hollywood's most important foreign outpost. Like *The Lives of a Bengal Lancer, The Charge of the Light Brigade* was a box-office winner. Bringing in around $1.5 million, it became Warners' top-earning film of 1936. Such success touched off a rush to release imitators. To paraphrase Dorothy Parker, studios believed in plagiarism. *The Lives of a Bengal Lancer* begat *The Charge of the Light Brigade,* which begat *Another Dawn* (1937), *Captains Courageous* (1937), *Wee Willie Winkie* (1937), and, a few years down the road, *Gunga Din* (1939).[9]

"Hollywood is doing very good work in selling the British Empire to the world," MPPDA foreign manager Frederick Herron told the State Department. Such imported tributes as *The Lives of a Bengal Lancer,* however, did not placate Anglos who desired "British films true to British life, accepting British standards and spreading British ideals." Partly because of concerns about cultural imperialism, momentum was building to replace the Films Act with more stringent legislation when it expired in 1938. In mid-1937 the British Board of Trade's prestigious Moyne Committee suggested bumping the film quota to 50 percent, imposing a quality test and minimum cost requirements to discourage quickie productions, pushing British financiers to back domestic studios, and confiscating exhibitors' licenses on their first quota violation rather than their third, as current law demanded.[10]

"The English situation is really quite serious," Will Hays told John Boettiger, his close friend and President Roosevelt's son-in law. Hollywood mobilized to head off the Moyne Committee's proposals. A stream of executives boarded ocean liners bound for the isles. Hays was already in London when the report appeared. Louis B. Mayer, Harry Warner, Jack Warner, and Adolph Zukor were not far behind. F. W. Allport, the MPPDA's European representative, discussed the document with members of Parliament, the Board of Trade, and the American Embassy. Roosevelt's nomination of former movie producer Joseph Kennedy as ambassador to Great Britain in early 1938 boosted Hollywood's morale. Studio heads, many of whom knew Kennedy well, were certain he would promote their British interests. FDR's selection also pleased Hays, a friend of the Kennedy family who affectionately called the new ambassador "the boss."[11]

Hays worked throughout the winter to bring the British negotiations to an acceptable conclusion. He urged FDR to incorporate movie issues into a larger Anglo-American trade agreement—the opposite of his approach to the Italians two years earlier—during a visit to Hyde Park. In February 1938 he convinced Cordell Hull, whose desire to tear down trade barriers jibed with the movie czar's agenda, to issue a thinly veiled threat just as the House of Commons prepared to vote on a revised Films Act. "I am confident," Hull wrote, "that the British Government will understand that an alteration to the disadvantage of the United States . . . in the status of so important a product as motion pictures could hardly fail to affect the attitude of my Government toward concessions to be offered certain important British exports to the United States."[12]

Although Hays did not know it, some within the British government endorsed his bid for favorable treatment. Some in Whitehall already anticipated war and wanted to ensure that the United States was on their side when it came. "The crucial importance of retaining the goodwill of the United States Government and public opinion in the event of a major crisis occurring in Europe is a matter which is keenly engaging my attention," Foreign Secretary Anthony Eden told Sir Ronald Lindsey, Britain's ambassador to the United States. Lindsey advised his superior to tread lightly, warning that "the watchdogs of isolation are very vigilant." He recommended creating goodwill with a subtle propaganda campaign emphasizing English grandeur, dignity, and history. Americans were unlikely to come out of their isolationist shell, but, Lindsey noted, "neutrality may be of many colors." Understanding film's potential as a publicity tool, Eden sought to accommodate the moguls.[13]

The 1938 Films Act established the outlines of Hollywood's relationship with Great Britain to Pearl Harbor and beyond. Rather than embrace the Moyne Commission's harsh recommendations, it set a relatively mild quota of 20 percent for 1939 that climbed to 30 percent in 1946. It eliminated quota quickies by establishing a minimum cost for each British-made project but rewarded studios with double or triple quota credits for more expensive productions. The multiple-credits clause made it worthwhile to produce bigger films in Britain, which had lower labor costs than the United States. MGM and Warners accordingly expanded their Denham and Teddington facilities outside of London. The act's minimum expense requirement and multiple-quota-credits clause encouraged studios to hire emerging British stars and make movies in Britain good enough to sell in the United States. In doing so, Hollywood produced a series of films that established a positive impression of the British in the American mind at a critical juncture in European history.[14]

MGM hit box-office gold with one of its first Denham releases, *A Yank at Oxford* (1938). It featured Robert Taylor as Lee Sheridan, a high-school track star from Kansas who wins an athletic scholarship to Oxford University's Cardinal College. The picture represented a new direction for Taylor's career. MGM wanted to remold the twenty-six-year-old actor's screen image from foppish playboy to beefcake he-man. *A Yank at Oxford* not only accomplished that, but it also helped to change images of Great Britain in the United States.

On one level *A Yank at Oxford* is typical college-film fare, replete with student high jinks and deans robed in academic garb. Befitting a production designed for a transatlantic audience, it also serves as a parable of Anglo-American cooperation. Oxford's snobbish, upper-crust students initially dismiss Sheridan as "another loud-mouthed American," and with good reason. He struts around campus like a victorious warrior and lustily pursues local girl Molly Beaumont (Maureen O'Sullivan). The picture uses Sheridan's conflict with fellow Oxford man Paul Beaumont (Griffith Jones) to personalize international tensions. Angered by the arrogant American's pursuit of his sister, Molly, Paul ostracizes the interloper. The two reconcile after Sheridan saves Paul from expulsion for having an affair with a college widow, played by future *Gone with the Wind* star Vivien Leigh. Both sides acknowledge their errors. Sheridan apologizes for his ebullient boorishness and Paul for his snootiness. They shake hands, then lead Cardinal's crew team to victory over Cambridge. Every synchronized pull of the oars symbolizes their determination to overcome cultural differences in the face of a common opponent.

A Yank at Oxford showed the England that Americans wanted to see. No grubby smokestacks or urban poverty here, the film declared. Its England had polished accents, charming avenues, and solid buildings that had stood for centuries. The British were decent, ordinary people, the kind of folks who made good friends. Similar representations pervaded MGM's next big Denham production, *Goodbye, Mr. Chips* (1939). It is hard to imagine a more likable movie. Director Sam Wood's adaptation of the James Hilton novel is a gentle romance wrapped inside an ode to the British educational system. Robert Donat's turn as a revered Latin teacher won him a Best Actor Oscar. Greer Garson's performance as Katherine Ellis, a free spirit who teaches the tightly wound Mr. Chips to love his students, launched her career.

Goodbye, Mr. Chips appeals to American audiences from its first scene, which reveals that the high-toned Brookfield School opened its doors in the magical year of 1492. From there the film recites comfortable British stereotypes as if checking them off a list. Brookfield comes equipped with cozy hearths, ancient classrooms, tea parties, and cricket matches. The quintessentially British Mr. Chips could only exist at Brookfield. His love for a dead language indicates his reverence for the venerable pathways the school represents. He speaks wistfully of the old days, of building character, of students long gone. He embodies British traditions, bringing the past to life for audiences just as he brings Latin to life for students.

The film's final scene, surely one of the great tear-jerking moments in screen history, reinforces the inexorable links binding present-day Britain with ancient tradition. A young student named Colley sits at Mr. Chips's deathbed. He is in fact the fourth generation of Colleys (all played by Terry Kilburn) to inhabit the teacher's classroom. The string of unchanging Colleys reinforces images of England as an ageless place, a nation of consistency and permanence. There is no doubt that, were Mr. Chips alive today, he would find yet another identical Colley waiting to hear his lesson.

Goodbye, Mr. Chips gave audiences another positive take on Great Britain. Class differences manifest themselves only once, when the third Colley brawls with a lowbrow vegetable delivery boy. In the end their dispute serves as an example of British egalitarianism, as the combatants quickly shed their social differences to become fast friends who serve together in the Great War. The war itself becomes a means for displaying British unity, courage, and stoicism. Mr. Chips contributes to the effort even though he is far too old to enlist. He comes out of retirement to serve as headmaster after the younger teachers volunteer for the army. Shots of him comforting terrified schoolboys during an air raid provide the film's most gripping moments and cannot help but stir sympathy for the United States' wartime ally.

Donat's bravura performance advanced *A Yank at Oxford*'s work of humanizing the British. The famous English reserve melted in the heat of Mr. Chips's romance with Katherine. British stuffiness becomes a virtue as the teacher reveals the tender heart beating beneath his starched exterior. American hearts reach across the ocean when Katherine's untimely death sends Mr. Chips into a deep despair. Queen Elizabeth cried when she watched the film with King George VI and their hosts, Joseph and Rose Kennedy. "Hollywood has gone Anglophile," the *London Daily Mirror* observed. "Hollywood has hauled down 'Old Glory,' the rather jazzy flag with the stars and stripes. And in its place Hollywood has run up the dazzling criss-cross of the Union Jack." *Goodbye, Mr. Chips* was the biggest tug on the flagpole cord, the picture that best promoted American sympathy for Britain in the months before the European war began.[15]

A Yank at Oxford and *Goodbye, Mr. Chips* were propaganda movies that worked, conveying pro-British messages without being message films. These enormously entertaining features illustrated Hollywood's desire to expand the British film market while spreading Anglophilic goodwill in the United States. Hollywood leaders thought little at this point about building a wartime Anglo-American alliance. Rather, they saw a pro-British United States as the best way to sell more domestic admissions to features that also performed well overseas.

MGM was not the only company exploring the pro-British genre in these months of intensifying European crisis. Like the MGM-Denham productions, Warner Bros.' *The Adventures of Robin Hood* (1938) fostered a sense of familiarity with the British. Although the studio shot the film in the forests of northern California, not its Teddington facilities, the Errol Flynn–Olivia de Havilland swashbuckler's rip-roaring jousts, archery competitions, and fancy swordplay endeared American audiences to their overseas cousins. The famous outlaw and his Merry Men were Technicolor emissaries who proved that the British could display as much dash, daring, and élan as any American serial hero ever mustered.

Robin Hood's band was the next in a line of historical figures the Warners used to construct antifascist parables. They were twelfth-century Emile Zolas battling a bow-and-arrow wielding branch of the Black Legion. Prince John (Claude Rains) illegitimately seizes power when his brother, King Richard, departs for the Crusades. The pretender's Norman thugs do a passable impression of Nazis as they deprive innocent Saxons of their rights and treasure. Robin Hood (Errol Flynn) serves as the voice of liberation. The righteous bandit mobilizes denizens of Sherwood Forest to "fight for a free England" before thwarting John's grab for the crown. King Richard's return sets the country on a path of freedom and tolerance. Richard banishes both his rebellious brother and "all injustices and oppressions which have burdened my people." Articulating a tolerant vision that contrasted with Nazi repression, the wise monarch decrees that "Normans and Saxons alike will share the rights of Englishmen."

At $1.9 million, *The Adventures of Robin Hood* was Warners' most expensive production to date. The studio could not take chances with such a big-budget feature. Its marketing campaign focused on the picture's action sequences, not its timely message. Its stars nevertheless understood the film's deeper significance. "We were preparing for another conflict," de Havilland remembered. "There really were the good guys and there really *was* a bad guy—and that was Hitler . . . and anyone who fought him became a kind of Errol Flynn." Warner Bros. created a thrilling picture that benefited from a progressive subtext instead of sinking under it, as *Blockade* did. Released about seven weeks before *Blockade,* *The Adventures of Robin Hood* became one of the biggest grossers of 1938. *Blockade* generated much more talk but much less money.[16]

American studios started wooing the British just as Anglo propagandists started doing the same to the United States. This did not imply a comity of interests or a coherent plan to forge an anti-Hitler alliance. At this point most moviemakers imagined Great Britain as a giant dollar sign floating in the North Sea. Concerns for the future of democracy or American military security barely entered their calculations. Neither was their confidence in Britain complete. Hollywood's close call with the recent Films Act angered executives. Chamberlain's pitiful performance at the October 1938 Munich Conference frustrated a broader range of industry voices. The HANL newspaper *Hollywood Now* called the prime minister "as great a menace to democracy and peace as the Nazi and Fascist dictators." Paramount's newsreel about Chamberlain's surrender of the Sudetenland was so scathing that Ambassador Kennedy intervened to have the offending material removed before the British retaliated.[17]

Chamberlain's collapse at Munich and the ensuing Paramount fracas left MPPDA European representative Harold Smith wondering whether Americans were too eager to back the Anglo horse. They never repaid our loans from the Great War, he reminded Hays, and they would make sure "good old Uncle Sam pays the bill" if war came again. The greedy

British "wouldn't throw us a life belt without charging us for it," Smith complained. Their regulations on American pictures served as "a fine example of the thanks our country receives for saving England." Hollywood needed the British, but on the whole, it did not yet have a sense of shared interest with them.[18]

❂ ❂ ❂

Hollywood added the pro-British film to its arsenal long before most Americans started considering the possibility of an Anglo alliance. A cycle of war pictures soon joined it on the world's screens. While the war film would become common in the early 1940s, it had fallen into disfavor after a run of popularity in the early 1930s. As the first signs of renewed unrest appeared in Europe, Warner Bros. looked to reinvigorate the genre with its 1938 remake of *The Dawn Patrol*.

The war film was a longtime staple of the movie screen. Although Civil War sequences had formed only a small portion of its whole, *The Birth of a Nation* (1915) had suggested the epic sweep a war movie could offer. The Great War era saw a spate of martial movies march across the screen. Eager to establish its patriotic credentials, Hollywood issued such anti-German diatribes as *The Prussian Cur* (1918) and *Kultur* (1918). D. W. Griffith showed the horror of war in *Hearts of the World* (1918). Charlie Chaplin made wartime audiences laugh with his satirical *Shoulder Arms* (1918). The brutal war's ambiguous end and the unpopular Treaty of Versailles that followed—a treaty the United States never ratified—set an unlikely stage for a cycle of heroic postwar pictures. Americans were unsure about what they had fought for and what they had won. Such confusion pervaded the antiwar dramas that appeared over the following years. *The Big Parade* (1925), *What Price Glory?* (1926), and *All Quiet on the Western Front* (1930) expressed the exhaustion of a world grown weary of bloodshed.[19]

Warners' original *Dawn Patrol* (1930) echoed the negativism of other World War I movies. Written by flying instructor John Monk Saunders with input from scenarist Seton Miller, dialogue ace Dan Totheroh, and director Howard Hawks, *The Dawn Patrol* was one of the grimmest features ever to hit theaters. It follows the psychological disintegration of a group of pilots forced to undertake daily suicide missions over enemy territory. The film resonates with Lost Generation cynicism. Patriotism, heroism, and authority figures are bunk. It peoples the military's most glamorous branch with desperate alcoholics who find solace in hollow bravado. "What a rotten war," Captain Courtney (Richard Barthelmess) mutters as he erases the names of dead flyers from the squadron's duty roster. The veterans never speak of their fallen comrades. Better to drink, sing, and wait for the next wave of recruits to get tossed into the meat grinder than to lament those beyond their help.[20]

The Dawn Patrol's box-office success reflected the public's disenchantment with old canards about the glory of war. Subsequent war movies recreated its dismal mood. Warners' *The Last Flight* (1931) followed emotionally shattered pilots who booze and whore around Paris. Paramount filmed Hemingway's antiwar *A Farewell to Arms* in 1932. MGM's *Men Must Fight* (1933) viewed war through the eyes of Laura Mattson (Diana Wynyard), a nurse impregnated by an American flyer (Robert Young) just days before the enemy blows him from the sky. RKO's *Ace of Aces* (1933) tells the story of Rocky Thorne, a spoiled young sculptor who becomes a dogfighting wizard after he enlists in the military's aviation section. His thirst for blood deepens as his kill numbers rise. "This is a great war," he tells his girlfriend, "and I'm having a grand time." In a scene reminiscent of *All Quiet on the Western Front,* Rocky finally comprehends the pain he has inflicted when he encounters one of his victims in a hospital. His forty-two kills become insignificant as he listens to the boy screaming for water and begging to die.

RKO released John Ford's *The Lost Patrol* the next year. Its breathtakingly simple story offered one of the most nihilistic features Hollywood ever produced. A British squadron gets lost in the Mesopotamian desert during the Great War. Unseen Arabs pick off the soldiers one by one while the unit fires futilely at their unseen tormentors. There is no noble cause, no grand strategy. There is nothing more than survival or death:

> *Sergeant (Victor McLaglen):* "Do you know where we are?"
> *Corporal (Brandon Hurst):* "No."
> *Sergeant:* "Do you know what we're here for?"
> *Corporal:* "No."
> *Sergeant:* "Do you know where we're going?"
> *Corporal:* "No."
> *Sergeant:* "Well, neither do I."

Their conversation summed up a generation's inability to grasp the war's purpose or to understand why the United States fought in it.

The lost patrol's shallow graves marked the temporary death of the war genre. After so many negative films, there seemed nothing new to say about the recent conflict. Popular conceptions of the Great War had frozen by 1934. That March, *Fortune* magazine published "Arms and the Men," a vicious exposé that accused arms dealers of sabotaging disarmament conferences, fomenting war scares, and prolonging conflicts to improve their bottom lines. "Without a doubt," *Fortune* concluded, "there is at this moment in Europe a huge and subversive force that lies behind the arming and counterarming of nations." Doubleday, Doran published the article as a book. Isolationist senator Woodrow Borah read excerpts on the Senate floor. Senator Gerald Nye sent fifty thousand copies to ministers, journalists, teachers, and lecturers and then convened hearings on international arms trafficking. Nye maintained that the merchants of death deceived the United States into joining the Allies. Few argued with him.[21]

The war no longer merited Hollywood's consideration, but the military itself remained a subject of fascination. Major studios venerated the military even as they condemned war. Eager for good publicity, the War Department allowed moviemakers to use its men, equipment, and facilities. Such generosity discouraged hostile movie treatments of the military. As typified by *Navy Blue and Gold* (1937), movies about the armed forces focused on pageantry rather than war. The film follows three Annapolis recruits—a pampered son of a wealthy family (Robert Young), a small-town rube (Tom Brown), and a navy mechanic who gets a crack at the officer corps (James Stewart)—through their first years at the Naval Academy. This varied cast anticipated the classic World War II movie, in which a platoon of diverse soldiers unite to achieve a goal. These cadets have a modest objective: to win the Army-Navy football game. *Navy Blue and Gold*'s reverence for the navy runs from the opening chorus of "Anchors Aweigh" to the closing shots of the academy's big win over Army. Characters interrupt the action to explain campus landmarks and traditions. Captain Skinny Dawes (John Barrymore) offers florid speeches about honoring the colors. The movie contains enough marching bands and parading soldiers to make the most retiring wallflower consider enlisting.

One reason studios liked service pictures is that military backdrops injected excitement into mundane genre pieces. Screenwriters fit service films into numerous molds. Often, as in *Suicide Fleet* (1931) and *Hell Below* (1933), they stocked them with comic scenes that humanized the armed forces while distracting audiences from the fact that the military exists to make war. Military settings also jazzed up otherwise-standard melodramas, such as MGM's *Hell Divers* (1932). The movie's outstanding aerial photography and exhilarating shots of planes landing on the USS *Saratoga* bracket a boilerplate romantic subplot that finds the jealous veteran pilot Windy Riker (Wallace Beery) trying to sabotage the hotshot upstart Steve Nelson's (Clark Gable) relationship with the beautiful Ann Mitchell (Dorothy Jordan).

Hell Divers and similar movies, including *Devil Dogs of the Air* (1934), *Here Comes the Navy* (1934), *West Point of the Air* (1935), and *Submarine D-1* (1937), rarely asked why characters enlisted or explained what they were preparing for. They address war in an abstract way, through drills or test runs for a fight that never comes. These features centered on personal rather than international conflict, tracing an individualistic malcontent's incorporation into a unified group. The one's inevitable merging with the many again foreshadowed plots from innumerable World War II flicks. Such narrative devices satisfied Hollywood's needs, filling the screen with action without delving into troublesome questions of war and peace. They also gave Hollywood a patriotic luster while deflecting potential charges of warmongering.

MGM's *They Gave Him a Gun* (1937) signaled Hollywood's renewed interest in the Great War. The picture recycled many of the war genre's tropes, then added a twist by becoming a gangster film halfway through. Hayseed draftee Jimmy Davis (Franchot Tone) stumbles his way through drills and wonders how he ended up in this mess. "I was taught 'thou shalt not kill,'" he complains. A fellow inductee, former carnival barker Fred Willis (Spencer Tracy), justifies the war with a barrage of patriotic gibberish that could have come from a Marx Brothers movie: "Now personally my only regret is that I got a life to lay down for my country," he tells Jimmy. "But will us dead have died in vain? Be yourself, remember the Alamo, remember the Maine, fifty-four forty or fight, don't give up the ship until you see the whites of their eyes! Are we going to stand for taxation without the pursuit of happiness? E Pluribus Unum! Hats off, Lafayette," he bellows; "we are here!"

Jimmy's skills as a sniper convince him that fighting is not so bad. Like Rocky from *Ace of Aces,* he turns into a bloodthirsty killer. His postwar career as an assassin seemed a logical jump to a nation disenchanted with fighting. Fred's efforts to get his friend back on the straight and narrow prove fruitless. Ironically, it is their old commander, Sergeant Meadowlark, who shoots Jimmy down at the end, upholding the gangster-film tradition that the antihero must die. The seductive power of war sent a good man to his destruction. Meadowlark expresses shock that one of his veterans went astray. Fred cuts him off. "You made a soldier out of him," he retorts, his voice filled with resignation. "You gave him a gun and told him how to be a hero. So why don't you pin a medal on him now, Sergeant Meadowlark? He was your star pupil." The strains of "Battle Hymn of the Republic" drip with sarcasm as they rise over the closing credits.

They Gave Him a Gun was a modest performer, an average if unusual film whose blending of the war and gangster genres made it difficult for audiences to pin down. It also suffered from the fact that war was still too distant to arouse much interest in a war picture, as opposed to a military picture. This was no longer true by the summer of 1938, when Warners producer Hal Wallis suggested remaking *The Dawn Patrol.* He planned to cut all possible corners, reusing exterior shots from the original, then shooting interior scenes with a new cast. Although Warners had staked out a position as Hollywood's most politicized studio, Wallis's interest was financial rather than ideological. "We could knock out a very great picture in a very short time," he told Jack Warner, "and one that I think would bring us a fortune now when the whole world is talking and thinking war and re-armament."[22]

Warner green-lighted the proposal. His studio's publicity department claimed the new *Dawn Patrol* was a million-dollar production. It actually cost less than half that amount. It was the kind of project Warners specialized in—a hastily made, no-frills action picture with a topical message. Editors snipped almost all its flying scenes from prints of the 1930 version. Workmen built just two sets for the remake, compared to around thirty for a normal feature. Seton Miller made only slight revisions to the 1930 script. Most of his work involved toning down the pilots' boozing to make it acceptable to the Breen Office, which did not exist when Warners made the first *Dawn Patrol*.[23]

The remake otherwise mimics the original's tone. Squadron leader Brand (Basil Rathbone) preserves the edgy nervousness Neil Hamilton brought to the role eight years before. "It's a slaughterhouse, and I'm the butcher," he moans after sending his compatriots on another suicide mission. Errol Flynn and David Niven play pilots Courtney and Scott with the same blend of bitterness, frustration, and world-weariness seen in Richard Barthelmess and Douglas Fairbanks Jr.'s earlier performances. The first *Dawn Patrol*'s antiwar message also survives intact. War, Courtney explains to a wide-eyed recruit, is "a great big, noisy, rather stupid game that doesn't make any sense at all. None of us know what it's all about or why." There is no glorious mission. Survival is their cause.

On the surface *The Dawn Patrol* endorses pacifism while denouncing the "criminal idiots" who start wars. Beneath its brooding cynicism, however, lies a more ambiguous reality. Like England in 1938, which was standing on the brink of war, the Royal Flying Corps of 1915 faced "an enemy of superior size, strength and experience." Warners brass envisioned the movie as a testament to the corps' determination in the face of desperate odds. The studio's casting of Niven and Flynn (whom audiences associated with plucky Britishness even though he was born in Tasmania) gave *The Dawn Patrol* a dynamic energy missing from the original. Publicity material stressed action, not angst. "Hell-Bent for Glory!" screamed one ad. "Gay, reckless, gallant, they fought, these eagles, for women they had never seen, and for the love they might never know!"[24]

The Dawn Patrol is an antiwar film that makes war look exciting. The movie, John Alden of the *Minneapolis Tribune* wrote, tried "to make it appear that war is not very lovely. But even so, when you leave the theater, you aren't remembering those sidelights. You're remembering only the heroic deeds of the fliers who died helping to kill off the Germans. Delete a few of those 'War-Is-Hell' speeches, and add a couple of not very complimentary references to the enemy, and you'd have an extremely fine piece of propaganda." War was a natural subject for motion pictures. It was in the headlines and on people's minds in the wake of the Sudetenland crisis. If done well, war and the military were almost sure profit makers. Such movies, however, exposed an anxious film community to charges of warmongering. Ignoring the gathering conflict, however, exposed Hollywood to charges of irrelevance and ignorance of current events.[25]

The Dawn Patrol exemplified the balance studios struck when dealing with war. For the moment, glamorized antiwar films made Hollywood both safe and relevant. Warners had no intention of releasing a prowar picture. Its executives, however, understood the dangers of reviving the World War genre at this unsettled moment, with Asia in flames and Europe headed toward the same. The studio kept a closer-than-usual eye on reviews, making a special effort to gauge responses in London and other important overseas centers.

The Dawn Patrol's solid box-office returns convinced Warner Bros. that the public could tolerate a certain kind of war film. Edith Lindeman of the *Richmond Times-Dispatch* called it "the opening gun of Warner Brothers' peace and Americanization program." Confident it was on the right course, the studio had already loaded the next salvos of its barrage. The rest of Hollywood stood in reserve, waiting to see whether Warners' attack would establish a beachhead in the realm of public favor or be repulsed by disinterested or offended moviegoers and politicians.[26]

Good Neighbors

THE ADVENTURES OF ROBIN HOOD, *Black Legion, The Life of Emile Zola,* and other disguised antifascist films represented a clandestine massing of the troops. The cinematic soldiers poured across the border in April 1939, just a few weeks after the Wehrmacht invaded Czechoslovakia. With the release of *Confessions of a Nazi Spy* and *Juarez,* the Warner brothers declared open war on totalitarianism.

These projects deviated from the timid political films preceding them, making their points overtly rather than concealing them within a web of metaphor. Recognizing the risks the Warners were taking, other studios closely monitored audience response to these productions. The White House also took a keen interest in the brothers' success or failure. At stake was public acceptance of the administration's prodemocratic foreign policy, which shaped the messages both pictures offered, and Hollywood's future ideological direction. *Confessions of a Nazi Spy* was a wakeup call to the American people, a warning that Hitler's grasp extended across the ocean. *Juarez* offered a more positive theme. In showing the triumph of democracy over autocracy in the Western Hemisphere it suggested historical roots for modern American antifascism.

Warners consciously designed *Juarez* as a goodwill gesture to Latin America. The studio's labors represented a case of cinematic necessity coinciding with political necessity. Most Hispanics viewed the Goliath to the north as a bully, an image grounded in decades of American filibustering missions to Central America, the seizure of northern Mexico after the Mexican-American War, and the United States' dominance of Cuba throughout the early twentieth century. Recognizing that military interventions undermined long-term international stability, the Hoover administration sought peaceful means of maintaining order in the region. Roosevelt expanded on Hoover's initiatives. His first inaugural address committed the United States to "the policy of the good neighbor—the neighbor who resolutely respects himself and, because he does so, respects the rights of others—the neighbor who respects his obligations and respects the sanctity of his agreements in and with a world of neighbors."[1]

Roosevelt's "good neighbor" policy evolved over the following years, eventually incorporating two major goals. First, the administration hoped to develop reciprocal trade programs with Latin American nations. Secretary of State Cordell Hull advocated lowering trade barriers as a way to diminish economic rivalries that caused wars. Hull announced his agenda in late 1933 to a receptive audience at the Seventh International Conference of American States in Montevideo, Uruguay. Roosevelt's considerable political capital facilitated the passage of legislation making it easier to cut tariff rates. The resulting pacts brought modest economic gains and perhaps some greater rewards in terms of improving hemispheric relations.[2]

The Good Neighbor program's second aim emerged amid the war scares of the late 1930s. An inheritor of Woodrow Wilson's internationalism, Roosevelt made collective security a priority. He believed a hemispheric defense system would contain future wars in Europe, unite democratic nations in a quest for peaceful prosperity, and counteract Axis efforts to establish footholds in Latin America. Even isolationists generally endorsed hemispheric defense as a means of keeping conflicts far from American shores. Their backing enabled Roosevelt to prepare the country for war without estranging an important constituency.[3]

Hollywood was also thinking about Latin America. Like Washington, the film capital had a dominant yet troubled position in the region. American studios had ruled the market during the silent era. They became even more powerful when the rise of talking pictures, which cost far more to shoot than silents, made production too expensive for Hispanic companies. Although distribution of such films was economically lucrative, Hollywood's cinematic supremacy reawoke long-standing fears of Yankee imperialism. Cuban legislators offered a bill to ban movies made in English. Other Latin American governments encouraged domestic production as a means of fostering cultural independence. Mexico nearly passed a quota law. Brazil exempted domestic studios from taxation and sponsored cash prizes for exceptional pictures. In the late 1930s lawmakers in Argentina, South America's largest movie market, debated a system of quotas, tax breaks, and censorship requirements similar to Germany's and Italy's. They also considered building a nationally funded studio in Buenos Aires.[4]

Hollywood shied away from Latin America during the mid-1930s. Europe had more theaters and money, and studios hesitated to invite further resentment from Hispanic nationalists. American studios released about fifty Spanish-language features in 1930 but only eight in 1937. They did not abandon the hemisphere altogether, however. Rather than produce films for Hispanic audiences, majors shifted toward distributing films made in Latin America. Movies shot in Mexico or Argentina were inexpensive and often outperformed their Hollywood counterparts because they better appealed to local tastes. United Artists won big with a deal to distribute the 1936 Mexican blockbuster *Allá en el rancho grande (Out on the Big Ranch)* throughout South and Central America. In contrast, two American-made films set in Argentina—RKO's *Hi Gaucho* (1935) and Fox's *Under the Pampas Moon* (1935)—never showed in South America for fear of adverse audience reaction.[5]

Previous experience supported the wisdom of withholding these movies. Hollywood had an unfortunate gift for caricaturing Hispanics. Annoyed by cinematic depictions of its people as ragged outlaws, Mexico briefly banned American films in 1922. The coming of talkies did little to improve the situation. Such films as *Captain Thunder* (1931) and *Viva Villa* (1934) perpetuated the bandito image and other Mexican stereotypes. Captain Thunder (Victor Varconi), a hot-blooded cattle rustler who spends his free time chasing women, lives in a world of siestas, gargantuan sombreros, comical public officials, and absurdly flamboyant clothes. When not gleefully breaking the law, he focuses his considerable store of lust on a temperamental cantina singer named Ynez (Fay Wray). While our hero thinks her quite fetching, Wray's absurd, jet-black wig and overwrought accent deprive her character of any believability. Captain Thunder is no model of authenticity himself, looking about as Hispanic as anyone named Victor Varconi—born Mihály Várkonyi in Kisvárda, Austria-Hungary—possibly could. It is a wreck of a film.

MGM shot *Viva Villa* in Mexico, but the picture's accurate setting did not translate into a realistic portrayal of Mexicans. Wallace Beery's Pancho Villa is a drunken slob with a wife in every town and an inability to grasp basic principles of government. His slavish devotion to president Francisco Madero reduces him to a comic lapdog even as his shocking ignorance transforms him into a typical Wallace Beery character—an uncouth, bumbling, yet likable buffoon. The film ostensibly traces how Mexico became "dedicated to justice and equality," but Villa's childlike glee at his power to print money and his growling threats to shoot anyone who defies his commands made such moralizing appear ridiculous. *Viva Villa* was no quick knockoff picture. It was pure A-list material, with recognizable stars (including a post–*King Kong* Fay Wray, again cast as the love interest of a good-hearted gorilla), expensive battle scenes, and epic shots of panoramic vistas. The industry honored the picture's caricaturing with four Academy Award nominations, including one for Best Picture. *Viva Villa*'s brave talk of liberty and claim to tell the "saga of the Mexican hero" spread a patina of self-importance over what was, in reality, a big-budget rehashing of *Captain Thunder*'s misrepresentations of America's good neighbors to the south.

Experts in the market lamented Hollywood's "continual underestimation of the Hispano-American's intelligence." Costumes and customs bore little resemblance to reality. Every film set in Latin America demanded the presence of at least one gaucho. Audiences complained about poor dubbing tracks and actors with inappropriate accents. Casting Mexican-born Dolores Del Rio as the fiery Brazilian who woos Fred Astaire in RKO's *Flying Down to Rio* (1933) was just one example of a studio acting as though all Latin Americans were the same. *Flying Down to Rio,* incidentally, contains one of the bawdiest lines from any 1930s movie. When Astaire snubs a gorgeous American to dance with Del Rio, the jilted peroxide blonde asks her friend, "What have South Americans got below the equator that we haven't?"[6]

The late 1930s brought new concern for Hispanic sensitivities. Economics provided the main motivation for Hollywood's interest. *Film Daily* ranked Brazil, Argentina, and Mexico as the three most important foreign markets of 1939. Central and South America's lack of theaters made them less-than-ideal outlets. These nations, however, represented the best opportunity to offset potentially crippling losses in Europe. "Storm clouds over the Old World are making that part of the New World on the other side of the equator look fairer, more alluring, more important than ever," *Motion Picture Herald* noted. Latin America already accounted for one-tenth of foreign grosses, but with little competition from domestic producers, Hollywood hoped to wring more from it.[7]

Hollywood's changing priorities coincided with Washington's desire to improve economic, cultural, and military ties with Latin America. Well aware that movies shaped foreigners' opinions of Americans, the government tracked what studios shipped south, particularly newsreels. Cordell Hull criticized the industry in 1934 for exporting newsreels that conveyed "an erroneous impression of American life and standards"—a diplomatic way of saying "bad news." Seeing little profit potential for newsreels in Latin America, studios paid scant attention to their content. Hollywood newsreels, consequently, "revealed North Americans as a nation of flag pole sitters, polar bear bathers, and people who were utterly and completely publicity mad." In contrast, Nazi filmmakers carefully crafted newsreels that stressed Germany's military might and cultural vibrancy, then distributed them for free or for a nominal fee throughout South and Central America. Hull asked Will Hays to further the Good Neighbor Policy by pushing studios to make newsreels containing more positive depictions of the United States.[8]

The administration expanded the Good Neighbor Policy's artistic side as it constructed a hemispheric defense system. Roosevelt launched the United States Film Service on the eve of the 1938 Munich Conference. This goodwill organization was part of Undersecretary of State Sumner Welles's program to promote democracy and pro-Americanism while counteracting totalitarian propaganda. The Film Service acted as a "celluloid ambassador" to the Hispanic world. Its tasks included equipping American embassies with projection equipment, hosting screenings for local dignitaries, and producing educational pictures that revealed the United States' glories to Latin American audiences. Although unsure of how they could help, the majors praised the Film Service. Movie moguls saw no harm and much to recommend in the agency. Because it focused on educational pictures, it did not compete with Hollywood. More important, closer ties with South and Central America benefited studios financially. Cooperation with the administration seemed especially advisable because, at that moment, the trust-busting Justice Department held the industry's economic future in the palm of its hand.[9]

Sensitive to charges of censorship, Washington had no interest in dictating the content of feature films. Newsreels were a different matter.

Somebody high up in the administration—probably Sumner Welles or Cordell Hull, possibly Roosevelt—asked Will Hays to send a team to chronicle Hull's 1938 appearance at the International Conference of American States in Lima. Fox Movietone's Anthony Muto headed the three-man expedition, which enjoyed full support from Hull's organization. Undersecretary Welles commanded his South and Central American staff to give the crew "all appropriate assistance" while keeping an eye out for newsreel-worthy events. "This project . . . should be of genuine value in the promotion of mutual understanding," he concluded.[10]

Armed with a letter of introduction from Hull and sponsorship from American embassies, the newsreelers found themselves engaged in an extended tour. Fox Movietone's first footage showed the Lima Conference endorsing Hull's Declaration of American Principles, a significant address that called for cultural exchanges, the peaceful resolution of international differences, and nonintervention in other states' internal affairs. While in Lima, the crew also filmed the Peruvian legislature in session and met with representatives from several Latin republics. From there it journeyed to Santiago with the conference's Chilean delegation before finalizing plans to visit Colombia, Ecuador, Bolivia, and Argentina. Over the coming months, Hollywood-based distributors fed this footage, along with coverage of an earthquake in Chile, interviews with prominent Hispanics, and joyful assertions of pan-American unity, into theaters throughout the hemisphere. In the meantime, American newsreel companies treated domestic audiences to a string of productions aimed at familiarizing them with Latin American people, places, and culture.[11]

Muto's expedition delighted Roosevelt, the State Department, and Will Hays, who bragged to the president that the newsreelers' work marked a new era of democracy and pro-Americanism in the region. *Variety* reported that producers planned to "insert the maximum of subtle propaganda and educational material" into future Latin American–themed installments. Always operating on multiple tracks, Hays considered whether Hollywood's service justified a try at overturning *Mutual Film Corp. v. Ohio,* the decision that opened the door to federal censorship.[12]

"No major industry in the United States has plumped more suddenly and completely for the objectives of the Good Neighbor Policy . . . than has Hollywood," the *New York Times* observed. A pro-Hispanic agenda made economic and political sense while making the moguls feel they were contributing to antifascism. Film was important in this unsettled world, which meant that filmmakers were important. At the same time, newsreel footage from Latin America was a safe investment. Shots of international conferences and natural disasters were inexpensive curios unlikely to rile the public. The true strength of Hollywood's resolve could not be measured until someone risked money on a big-budget feature trumpeting the Good Neighbor's pan-Americanism. Not surprisingly, the Warners stuck their necks out first.[13]

✿ ✿ ✿

The odyssey of *Juarez* began in August 1937 when Jack Warner paid $5,000 for the screen rights to *The Phantom Crown*, Bertita Harding's study of Mexico's emperor Maximilian, a puppet of Napoleon III, and his fight against Benito Juarez, a humble-born Mexican Indian who brought democracy to his native country when he overthrew the pretender in the 1860s. The project hit its first snag when Warners sent the book to the Production Code Administration for preliminary review. An anonymous PCA reader blasted Harding's work as "a prize package of cheap sneers against religion, the church, the Bourbons, the Hapsburgs, the Bonaparts [*sic*], the Coburgs, monarchy, government, sincerity, Napoleon III, Eugenie, Queen Victoria, Pius IX and Archbishop Labastida." A movie based on the book seemed certain to offend the French, the British, the Italians, Latin Americans, and Catholics. Breen's reader advised Warners to drop the idea.[14]

Believing it could overcome the PCA's objections, Warners handed *The Phantom Crown* to a promising young screenwriter named John Huston. The assignment delighted Huston, an aficionado of all things Mexican. Along with first-time screenwriters Wolfgang Reinhardt and Aeneas MacKenzie, he threw himself into researching Maximilian and Juarez. Interpreting their dispute as "a conflict of ideologies," Huston focused on the contest between monarchy and democracy implied within the drama. Warners encouraged Huston to establish unmistakable connections to present conditions. "Every child," remarked one executive, "must be able to realize that Napoleon, in his Mexican intervention, is none other than Mussolini plus Hitler in their Spanish adventure." Huston should cast Juarez as a "Mexican Lincoln."[15]

Huston's team handed in a first draft in the summer of 1938, just as Warners was starting *The Dawn Patrol* and Walter Wanger was wrapping *Blockade*. Executive producer Hal Wallis liked their work but found himself in a touchy legal situation. The script resembled Franz Werfel's 1924 play *Juarez and Maximilian,* which toured extensively in Europe and mounted a brief run in the United States with a then-unknown Edward G. Robinson in the cast. Studios routinely paid authors to protect themselves from litigation. *Juarez and Maximilian*'s copyright, however, belonged to German publisher Paul Zsolnay Verlag. The prospect of negotiating with Nazis left Harry Warner fuming. "Don't give them one dollar," he insisted.[16]

The issue lingered for weeks as Warner browbeat his lawyers to find a way to acquire the rights without offending his morals. Always more levelheaded in matters concerning the Nazis, Jack convinced Harry to bite his tongue and pay off the Germans. Warner Bros.' $1,020 check to Paul Zsolnay Verlag galled Harry so much that everyone involved in the transaction denied culpability for fear of his wrath. "You may be sure that I have no desire to give any of our good money to the blonde beasts," apologized studio lawyer Morris Ebenstein, who arranged the deal. "It was an unfortunate situation in which we had no choice."[17]

Knowing the film's success depended on strong Latin American returns, Warner Bros. assured the Mexicans that it would respect their national hero. Producers Hal Wallis and Henry Blanke, director William Dieterle, and actor Paul Muni spent six weeks examining locations and spreading cheer in Mexico. Warners regularly updated the Mexican government on script changes. Joseph Breen did the same with well-connected Los Angeleno Father Jose Conseco. Suspicions remained despite assurances that "Juarez and the Mexicans will be glorified in this picture to the highest degree." Most in Mexico City assumed Hollywood would screw it up again.[18]

Mexico's reservations involved more than Hollywood's past ineptitude. President Lázaro Cárdenas's nationalistic policies had brought relations with the United States to one of their periodic low points. Cárdenas, a radical populist devoted to land reform and educating the poor, resented the power of British and American oil companies operating in Mexico. In a thrust against foreign control of domestic resources, his administration ordered Standard Oil and other corporations to raise wages, shorten workdays, and institute a pension program. When they refused, Cárdenas declared them in rebellion. He seized the oil fields in March 1938, a provocative action that sent jubilant Mexicans parading through the capital city. Mexico severed diplomatic relations with Great Britain after Prime Minister Neville Chamberlain tried to mobilize worldwide protest. Roosevelt played the middle, applying mild economic pressure but not risking a rupture that might disrupt the Good Neighbor Policy.[19]

Word of *Juarez*'s prodemocracy, pan-American message sped around Hollywood. Liberal actors lined up for parts. Edward G. Robinson begged for the lead. Melvyn Douglas desperately wanted to play Maximilian. Gale Sondergaard, a fervently anti-Nazi actress married to equally anti-Nazi screenwriter Herbert Biberman, won the role of Napoleon III's wife, Empress Eugenie. Bette Davis fought to portray Maximilian's wife, Carlotta, even though the small role seemed beneath Warner Bros.' biggest female star. Her instincts were right on. Davis's gift for depicting strong yet slightly unhinged women gave her scenes a loopy intensity missing from the rest of *Juarez*. The role of Maximilian went to Brian Aherne, whose dignified performance garnered sympathy for the doomed monarch and an Academy Award nomination as the year's best supporting actor.[20]

Despite Robinson's lobbying, the casting of Benito Juarez was never in doubt. Paul Muni, Warner Bros.' master of disguise, had the part sewn up from the beginning. The actor was born Muni Weisenfreund in 1895 in the Austro-Hungarian village of Lemberg. His parents, both traveling performers, brought him to the United States when he was six. Muni followed his family to the stage, immersing himself in New York's Yiddish theater as a teenager. He gained some fame on Broadway after moving into English-speaking roles in the 1920s. Muni always envisioned himself as a theater man rather than a movie star despite a thirty-year film career. A member of the Hollywood Anti-Nazi League, Muni coveted roles that addressed current events while showcasing his talent for mimicry. He was built for versatility. One could never exactly place him as being either this or that. His black hair, swarthy complexion, and slight frame looked vaguely Italian, barely Asian, faintly French, and slightly Hispanic. He played them all onscreen—as *Scarface*'s Tony Camonte, *The Good Earth*'s Wang Lung, Louis Pasteur, and Benito

Juarez. His performances in *The Story of Louis Pasteur* and *The Life of Emile Zola* established his ability to play historical figures in prestige films. Reuniting him with William Dieterle, who had directed *The Story of Louis Pasteur* and *The Life of Zola,* gave *Juarez* instant cachet.[21]

Juarez challenged even Muni's considerable skills. He subjected himself to three hours of makeup a day, arriving at six o'clock every morning to be fitted with a wig and prosthetic nose. In turn, he subjected Warners executives to his perfectionism. He demanded endless script rewrites, with each new version enlarging his role, and indulged his well-deserved reputation for prickliness. He constantly complained about setups and dialogue. As always, he insisted that his wife, Bella, watch from behind the camera. A shake of her head caused Muni to call for a retake. As the film's costs rocketed past $1.2 million, a furious Jack Warner promised he would never again allow an actor to have so much control over a shoot.[22]

Muni wanted scriptwriters to make Benito Juarez's similarities to his contemporary, Abraham Lincoln, more overt. Lincoln's spirit pervades the film from Muni's first scene, in which Juarez reads a letter from the American president. "The defense of democracy is an imperative duty," the Great Emancipator writes, "since it is the defense of our own honor, the dignity of our wives and children, the honor and dignity of all men." A portrait of Lincoln hangs on the wall over Juarez's shoulder. The painting accompanies Juarez throughout his travels, providing comfort as Maximilian's forces obstruct his democratic quest to free Mexico from European domination. Muni's Juarez truly is the Mexican Lincoln, right down to his shuffling walk, ill-fitting frock coat, unassuming bow tie, and stovepipe hat. He is pan-Americanism embodied, a visual image of the ties between the two republics.

Juarez's single focus is his democratic revolution against authoritarianism. "We represent irreconcilable principles, one or the other of which must perish," he says of Maximilian. As he had predicted, monarchy devolves into fascist-style tyranny. Maximilian signs a decree ordering capital punishment for any Mexican found with a weapon. The emperor pours sealing wax on the document like blood from a vial, then brings down his stamp with an ominous thud that foreshadows the executions to come. Rather than allow despotism to spread to its border, the Lincoln administration dispatches General Ulysses S. Grant's army to assist Juarez's rump government. America's defense of Latin American democracy topples Maximilian's regime, clearing the way for a new epoch of freedom, democracy, and regional cooperation.

Warner Bros. took a huge financial risk with *Juarez*. Costume dramas about foreign revolutionaries were hardly box-office guarantees, and *Juarez* seemed particularly likely to fail. There is precious little action for a movie revolving around war and ideological conflict. It is instead a brooding picture, never in a hurry and prone to wallowing in flowery language. *Juarez*'s dialogue was heady stuff on the page but sounded awkward on the screen. Americans' aversion to propaganda films added to Warners' perils. *Juarez* is clearly propaganda. Pro-American, prodemocracy propaganda, to be sure, but propaganda as obvious as *Triumph of the Will*. The movie sings democracy's praises from the beginning, when the haughty Napoleon III chides "the rule of the cattle by the cattle for the cattle," to the end, when Juarez stands over the executed Maximilian's coffin, a symbol of the triumph over monarchy. One of Warners' South American representatives cautioned before shooting began that the film could be either "the biggest money maker" or "the biggest flop" in history. Others within the organization had more faith. *Juarez* fit "the spirit of the times," Morris Ebenstein said, because it sold democracy.[23]

Warners executives celebrated the completion of "a motion picture classic" when *Juarez* wrapped in February 1939, only to discover that *Juarez*'s first preview audience disagreed with their assessment. The screening at Grauman's Egyptian Theatre on Hollywood Boulevard was a disaster. People walked out early and laughed at inappropriate times. Word that the studio had a flop on its hands permeated nearby watering holes. Warners chopped twenty minutes from the film and held its collective breath. *Juarez*'s next preview went better, and Warners began preparing a publicity barrage for the picture's premiere. Press releases stressed the film's democracy theme by tying Juarez to notable American figures and traditions. One canned story compared the hut Juarez was born in with Lincoln's log cabin. Another equated Juarez with Andrew Jackson, observing that "each time that the future of an American country's free institutions was wavering in the balance, a great frontiersman stepped forward from obscurity and swept the foreign invasion back." A third article more clearly linked Juarez's struggle to current events.

"There were two great international crises in the western hemisphere during the 19th century," it declared, "in each of which the tide of European aggression washed the shores of America and ate away at the fabric of democracy which had been established there." It is unlikely readers who encountered this statement in April 1939, just days after Germany swallowed Czechoslovakia, had the War of 1812 and the French imperial adventure in Mexico—the two crises the piece referred to—on their minds.[24]

Warners arranged a private showing of *Juarez* for the Mexican consul in Los Angeles on April 20 before debuting it at Broadway's Hollywood Theatre five days later. Representatives from twelve Latin American nations packed the house. A special train brought dozens of diplomats from Washington, D.C. Juarez's great-grandson, Pablo Prida, took a bow. The opening-night crowd received *Juarez* with respectful admiration—the kind of response one has when viewing fine art while wishing they were reading a comic book. Critics felt the same, applauding the picture's substance but questioning its style. *Brooklyn Eagle* reviewer Herbert Cohn called it "the frankest and sincerest defense of democratic principles that the American screen has ever attempted." He did not call it an entertaining movie or even a good movie. Ed Sullivan admired Muni's performance but found the movie "stiff and wooden." *Nation* admired the film not for its cinematic merits so much as for its willingness to say what *The Life of Emile Zola* and *Black Legion* only hinted at. "Clearness of purpose is reached," the magazine cheered.[25]

Harry Warner especially reveled in praise from the administration. Sumner Welles congratulated the mogul for advancing the Good Neighbor Policy. Roosevelt did not comment directly but offered a general blessing of Hollywood's turn toward projects that promoted hemispheric goodwill. That was enough for Warner, who hoped *Juarez* would benefit his company's relations with the government. He implored Undersecretary Welles to notify him should the State Department find another Latin American–themed project his studio could use. Warners exploited its political connections as it prepared for *Juarez*'s international release, dragooning State Department representatives into joining officials from Latin American embassies for a shortwave broadcast about the picture. Invited dignitaries lauded the picture's contribution to international solidarity and called for more of the same.[26]

The State Department did not dispatch operatives to scour the Hispanic world for plot ideas but, recognizing that movies could bolster the administration's Latin American policy, it did take a strong interest in *Juarez*'s overseas success. Welles, likely with Roosevelt's approval, ordered South and Central American embassy staffs to monitor the film's reception. Reports from Costa Rica, El Salvador, Uruguay, and Venezuela were hopeful. *Juarez* drew positive press coverage and large audiences in these places, especially from among the lower classes.[27]

The response from Mexico was more mixed. *Juarez* had a promising opening night at Mexico City's Palace of Fine Arts, where American ambassador Josephus Daniels joined an appreciative audience of local power brokers and government officials. The ambassador noted that Warners excised a scene where an American diplomat lectures Napoleon III about the Monroe Doctrine. This was a good decision, Daniels observed, because Mexicans failed to appreciate "how much all nations south of the Rio Grande owe to the Doctrine." The American Consulate in Ciudad Juarez arranged a viewing for President Cárdenas, who raved about Muni's performance. On the other hand, *Juarez* flopped in San Luis Potosí. Attendance there was so low the theater manager invited people to watch for free during its five-day run. That topped its performance in Monterrey, however, where it received only one showing. Unusually high ticket prices accounted for some of the apathy. Mexico's oil-inspired animosity toward the United States added to it. Hispanic audiences derided the film's proposition that Lincoln's military intervention saved Mexico sixteen years after the Americans seized half the country in the Mexican War. Finally, for all its good intentions, *Juarez* was a ponderous history lesson that lacked the zip theatergoers expected from Hollywood films.[28]

Studio accounting wizardry makes it difficult to be sure, but *Juarez* probably lost money. Muni's previous biopic, *The Life of Emile Zola*, had cost about $830,000 to make and had grossed over $2 million. Warners spent more than $1.2 million shooting *Juarez* and took in about $1.6 million. Distribution expenses made it a wash at best. Warners put a brave face on *Juarez*'s lackluster performance, promising more progressive features in the future. Studio executives even considered purchasing *It Can't Happen Here* from MGM. Industry watchers were less optimistic. Many thought the Latin American film market was saturated and saw little hope of finding projects that appealed to both domestic and overseas audiences.[29]

Whether for ideological, political, or economic reasons, Hollywood was not ready to give up on Latin America. Tinseltown's drive to be a cinematic good neighbor continued as studios put more Latin American–themed projects into production, albeit with smaller budgets than *Juarez*. Even so, the moguls recognized that Warners' swing at pan-American unity missed its target. *Juarez* was propaganda that did not entertain, and moviegoers wanted above all else to be entertained.

CHAPTER SEVEN

Serving America

J ACK WARNER SOLD DREAMS, fictional visions of America and the
world. His interpretation of his own life merely extended the myth-
making that informed his professional existence. According to his autobiography, he first publicly mentioned *Confessions of a Nazi Spy* at the
1937 Venice Film Festival after the Fascists cancelled a screening of *The
Life of Emile Zola*. As Warner remembered it, he angrily promised
Countess Dorothy di Frasso and her friend mobster Bugsy Siegel that he
would exact his revenge by making a movie that denounced Mussolini's
allies, the Nazis, as lawless thugs. Moved by Warner's conviction, Siegel
offered to bump off Joseph Goebbels and other top Nazis. Countess di
Frasso informed Warner a few days later that Goebbels had not only
expressed interest in the project but also offered to play himself for free.
Scoffing at the proposal, Warner made the film at great personal risk to
himself and his family. Warner later learned that Hitler placed him on
an "extinction list" after the dictator viewed *Confessions of a Nazi Spy*
in his Berchtesgaden retreat.[1]

As with so much Jack Warner said, the story was utter nonsense, bearing no relation to reality except that *The Life of Emile Zola* did not show
in Venice. Yet his flawed memory—to put a generous spin on his fanciful
autobiography—is revealing, as it underscores the importance he and his
studio placed on *Confessions of a Nazi Spy*. Jack wanted to be a hero for
making it. His invented chronology pushed him into the vanguard of
American anti-Nazism. In his version Warner Bros. committed to the first
movie to overtly denounce Nazism before Hitler annexed Austria and the
Sudetenland, before the release of *Blockade,* and before the antitrust suit
sent executives scrambling to appease the Roosevelt administration.

That *Confessions of a Nazi Spy* has more pedestrian origins does not
lessen its impact or diminish its revolutionary nature. "Here is propa-

ganda, unquestionably," observed the *Hollywood Reporter*. "It serves notice on the American public that each and every citizen must look into his own heart and those of his neighbors." The picture's cast and crew truly believed they were participating in a noble venture. Detractors thought Warners' step into the cinematic abyss put lives in the balance. *Confessions of a Nazi Spy* divided opinion makers across the United States and around the world. Released three days after *Juarez* and four months before the war in Europe began, it was the second barrel of Warners' wakeup blast, Hollywood's first test of whether theatergoers would pay to see a movie bashing a movement they disliked but did not wish to oppose with bullets.[2]

Confessions of a Nazi Spy would have been a natural for Warner Bros. even had Jack and Harry not been ardent anti-Nazis. It fell within the studio's tradition of gritty gangster movies and socially conscious films. A fast-paced thriller that plugged into real-world affairs, *Confessions of a Nazi Spy* was *G-Men* (1935) or *Bullets or Ballots* (1936) with a heavy dollop of anti-Nazism. But this new ingredient was the movie's raison d'être, not mere icing on the cake. The picture's success rested on the willingness of audiences to accept its strident philosophy. There were no camouflaged messages here, no antifascist parables or metaphors. Only someone who hated the Nazis could love *Confessions of a Nazi Spy*.

As with so many Warners pictures, *Confessions of a Nazi Spy* was born in newspaper headlines. J. Edgar Hoover's FBI busted a New York City–based Nazi spy ring in February 1938. Special Agent Leon Turrou, already famous for his work on the Lindbergh baby kidnapping, led the well-publicized investigation. The public paid close attention to the case, which offered the first real evidence of Nazi ambitions in the United States. Always eager to show his agency in a positive light, Hoover suggested to producer Hal Wallis that Warner Bros. make a film about the incident. Wallis found the idea intriguing, as did Jack Warner, who received at least tacit approval from Roosevelt before proceeding.[3]

Studio researchers assembled a massive clippings file on the espionage trial. Wallis liberated outspoken anti-Nazi screenwriter Milton Krims from a going-nowhere biopic project about Beethoven and assigned him to the Nazi movie. Warners concealed Krims's new job, billing him on "Beethoven's" budget even as he shuttled between Hollywood and New

York to conduct research and furtively attend meetings of the German-American Bund, the United States' most prominent pro-Nazi organization. Krims handed in a preliminary treatment for "The World Is Ours" in September 1938, a few months after Huston's script for *Juarez* arrived and a few months before *The Dawn Patrol* hit theaters.[4]

Krims revised his draft as he sat in on the spy trial, which opened in October. The proceedings revealed a bizarre cast of characters. Government attorneys introduced Jessie Jordan, a mild-mannered Scotswoman who funneled information from agents in Germany to their American counterparts; Dr. Ignatz Griebl, an obstetrician and former head of the Friends of New Germany, a New York–based predecessor to the German-American Bund; and Guenther Rumrich, a United States Army deserter who launched a ridiculous scheme to acquire blank passports. Along with the loosely organized network's other members, these head-liners operated more like figures in a bad movie than a disciplined band of espionage artists. Although the ring never acquired any sensitive information from the American government, it did embrace the worst tropes of the spy genre, including the use of codes concealed in matchbooks and, yes, blueprints hidden inside a violin case. A jury convicted four defendants in November. Fourteen indicted agents escaped the country.[5]

Word of Warners' project got around even though the studio tried to keep its script, code-named "Hot Lips," under wraps. Edward G. Robinson began lobbying for a role even before the trial concluded. *"I want to do that for my people,"* the Jewish actor told Wallis. Dr. Georg Gyssling, the German consul in Los Angeles, fired ominous letters at Joseph Breen after seeing an item about the film in the *Hollywood Reporter.* Gyssling kept his threats implicit but clearly expected the PCA chief to muzzle those bothersome Warners.[6]

It is difficult today to understand how dangerous *Confessions of a Nazi Spy* seemed at that particular moment. Its overt anti-Nazism ran counter to America's profoundly isolationist mood, and most producers believed the only way to survive was to cater to public tastes. Warners was thumbing its nose at many of the domestic and overseas elements currently arrayed against Hollywood. Civic and religious groups leaped at perceived violations of Will Hays's promise of an unbroken stream of pure entertainment. Congress regularly debated censorship bills and other hostile legislation. Thurman Arnold's antitrust brigade sought to divorce studios from their theaters. Foreign governments were tightening censorship rules, imposing quotas, and limiting revenues. Italy's ENIC monopoly edict coincided with Krims's appearance in the New York courtroom. *Confessions of a Nazi Spy* could blow the powder keg sky high, prompting new calls for federal supervision of films, driving away theatergoers, and causing trouble in critical overseas markets. The movie might even arouse a new round of Nazi anti-Semitism. Paramount's foreign department predicted that "Warners will have on their hands the blood of a great many Jews in Germany" if it made the picture. Such fears of reprisal gained strength as Americans learned about the bloody brutality of November 1938's *Kristallnacht.*[7]

Jack Warner countered the project's detractors by calling for a heightened sense of Americanism, which to him meant faith in democracy and tolerance, the very issues Warner Bros. would explore in *Confessions of a Nazi Spy.* "We know from personal experience the value of the American philosophy," he told reporters in early 1939. "We are descendents of immigrants and we know why our father came to America. Possibly we have a more acute appreciation of these ideals than those who accept American freedom as a matter of course. We believe that anyone who is anti-Semitic, anti-Catholic, anti-Protestant or anti-anything that has gone into the building of this country is anti-American."[8] With audiences numbering in the tens of millions, he concluded, movies were the ideal medium for disseminating these ideals. In a way this perspective dovetailed with what Will Hays and other "pure entertainment" advocates argued. Everyone in Hollywood agreed that motion pictures should promote Americanism. Warners, however, was changing the rules of the game. Linking Americanism with anti-Nazism demanded a new understanding of "Americanism," a redefinition of the Production Code's national feelings clause, and a readiness to risk revenues in the name of a divisive message.

Warner Bros. bulked up its security in response to Gyssling's cautions but refused to slow its pace. Speed was of the essence; the studio had to get the picture out before audience interest in the spy case waned. Work on the project took on even more immediacy in December, when the *New York Post* began publishing Agent Turrou's memoirs. Wallis pulled screenwriter John Wexley off *Footsteps in the Dark,* a trifle of a crime comedy, to help Krims with "The World Is Ours," now renamed "Storm over America." A leftist member of the Hollywood Anti-Nazi League and future victim of the red scare–era blacklist, Wexley felt a special connection with *Confessions of a Nazi Spy,* not only because of his political leanings but also because his wife was Austrian. He later called his time on the project "the most exciting and exhilarating work I had ever done in Hollywood." Warners made sure to keep Washington in the loop during the scriptwriting process.[9]

Confessions of a Nazi Spy's timeliness naturally lent it a sense of authenticity. Warners looked to enhance that quality by shooting the film in a documentary style. The studio dispatched photographers to shoot the New York restaurants, Western Union stations, docks, government offices, and meeting halls where the real drama occurred so that set designers could copy them on the West Coast. Armed with these visual guides, studio staffers in Burbank began conducting sound and photo tests on December 22. Warners sent a preliminary script of "our anti-Nazi picture" to Joseph Breen two days later. The studio's cloak-and-dagger atmosphere accompanied the treatment. Producer Robert Lord implored the Production Code Administration to guard the document closely. "The German-American Bund, the German Consul and all such forces are desperately trying to get a copy of it," he reported.[10]

"Storm over America" hit the PCA office like a grenade. The script was unlike anything Breen had ever read. He could almost see lawsuits and international confrontations leaping off the page. Spies appeared under their real names. Ignatz Griebl offered an anti-Semitic tirade that shattered Hollywood's code of silence on all things Jewish. The final sequence of "Storm over America" had a German general insisting that the espionage ring's demise was but a temporary setback in his nation's inevitable march to global domination. "Tomorrow the world is ours!" he shrieks as the screen fades to black.[11]

Breen shrank at the prospect of such inflammatory material on the screen. He advised Jack Warner that, while the studio might yet bring the script into conformity with the code—although the all-encompassing "National Feelings" clause posed a difficult hurdle—"Storm over America" raised questions of "general industry policy." Its direct attack on another country transcended the PCA's typical focus on sex, language, and violence. Breen informed Warner that the "highly controversial nature of this subject matter" made it a certain target for both foreign and domestic censors. "Storm over America" endangered Hollywood's pure-entertainment philosophy and self-image as a global unifier. Breen predicted the movie would enrage theatergoers around the world. He wanted the movie magnate to think long and hard before single-handedly destroying everything Hollywood had built up. He took the additional, unusual step of alerting Will Hays, the industry's chief political fixer, to the studio's plans.[12]

"Storm over America" mellowed with rewrites. Warner Bros. lawyers seconded Breen's concern that using defendants' real names invited libel suits and reported that Hapag Lloyd Company, which operated the *Europa* and the *Bremen,* the ships that transported German agents and propaganda across the ocean, would sue if the picture depicted its crews as spies. Wallis's crew incorporated this prudent advice into their revisions.[13] Unlike MGM's simultaneous neutering of *Idiot's Delight,* however, these were cosmetic changes that forestalled lawsuits without altering the film's central thrust. Dr. Ignatz Griebl became Dr. Karl Kassell.[14] U.S. Army deserter and inept German spy Guenther Rumrich became U.S. Army deserter and inept German spy Kurt Schneider, and so on.

Now entitled "Confessions of a Nazi Spy," the revised draft did not impress the Breen Office. "I fear it will be one of the most memorable, one of the most lamentable mistakes ever made by the industry," PCA reader Karl Lischka told Breen. Lischka found the script's hostility toward Hitler "manifestly unfair." He clinched his point by parroting Will Hays's oft-stated endorsement of noncontroversial pictures. "Are we ready," he wondered, "to depart from the pleasant and profitable course of entertainment, to engage in propaganda, to produce screen portrayals arousing controversy, conflict, racial, religious and nationalistic antagonism, and outright, horrible human hatred?" Although unaware of Lischka's outrage, Adolf Hitler confirmed his fears. During a two-hour address to the Reichstag delivered the same month "Confessions" appeared in Breen's office, the Führer warned that Germany would answer anti-Nazi movies with anti-Semitic movies.[15]

Members of the State Department shared the PCA's concerns. Staffers in the agency's Cultural Relations Division quailed at signs that Hollywood was preparing an anti-Nazi barrage, a development certain to strain affairs with Germany. Some in the department urged Secretary

Hull to inform the Hays Office of his displeasure. In the end, however, Hull's men decided the best course of action was to keep their distance from *Confessions of a Nazi Spy*. If made public, they concluded, any intervention might lead to charges of government censorship or suggest administration support for the film. So the show went on.[16]

Warners did an exceptionally shrewd job of casting *Confessions of a Nazi Spy*. The studio's decision to fill the picture with members of Hollywood's émigré community subtly reinforced awareness of Nazi tyranny. These largely unknown actors gave heartfelt performances born from personal suffering. Francis Lederer, who starred as New York–based spy Kurt Schneider, was born in Prague, which fell just before shooting wrapped. Paul Lukas (Karl Kassell) grew up in Budapest. Hedwiga Reicher, who played Mrs. Kassell, and Lya Lys, cast as Dr. Kassell's mistress, came from Germany. Anatole Litvak, the film's director, was a Russian Jew who resettled in Berlin only to be forced out in the mid-1930s.

The cast's anonymity contributed to the movie's documentary feel. Modern cinephiles might recognize Ward Bond and Grace Stafford, who later voiced Woody Woodpecker, in small roles; but with the exception of Edward G. Robinson, who got his wish to play Leon Turrou (thinly disguised as FBI agent Edward Renard), the film featured bit players whom audiences could not associate with a particular screen image. In a remarkable display of humility for status-conscious Hollywood, the director, actors, and screenwriters deferred onscreen billing until the end. *Confessions of a Nazi Spy* opens with an announcer laying out the spy plot newsreel-style rather than opening with credits. Its use of minor performers also allowed the budget-conscious Warner Bros. to make the film on the cheap, no small consideration given its chances of flopping. Litvak cost $55,000 and Robinson $50,000. Francis Lederer, who earned $16,500, took the next-highest salary. The entire production cost around $600,000, on the low end for a Warner Bros. A-release. *Juarez* cost the studio twice as much.[17]

Warner Bros.' determination to produce *Confessions of a Nazi Spy* surpassed the Breen Office's and State Department's desire to stop it. Such rebelliousness hinted at the possibilities of this new era. "National Feelings" clause or no, studios could release anti-Nazi films under the Production Code if they stuck to their guns. An increasingly anti-Nazi federal government would not prevent Hollywood from dabbling in politics. Hollywood, moreover, had less to lose than before. Although parts of Europe remained viable, the twenty-nine American movies that cleared German censorship in 1938 earned a negligible sum. Germany still threatened to pressure other nations to ban American films, but by now even Will Hays was emerging from his political shell. While holding to his "pure entertainment" vocabulary, he started privately accumulating material on the Nazis' abuse of German Jews.[18]

Hays's collection paled in comparison to Harry Warner's. The mogul's infatuation with the Nazi and American Nazi movements inspired him to compile a thick dossier of newspaper clippings, pamphlets, and anti-Jewish propaganda. *Confessions of a Nazi Spy* fueled his fixation so much that he teetered on the brink of a nervous breakdown by January 1939. Harry's condition was so perilous that the self-centered Jack ordered his subordinates to protect his brother's peace of mind by cutting off shipments of inflammatory material. "He's really not well," Jack explained, "and the worrying he does about world problems, etc. constitutes a very definite threat to his health."[19]

With Harry laid up and Jack holding the reins in Burbank, *Confessions of a Nazi Spy* sped through the Warner Bros. pipeline, although the shoot did not lack for intrigue. Actors received the script a few pages at a time because producers feared leaks to hostile parties. Considering the bunker mentality pervading the studio, a hostile party was pretty much anyone whose paycheck was not signed by Harry Warner. Shrugging off Consul Gyssling's warning of "trouble ahead," the production wrapped on March 18, 1939, two days ahead of schedule. Breen reluctantly granted a PCA seal of approval three weeks later.[20]

A rejuvenated Harry Warner opened the publicity campaign for *Confessions of a Nazi Spy* during a St. Patrick's Day address to the Ancient Order of Hibernians. "You are not presenting yourselves as Irish-Americans," he told the crowd. "You are Americans. I am not accepting your hospitality as a Jewish-American," he continued. "I am here as an *American*." And it was this very notion, this concept of an inclusive spirit of Americanism, that the Nazis and New World sympathizers like the German-American Bund so endangered. "I wonder what is happening when I hear of American radicals wearing a foreign emblem on their sleeves and drilling and marching in a foreign style," Harry lamented.

He called on Americans to unite behind their shared national identity in the face of a common menace. Warner Bros. would lead the way by promoting democracy through their films. "And so," Warner concluded, "our producing company is making right now a picture revealing the astonishing length to which Nazi spies have gone in America. We are making this—and we will make more like it, no doubt, when the occasion arises. We have disregarded, and we will continue to disregard, threats and pleas intended to dissuade us from our purpose. We have defied, and we will continue to defy, any elements that may try to turn us from our loyal and sincere purpose of serving America."[21] Warner's St. Patrick's Day speech refined the ideas that had long defined him—patriotism, the desire to assimilate into mainstream America, the need to protect Jewish interests, and the belief that motion pictures could enlighten the masses.

Confessions of a Nazi Spy premiered at the Warner Bros. Beverly Hills Theatre on April 27, 1939, three days after *Juarez* opened. Hundreds of plainclothes policemen milled about, looking for any sign of trouble. Their (well-publicized) vigilance proved unnecessary, as the event passed without incident. The crowd of three thousand lustily applauded the movie. Warners executives crowed. *Confessions of a Nazi Spy* marked "the coming of age of the motion picture," exclaimed studio producer Lou Edelman. "From now on, with this as a beginning, motion pictures will grow to greater and stronger manhood, and have more and more to say." Jack Warner hoped to parley his success into an even bigger splash. He asked his "old and good friend" in the White House to see his studio's "great American document of civilization." Warner yearned for official endorsement of *Confessions of a Nazi Spy*. He received a polite but non-committal reply from presidential secretary Stephen Early.[22]

The enthusiasm permeating Warner Bros. was not universal. Many studios avoided the controversial opening, keeping their valuable leading players clear of a potential public-relations disaster. Louis B. Mayer fashioned the most creative dodge, celebrating the release of *Confessions of a Nazi Spy* with a surprise birthday party for fading MGM actor Lionel Barrymore. Attendance at the bash was mandatory for MGM stars, keeping them safely away from the cameras and reporters at the premiere.[23]

Mayer's guests missed a movie like no other in recent memory. *Confessions of a Nazi Spy* culminated the first stage of Hollywood antifascism, finally tackling the Nazi menace head-on after months of motion pictures that tiptoed around it. Dr. Karl Kassell, a physician who moonlights as the head of the German-American Bund's New York City branch, serves as the film's introduction to American Nazism. The film poses Kassell as a surrogate Hitler. He sports military regalia as he addresses a Bund rally from a podium crowded with Nazi and American flags. His overblown oratorical style matches the Führer's. He pounds the lectern as he mocks democracy and racial equality, his voice swelling to a frenzied pitch when he talks of creating a new Germany in the United States.

Kassell's adulterous relationship with Erika Wolf illustrates the moral depravity lurking behind his ravings. His followers are equally flawed. Like Humphrey Bogart's Frank Taylor in *Black Legion,* the Bundists in *Confessions of a Nazi Spy* are small men who dream of power. Kurt Schneider has no ideology other than a vague desire to serve his place of birth. Kassell's hateful rhetoric inspires Schneider to approach German Naval Intelligence, which improbably accepts him as an agent. His first assignment—stealing a military code and troop-strength numbers for the New York area—gives him visions of escaping his pedestrian life.

Schneider is not a secret agent so much as a loser pretending to be a secret agent. He stalks the streets in a fedora and rumpled trench coat. His cockeyed schemes succeed only because the United States has no counterespionage program. America's guard is so lowered that a military courier hands Schneider a sheaf of reports even though he is wearing civilian clothes, has no identification, and is standing on a street corner. Such triumphs inflate Schneider's self-worth. He assures a friend that he receives orders directly from Hitler and will soon be a big wheel in the espionage game, even though he lives in the same cramped apartment as before and receives a mere fifty dollars a month from his contact in German Intelligence, Franz Schlager.

Schlager (George Sanders) is the primary link between the Bund, Schneider, and Germany. Backed by Gestapo enforcers, he supervises Kassell's spy network and issues Schneider's orders. He is a true believer with a face torn from an Aryan propaganda leaflet. "Tomorrow the world is ours," he reminds the party faithful. Demanding "blind obedience to party discipline," the fanatical Schlager labels any German with less-than-total devotion to Hitler a traitor. He commands by intimidation, collecting names of the potentially disloyal, bullying countrymen who question Hitler's infallibility, and spying on subordinates exhibiting signs of ideological wavering.

The scope of the German threat widens when the Nazis summon Kassell for his first trip home in ten years. Hitler's stranglehold on the nation's newspapers, literature, religion, and politics delights Kassell. He imagines that one day the United States will follow the same path. Joseph Goebbels (Martin Kosleck) gives him a blueprint for doing just that. The propaganda minister tells Kassell that the German-American Bund must start promoting Nazism as an all-American ideology. While assuming this patriotic guise, Kassell's organization should fracture the United States along racial and class lines by implementing a disinformation campaign masterminded by Berlin. The duped masses will be left searching for a new ideology, a new definition of Americanism. This confusion, Goebbels concludes, "is a formless iron that we will beat into another swastika."

Karl Kassell's real-life counterpart, Ignatz Griebl, had no connection to the German-American Bund. He briefly led the Friends of New Germany before members forced him out amid scurrilous rumors that his wife was Jewish. In Kassell, Warners conflated the spy Griebl with Fritz Kuhn, the bund's current leader, then further improved on reality for the sake of heightening drama. Hitler considered the bundists an embarrassment whose bombast created more anti-Nazi than pro-Nazi sentiment in the United States. He stood for a photograph with Kuhn during the 1936 Berlin Olympics but saw little importance in the meeting. His subordinates were similarly dismissive. "Nothing has resulted in so much hostility toward us in the last few months as the stupid and noisy activities of . . . the German-American Bund," reported Ambassador Hans Dieckhoff in late 1937.[24]

The bund seemed more powerful than it really was, an illusion that lent *Confessions of a Nazi Spy*'s portrait of imminent domestic peril an added layer of apparent veracity. Kuhn suggested an intimate relationship with Berlin long after Hitler dismissed him as a troublemaker. Although the group's New York branch had only nine hundred members, mainstream journals often cited or reprinted fire-breathing stories from its newspaper, *Deutscher Weckruf und Beobachter*. Its February 1939 celebration of Washington's birthday drew twenty-two thousand to

Madison Square Garden. At this so-called "Pro-American Rally," Kuhn blasted Roosevelt, likened Hitler to George Washington, and predicted the nazification of the United States. Publicity from the event provided a short-term boost to the group's prospects and, coincidentally, enhanced the timely appeal of *Confessions of a Nazi Spy*.[25]

The film characterized America's Nazi problem as the product of a few malcontents rather than an entire ethnic group. In doing so, it preserves a comforting image of a heterogeneous yet harmonious republic where minorities are reliably patriotic. Restoration of true Americanism is a matter of excising a cancerous tumor, not launching a witch hunt. Kurt Schneider's wife, Helen, serves as the voice of most German Americans. "Aren't we all supposed to be Americans in America?" she asks her husband. Even the spies recognize their unpopularity. "The vast majority of German Americans are ashamed at the black name we are giving them," moans one agent.

Confessions of a Nazi Spy pulls its punches only when dealing with anti-Semitism. As it did in *The Life of Emile Zola,* Warner Bros. sidestepped the Jewish issue despite the brutal repression of *Kristallnacht.* Characters mention concentration camps a few times, but no one utters the word *Jew.* FBI agents raiding Ignatz Griebl's office found files on important American Jews, but in the movie version agents discover Karl Kassell's files on "prominent Americans." This omission reflected the studio's fear that forcing audiences to confront anti-Semitism might distract them from the picture's main point—that the Nazis aimed to destabilize the United States. Highlighting Nazi racial policies might also lead to charges that Hollywood was part of a Jewish conspiracy to bring the United States into conflict with Germany.

Confessions of a Nazi Spy interrupts its dramatized retelling of factual events with a series of newsreel-style interludes that present a more panoramic perspective on the evils of Nazism. Backed by narrator John Deering's authoritative voice, these featurettes appropriated the look of newsreels to distill the movie's themes into chunks of anti-Nazi propaganda no moviegoer could misinterpret. One interlude, for example, shows a swastika impressed on a spinning globe. The swastika grows larger until it finally overshadows the entire Western Hemisphere. As this occurs, Deering explains that Hitler's regime has created "a new fascist society based on a devout worship of the Aryan superman; a new fascist culture imbued with a glorification of conquest and war; a fascist system of life, where every man, woman, and child must think alike, speak alike, and do alike, a rigidly censored press, with all news colored by the Ministry of Propaganda; a fascist literature, shorn of its greatest writers and poets; a new religion, ridiculing the brotherhood and equality of man before God." Another newsreel feature illustrates the penetration of Nazi propaganda into "every nerve and fiber of American life, inciting racial prejudice, ridiculing democracy, striving to shatter that attitude of tolerance and respect for minority rights which entitle people to consider themselves as civilized human beings." Agents slip leaflets into mailboxes and under doors. Propagandists drop pamphlets from an airplane. A schoolboy finds a Nazi handout in his lunchbox.

In a tightly packed 104 minutes of screen time, *Confessions of a Nazi Spy* constructs a conspiracy so immense as to be almost overwhelming. The film then dispels the gloom by suggesting ways theatergoers can combat un-American philosophies. The picture's insistence that most German Americans are loyal offers some hope, as does the good work of such patriotic organizations as the American Legion. One veteran (Ward Bond) paraphrases Harry Warner's 1938 message to the legionnaires as he disrupts a bund meeting. "We don't want any isms in this country except Americanism," he shouts before bundists mob him. *Confessions of a Nazi Spy* also depicts the slow awakening of the United States' counterespionage machinery. Once vulnerable to amateurs like Kurt Schneider, law-enforcement agencies gain expertise as the film rolls on. British military intelligence arrests Mary McLaughlin, the spy ring's mailbox in Scotland. New York City police prevent Schneider from obtaining blank passports. FBI agent Renard's cunning questioning lures the pathetic spy into naming his superiors, who are soon either caught up in the dragnet or flee across the ocean.

Renard's heroic work marked a first step toward expelling Nazi influence, but, the film argues, America cannot defeat the foreign menace once and for all until every citizen assumes responsibility for protecting it from alien ideologies. In a reflective mood over coffee with the district attorney (Henry O'Neill) after the trial, Renard wonders why Germany orchestrated the absurd spy plot. It is "absolutely insane," he concludes, for Nazis to think they could topple the United States. Still, considering recent events in Europe, Renard worries about future espionage campaigns. The DA is more confident. "It's true we're a careless, easygoing, optimistic nation," he says, "but when our basic liberties become threatened, we wake up." And Americans are waking up. Everyone in the diner is buzzing about the trial and promising greater awareness of Nazi conspiracies. After offering this upbeat resolution, the movie closes with the strains of "America" and, finally, the credits.

Reviewers generally appreciated *Confessions of a Nazi Spy* but wondered where it might pull the movies and the nation. It is "more than entertainment," *Variety* said. "It is a venture in the permitted privileges of the screen, the extent to which the freedom of the film may be employed in discussing matters of moment." *Time* called it "Hollywood's first outright assault on the dictators' totem." Critics tagged the film as propaganda but, after hearing Hays and others denounce propaganda for so long, could not decide whether that was a good thing. *Motion Picture Daily* saw it as "propaganda for the institutions and traditions of the United States of America," whereas *New Republic*'s Otis Ferguson labeled it "a hate-breeder if there ever was one." Memories of World War I–era anti-German blasts remained vibrant. With a new cycle of similar films on the horizon, Ferguson was among those who wondered whether the movie industry would again contribute to American involvement in a European bloodbath.[26]

Despite its peaceful opening night, predictions that the movie would cause trouble proved true. Patrons of a Cleveland movie house slashed seats with razors. German Americans in Milwaukee torched a theater showing the picture. Other cities experienced picketing and protests. Radio priest Charles Coughlin cited *Confessions of a Nazi Spy* as evidence of a communist-Jewish plot against America. The German-American Bund had a predictably strong response. *Deutscher Weckruf und Beobachter*'s examination of the closing credits told readers all they needed to know about the production: "*Confessions of a Nazi Spy;* produced by Jew Jack Warner, story by Jew Milton Krims, acted by Jew Emmanuel Goldenburg (Edward Robinson), Communist supporter of Leon Trotsky, acted by Francis Lederer, Communist 'peace' advocate; directed by Jew Anatole Litvak, sponsor of Communist Hollywood Anti-Nazi League, technical advisor Jew Rabbi Herman Lissauer, founder of Communist 'Liberal Forum,' historical director Jew Leon Turrou, former employee of Jacob Stern." Fritz Kuhn filed a temporary injunction against the picture and initiated a $5 million libel suit. Neither petition went anywhere. German diplomats complained to the State Department, which forwarded the angry dispatches to the MPPDA without comment.[27]

Letter writers inundated Warner Bros. Some commended the studio's stand against totalitarianism. To them, *Confessions of a Nazi Spy* stimulated "those who attend your theatres to be loyal and unswerving in their devotion to America and American ideology." Others disagreed. "I call the picture gross Jewish Propaganda," objected J. P. Thompson of St. Louis. "A Jew produced it to show his hatred." Soon after the film opened, Los Angelenos discovered posters allegedly created by the Hollywood branch of the "Committee on Unemployment" tacked to walls around town. The broadside ripped "Un-American, JEWISH practices of spreading propaganda of HATE and WAR." It claimed that *Confessions of a Nazi Spy* created unemployment by destroying foreign markets and urged patriotic citizens to oppose the "ARROGANT, VICIOUS POLICY of the JEWISH MONOPOLY of the Industry."[28]

With its pretentious dialogue and heavy-handed message, *Confessions of a Nazi Spy* was not the kind of movie that typically raked in money. As Breen foresaw, censorship boards around the world blocked the film. Germany banned it, as did Brazil, Chile, the Dominican Republic, Holland, Norway, Peru, Sweden, Switzerland, and other countries. Yet, assisted by the hullabaloo surrounding it, the picture did big business in London, Paris, and Warsaw, at least until Poland fell in September, and it did well enough in the United States to make it a success. *Confessions of a Nazi Spy* brought in $1,531,000 against a total cost of $681,000, a healthy profit for a studio that tackled an issue no one else wanted to put onscreen. Industry observers believed more of the same was on the way.[29]

And at that moment not one of Berlin's first-run theaters was showing an American film. There had been no official ban, just a sudden refusal to approve any Hollywood product. German officials offered many reasons for the blackout. The Nazis claimed Hollywood majors shut German features out of the United States and protested the "incessant agitation against the Third Reich in the United States." Germany also cited the importance of placing more homegrown pictures in its domestic market and its conviction that Hollywood's Jewish oligarchy made pictures contrary to Aryan ideals. Although the embargo loosened slightly over the coming months, American studios never again took significant profits from Nazi Germany.[30]

Hitler's 1938 seizures of Austria and the Sudetenland brought around eleven hundred more theaters under the Reich's restrictive system. The Ministry of Propaganda applied Germany's microscopic importation quotas to annexed territories and barred any production considered harmful to German prestige—a nebulous category Goebbels defined on a case-by-case basis—or deemed "artistically inferior." Because companies needed the Reich Film Chamber's permission to build a theater or establish a distribution network, American studios had no chance of expanding their presence in the German empire. As of January 1, 1939, Jews could not attend or own movie theaters. American studios still distributing in Germany—Fox, MGM, and Paramount—hung on slender financial threads. The Nazis imported just enough features to bridge the gap between domestic demand and what German filmmakers could supply.[31]

As the only mass-culture medium with a global reach, motion pictures were uniquely vulnerable to economic pressure applied by foreign governments. This fact, along with the considerable time it took for an idea to move from script to screen and the large amount of money involved in every production, kept Hollywood slightly behind the cultural curve. Notable as it was, *Confessions of a Nazi Spy* was nothing new in the greater universe of popular culture. Industries across the cultural spectrum were already deeply engaged in antifascism. Mass-market magazines often ran anti-Nazi or pro-American pieces. *Ladies' Home Journal* hired noted anti-Nazi columnist Dorothy Parker in 1937, the same year it ran "Once to Every Woman," a short story about the Gestapo's thuggery. *Life* magazine printed extensive photo-essays on the Spanish Civil War and Sino-Japanese War, took readers inside the German-American Bund, and speculated on the result of a German invasion of Great Britain months before *Confessions of a Nazi Spy* appeared. Many prominent radio commentators openly opposed the Nazis. Even radio serials got in on the act. A January 1938 episode of *The Shadow* featured Orson Welles's mysterious hero dismantling a German sabotage ring responsible for destroying several American naval vessels.

That Hollywood neither fought alone nor was first into the fight does not lessen its ultimate impact on public sentiments toward fascism, democracy, and the war. These factors do, however, indicate the pervasive caution of the industry's leaders and the difficulty of moving corporatized, globalized, culture-making institutions in new directions. Joseph Breen and like-minded movie people wanted to shove the anti-Nazi genie back into the bottle. Or rather, they wanted the genie to voluntarily return to the confinement of pure entertainment. It remained unclear whether other executives wanted to close the door that Warner Bros. had kicked open.

Juarez and *Confessions of a Nazi Spy* nevertheless made democracy and antifascism legitimate topics for screen fare. The first brought the studio prestige and publicity. The second brought it both those and, as an added benefit, profits. A town that ruthlessly copied success seemed certain to produce similar films in the near future. Political pressure or appeals to economic self-interest, however, might stem the tide of so-called propaganda pictures. With more film folk adopting Harry Warner's and the Hollywood Anti-Nazi League's gung ho antifascism, it seemed equally likely that ideologically driven projects inspired by moviemakers' concern for the United States' long-term security would carry the day. Europe was technically at peace, but Hollywood was already choosing sides.

CHAPTER EIGHT

The Widening Campaign

❧ ❧ ❧

Harry Warner declared war on September 19, 1938, almost one year before Britain and France did the same. John Huston had just turned in his *Juarez* script and Milton Krims was polishing his treatment of "The World Is Ours" when a delegation of 150 American Legionnaires descended on Burbank for lunch and a tour of Warner Bros. They got more than they expected. Harry Warner hit them with a speech that shook them to their patriotic cores and served as the first public announcement of his studio's new direction. Praising the legion as "the watch dog of democracy," he urged it to continue supporting the American system through the critical times ahead. Democratic Europe's fight for liberty and against intolerance has spread to our shores, Warner said. "Unwelcome, un-American forces," working in tandem with "various foreign governments," were flooding the nation with propaganda intended to destabilize the national way of life by sowing "the seeds of discontent, of intolerance, and national destruction."[1]

Warner proclaimed his studio's willingness to aid the legion's defense of democracy. "We have been trying in our humble way," he told them, "to contribute to the welfare and peace of our country through the pictures we make," and more of the same was coming. He closed with a call for national purification that drew from the biblical rhetoric the devout Jew loved to scatter into his speeches. "Drive them from their secret meeting places," he demanded. "Destroy their insidious propaganda machines, drive out their 'Bunds' and their Leagues, their clans and Black Legions, the Silver Shirts, the Black Shirts and the Dirty Shirts." He made no apology for his intemperate talk. "If this is flag waving," Warner concluded, "I, for one, am proud of it. We need more flag waving." The mogul was so pleased with his oration that he sent Roosevelt a copy. He had staked out a position far in advance of other Hollywood executives and, in fact, well beyond anything the president could say, and this was still months before *Confessions of a Nazi Spy* appeared.[2]

Warner Bros. was Hollywood's Maginot Line of anti-Nazism. The studio stood in harm's way, exposing itself to economic retaliation and dragging the rest of the industry along with it. It pursued a risky policy. Italy was sealing its cinematic borders, and Germany's expansion put ever more theaters into Nazi hands. People concerned about Jewish domination of American culture or fearful of Hollywood's miring the United States in a foreign morass were unlikely to differentiate between one studio and another. Every admission ticket counted, and Warners was daring anyone who objected to its foreign policy to leave the theater.

Although Warners stood alone for now, reinforcements were on the way. Anti-Nazi brush fires broke out in the film community as *Juarez* and *Confessions of a Nazi Spy* wended their way through the studio's pipeline. Although most executives kept themselves on safe ideological ground, their employees' actions during late 1938 and early 1939 marked the first evidence of a gathering storm that eventually thundered through Hollywood, the halls of Congress, and the screens of the world. Liberal film folk threw themselves into the battle without regard for the moguls' trepidation. Their overt antifascism stirred counterforces that assailed Hollywood for trying to subvert the nation's basic values by derailing American isolationism.

America's favorite screen comedian was among the new combatants. In 1937 British filmmaker Alexander Korda told his friend Charlie Chaplin that the Führer's physical similarities with the Tramp, who sported a Hitlerian mustache years before the dictator, practically demanded a mistaken-identity farce. Chaplin closely followed international events and held strong opinions on the emerging ultranationalist movements. He despised the Nazis, backed the Spanish Loyalists, and feared the consequences of a Japanese victory in Asia. For the moment, however, Chaplin dismissed Korda's proposal as premature, an idea likely to feel outdated by the time it reached screens.[3]

Chaplin reconsidered as the fascist cloud darkened over Europe. As Warners worked on *Juarez* and *Confessions of a Nazi Spy,* he revealed that his next film would be "The Dictators." Although the plot was vaguely defined at this point, it did not take much imagination to determine where Chaplin had aimed his satirical sights. His announcement brought a quick response from German consul Georg Gyssling, who cautioned Joseph Breen that mocking Hitler would "lead to serious troubles and complications." The consul's anger surprised Breen, who was unaware of Chaplin's plans. Gyssling seemed to have a better handle on Hollywood affairs than the industry's chief censor. With no script to critique and no guarantee the mercurial Chaplin would follow through on his announcement, Breen could do nothing to pacify the Germans.[4]

After overcoming some additional reservations, Chaplin finally committed to "The Dictators" in early 1939. Its plot remained sketchy, but the very idea of an antifascist comedy scared those still hoping to keep politics out of movies. James Brooke-Wilkinson, secretary of the British Board of Film Censors, informed Breen that "The Dictators" could cause a "delicate situation" in his country. Breen, who sensed the industry sliding from the safety of pure entertainment, shared his colleague's concern. "There is an unsettled feeling in the air," he told Brooke-Wilkinson. "We are hopeful, of course, that matters will soon right themselves."[5]

Consul Gyssling's relations with Hollywood further deteriorated when famed director Leni Riefenstahl arrived in New York in November 1938. Movie people knew the German filmmaker well. *Triumph of the Will* (1935), her landmark, avidly pro-Hitler documentary of the 1934 Nuremburg Rally, largely created the world's image of Nazism. She came to the United States searching for an American distribution contract for *Olympia*, her record of the 1936 Berlin Olympics. Riefenstahl had no inkling of the ideological ferment brewing on the West Coast. She anticipated a warm welcome from her cinematic colleagues.[6]

Riefenstahl stepped off the luxury liner *Europa* to find a gaggle of reporters waiting for her. She spent most of her thirty-minute dockside press conference deflecting their half-jesting efforts to paint her as Hitler's girlfriend. Their sparring masked troubling developments. A federal court a few miles away prepared to convict Nazi spies. Hollywood executives seething over Italy's recent ENIC declaration showed little interest in welcoming an associate of Mussolini's chief ally. Riefenstahl's disembarkation also coincided with initial reports of *Kristallnacht*. Hitler's talk of peace at the previous month's Munich Conference rang false as news of the Nazi pogrom spread. Unaware of the happenings in Germany, Riefenstahl denied rumors of violence. Good feelings prevailed for the moment. Director King Vidor flew from the West Coast to greet her, she toured Radio City Music Hall, and the newspapers remained benevolent.[7]

She found more friends during her swing through the Midwest. American Olympic Committee president Avery Brundage arranged a screening of *Olympia* in his Chicago home. Henry Ford invited her to Detroit, where he showed off his assembly line while raving about Hitler's elimination of unemployment. Riefenstahl then journeyed to the Grand Canyon, tossing out smiles and upbeat statements all the way.[8]

Despite her pleasant facade, however, the mood around her darkened with every step west. Journalists grew increasingly hostile as evidence of Nazi brutality trickled in, eventually branding her as "Hitler's honey." Hollywood Anti-Nazi League members arranged a rude welcome for her in Los Angeles. "There is no room in Hollywood for Leni Riefenstahl," declared one HANL broadside. "In this moment when hundreds of thousands of our brethren await certain death, close your doors to all Nazi agents." HANL used her visit to publicize its demand for an economic embargo of Germany. Unwilling to risk bad press, none of the majors invited her to tour their facilities. The German Consulate hastily arranged some events to keep her holiday from turning into a social disaster.[9]

Riefenstahl could not understand why America rejected her. She insisted that her trip had nothing to do with Hitler or the Nazis. "I am an independent artist," she asserted. Independent or not, few wanted to be seen with the accomplished director, who cooled her heels in Palm Springs and waited for the phone to ring. Producer Winfield Sheehan hosted a sparsely attended screening of *Olympia*. Walt Disney showed Riefenstahl sketches of his new production, *Fantasia,* and then later told inquiring reporters that he had not known who his guest was.[10]

The industry's collective cold shoulder marked another victory for Hollywood anti-Nazism. "Vittorio Mussolini at least got onto the movie lots so that he could see the stars," HANL's newspaper laughed. "The only thing Hollywood gave Leni Riefenstahl was deep, frigid silence and 24 hours a day to see the scenery." She left town without her coveted distribution contract. "I hope next time it will be different when I come, yes?" she lamented as she boarded her train for New York. Hollywood's treatment of Riefenstahl incensed Joseph Goebbels. "We shall get nowhere there," the propaganda minister wrote in his diary. "The Jews rule by terror and bribery. But for how much longer?"[11]

Hitler and Mussolini's efforts to unite the Old World under their banners divided Hollywood, the magical city of the New World, into competing ideological camps. Most producers—along with the politically apathetic—clung to Will Hays's prudent mantra of pure entertainment. With less to lose and no responsibility to stockholders, their underlings simultaneously lobbed grenades that threatened to explode the fragile framework holding the dream machine together. Once a bastion of economic conservatism and lazy indifference to social issues, Hollywood saw its political locus veer to the left as new organizations extended the industry's progressive, internationalist critique of current affairs already embraced by Chaplin and HANL.

The Motion Picture Democratic Committee (MPDC) marked studio workers' revenge against the producers' heavy-handed opposition to Upton Sinclair's 1934 gubernatorial campaign. Its formation represented another step toward a politically energized film community. The MPDC came together in summer 1938 at a party hosted by the actress Miriam Hopkins. The assembled screenwriters, actors, and technical workers still resented the machinations that landed conservative Republican Frank Merriam in the governor's chair four years earlier. "We couldn't let our motion picture producers lead us by the nose into the camp of latter-day Hoovers, as they did in 1934," grumbled actor Maurice Murphy. Adopting "Merriam for Ex-Governor" as its slogan, the group resolved to endorse liberal, antifascist New Dealers in the upcoming elections. Membership in the MPDC soon swelled to twenty-four hundred.[12]

Screenwriters led the way in the new organization. Philip Dunne, Dashiell Hammett, Dudley Nichols, and Donald Ogden Stewart sat on its executive board, which read like an all-star list of Hollywood progressivism—Melvyn Douglas, John Ford, Miriam Hopkins, Fredric March, and Gloria Stuart filled out its ranks. After settling on state senator Culbert Olson as its preferred candidate in the 1938 governor's race, the MPDC backed his campaign with personal appearances, radio shows, pamphlets, and a pro-Olson movie projected on screens attached to trucks that patrolled the state in search of voters.[13]

Most executives disliked Olson, an avid New Dealer, but did not loathe him as they had Upton Sinclair. Governor Merriam, who raised income taxes during his term, did not endear himself either. Freed from the moguls' determined resistance, their employees carried the day by contributing to a convincing Olson win. Liberal Hollywood had its first major political victory and an ally in the statehouse.[14]

Imbued with a sense of new possibilities, the MPDC expanded into a fund-raising and public relations arm of the Roosevelt administration, a role that included endorsing the president's cautious criticism of totalitarianism. Members of the MPDC passed a Declaration of Policy in early 1939 reaffirming the group's faith in democracy and calling for stronger opposition to dictatorship. This seemingly innocuous measure did not pass as easily as expected; presaging future difficulties, communists in the MPDC delayed the resolution until members removed language condemning Stalin alongside Hitler and Mussolini. Even with these ominous divisions, the MPDC marked another step forward for Popular Front Hollywood that inspired a bevy of new organizations over the next few years. Its liberal offshoots included the Actors' Refugee Committee, the Spanish Child Welfare Organization, and the Hollywood Committee for Polish Relief.[15]

Actor and MPDC board member Melvyn Douglas was fast emerging as one of Hollywood's most articulate antifascist voices. In contrast to his friend Franklin Roosevelt's guarded rhetoric, Douglas ripped Germany and its allies as "Jew killer countries," and he implored Americans to take an active interest in global affairs. "We cannot draw into our national shell," he told the American Union for Concerted Peace Efforts in early 1939. "Isolationism and appeasement are the characteristics of individuals who are tired of the struggle for progress." Such statements enraged Douglas's employer, Louis B. Mayer, who discouraged the actor's politically charged activities.[16]

Douglas played an important role in the Committee of 56, perhaps the most controversial of Hollywood's new antifascist operations. Along with James Cagney, Edward G. Robinson, Gloria Stuart, and other HANL stalwarts, Douglas formed the committee in late 1938 to write a "Declaration of Democratic Independence," asking Roosevelt to sever trade ties with Germany. The declaration, which the committee planned to circulate around the country, collecting millions of signatures before submitting it to the president, supplemented HANL's recent call for an economic embargo. A *Variety* editorial blasted the petition as "sincere but mistaken zeal" and advocated caution, suggesting the committee focus on such safe causes as aid to refugees. *Variety*'s response, incidentally, appeared a few pages from a headline announcing: "WB to Unloose Flood of Anti-Nazi Pix." Words and deeds, moving in two directions.[17]

Melvyn Douglas became the committee's chief publicist, promoting its cause in a series of speeches and radio addresses that garnered mixed reviews from fans. "I should like to know why none of your organizations commit themselves to actual American loyalty by speaking, at least, one tiny little word against Communism," one writer asked of Douglas and his wife, future congresswoman Helen Gahagan Douglas. "You would surely not like it if your pictures were being boycotted," observed another critic. Even sympathetic correspondents expressed confusion over why a mere movie actor felt compelled to offer his political views. Policy, they argued, should be left to policy makers. Douglas's public discussion of war and peace also aroused the ire of American anti-Semites—exactly the response so many dreaded. "We never knew before that you are Jewish and needless to say you no longer hold the affectionate position in our esteem which you formerly held," one anonymous collection of female ex-fans wrote. "We shall support in the future some leading man who is white."[18]

Along with the rest of the Committee of 56, Douglas signed the Declaration of Democratic Independence in December 1938 on a flag-filled stage flanked with portraits of Washington and Lincoln. As newsreel cameras whirred, one star after another inked their autographs on a document that slammed Germany's militarism, oppression of minorities, persecution of religious figures, and attempts to export its philosophy through bunds and espionage networks. The petition appropriated rhetoric from the American Revolution and the First Amendment—the most important amendment for an industry obsessed with censorship—to make the committee's case against the Nazis. "They deny the rights of man," it proclaimed. "They destroy Freedom of Speech, Freedom of Worship, Freedom of the Press, and the Right to Peaceful Assembly."[19]

Fifty-six names adorned the document, the same number that appear on the Declaration of Independence. Douglas assumed the John Hancock role, placing his signature directly beneath the petition's demand for an economic boycott until such time as Germany adhered to "humane principles of international law and universal freedom." Other signatories represented a broad range of Hollywood liberals. Popular Front screenwriters Herbert Biberman, Philip Dunne, and Donald Ogden Stewart signed, as did liberal actors Henry Fonda, Groucho Marx, Paul Muni, Edward G. Robinson, and Gale Sondergaard. Directors George Cukor, John Ford, and Josef von Sternberg were also there. Former Universal executive Carl Laemmle Jr.'s name appeared to the right of Walter Wanger's. Jack and Harry Warner signed even though they refused to sign next to each other. Their studio's biggest malcontent, James Cagney, must have been a little nervous as he placed his name between theirs. His signature is tiny, as if cowering from the sparring that broke out whenever the brothers were together. But it was there, and although the petition did not alter Roosevelt's course, it was becoming clear that Douglas and his cohorts were gaining strength within the film community.[20]

By revealing the breadth of Hollywood liberalism, Popular Front groups like the Committee of 56, HANL, and the MPDC fed concerns that moviemakers were churning out propaganda rather than entertainment. Among the industry's chief detractors was Martin Dies, a powerful Texas Democrat who headed the House of Representatives' Committee on Un-American Activities (HUAC). Formed in 1934 to investigate Nazi activity in the United States, HUAC was transformed by Dies to match his right-wing agenda when he assumed its chairmanship in 1937. The congressman militantly opposed immigration and disliked Jews, but he reserved his greatest hatred for communists. Dies foresaw an epic collision between Marxism and Christianity, and he aspired to give the world a Hollywood-style ending by ensuring the good guys won. Rather than a dream factory, he saw Hollywood as a refuge for communists who polluted the national dialogue with Soviet-style harangues and un-American propaganda. After all, he reasoned, when was the last time a major studio criticized the Soviet Union?[21]

The Texan took action in fall 1938, dispatching HUAC investigators J. B. Matthews and Edward Sullivan to root out subversives on the West Coast. "All phases of radical and Communistic activities are rampant among the studios," Sullivan reported soon after arriving. He and Matthews claimed that reds tricked stars into contributing to communist fronts and endorsing communist publications. Matthews cited Clark Gable, James Cagney, Robert Taylor, and Shirley Temple, who had sent greetings to *Ce soir,* a French newspaper run by the Communist Party, as examples. Matthews saw these stars as patsies, not revolutionaries, who unwittingly allowed their names "to further the cause of communism." Dies added his own charge by denouncing HANL as a red organization.[22]

These warning shots shook the highest reaches of power. Roosevelt administration officials worried that Dies planned to discredit the White House's political and financial ties with Hollywood by painting the industry with a red brush, but they maintained public silence. Feeling no such constraints, screenwriter Donald Ogden Stewart fired back on Hollywood's behalf. Accusations of communism, he said, were themselves "a threat to democracy." He recommended that Dies probe American Nazism "instead of attacking the organizations formed for the purposes of taking such action."[23]

Dies's probe fizzled, starved by a lack of funds and doomed to ridicule by Matthews's implication of Shirley Temple as a supporter of communist causes—an accusation the Hollywood press inflated to ridicule the investigation and win public favor. *Variety* bid a not-so-fond adieu to the "one-ring Congressional circus," but Dies was not finished. The congressman used a January 1939 HUAC report to take another swing at Hollywood. While not naming names, the document warned that "communists have made great strides" within the film community. Their infestation was "so serious that it would require many months of diligent investigation and courageous exposure to correct." For the time being, Dies could only search for new appropriations and promise Hollywood that his inquiry had not concluded.[24]

Martin Dies was not the only one concerned about Hollywood communism. Many studio liberals were uncomfortable with their Popular Front coalition. Communists seemed misplaced in such a clannish, well-heeled community. They "would have looked far more at home organizing longshoreman strikes . . . or Molotov cocktail parties" than giving actors economics lessons, producer Jesse Lasky Jr. thought. Cameramen and movie stars could not equal communists' discipline. Hard-core leftists used parliamentary chicanery to stretch meetings into the wee hours, passing resolutions long after the less-dedicated trooped off to bed. "These lads had iron bottoms," Lasky recalled, "because they never went home." Hollywood liberals were in a difficult position. They knew associating with communists exposed them to attacks from people like Dies. At the same time, they saw communists as allies in their fight against Hitler. Antifascist groups needed their recruiting, bureaucratic, and propaganda skills to keep day-to-day operations running smoothly.[25]

✿ ✿ ✿

Liberals and communists coexisted for the moment. With Dies's committee out of money, the communism issue appeared to be resolved. Hollywood soon seized an opportunity to lay another problem—its legal difficulties—to rest. In doing so, movie folk unexpectedly furthered their halting anti-Nazi campaign by tightening their relationship with the Roosevelt administration. Escaping from Assistant Attorney General Thurman Arnold's antitrust suit demanded, among other things, a stronger commitment to the antifascist agenda Hollywood progressives and the Warner brothers were already promoting.

The next phase of the antitrust suit opened, oddly enough, when commerce secretary and presidential confidant Harry Hopkins addressed the Iowa State Legislature in February 1939 on the importance of foreign commerce. After reading a report of the speech, Harry Warner seized on the secretary's references to reciprocal trade agreements and new overseas trade, and dashed off a ten-page, single-spaced letter to Hopkins. "The obvious corollary" to expanding foreign commerce, Warner wrote, is that the government should redouble efforts to maintain existing trade, particularly in goods not already protected by commercial pacts. Motion pictures just happened to be one such item. Having established his logic, Warner quickly came to the point. "I am taking the liberty of bringing your attention to the threatened destruction by another Department of the Government of the foreign trade in American films," he wrote. Thurman Arnold's obsession with theater divorcement challenged the movie industry's financial underpinnings. Without theaters, major studios could no longer produce the "big quality films" that constituted "the backbone" of Hollywood's export business.

Saving theaters, Warner continued, meant more than staving off financial disaster for corporations like Warner Bros. He argued that Hollywood pictures actually sold America to the world. Without these celluloid ambassadors of goodwill, foreign audiences would never learn to lust for American products and lifestyles. Trade, in Warner's eyes, followed the film. Studios yearning to sell Americanism overseas were caught in a nationalist web of quota laws, exchange restrictions, and censorship. In this climate, "the threat of demolishment at the hand of its own government" was too much for Hollywood to bear. Help us keep our theaters, Warner pleaded.[26]

Hopkins sympathized with the industry's economic problems. He also knew he had leverage over the movie moguls. Assistance in the antitrust matter might guarantee Hollywood's loyalties through the troubling times ahead. With this plan in mind, Hopkins brought Warner's missive to Roosevelt's attention. FDR agreed with his adviser's argument that the Commerce Department could play a useful role in ending the lawsuit. Hopkins quickly arranged a meeting with Will Hays to thrash out the outlines of a deal. Hays promised to give the Commerce Department access to whatever information it needed to compose a settlement. For his part, Hopkins assented to Hays's demand that the resulting consent decree must allow studios to keep their theaters.[27]

In the wake of this arrangement studio heads were eager to demonstrate approval for the administration's foreign policy. The Warners hoped a Washington, D.C., screening of *Confessions of a Nazi Spy* for Hopkins and other officials would sufficiently reaffirm their support. Studio attorney Joseph Hazen, the only man Jack and Harry trusted with "the Hopkins matter," postponed the performance when the commerce secretary fell ill. "I definitely want him present when the picture is shown for reasons which you may readily understand," he told Jack. Hopkins's slow recovery forced Hazen to show the film without the secretary in attendance. He assured Jack the master plan was nevertheless intact. "I checked up this morning," he said, "and find that [Hopkins] is still determined to go ahead with working out a solution of this industry's problem and it will be the first job which he will tackle when he gets back to work."[28]

Hopkins assigned Commerce Department agents to Hollywood soon after regaining his health. Negotiations for a settlement proceeded through the spring of 1939. Producers made their final vow of fealty to Roosevelt and Hopkins on June 6, when Hays, Hazen, Sidney Kent, Harry Warner, RKO's George Schaefer, and Loews/MGM's Nick Schenck (Louis B. Mayer's boss) trooped into the secretary's office for a two-hour discussion of, as a press release blandly put it, "problems affecting the motion picture industry in its relation to the general economic structure." This stilted language concealed the meeting's real purpose, which was to establish a framework for a consent decree that preserved as much of the majors' existing production, distribution, and exhibition system as possible.[29]

The Commerce Department was on Hollywood's side, meaning that Harry Hopkins was on Hollywood's side. And behind Hopkins stood Roosevelt, who never directly involved himself yet influenced the course of talks from behind the scenes. It is tempting to see these events as a simple trade-off—an escape from divorcement in exchange for cooperation in foreign policy. That is too easy and Machiavellian. If Hopkins came through, however, Hollywood would owe the administration a huge debt, one that demonstrated that the industry's best hope of survival lay with the man in the White House.

❧ ❧ ❧

Hollywood's difficulties with the federal government appeared to be easing in the spring of 1939. From the perspective of industry liberals, the news everywhere else was bad. The economic, cultural, and political freedom Hollywood needed to be financially successful was disappearing from Europe. The Spanish Loyalists surrendered in March 1939, their battered forces symbolizing the beating antifascism was taking in Europe. "Our hearts sank" when Hollywood progressives heard the news, Gale Sondergaard remembered. "It was the death knell for democratic life. Fascism was on the march." Hitler's recent triumphs, including his conquest of Czechoslovakia in the same month the Loyalists capitulated, left the continent's future in his hands. *Kristallnacht* indicated that more violence lay ahead.[30]

Troubling events overseas renewed movie liberals' desire to arouse American antifascists but did not send the majors scrambling for anti-Nazi material. In fact, some in Hollywood still hoped to salvage the German market. As American studio executives saw it, giving up would leave European cinema wide open to Nazi domination, and a German stranglehold on the continental market might well outlive Hitler. Hollywood was not yet ready to commit to a policy that might jeopardize its long-term financial well-being. Louis B. Mayer went so far as to invite a group of Nazi film editors to tour MGM in the summer of 1939. His accommodating gesture infuriated such Hitler-haters as Harry Warner, who demanded an explanation. "I just can't bring myself to believe that your people would entertain those whom the world regards as the murderers of their own families," he told one MGM executive. Warner already suspected that Mayer, who gave sparingly to Jewish charity drives, was a traitor to his religion. Opening MGM's doors to Nazis confirmed his suspicions. "I consider it a waste of time to write him," Warner groused.[31]

The fate of Europe's Jews certainly affected film folk in very personal ways. Samuel Goldwyn helped his nephew and three nieces escape Poland before the invasion. His sister and brother-in-law, who refused to be relocated, died in the Treblinka concentration camp. Walter Wanger spent much of 1939 working to get his cousins out of Germany. Fears of German pressure on European exhibitors and public disfavor at home, however, kept anti-Nazism off the screen even after *Confessions of a Nazi Spy*. In the spring of 1939 some studios again considered, then rejected, a screen adaptation of Albert Nesor's strongly anti-Nazi novel *Mad Dog of Europe*. As he had in 1933, Breen found *Mad Dog of Europe* "enormously dangerous from the standpoint of political censorship outside the United States." MGM displayed similar trepidation when it briefly revisited *It Can't Happen Here*. The studio quickly discovered that the project's time in production limbo had done little to remove the stink surrounding it. Breen shot off another series of warnings about the production's likely demise overseas. MGM's New York office received a tepid response when it sent presidential secretary Stephen Early a copy of the treatment to gauge the White House's attitude. MGM surrendered when Breen warned that the final script might be too violent to receive PCA approval.[32]

Screenwriters and executives were skilled at meeting or circumventing Breen's objections when they wanted approval of high-priority pictures. *It Can't Happen Here* apparently did not fall into this category. MGM's reluctance to denounce fascism spawned a song whispered around the MGM lot:

Oh, it can't happen here; it can't happen here!
It can happen in Siberia; it can happen in Liberia;
It can happen over here; it can happen over there
But Metro-Goldwyn-Mayer
Says it can't happen here.

Music alone could not change minds. The script disappeared into MGM's vaults, never to be exhumed.[33]

It Can't Happen Here had too much potential to divide. Moviemakers preferred releases that made useful points without provoking the kind of controversy that progressive organizations such as the MPDC and the Committee of 56 engendered. In a time of rising nationalism, flag-waving seemed a sure winner at the box office and a convenient way to clothe the industry in patriotic garb. By the spring of 1939 producers were projecting Will Hays's oft-repeated argument that "the screen is distinctively the product of the American spirit—vision, initiative, enterprise, and progress" into theaters around the world. "The most conspicuous 'theme' in the movies today is Americanism," the *Norfolk Virginian-Pilot* observed in April 1939.[34]

Major studios released a spate of films during the last months of European peace that crafted a narrative of United States history centered around the growth and preservation of democracy. The French and Indian War provided the background for RKO's *Allegheny Uprising* (1939), in which a John Wayne–led cast of Pennsylvania backwoodsmen take up arms to defend their liberty from savage Indians and unscrupulous arms dealers. They fight to protect their land from interlopers and preserve civilian government in the face of attempts to impose martial law.

Allegheny Uprising appeared alongside Twentieth Century–Fox's *Drums along the Mohawk* (1939), a far more prestigious production that nevertheless raised similar ideas. Fox openly approached this story— a tale of backwoodsmen who take up arms to defend their homesteads from savage Indians during the Revolutionary War—from a current-events perspective. Lamar Trotti, one of the screenwriters for *Drums along the Mohawk,* wanted to see the revolution in theaters because, "in the light of recent history," audiences needed to understand the origins of "the American form of Democratic government." Fox head Darryl F. Zanuck agreed but saw danger in the film's obligatory depiction of redcoats as bad guys. "Whenever possible, keep [the] British out of brutality," he ordered. Zanuck, who was sliding from isolation to internationalism, wanted to elevate Great Britain's status in the American mind, or at least do no harm to it.[35]

Drums along the Mohawk concludes with a scene that foreshadowed the coming emphasis on an American unity that transcended class, ethnic, and racial barriers. After helping win the war by defeating marauding Iroquois, Gil and Lana Martin (Henry Fonda and Claudette Colbert) watch a troop of patriot soldiers march the new republic's flag into a garrison. The banner transfixes the diverse community—a black woman, a beefy blacksmith, a Native American, and the Martins. "It's a pretty flag, isn't it?" Lana asks as "America" wafts through the background. "I reckon we better get back to work," Gil says. "There's gonna be a heap to do from now on." Freedom did not come cheaply, and preserving freedom promises to be an even more challenging task than winning it. Director John Ford's patriotic flourish exposed a rare miscalculation in Zanuck's usually sure sense for moviegoers' tastes. "Pictures that wave the flag are poison at the box office," he had warned Ford during shooting. *Drums along the Mohawk* was a hit despite its literal violation of the mogul's maxim. Zanuck and his peers absorbed the lesson, making displays of red-meat patriotism a recurring feature in movies over the next few years.[36]

The Civil War era also provided a historical backdrop for pictures designed to build national unity through glamorizing the past. Before shooting *Drums along the Mohawk,* John Ford teamed up with Henry Fonda on *Young Mr. Lincoln* (1939). Fonda's Abraham Lincoln epitomizes the self-made man, a rugged individual who relies on honesty, hard work, and common sense to lift himself from obscurity to respectability. His folksy courtroom performance frees an innocent man accused of murder and heals a town rife with the dissention the case spawned. An even more popular film, David O. Selznick's *Gone with the Wind,* eliminated most of the anti-Yankee and antiblack sentiment from Margaret Mitchell's novel while relegating its gruff, lower-class characters to the cutting-room floor. The result is a sanitized South bereft of regional, racial, and class fissures, a romanticized interpretation of history palatable to all Americans.

The West had been a popular topic for filmmakers since the early days of cinema. Cecil B. DeMille's *The Squaw Man* (1914), often credited as the first feature made in Hollywood, was a western. The genre remained popular through the silent era before falling into disfavor with the birth of talkies. It rarely appeared outside of slapdash serials and B-movie oaters until John Ford's *Stagecoach,* Warners' *Dodge City,* and Paramount's *Union Pacific* reinvigorated it in 1939. Each of these pictures played on national unity—although *Stagecoach* excluded greedy capitalists and moralizing bluenoses from its emerging frontier community—and, to varying extents, the civilization of the West.

Union Pacific presented these ideas most clearly. DeMille's epic of the transcontinental railroad celebrates a "young, tough, prodigal, and invincible" nation's determination to fuse its vast reaches into a single whole. President Lincoln himself sanctions the audacious plan to build a railroad between Omaha and California, a project he believes will "bind us together, east and west, forever as one people." Hardworking Americans (and a smattering of thoroughly Americanized Irish immigrants) struggle against harsh weather, Indian attacks, and industrial saboteurs to bring Lincoln's dream to fruition. Towns spring up almost overnight along the route, with each new settlement representing another victory for civilization over the dark forces of savagery. DeMille's recreation of the epic meeting at Promontory Point, marking the completion of the transcontinental railroad, merges seamlessly into a shot of a modern engine roaring over the rails, backed by the rousing tones of "Stars and Stripes Forever." This pairing of images symbolizes the nation's indelible connection to its pioneering past. It calls on viewers to honor those who risked their lives to forge a unified American republic by emulating their can-do spirit and tireless love of country.

DeMille further contributed to Hollywood's patriotic surge by compiling, at the Hays Office's request, *Land of Liberty,* the industry's contribution to the 1939 New York World's Fair and the San Francisco Exposition. DeMille created a cut-and-paste job of epic proportions, snipping footage from scores of earlier releases to create a panoramic history of the United States from the colonial era to the 1920s. Not surprisingly, considering Hollywood's long-standing reverence toward the American past, *Land of Liberty* offers a triumphant interpretation of history that fueled nationalistic fires while demonstrating that Hollywood had engaged in flag-waving since its early years. MGM distributed a shortened version to theaters early in 1941, donating profits to the American Red Cross, the RAF Benevolent Fund, and charities benefiting British air-raid victims.[37]

"Hollywood's current preoccupation with American history," *Life* magazine declared, "springs partly from a nationwide resurgence in patriotism." The screen's interest in exploiting the past was indeed a response to existing cultural trends. Hollywood was reacting to, rather than initiating, a rise in nationalist sentiment. Late-1930s Americans yearned for a coherent set of beliefs capable of withstanding economic depression and rising totalitarianism. "Americanism" infused the popular culture landscape like oxygen forced into a sealed room. Mass-circulation magazines delved into American history and proclaimed the virtues of democracy. Public-opinion polling grew more common and sophisticated as organizations sought to quantify how Americans viewed the world. Book publishers also hopped aboard the nostalgia train with a string of sympathetic biographies of great Americans. Bernard DeVoto's *Mark Twain's America* (1932), Van Wyck Brooks's *Life of Emerson* (1932), Douglas Southall Freeman's *R. E. Lee* (1934–1935), Marquis James's *Andrew Jackson* (1933–1937), and Carl Sandburg's *Abraham Lincoln: The War Years* (1939) all sold well. Novelists followed the turn toward the past. *Drums along the Mohawk* and *Gone with the Wind* climbed best-seller lists before appearing onscreen, as did such releases as *Northwest Passage*.[38]

Peddling patriotism was a no-lose proposition. It projected the moguls' instinctive sense of the United States as a place of opportunity, furthered Hollywood's desire to package itself as an all-American institution, and refuted calls for censorship or other economic restrictions. Major studios' new interest in the past, moreover, situated them within the mainstream in a nation looking for answers to complex questions. No less important, early returns suggested that patriotic films brought people to the box office. Audiences felt good about watching movies that venerated their past without diving into what they saw as propaganda.

The dream factory's salute to the colors surprised critics accustomed to its neglect of current events. "Hollywood may be forgiven many of its sins if it is actually coming down with a sense of responsibility and social consciousness," observed the *Albany Knickerbocker News*. Skeptics dismissed the new patriotism as "a lot of phony flag waving," a ploy to curry popular favor while enhancing revenues. "The motion-picture industry has never been proved guilty of high-mindedness," sniffed *Nation*'s Frank Nugent. Such doubts reveal an increasingly prickly sense of national honor, a growing desire to separate patriots from pretenders. Purists insisted that moviemakers could never really act idealistically because their quest for profits forever sullied their Americanism. Short of making pro-American jeremiads that tanked at the box office, studios had no real way to escape this paradox.[39]

Suspicions that Hollywood acted from less-than-pure motives were well-founded; film executives indeed hoped to catch a profitable wave of nationalism. Even so, signs of Hollywood's patriotic fervor multiplied as 1939 went on. By that summer most theaters in larger chains and all Warners theaters opened and closed programs with "The Star-Spangled Banner." The Allied States Association of Motion Picture Exhibitors, a trade group for independent theater owners, prepared patriotic trailers to show before features. Allied president Abram F. Myers informed President Roosevelt that his members "realize as never before the blessings of American citizenship and . . . feel that the audiences they serve appreciate being reminded of those blessings."[40]

Short subjects at the front of the bill increasingly displayed this same awareness of America's blessings. At Harry Warner's order, Warner Bros. initiated its "Old Glory" series of two-reelers with 1936's tribute to Patrick Henry, "Give Me Liberty." The studio released "The Romance of Louisiana," the story of the Louisiana Purchase, the next year and then "The Declaration of Independence" in 1938. The Old Glory series often focused on moments when the fate of the nation hung in the balance. Its celebration of Americans who overcame impediments to national greatness perpetuated the heroic version of history seen in features. Warners bracketed these shorts with additional displays of patriotic fervor. Harry's onscreen preface to the series declared that "these films are produced for your entertainment—but primarily to remind you, and all Americans, of that magnificent heritage which is yours to enjoy and PRESERVE." Each Old Glory entry ended with a shot of the American flag waving in a gentle breeze that seemed somehow insufficient considering the nationalistic gale the company hoped to inspire.[41]

Warner Bros. accelerated production of the Old Glory series in 1939, releasing "The Monroe Doctrine," "The Bill of Rights," "Lincoln in the White House," "Old Hickory," and "Sons of Liberty." These were prestige shorts, Technicolor films replete with location shots, lavish sets, and period costumes. They employed such stars as Donald Crisp, Claude Rains, and Gale Sondergaard, actors who would never have been asked to appear in ordinary shorts. Still an unknown, future Superman George Reeves played a young Buffalo Bill Cody in "Pony Express Days" (1940).

That most of these films lost money did not deter Harry Warner from making more. For him, the message was more important than money.[42]

Jack shared some of Harry's fervor, although he was never as enthusiastic about the Old Glory shorts as his brother. Jack's incurable sycophantism, however, led him to use the series to curry favor with the White House. He informed presidential secretary Marvin McIntyre that Warner Bros. would continue to make two-reelers "which we feel will do some good in the patriotic fervor that has justly come to these grand United States." As confirmation, he sent Roosevelt a series of obsequious letters soliciting story ideas or offering to send prints of recent installments. Jack also arranged a screening of "The Monroe Doctrine" for State Department officials, but he struggled to comprehend their concern that the subject might be unpopular in Latin America (the studio did not release it in Mexico or South America).[43]

MGM contributed "Yankee Doodle Goes to Town" (1939), a one-reeler depicting Yankee Doodle taking a cynical American on a trip through the past to demonstrate the perseverance of democracy, to the parade of patriotic shorts. Warners, however, dominated the field. "Teddy the Rough Rider" (1940) made the former president's desire for a strong national defense relevant to the contemporary world. In its climactic scene the great man, fresh from his victory at San Juan Hill, turns to the camera to give the viewer a mission. "Our next business," he says, "will be to help guarantee a peace of justice for all the world. . . . Let us not forget that the surest promise of peace lies in our constant preparedness to meet all eventualities from without, and to destroy all subversive elements from within." Such chest-thumping sentiments earned "Teddy the Rough Rider" an Oscar for Best Short Feature.[44]

Even animated characters joined the cause. Between 1937 and 1941 Warners produced twenty-three cartoons dealing with the war or national defense. Its *Merrie Melodies* cartoon "Old Glory" (1939) was among those pushing a preparedness message. Exhausted by his frustrating inability to memorize the Pledge of Allegiance, Porky Pig collapses and falls asleep. Uncle Sam appears in his dream to provide a guided tour of American Revolution sites. Stressing the revolutionary generation's sacrifices for freedom, Uncle Sam explains that Americans have often defended the liberties the flag represents. When Porky Pig wakes up, he can recite the pledge without a stumble.[45]

Hollywood was moving in multiple directions as the summer of 1939 wore on. *Confessions of a Nazi Spy*'s anti-Nazi blast quieted into a more muted call for increased patriotism. While pro-Americanism implied anti-Nazism, the two did not necessarily coexist. Simultaneously relevant and nonthreatening, patriotic pictures offered producers a middle ground between apathy and activism. At the same time, however, liberal studio employees were embracing more militant rhetoric, unabashedly demanding a more vigorous response to fascism.

This gap between onscreen and offscreen Hollywood reflected the perceived limits of the industry's ability to speak out. Most producers, on the one hand, opposed the dictators but did not want to risk their own empires by running afoul of public opinion or foreign and domestic governments. Directors, actors, and craftsworkers, on the other hand, lacked the power to consistently express their sentiments in feature films. As summer turned to fall, however, studios once again recalculated the delicate balance between financial and ideological interests. Their small Asian profits freed them to essentially ignore the ongoing Sino-Japanese conflict. A war in Europe was a different matter altogether.

CHAPTER NINE

A Fine Pickle

❧ ❧ ❧

E VERYONE IN THE KNOW suspected that war was coming to Europe. The question was when, not if. Neville Chamberlain's post-Munich promise of peace in our time appeared increasingly ludicrous as the German military buildup continued unabated. Hitler could not imagine Britain and France upholding their commitment to defend Poland after yielding on the Rhineland, Austria, and the Sudetenland. He ended the suspense by unleashing his *Wehrmacht* on Poland in the predawn hours of September 1, 1939. German planes caught Poland's air force on the ground, and its *Panzers,* the metallic monsters of modern combat, brushed aside overmatched Polish cavalry units. Britain and France declared war on Germany two days later. Appeasement had failed. Weapons, not words, would determine Europe's future.

News of the Polish invasion depressed FDR. He knew the Allies stood a good chance of losing the war. His first moves came swiftly, the actions of a man who had already plotted his response to this event. He summoned Congress into special session and laid the groundwork for a Pan-American security zone to discourage Nazi attacks on shipping in the Western Hemisphere. Taking to the airwaves on September 3, Roosevelt informed Americans that their country was neutral in deed if not in thought. "Even a neutral cannot be asked to close his mind or his conscience," he explained. The president invoked the Neutrality Act while simultaneously pushing Congress to repeal its arms embargo provision. It did so two months later, opening the door to deliveries of war materiel to the Allies.[1]

Germany's invasion and Roosevelt's reaction stirred the isolationist embers that burned throughout America's history. On the same day that the *Wehrmacht* crossed into Poland, former president Herbert Hoover told NBC listeners that "America must keep out of this war. . . . We can be of more service to Europe and to humanity if we preserve the vitality and strength of the United States for use in the period of peace which must sometime come." Speaking a few weeks later in support of continuing the arms embargo, Senator William Borah flatly stated that "these wars are not our wars." To these critics intervention represented a surrender to the same spirit of militarism that had toppled Europe into bloody disarray.[2]

The publicity-shy aviator Charles Lindbergh emerged as the isolationists' most popular spokesman. He had many motivations for putting himself in the spotlight, including his genuine hatred of war, belief that the new conflict was merely another of Europe's periodic disputes over power, desire for Europeans to unite against supposedly inferior African and Asian races rather than fight among themselves, and fear that the Soviet Union would exploit the crisis to spread communism. Anti-Semitism also informed Lindbergh's thinking. While keeping his feelings private for the time being, he wondered whether powerful Jews with influence over "our press, radio, and motion pictures" might eventually maneuver the United States into the conflict. Finally, he saw involvement in the European war as a first step toward a permanent American presence on a continent beset with intrigue and backstabbing. The United States should instead wall off the Western Hemisphere, leaving the Old World to destroy itself.[3]

Some noninterventionists, including the German-American Bund and the Silver Shirts, sympathized with the Nazis. Most did not. While Lindbergh had a complicated relationship with the Nazis, he and like-minded people saw themselves drawing from American traditions, not endorsing Hitler's regime. George Washington's admonition to "steer clear of permanent Alliances, with any portion of the foreign world" resonated in the geographically isolated nation. With oceans on either side, no menacing neighbors, and abundant natural resources, Americans saw little need to engage a continent many saw as corrupt and aristocratic. The disillusioning experience of the Great War, supposedly a noble democratic crusade ruined by backstage dealings at Versailles, confirmed suspicions that Europeans exploited American virtues for their own selfish ends.[4]

✿ ✿ ✿

Hollywood's response to the European war's opening salvos ranged from despair to disregard. "Movies aren't enough," moaned Sam Goldwyn, "now I've got the whole World War on my hands!" Warners banned the German language from its lot. The Hollywood Anti-Nazi League echoed the Roosevelt line, backing the president's call to repeal the Neutrality Act's arms embargo. "Americans can be neutral from a military point of view," declared an editorial in *Hollywood Now,* "but its citizens cannot be neutral in the face of an unprovoked aggression against a peaceful nation." MGM producers, however, maintained a business-as-usual approach. Shooting on their sets continued uninterrupted, leaving distracted casts and crews to crowd around radios to hear the latest news between takes.[5]

Others in Hollywood took the news with less equanimity. Laurence Olivier learned that his native Great Britain had declared war as he cruised on a rented yacht off Catalina Island with Douglas Fairbanks Jr. and other friends. The debonair star of *Wuthering Heights* got roaring drunk, commandeered a dinghy, and rowed past other ships while shouting, "You're all finished! Done! Drink up! You've had it! *This is the end!*"[6]

The war finished off the film industry's already wobbling Popular Front alliance. Communists began their breakup with New Deal liberals after the August 1939 Nazi-Soviet Pact. In one of the most cynical accords ever concluded, Germany and the Soviet Union pledged not to attack each other and to remain neutral should the other become involved in a war. A secret protocol called for the two powers to divide Poland between themselves. Hollywood liberals argued long and loud over the deal. Most hard-core communists followed the party line and backed Stalin's move. Communist screenwriter John Bright called the pact "logical and inevitable." With Stalin now allied to Hitler, leftists who previously cheered Roosevelt's anti-Nazi rhetoric abruptly reversed course and began accusing the president of warmongering. Less doctrinaire Popular Frontists abandoned their radical colleagues for the Democratic Party's safe, mainstream liberalism.[7]

Congressman Martin Dies's ongoing inquiry further marginalized Hollywood communists. Dies had investigators sniffing around town as news of the Nazi-Soviet Pact broke. J. Edgar Hoover's FBI was also checking into reports of Hollywood communism by placing moles within the Hollywood Anti-Nazi League and other groups. In November it acquired a copy of the subscriber list for *Hollywood Now,* HANL's weekly newspaper. Apparently unaware of Hoover's machinations, HANL again shot back at Dies, blasting the Texan as a publicity hound who was inadvertently doing "the bidding of Hitler, Mussolini and the Mikado by seeking to divide and destroy the defenders of free popular expression, constitutional rights, education and culture." HANL never denied its communist leanings.[8]

These pressures collapsed Hollywood's Popular Front groups. The Motion Picture Democratic Committee disintegrated after communists on its executive board rejected Melvyn Douglas's motion to reaffirm support for Roosevelt's foreign policy and then smothered Philip Dunne's resolution denouncing the Soviet Union's November 1939 invasion of Finland. Noncommunists similarly abandoned HANL when members failed to agree on a response to Stalin's Poland and Finland incursions. Many foreign-born members shifted their energies to the European Film Fund, an agency that provided refugees with financial and career assistance, leaving the last radical HANL holdouts to reorganize as the new, pacifist Hollywood League for Democratic Action. Hollywood communists returned to the antifascist fold after Germany invaded the Soviet Union in June 1941 but never reforged their earlier ties with conventional liberals.[9]

There was a sense around town that an era had ended. Nobody could predict the war's impact on foreign revenues, distribution practices, wages, costs, or budgets. Income from foreign markets, which produced nearly half of gross revenues, had dropped 8 percent in 1938. A greater plunge seemed certain for 1939. "This is the biggest problem the film industry has ever faced," reported Paramount vice president John W. Hicks. Studios scaled back expensive productions in progress. Fearful of violating the Neutrality Act, Warner Bros. postponed two anti-Nazi projects, *Underground* and *The Bishop Who Walks with God*. Hollywood optimists hoped the war would force Italy to reopen its market in response to a lack of domestic supply.[10]

The future of French and British actors working in American studios was equally unclear. Gossip columnist Louella Parsons reported that Anglo actors had orders to come home once the fighting started. Such a desertion would spell disaster for such producers as David O. Selznick, who was preparing to shoot *Rebecca* with British citizens Laurence Olivier and George Sanders. "We would be in a fine pickle if they walked out in the middle," he worried. "Not so much of a pickle as Poland, I grant you, but still a pickle." Like many of Parsons's predictions, this one did not materialize. Deciding that Hollywood's émigrés could do more good in Hollywood than in London or Paris, the Los Angeles consulates advised them to stay put. David Niven, a graduate of the elite Sandhurst Military College, ignored this advice and went home to fight. Niven's employer, Samuel Goldwyn, promised to "cable Hitler and ask him to shoot around you."[11]

London-born actor Leslie Howard had left a few weeks before the invasion of Poland, soon after wrapping his work in *Gone with the Wind*. He hoped to aid Britain's cause by making movies that pulled the United States closer to his homeland. "I am quite certain that, properly camouflaged, the message we want to deliver can be carried direct to the American people," he told the Ministry of Information's Duff Cooper. "After all, most of them are intensely sympathetic to our cause, they are 'rooting' for us, they want us to win." Over the next few years Howard appeared in such propaganda pictures as *49th Parallel* (1941), *In Which We Serve* (1942), and *War in the Mediterranean* (1943). He died in 1943 when a German fighter shot down a plane carrying him home from a visit to Portugal.[12]

Hollywood's British colony was more cohesive than its other émigré communities. Transplanted Britons devoured imported copies of the *Times* of London at the Hollywood Cricket Club in Griffith Park, not far from where D. W. Griffith filmed the battle scenes for *Birth of a Nation*. Many gathered around the radio every December 31 to hear Big Ben toll in the new year. War transformed these social events into patriotic obligations. The group's ringleader was C. Aubrey Smith, a six-foot-four-inch ramrod of an actor who was the first choice of any casting director seeking a distinguished representative of the British Empire. Tall and lean, with hawklike eyes and a fiercely aristocratic nose, he was so impossibly British that one could not see him onscreen without envisioning the Union Jack. Prime Minister Chamberlain's weak response to Hitler infuriated the Cambridge-educated Smith, who led the calls for his countrymen to work on Britain's behalf. He joined Nigel Bruce, Herbert Marshall, Basil Rathbone, and other transplants in fund-raising and goodwill campaigns that kept Britain's plight near the forefront of Hollywood's collective mind.[13]

Hollywood worried that the conflict would close Britain, which accounted for roughly half of overseas revenue, to American films. As prewar restrictions on currency exports had essentially achieved this in France, losing Britain as well would spell disaster for motion picture companies. Chamberlain's declaration of war sent employees of American studios' London offices scrambling out of town. MGM had closed its Denham studio's doors months earlier amid invasion rumors. Warner Bros. temporarily shuttered Teddington Studios. More damaging than the resulting production delays was the loss of theater revenue caused by the opening of hostilities. British movie houses closed for fear of German air raids. Although most reopened with reduced hours over the next several weeks, the war took a toll. Theaters in Middlesborough, on London's northeast outskirts, required patrons to bring gas masks with them. Exhibitors' curtailing of evening performances cut profits by around 40 percent in urban centers and 20 percent in smaller towns. A worried Will Hays reminded Secretary of State Hull of Britain's importance to the film industry. Hull, who was attending to far more pressing matters, testily assured the MPPDA president that his department would lend Hollywood "every appropriate assistance" in its time of need.[14]

Harry Warner hoped for more concrete help. He was onboard the *Queen Mary* when Hitler invaded Poland, halfway home to New York after spending two weeks examining his British and French offices' preparations for war. He dashed off a confidential letter to President Roosevelt moments after his feet touched the pier. Warner poured his heart out to his ally in the White House, explaining that the anticipated loss of European income might well tip his studio into bankruptcy. Then, making an incongruous yet not completely unexpected leap, Warner shifted his missive into an assault on Thurman Arnold, whose expensive antitrust lawsuit robbed Warners executives of "the time, attention and energy" needed to address the international crisis. The only way to save the studio—and to keep its pro-American and anti-Nazi messages on theater screens—was to free it from "the overwhelming burden and non-productive effort and expense" the suit created. Unlike his earlier letter to Harry Hopkins, Warner's effort achieved nothing, as his extraordinary missive never made it into FDR's hands. Roosevelt's secretaries diverted it to Attorney General Frank Murphy, who drafted a polite yet noncommittal reply. They knew that, for the time being, the president was unwilling to apply more pressure on Hopkins to work out a deal.[15]

Will Hays provided Hollywood's official reaction to the war. The MPPDA president flew from New York to Los Angeles as soon as hostilities started. He asked studio heads to observe strict neutrality, which to him meant avoiding international affairs altogether. "Today, with European nations once more at each other's throats," he warned, "our responsibility is emphasized to keep genuine screen entertainment flowing— undeflected by wartime propaganda." A flood of war-themed movies would invite federal regulation and create a warlike spirit in the United States. Hollywood must not "assume the dreadful responsibility of sending the youth of America to war." Hays made the industry's position public during his return trip to New York. Pausing to speak with reporters in Chicago, he promised an uninterrupted flow of motion pictures despite the probable loss of additional foreign markets. Hays then articulated a Frankenstein's monster of a wartime doctrine, a homily seemingly constructed from fragments of earlier speeches: "There will be no cycle of 'hate' pictures. The primary purpose of the essential service of motion pictures is entertainment—entertainment which will be effective as such and entertainment which is, at its best, inspirational. There may be pictures in which war is an element, as love or crime is an element, but 'hate' pictures, made for the purpose of stirring up animosity, have no place, in our opinion, on the American screen and certainly are no part of the purpose of the organized motion picture industry." Hays forwarded his "hate pictures" comments to all of Hollywood's most important producers, giving them a not-so-subtle hint for how he wanted them to conduct themselves during the conflict.[16]

The savvy ex-politico's comments left some wiggle room. While not rejecting war movies outright, he limited studios to war movies that shunned realistic violence, upheld rather than challenged audience preconceptions, and offered no specific course of action for the United States. His was a practical approach that appealed to public interest in the conflict without making people feel uncomfortable about it. From Hays's perspective, this was all Hollywood could hope to do. His instincts for national sentiment were solid. Americans had little problem choosing sides, indicating that they saw the war as in some way relevant to them. A September 1939 *Life* magazine poll showed that 83 percent of respondents wanted the Allies to win the war, as opposed to 1 percent wanting Germany to win and 16 percent expressing no opinion. At the same time, Americans did not want to get too close to the fighting; the same survey showed that only 3 percent wanted the United States to immediately join the Allies.[17]

Most movie moguls willingly followed Hays. Republic Studio's Herbert Yates told the *New York World-Telegram* that his company would "veer away from pictures of war." Murray Silverstone, United Artists' chief of worldwide operations, argued that "the public, given a choice between news of the war and entertainment on the screen, will definitely gravitate towards the latter." Jack and Harry Warner, however, seemed to more accurately catch the true spirit of American public opinion. Although Jack promised "no propaganda pictures from Warner Brothers," Harry modified his brother's stance, declaring that the freedom "we fought the British to obtain we will have to fight with them to retain." Between them the brothers offered a special kind of neutrality: a pro-Allied neutrality.[18]

Studios at every point of Hollywood's compass had historical or patriotic subjects in the works when war broke out, projects that for the most part endorsed Hays's "no hate films" proclamation while continuing the flag-waving seen in *Allegheny Uprising* and other recent releases. Frank Capra was wrapping *Mr. Smith Goes to Washington* on the Columbia lot, a picture the Breen Office hailed as a "strong preachment in favor of democracy, Americanism and clean politics." RKO was filming its adaptation of Robert Sherwood's Pulitzer Prize–winning *Abe Lincoln in Illinois* a few blocks south. Over in Culver City, MGM had enlisted Spencer Tracy to headline its version of *Northwest Passage,* Kenneth Roberts's best-selling novel of the French and Indian War. Up in Burbank, Warner Bros. was shooting tests for its next World War I feature, a James Cagney vehicle entitled *The Fighting 69th.*[19]

There were, however, signs that Hollywood was also stirring in directions that defied Hays's pronouncement. The financial blackout settling over continental Europe convinced some studio activists that now was the time to follow up *Confessions of a Nazi Spy* with additional antifascist productions. Charlie Chaplin completed the script for *The Great Dictator* on September 3, the day Great Britain declared war, and assembled his crew at Chaplin Studios on the corner of La Brea Avenue and

Sunset Boulevard soon after. Twentieth Century–Fox writers polished a treatment for Oscar Schisgall's short story "I Married a Nazi." Warners debated whether to restart *Underground,* which examined the German resistance. The studio begged Joseph Breen to keep the screenplay secret for fear "local Nazis" might get their hands on it. Breen warned Hays about *Underground,* as he did with any proposal raising "an important question of industry policy," Breen-speak for violating Hays's no-hate-film decree. The movie community was dividing on the war issue, in essence splitting between backers of Will Hays and Harry Warner. Even individual studios found themselves torn in opposite directions. MGM put two anti-Nazi projects, *Escape* and *The Mortal Storm,* into its pipeline just as it rejected *It Can't Happen Here.*[20]

Some Hollywood detractors expected studios to unleash a barrage of war-themed pictures the moment fighting began, as if moviemakers could will pictures into existence with the snap of a finger. Senator Elmer Thomas of Oklahoma hoped to spike the industry's guns before they fired. Reasoning that "the only way to be neutral is to be neutral all the way," he mulled a resolution to ban war-themed features and newsreels. Thomas worried that such projects might imperil neutrality by inspiring war hysteria. Hays took personal charge of mollifying the senator, eventually convincing him to drop his proposal by repeatedly promising to keep war propaganda out of theaters.[21]

The cinematic torrent Thomas feared did not materialize. Although *The Great Dictator* and similar projects moved forward, the film community as a whole settled into its version of the "Phony War," as some called the tense period of inactivity in Europe following the fall of Poland. Prowar or anti-Nazi pictures, observed Hays's friend and *Nashville Banner* editor James Stahlman, might "disturb the equilibrium of the judgment of the people." No one knew how much war audiences wanted to see or how best to make money under wartime conditions. Americans disliked combat movies, Breen told Twentieth Century–Fox's Jason Joy. More films like *Confessions of a Nazi Spy* might "ignite a nation-wide conflagration of protest against the screen as an institution, which may cause the industry, as a whole, very serious worry."[22]

Besides being a noble goal, peace sold better than war. MGM responded to the blitzkrieg with "Peace on Earth," an animated short released at Christmastime of 1939. It was one of the most heartfelt films made during this era and one that must have traumatized young theater-goers. Three squirrels sing "Hark the Herald Angels" as the scene pans a bombed-out church, snowbound cannons, and helmets strewn about the ground. An elderly squirrel (Mel Blanc) tells his grandchildren about the last days of humankind, which obliterated itself in a pointless war. The screen fills with ghastly images of men in gas masks, roaring artillery, and devastated cities. There are no identifiable causes here, only "Vegetarians" and "Meat-Eaters" locked in a senseless global death match. Neither army wins the brutal conflict. The last two men on Earth shoot each other from muddy trenches that slowly swallow war's final victims. With humanity extinct, rabbits, birds, squirrels, and chipmunks emerge from hiding to investigate the blasted landscape. They discover a Bible resting in a church. Humans did not adhere to its commandments, but they will. The wise little creatures transform the wasteland into "Peaceville," turning helmets into houses and daggers into lamp posts. Humanity fades into the past, its existence no more than a fairy tale meant to scare children.

"Peace on Earth" was nominated for an Academy Award and the Nobel Peace Prize. Two years later many of its animators went to work on promilitary shorts.

CHAPTER TEN

A Winter of Discontent

A MOVIE PRODUCER'S ATTITUDE toward the public "is very like that of the sailor towards the sea," explained Margaret Farrand Thorp in 1939's *America at the Movies.* "The sailor may guess what the sea is going to do but he can never be sure. So the producer." Current events magnified the producers' perpetual uncertainty about the tastes of future audiences. "Inasmuch as it is impossible to tell which way the war wind is blowing," *Variety* observed, "producers don't want to be left on a limb." The war stood foremost in everyone's mind, but Hollywood faced many problems between fall 1939 and spring 1940. Foreign and domestic adversaries inflicted a thousand cuts that left the dispirited movie community desperate for a sense of direction. Movie producers had important voices but did not know what to say to a war-torn world. Their predicament resembled Jim Casy's, the Okie preacher from John Steinbeck's *Grapes of Wrath.* "Here I got the sperit sometimes an' nothin' to preach about," Casy told Tom Joad. "I got the call to lead people, an' no place to lead 'em." Hollywood seemed to be waiting for a Roosevelt, a Churchill, anyone to rally it into action.[1]

Industry executives could make no long-term plans until they resolved the Department of Justice's antitrust suit. The movie moguls fumed that the government singled them out for scrutiny despite their long service to the country and, as they saw it, immaculate record of voluntary self-regulation. Continued collaboration with Harry Hopkins's Department of Commerce offered the best means of escaping Thurman Arnold's crusade with their theater chains intact. Studio lawyers worked with Commerce Department officials throughout 1938 and 1939 to convince Arnold to settle the case.

After innumerable meetings and countless drafts, Hollywood unveiled its proposal for a new trade practice code a few weeks before the invasion of Poland. Industry attorneys hailed the document with a hyperbolic zeal akin to an overenthusiastic studio publicity department's praise for a formulaic genre flick. Rather than making a serious effort to satisfy Hollywood's legal problems, the code instead suggested a business delaying action in the hopes of making the issue disappear. Not only did it ignore Arnold's top demand—divorcing exhibition from production and distribution—it also clung to Will Hays's Hooveresque notion of self-regulation. Acceptance of the code, which merely offered small concessions on block booking and other tangential matters, was voluntary for studios. The Justice Department dismissed the trade practice code, and the months of work that went into it, with hardly a second thought.[2]

Arnold's insistence that the majors change their underlying, monopolistic structure outraged Hollywood executives. *Variety* interpreted the Justice Department's rejection of the code as part of a "campaign to punish the film industry." Such cries of "legal ambush" were disingenuous. Arnold's men never showed any interest in the majors' latest bid for self-regulation. They ignored the fifteen-month-long code-writing process, refusing to comment on drafts studio lawyers sent them. Arnold's rebuff also angered Commerce Department negotiators. Sharing Hollywood's hopes of improving the government's relationship with business in an unsettled wartime climate, Hopkins's delegation pushed the assistant attorney general to resolve the suit but did not succeed. Holding to his insistence on divorcement, Arnold continued preparing for a trial.[3]

The collapse of foreign markets and the initiation of European hostilities made Hollywood's control over domestic theaters more important to its bottom line than ever. Accordingly, Will Hays, who had played only a minor role in the code talks, now leapt into the fight to save the majors' theaters by slipping into Washington to ask Roosevelt to nudge the Justice Department into softening its stance. Hays chatted with Attorney General Frank Murphy a week later to smooth any feathers the studios' public outcry may have ruffled. Murphy wanted an amiable agreement but also wanted to give Arnold time to extract more concessions. The attorney general stalled, turning the talk toward Hollywood's depictions of G-Men and federal prisons and parrying Hays's efforts to get the conversation back on track. As Murphy had intended, the meeting accomplished nothing.[4]

Hays had a better chance of winning over Roosevelt, who had already privately endorsed Hollywood's desire to have Hopkins's men negotiate a compromise. After their inconsequential face-to-face meeting Hays tried to sway the president again with an October 1939 letter. His appeal applied the same tactics he had used with Mussolini three years earlier. Hays opened with flattery, congratulating the president for winning repeal of the arms embargo, and then made his pitch, begging FDR to keep Arnold from "forcing his own theories . . . on Harry's people before their recommendations are made." With Hopkins again away on sick leave, Hays worried that the Justice Department would fill the power vacuum his absence created. He was right. Distracted by the war, Roosevelt had neither the time nor the desire to meddle in an interdepartmental dispute, and Hopkins was not there to defend his department's interests. The president responded to Hays's well-crafted missive with a bland, noncommittal note drafted by the attorney general's office.[5]

The war made it all the more important that studios survive the antitrust suit intact while staying in the president's good graces because Hitler's advances imperiled overseas resources even as the moguls fought to keep their domestic empires intact. The war also added impetus to Hollywood's drive to use the screen to shore up reverence for democracy. In a time of frayed nerves and patriotic fervor, the powers in Washington had little tolerance for any picture that could be interpreted as mocking the American form of government. Opening during the first weeks of conflict and in the wake of Arnold's rejection of the code proposal, *Mr. Smith Goes to Washington* therefore could not have appeared at a worse time. Director Frank Capra's critically acclaimed and commercially successful film outraged many of the politicians who held Hollywood's fate in their hands.

Studios battled for the screen rights to Lewis Ransom Foster's novel *The Gentleman from Montana*. Columbia came out on top, winning a title that held both promise and peril. "It is particularly fortunate that this kind of story is to be made at this time," Joseph Breen told Hays, because it stressed "the importance of a democracy" and America's "rich and glorious heritage." Breen also anticipated problems. Foster's portrayal of corrupt congressmen beholden to greedy lobbyists lent his book an antidemocratic flavor that could be "dynamite . . . for the motion picture industry, and for the country at large" if handled poorly. The PCA head convinced Columbia to moderate the story's negativity.[6]

Capra believed his movie idealized democracy, but the October 17 premiere of *Mr. Smith Goes to Washington* had the markings of a disaster. A throng of four thousand—including 45 senators, some 250 congressmen, Secretary of State Cordell Hull, Attorney General Frank Murphy, Supreme Court justices, and members of the press—packed Washington's Constitution Hall. Capra sat beside one of the Senate's staunchest isolationists, Montana's Burton K. Wheeler. The crowd watched Jimmy Stewart's accidental senator, Jefferson Smith, discover that Washington, D.C., is thick with cynical newsmen and crooked power brokers more interested in self-enrichment than the common good. Although the screening went better than Capra had anticipated, the film's criticism of politicians and the press left some attendees "looking as if they'd been through a tough session with a traffic cop."[7]

Columbia executives heard little dissatisfaction that night but took notice when the *Chicago Tribune* reported a few days later that many congressmen were privately fuming about the film. The paper's observation prefaced a stream of angry testimonials from angry congressmen. "It won't do the movies any good," grumbled House Majority Leader Sam Rayburn. "It was as grotesque as anything I have ever seen," agreed Senate Majority Leader Alben Barkley. South Carolina senator James F. Byrnes called it "outrageous, exactly the kind of picture that dictators of totalitarian governments would like to have their subjects believe exists in a democracy."[8]

Senators felt "ridiculed and maligned by the motion picture industry," the *Indianapolis Star* claimed, "and the more those august members of that body think back on the story and action, the madder they get." Angry legislators sought revenge by asking the House to revive Senator Matthew Neely's anti-block-booking bill, which had already passed the Senate before foundering in the House Interstate Commerce Committee. Ironically, Capra favored Neely's bill, which he thought would ease the way for him to enter independent production. His superiors, however, were horrified. Once safely dead, the bill now became a topic of national conversation. Hays's men fanned out on the offensive, using their media and political connections to put the monster back in chains. Despite their efforts, hearings on the bill resumed in April 1940 only to collapse when civic reformers failed to agree with owners of independent theaters on a viable alternative to block booking.[9]

Mr. Smith Goes to Washington also tested Hollywood's relationship with the State Department, whose officials worried that the film might harm America's image overseas. J. Holbrook Chapman, the department's charge d'affairs in Bangkok, thought it "should never be permitted to be shown outside of the borders of the United States" because it undermined faith in democracy. Bureaucrats in Washington agreed. Although careful to avoid direct censorship, they urged Hays to dissuade Columbia from an international release. Ambassador Kennedy, who called *Mr. Smith Goes to Washington* "one of the most disgraceful things I have ever seen done to our country," warned Columbia head of production Harry Cohn that the movie would "definitely discredit American Government and American civilization in the eyes of the English public." The State Department saw its caution not as an isolated attack on a single movie but rather as part of a broader effort to alert businesses to the dangers of operating in wartime. Its harsh critiques aimed at better cooperation, not government censorship.[10]

The department's concerns proved unfounded, as American politicians were apparently more sensitive than foreign viewers. *Mr. Smith Goes to Washington* performed well overseas, and its likable hero became a symbol of everything right with the United States. James Hilton wrote in the *London Sunday Graphic* that *Mr. Smith Goes to Washington* was "just about the best American patriotic film ever made." A State Department official in Zürich (named, oddly enough, James Stewart) told Secretary Hull that Swiss audiences saw the fictional senator as a "symbol of democracy."[11]

Its patriotism thus confirmed, *Mr. Smith Goes to Washington* joined *Union Pacific, Young Mr. Lincoln,* and other contemporary pro-American releases opening across the country. Even with all these efforts, however, some still wondered whether Hollywood sufficiently embraced what the *Boston American* called "REAL American democracy." The same war-inspired zeal that produced Capra's masterpiece prompted renewed demands for the movie capital to cleanse itself of un-American presences— namely communists. Critics charged that communist influence made Hollywood quick to jump on the anti-Nazi bandwagon yet reluctant to condemn Stalin. FBI informants in the Hollywood Anti-Nazi League suspected that communists in the group were actually using anti-Nazism as a tool for indoctrinating the naive with red propaganda.[12]

Studios had in fact made few pictures about Russia, including the czarist-era spy drama *The Emperor's Candlesticks* (1937) and the mildly anticommunist *Balalaika* (1939). MGM tried to fill the anticommunist void with Ernst Lubitsch's comedy *Ninotchka* (1939). Greta Garbo's delightfully wooden performance as a hard-line Soviet envoy in Paris cast life under communism as grim, loveless, and hardscrabble. The famous shot of Ninotchka cavorting about in a ridiculous French hat she had previously denigrated as evidence of capitalism's impending demise said more about capitalism's merits than any heavy-handed propaganda picture.

This example of the famed "Lubitsch touch" did not keep anticommunist fanatics away from Hollywood. Congressman Martin Dies relaunched his red-baiting crusade in early 1940 with support from the Hearst press and, much more quietly, from Hays, who lamented the "reprehensible" presence of communists in the film business. The congressman announced his move with a pair of articles in *Liberty* magazine, asserting that scores of prominent movie people were either members of the Communist Party, communist sympathizers, or contributors to communist causes and reiterating the charge that studios avoided making anticommunist pictures. Dies's conclusion that Hollywood was a "powerhouse of Communistic activities and propaganda" left Hollywood's leading anticommunist, Louis B. Mayer, to defend the industry. "When you can bring me a book, a good book, dealing with the drama in the Communist regime I'll buy it and pay good money for it," he retorted.[13]

Although some dismissed Dies's attack as a stunt, his charges resonated. "We hope Mr. Dies can in some way bring the picture industry to realize that they should rule out pictures which are of a character which influence a disregard for American institutions, or its laws, and that the actors and actresses who are communists are shown up," opined one editorialist. The Texan repeated his accusations at a Hollywood luncheon arranged by the big producers—a luncheon at which prominent leftist actors and screenwriters were conspicuously absent. The guest of honor refused to name names, preferring to keep the moguls guessing about who was in his sights. He nevertheless promised hearings on the subject in the near future.[14]

Screenwriters and Hollywood crafts unions answered Dies's visit with a rally at the Los Angeles Philharmonic Auditorium. Donald Ogden Stewart was among those urging the industry to reject anticommunist fear-mongering by aggressively highlighting its Americanism. The moguls, on the other hand, cowered in silence. Anticipating the logic applied during the cold war–era red scare, they believed opposing Dies would mark them as either procommunist or, at best, apathetic to communism. As the *Springfield Evening Union* put it, "If Hollywood is innocent it has nothing to fear." With Stalin and Hitler allies and democratic passions running high, now was not the time to appear un-American—whatever that meant, and no one felt the need to define this oft-used word. Dies's explanation for why there were so many communists in Hollywood further intimidated executives. "Most of the producers are Jews," he wrote in his second *Liberty* article. "They are therefore anxious to do everything within their power to prevent the spread of Nazism and Fascism." Judaism was the third rail of Hollywood politics, one not even Harry Warner wanted to touch at this moment.[15]

Martin Dies's shadow loomed over the dream factory for months to come. He returned to California in the summer after former-communist-turned-red-baiter John Leech accused forty-two members of the film industry of contributing to or recruiting for communist causes. Dies set up in the Waldorf-Astoria Hotel as a one-man subcommittee of HUAC to grill the people on Leech's list. He cleared Humphrey Bogart after the actor came to plead his innocence. Fredric March, Luise Rainer, and Franchot Tone also knocked at the congressman's door. James Cagney cut short his vacation on Martha's Vineyard and flew cross-country to defend himself. Robert Montgomery received his absolution over the phone; Melvyn Douglas's came by telegraph. Dies's investigation produced much heat but no light, failing to prove the existence of a malicious, well-financed conspiracy of cinematic communists. It did, however, keep Hollywood on edge, anxious that any ideological misstep could bring down the powerful Texan's wrath.[16]

❧ ❧ ❧

The movie industry's problems were legion in the winter of 1939–1940. An intensifying antitrust suit, the reappearance of the Neely bill, and the anticommunist witch hunt—difficulties that all grew to some extent from the international crisis—threw producers on the defensive. Overlapping these concerns were ongoing overseas economic issues that also stemmed in large part from the wars in Europe and Asia. Marching armies and falling bombs shook up regions crucial to Hollywood's survival. Studios attempted with mixed success to preserve markets caught up in the conflict while expanding their dominance in nations still at peace.

Great Britain's film business rebounded quickly after the war began. Hollywood accountants breathed a sigh of relief as British movie houses reopened their doors. Perceiving that entertainment was essential for morale and that theaters were crucial outlets for war news and propaganda, the British government encouraged citizens to return to the movies. But crowded theaters did not mean all was well. Wartime conditions made producing in Britain a hazardous proposition. American studios reopened their British facilities—MGM executive Eddie Mannix promised to keep shooting "until bombs and parachute troops began raining on the studio"—to fill quota requirements and maintain goodwill yet hesitated to send their headliners into harm's way. Robert Montgomery stayed in England, but most American actors and directors avoided assignments to Denham and Teddington.[17]

As if the fear of bombs was not bad enough, Great Britain's wartime financial priorities further endangered Hollywood's operations on the island. Britain's Board of Trade wanted to freeze a portion of American studios' profits to prevent a currency exodus that might damage the United Kingdom's already fragile fiscal health. Whitehall's desire to horde currency developed in part from the United States' Neutrality Acts, which required nations at war to pay cash for American goods. Ambassador Joseph Kennedy served as the moguls' chief proxy in fighting the effort to control studio assets. American production in Britain required access to profits, he told Anglo negotiators, and the Board of Trade's plan might prompt studios to boycott their country. Kennedy's belief that Britain would likely lose the war informed his hard-line stance. Hollywood's frozen funds would melt away forever if, as he predicted, the Germans triumphed. Free-trader Cordell Hull also objected to London's meddling, warning Lord Lothian, Kennedy's counterpart in Washington, that "the British Government will soon reach a stage where the advantages of these discriminations and restrictions will be decidedly less than the bad reactionary effects in this country."[18]

Neither side wanted a break in relations. Hollywood was committed to a pro-British line, and the Board of Trade desperately needed the United States on its side. Its members sought compromise even though they thought Kennedy was bluffing. After a series of tough talks, Kennedy brokered a deal in November 1939 that allowed Hollywood studios to export $17.5 million per year from Britain, about half of their normal earnings there. Studio executives applauded the deal even though it required them to make serious financial sacrifices. "It literally means almost the life" of some companies, Will Hays exulted. A delegation from the MPPDA greeted the ambassador like a conquering hero when his seaplane touched down at Port Washington, Long Island, a few weeks later. Producers feted Kennedy during his stay, knowing their former peer had averted disaster.[19]

Kennedy's tough bargaining kept Hollywood operating in England. It did not change the ambassador's opinion that British defenses were "appallingly weak" and that incoming prime minister Winston Churchill possessed "energy and brains but *no* judgment." Nor did the deal revive the industry's declining economic fortunes. After netting $13.5 million from worldwide film rentals in 1938, the majors (excluding United Artists) saw their net profits sink to just under $9 million in 1939. They lost around $2.4 million in 1940. Exchange restrictions and Axis domination of key markets decimated their bottom line. Non-European revenues remained ominously level despite Hollywood's campaign to extract more from Latin America. Gross profits from Europe fell from about $44.5 million in 1938 to around $21 million in 1940.[20]

Great Britain was not alone in adopting a nationalistic monetary policy. In summer 1940 studios had money frozen in Australia, Belgium, France, Holland, New Zealand, and throughout Scandinavia. Bankers who financed Hollywood counseled fiscal conservatism, a financial drawing in of the horns. Studio executives talked of making fewer, less-expensive films. Some advocated dissolving their foreign departments to save money. Twentieth Century–Fox and MGM laid off hundreds of employees. "The economic impact of the war," *New York Times* movie correspondent Douglas Churchill wrote, "has created a state of utter confusion in Hollywood." Even Will Hays accepted a pay cut that dropped his annual salary from $100,000 to $80,000.[21]

Hollywood faced equally acute problems in Asia. Japan was a relatively unimportant market, accounting for slightly more than 1 percent of foreign revenues. Even so, the disintegration of the 1938 Yokohama settlement added another item to an already crowded overseas agenda. Contrary to its agreement, Japan deposited no funds in San Francisco's Yokohama Specie Bank after late 1938, leaving more than $1 million frozen in the home islands. Japan locked up an additional $2 million in profits by mid-1940 while taking steps toward fascist-style control of its screens. Although Hollywood product remained popular, the government hoped to dominate the medium for its own purposes. An April 1939 law required domestic producers to obtain government approval of scenarios. Japanese officials squeezed out alien competition by issuing fewer import permits and, as of 1 January 1940, forbidding theaters from showing more than fifty new foreign films per year.[22]

The prospect of improving relations and cash flow took another hit when President Roosevelt renounced the 1911 Treaty of Commerce and Navigation, which regulated trade between the two nations, in July. FDR's action satisfied Americans' demand for retaliation against Japanese militarism in China while acknowledging their desire to avoid provocation. Abrogating the treaty did not halt trade; the move merely alerted Japan to the United States' displeasure. Studio executives saw no need to sever ties with Japan so long as there was still some money to be made. Selling to the Land of the Rising Sun lacked the ideological stigma of selling to the Land of Hitler's Brownshirts. Hollywood was staying until the Japanese threw them out.[23]

Unfriendly governments in Asia and Europe made Latin America Hollywood's most reliable overseas market. Producers were thankful it was holding up under the pressures of war yet disturbed that their drive to boost profits there had little impact. Hollywood's obsession with Latin America also triggered an unanticipated backlash. Fearing Yankee cultural domination, the Mexican government passed an ordinance directing theaters to show a homegrown feature for at least one week of every month. Some Hispanics worried that a greater American film presence might upset the Germans, who were establishing their own cinematic foothold in the region. Censors in Venezuela, for example, clamped down on Hollywood films that the German consulate there declared anti-Nazi.[24]

Movie producers who claimed to speak in a global language could not figure out how to communicate with the Hispanic world. It is a measure of Hollywood's desperation that the trade press actually considered advice from George O'Brien, a silent-era star who had since fallen into B-movie anonymity. After a ten-week visit to South America the actor concluded that the film business's difficulties there resulted from studios casting women who were "too frail" for Latin tastes. "You are a beeg man," he quoted one Bolivian exhibitor, "you need a beeg woman." Hollywood's confusion reflected its parochialism and, on a larger scale, Americans' ignorance of their neighbors. Pious claims of good neighborliness and well-meaning campaigns to build a hemispheric defense network served the Good Neighbor Policy's political and military needs but had failed to achieve its cultural objectives.[25]

Juarez remained the exception when it came to onscreen depictions of Latin Americans. Nobody immediately followed up on Warners' A-budget, prestige production. For all Hollywood's talk of hemispheric harmony and cultural sensitivity, its Hispanic characters continued to be *characters,* colorful stereotypes who added broad comedy or over-the-top ethnic flavor to B-grade productions such as George O'Brien's *The Fighting Gringo* (1939). Made before the actor's trip south and therefore bereft of "beeg" women, the RKO western met the expectations of small-town matinee audiences while ignoring contemporary political currents. Its Mexicans are neither lazy nor villainous, but they are caricatures. Rancher Don Aliso del Campo (Lucio Villegas) favors the same velvet bullfighting garb that Captain Thunder had donned several years earlier. Hat dancers and mariachi bands materialize from nowhere. Anglos intermingle with Mexicans yet are visually distinct. Gringos are clean shaven and wear respectable clothes, while their darker-skinned compatriots sport scruffy beards and shabby cowboy hats so absurdly voluminous they could conceal an entire herd of rustled cattle.

Singing cowboy Gene Autry's *South of the Border* (1939) merged the incipient interest in Latin America with post-blitzkrieg fears of fifth columnists. Federal agents Gene Autry and Frog Millhouse (Smiley Burnette) stumble on an unnamed foreign power's scheme to wreck pan-American neutrality by fomenting a revolution in the South American nation of Palermo.[26] Ostensibly designed to build hemispheric friendships, *South of the Border* repeated Hollywood stereotypes despite Joseph

Breen's plea to Republic Studios to remove language "pretty sure to give offense to Latin Americans." Like other films, for example, it insisted that Latinos typically wore fancy jackets, colorful sashes, and festive formal dresses. While such imagery was not necessarily disparaging, it miscast America's neighbors as frivolous, well-dressed partiers who had little time for actual work, a depiction roughly equivalent to a movie starring tuxedo-wearing coal miners.[27]

More damaging was *South of the Border*'s amalgamation of Latin Americans into a single type, a convenient if misguided dodge for studios reluctant to market films associated with a particular country throughout the hemisphere. Hollywood's—and America's—profound ignorance of Latin America's variegated culture paved the way for the opening song, "Come to the Fiesta." "Do the step they call the tango," Autry told the Mexicans swarming around him. He plowed on, suggesting they also do "the rumba and mandango." Like the use of overblown costumes, Autry's terpsichorean imprecision in "Come to the Fiesta" was a small piece in a larger pattern of inaccuracy that diluted his movie's good intentions.

Autry and Republic made similar missteps in their next Latin-themed effort, *Gaucho Serenade* (1940), a picture in which Gene and Frog never come close to Argentina. The title song is a mélange of Hispanic images, a continent blended into homogenous soup by Hollywood's cultural Cuisinart. "Every night when the moon is shining bright down in Rio de Janeiro," Gene croons to a band of festive Mexicans, "Comes a gent with a mellow instrument and a colorful sombrero." The Mexicans in the Gaucho Cantina celebrate Gene's sentiments with a sizzling dance involving capes, ruffled shirts, and fiery rhythms.

Gaucho Serenade tried sincerely to capitalize on Americans' interest in all things Hispanic, but merely showing an interest did not translate into verisimilitude. The limitations of post-*Juarez* features indicate Hollywood's sluggishness in adopting new perspectives. Judging from the lack of outcry against these films within the United States, B-movie audiences felt a similar disinterest in challenging comfortable ethnic labels even when they undermined President Roosevelt's geopolitical priorities by reinforcing images of Yankee arrogance toward other nations.

MGM screenwriter Dore Schary wanted to break this impasse with a picture that presented the Good Neighbor Policy in a manner that appealed to theatergoers throughout the Western Hemisphere. In early 1940 he began a screenplay on the life of Simon Bolivar, a Venezuelan whose success in winning independence for a half-dozen nations made him, in Schary's eyes, the "George Washington of South America." Schary envisioned an ideological sequel to *Juarez*. Like Warners' film, a Bolivar biopic could show South America liberating itself from European military tyranny, establishing democratic republics, and embracing the ideals embodied within the Declaration of Independence.[28]

Schary developed his outline with such Catholic leaders as Bishop James Ryan of Omaha and Father Maurice Sheehy, head of the religious education department at Catholic University of America and an intimate of the president. Ryan and Sheehy introduced Schary to South American envoys and arranged a meeting with Undersecretary of State Sumner Welles. While unable to offer official approval, Welles expressed enthusiasm for "Bolivar" and promised to assist "in any way possible." Schary's promises of a historically accurate film that treated the Liberator respectfully while advancing pan-Americanism convinced skeptical diplomats to lend their backing. Dr. Don Eduardo Garland, the Peruvian Embassy's counselor, suggested Leslie Howard for the title role.[29]

"Bolivar" was a perfect project for 1940. It dealt with timely issues, conveyed a message of peaceful internationalism, furthered the White House's foreign agenda, and fulfilled the industry's desire to win over Hispanics. Schary's well-intentioned picture, however, became another victim of Hollywood's focus on the bottom line. MGM doubted the picture could find an audience in Argentina or Brazil, South America's two largest movie markets, because Bolivar had not personally touched those countries. Executives also feared the prohibitive cost of a historical costume drama. "Bolivar" held questionable appeal for the domestic market, as Americans had, at best, a passing familiarity with the Liberator. Jack and Harry Warner took a chance when *Juarez* faced similar obstacles. Mayer's MGM did not. Its primary commitment was to stockholders, not to abstract and potentially unprofitable notions of international harmony.[30]

✿ ✿ ✿

Hollywood was in an unenviable position during the first winter of war. Its studios faced dismal economic forecasts, made pictures that angered powerful politicians, reeled from charges of harboring communists, and struggled to settle on a workable foreign policy. One correspondent noted that "while Hollywood has always been given to hysteria over its own plight, it is probable that the industry never faced blacker days."[31]

Executives also spent the winter searching for an end to the Justice Department's antitrust suit. Although the Commerce Department's negotiations with Thurman Arnold's staff continued, prospects for a settlement were dim. Arnold's men stubbornly held that "the evils of the industry can never be permanently eliminated until there is complete separation of exhibition from the production and distribution branches." In January 1940 the government appointed Judge Henry Goddard, a veteran jurist well versed in antitrust issues, to preside over the upcoming trial. Major studios expected to spend between $6 and $8 million on defense lawyers. Nobody in Hollywood seemed to be taking charge. Will Hays, the industry's putative leader, offered only unconvincing platitudes about fixing trade problems through self-regulation. Preparations for a trial continued through the spring, as did the Commerce Department's talks with the Justice Department. Divorcement remained the sticking point.[32]

"The tide seems to be running very strongly against us," Commerce Department representative E. A. Tupper told Harry Hopkins in April. In reality, the tide was running against Arnold, who could not match Hopkins's influence with Roosevelt. On a grander scale the course of the New Deal was flowing in Hopkins's direction. After a noisy start, the president's antimonopoly crusade quieted to a desultory hum. The much-anticipated Temporary National Economic Committee hearings produced little public excitement and no solutions to the monopoly problem. In the wake of the 1937–38 Roosevelt recession, many New Dealers now looked to prime the economy by increasing government spending rather than dismantling monopolies. Wartime economics played an important role in this shift, as the nascent defense buildup tightened the government's relationship with big business, making it harder to gain momentum for trustbusting.[33]

Recognizing his deteriorating position, Arnold joined forces with industry nemesis Matthew Neely in spring 1940, just as Hopkins reengaged in the antitrust fight. Motivated in part by the *Mr. Smith Goes to Washington* uproar, the anti-block-booking senator introduced a bill requiring producers to sell their theaters within eighteen months or else face heavy fines and possible jail terms. E. A. Tupper scribbled "this appears to be Sen[ator] Neely's notice that he is against any settlement" across his copy of the bill. Hays saw Arnold behind this new attack. The lawyer declined to accept responsibility, but his statements before a Senate judiciary subcommittee conducting hearings on the bill—a subcommittee comprising Neely and one other senator—suggest his involvement. Blasting Hollywood for causing "interminable delays" in reaching a settlement, Arnold used his testimony to promote divorcement as the only way to break the majors' monopoly.[34]

Hays organized the industry's resistance, dispatching attorney C. C. Pettijohn and industry lobbyist Jack Bryson to work their contacts. Senate Interstate and Foreign Commerce Committee clerk Elton Layton quietly cooperated with the MPPDA, offering an insider's perspective on the proceedings. Although Hays's counterattack and the waning of the imbroglio surrounding *Mr. Smith Goes to Washington* helped to shelve the bill, Arnold obviously intended to hold his position to the bitter end.[35]

A gloomy mood surrounded Hollywood as the June 3 trial date neared. The moguls felt betrayed by Arnold's criticism of their arrangement with the Commerce Department. They could not understand his intransigence in the face of the war's economic dislocations. In their eyes Arnold's reckless obsession threatened a patriotic, proadministration industry. "The whole structure of this essential business, with its 300,000 employees and billion dollar box office business is in jeopardy," Hays complained, "and yet it is subjected to this harassment in spite of its course during the last 2 years to do everything possible to work out an arrangement with its government."[36]

These were troubling times for Hollywood. Angry congressmen, red scares, economic difficulties, and a half-benevolent, half-vindictive government plagued studio heads. To varying degrees these problems all sprang from a war the United States was scrupulously avoiding. Hollywood bosses felt like Dorothy Gale, a troubled Kansas farm girl whose hopes for escape touched movie audiences even as political and economic tornadoes touched down that winter. She sang of a magical land "over the rainbow," where troubles melted "like lemon drops." She sought the freedom to fly from her troubles, the power to dispatch her worries with a song.

Movies had peddled such fantasies for years. But there were no wish-granting stars in the real world, the world of guns, money, and politics. Filmmakers had to face their problems, not flee them. They approached their foreign and domestic difficulties as both businessmen and idealists, their thoughts divided between gold and country. When it came to film content, they recognized that their productions needed to more clearly reflect those dark times. If done properly, pictures that addressed contemporary issues without alienating important constituencies could serve their economic needs, by performing well at the box office and confirming Hollywood's ties to Washington, as well as their ideological needs, by proving their industry's cultural relevancy and striking blows against dictatorship. Whether for one cause or another, Hollywood executives needed to change their cinematic directions. Their hearts and their wallets depended on it.

CHAPTER ELEVEN

Leading the Way

ஓ ஓ ஓ

A UDIENCES DO NOT GO to the movies out of habit or just to pass the time," Darryl F. Zanuck scolded Twentieth Century–Fox producers in early 1940. "They *only* go when there is something playing that they definitely *want* to see. . . . Not the greatest cast in the world can make them go to see a subject that they don't like." Throughout Hollywood's winter of troubles, the content of the silver screen suggested that audiences did not want to see the war. Dorothy dreamed of going home in *The Wizard of Oz*. Nick and Nora Charles cracked a murder mystery and a few bottles of booze in *Another Thin Man*. Charles Laughton nearly equaled Lon Chaney's interpretation of *The Hunchback of Notre Dame*. The silver screen's apparent disjuncture from the front page was deceptive. Feature films were like babies, not just in a creative sense but also chronologically. It took a mother-studio about nine months to move a film from conception to delivery. Any war-related picture appearing in early 1940 had to be in production in summer 1939, months before the invasion of Poland. Most studios were not so reckless as to anticipate a conflict, guess at the parties involved, or imagine how Americans would respond to it.[1]

Producers' understandable lack of foresight left the war-movie field open to Warner Bros. *Confessions of a Nazi Spy* committed the studio to a propreparedness, anti-Nazi slant, and *The Dawn Patrol* demonstrated Warners' interest in the combat genre. Harry and Jack Warner released a number of films during the first months of the European war that furthered their self-appointed mission of alerting Americans to overseas dangers. Warners set *Espionage Agent, Murder in the Air,* and *The Fighting 69th* in motion while its competitors sat on the sidelines. As executives green-lighted these pictures during peacetime, Adolf Hitler's invading armies, not the Warner brothers, made them wartime pictures.

Filmed during the summer of 1939, *Espionage Agent* reiterated the warnings embodied in *Confessions of a Nazi Spy,* placing the earlier film's theme of destruction from within at center stage once again. The conventional narrative style of *Espionage Agent* robbed it of the documentary veracity of *Confessions of a Nazi Spy,* but the fortuitous timing of its release—it appeared about six weeks after fighting began in Europe—lent it an immediacy that *Confessions of a Nazi Spy* could not match. The picture wasted no time in establishing its relevance to audiences. It opens in 1915, with Europe at war and the United States at peace. Americans' disinterest in domestic security allows saboteurs to run wild. Foreign agents plant bombs in munitions plants, warehouses, factories, and mines. The secretary of state (Edwin Stanley) implores a complacent Congress to pass strong counterespionage laws. "Will we as a nation ever learn the difference between tolerance and stupidity?" he fumes. America's failure to crack down on spies leads to more attacks, whipping up an antiforeign fever that contributes to U.S. intervention in the Great War.

Following this introductory segment, *Espionage Agent* jumps to the present, quickly reestablishing its theme of vigilance against foreign operatives as another war looms. It does this through lionizing the State Department—not a bad idea considering the agency's work on Hollywood's behalf. Barry Corvall (Joel McCrea) is a minor department official, the son of a career foreign service agent who had joined the calls for action twenty-five years earlier. Corvall has apparently failed to embrace his father's alertness, as his new bride, a European refugee named Brenda Ballard (Brenda Marshall), is actually a spy. *Espionage Agent* never says where Brenda comes from, though the fact that she reports to the highly Teutonic Karl Müller (Martin Kosleck, fresh from his turn as Joseph Goebbels in *Confessions of a Nazi Spy*) rather gives away the secret.

Corvall spends the bulk of the picture uncovering his wife's deceitful past and—shades of 1915—unraveling a spy network infiltrating American war industries. Along the way *Espionage Agent* becomes an advertisement for Roosevelt's armed neutrality strategy and a critique of staunch isolationists. "Isolation is a political policy and not a brick wall around the nation," declares fellow foreign service agent Dud Garrett (George Bancroft). "What's the use of defending our American rights abroad if no one bothers to defend them at home?" Corvall asks as he ponders his countrymen's indifference to domestic spy rings. Should the nation go to war, "it will be because of those human ostriches who keep their heads buried in the sand." Such calls for the United States to head off foreign threats implied a nationalist agenda that stopped well short of endorsing action overseas. It followed the spirit of the recently signed Declaration of Panama, in which twenty-one American republics insulated themselves from war by banning belligerent naval activities within three hundred miles of their shores.[2]

The stilted language and confusing plot of *Espionage Agent* impressed neither theatergoers nor critics. Its clunky story accounted for most negative reviews, but some critics saw larger problems with it. *New Republic*'s Otis Ferguson wondered whether such a proneutrality production might actually lead the nation to war. Like other liberals, Ferguson had long criticized Hollywood for ignoring contemporary events. Now that the tide was shifting, he fretted that studios were becoming *too* contemporary. He compared the picture to a newspaper headline written by Churchill or another British hawk. Its demand that Americans prepare for Germany's inevitable machinations might prompt violent anti-Nazism. "First thing you know," he wrote, "the more impressionable are going to want to get out and kill somebody."[3]

Such concerns did not slow Warners' drive to showcase armed neutrality. Ferguson's piece appeared as the studio was shooting *Murder in the Air* (1940). Originally titled "Uncle Sam Awakens," then "The Enemy Within," the fourth in a series of B movies starring Ronald Reagan as Secret Service agent Brass Bancroft brought *Espionage Agent*'s message to a Saturday-matinee audience. The service assigns Bancroft to recover stolen plans for the navy's Inertia Projector, a defensive weapon that will make the United States "the greatest force for world peace ever." When operational, the device will emit electrical currents capable of stalling enemy ships and knocking planes from the sky long before they reach America's coasts. *Murder in the Air* includes a nod to Congressman Martin Dies, as it notes that the "Rice Committee on Un-American Activities" was closing in on the leader of the espionage gang that stole the blueprints. After some exciting fistfights and dogfight scenes guaranteed to thrill young theatergoers, Bancroft succeeds in his mission. American forces destroy the spies' plane and the stolen blueprints, guaranteeing that the United States will maintain sole possession of the Inertia

Projector. Bancroft's triumph places the final brick in an impregnable Fortress America. The country will never again be dragged into a foreign war.[4]

Warners' fascination with spy stories also produced such features as *Code of the Secret Service* (1939), another Brass Bancroft flick, and *British Intelligence* (1940), which starred Boris Karloff as a German agent operating in London during World War I. As with *Espionage Agent* and *Murder in the Air,* both intended to rouse Americans to the threat of enemy subversion. *Code of the Secret Service* has Bancroft busting up a ring of foreign agents who flood the United States with counterfeit currency. *British Intelligence* is a far more interesting film, even if Warners' did make it on the cheap—the studio snipped the picture's aerial footage from previous releases, including some it had already reused in *The Dawn Patrol.* Besides having some nice twists and a typically creepy performance from Karloff, *British Intelligence* drew direct parallels between Germany under the Kaiser and Germany under Hitler. "We have but one objective: to win the war," declares one helmet-wearing, waxed-mustachioed German officer, "even if we have to fight the entire world! No nation, no group of nations can stop our advance, and the advance of German culture. We are destined to conquer the world! If our Kaiser's taken from us, a new leader will arise. I may not live to see it, but someday, someday, Germany will own the world!"[5]

Though not war pictures, these inexpensive, minor features assumed contemporary relevance because they appeared during wartime and pushed American theatergoers to strenuously defend their national liberties. *The Fighting 69th* (1940) approached war from a different perspective. In continuing *The Dawn Patrol*'s revival of the world war genre, the picture exposed audiences to the grim realities awaiting should the United States actually enter the current fight. It straddled the divided sentiments of a nation opposed to war yet doubtful that it could avoid it. The depictions of trench warfare in *The Fighting 69th* matched the intensity of the harshest scenes in *The Big Parade* and *All Quiet on the Western Front,* validating the pacifist argument that war was a horrific thing. At the same time, its call for national unity and a commitment to a cause that transcends self-interest spoke directly to a country debating the domestic consequences of European totalitarianism. While trying to please everyone, *The Fighting 69th* feels like a wartime movie.

Its balancing act paid off, as it racked up more than $2 million in ticket sales against costs of just over $900,000.[6]

The 69th New York Infantry was one of America's legendary regiments. Initially a militia unit during the Revolutionary War, an influx of immigrants lent the 69th a heavily Irish flavor through its service in the Civil War and Spanish-American War. It acquitted itself well in France during the Great War, gaining further renown for the bravery of its "fighting chaplain," Francis Duffy, who coolly performed his ministerial duties under heavy fire during the Meuse-Argonne offensive. Recognizing the cinematic potential in such drama, both Warner Bros. and Twentieth Century–Fox, Hollywood's two most politicized studios, vied for the movie rights. Jack Warner's long-standing enmity toward Darryl F. Zanuck lent a hard edge to negotiations. At one point Warner accused his former employee of resorting to Nazi tactics.[7]

Warners had an unexpected ally in the dispute. William "Wild Bill" Donovan, who commanded the 69th during the war, suggested the studio outflank Fox by staging a reunion dinner for the unit. Donovan addressed the New York gathering, lauding Warner Bros.' patriotism and ability to make truthful, respectful war films. At his suggestion, attendees signed waivers granting Warner Bros. the exclusive right to depict them onscreen, threatening legal action against Fox if Zanuck proceeded with his proposal for "Father Duffy of the Sixty Ninth." Checkmated, Zanuck abandoned his project after Warners gave him a settlement check for $15,000, roughly half of Fox's preproduction costs.[8]

Warners cast James Cagney as Jerry Plunkett, a self-absorbed lone wolf who rejects army discipline, his peers, and his Irish Catholic roots. One of *The Fighting 69th*'s screenwriters, Norman Reilly Raine, described Plunkett as having "no friends, no faith, no illusions, and an appallingly complete disbelief in spiritual grace." Cagney was a smart choice, given that he had already perfected his outsider, tough-guy image in such films as *The Public Enemy* (1931), *Taxi!* (1932), and *The Roaring Twenties* (1939). His performance in *The Fighting 69th* had a gritty authenticity that no other actor could have matched. It was almost inevitable that Pat O'Brien would play Francis Duffy. O'Brien was to military movies what C. Aubrey Smith was to British Empire films. His performances in *Here Comes the Navy* (1934), *Devil Dogs of the Air* (1935), and *Submarine D-1* (1937) established his persona as a gentle yet determined father figure who steered troubled young men down the path of righteousness.[9]

Cagney and O'Brien represent polar opposites in *The Fighting 69th*. Their antagonistic relationship was familiar to moviegoers who had watched them tangle in *Ceiling Zero* (1936) and *Angels with Dirty Faces* (1938). Plunkett demonstrates the damage a reckless malcontent can inflict on the community. Duffy tries to integrate the maverick into the group by appealing to Plunkett's religious roots, the Irish Catholic heritage so important to the regiment's rich history. Plunkett is uninterested in Duffy's ministering. "I can take care of myself," he snaps after the chaplain describes the protective powers of the saints. The untested private is full of big talk about his eagerness to see battle but turns tail when the actual shooting starts. His cowardice disgraces the group and, worse, causes the deaths of several comrades. The army court-martials him, sentencing him to death for dereliction of duty. Plunkett, a proud, stubborn individualist, is now truly alone. His peers are indifferent to his fate, never deigning to comment on his impending execution.

In contrast to Plunkett, Father Duffy serves as the center of the community, evidence that the army can create harmony from discord. Soldiers rise respectfully when he enters. His priestly presence calms their nerves when they face heavy fire. Duffy's Catholicism poses no barrier to group unity—he supplements his masses with Protestant services for the regiment's non-Catholics. His all-embracing version of Catholicism trumps the 69th's religious, ethnic, and regional divisions. Although largely Irish, the regiment consists of the smorgasbord of stereotypes that populated the screen throughout World War II. The New York City brat, the southerner, and the WASP-y New Englander serve alongside the Sons of Erin without causing friction. "You know, Colonel," Duffy tells Donovan (George Brent), "if a lot of the people back home knew how well the various faiths got along together over here, it would cause a lot of scandal to some biased minds." On Christmas Eve the 69th—minus Plunkett—joins Duffy for an inspired version of "Silent Night." Soldiers' separate voices blend into a pitch-perfect whole that soars above sectarian disputes, transforming the uniformed many into a seamless one.

Duffy stands at the head of a competent, compassionate military establishment. Colonel Donovan pushes his regiment hard because he knows the terrible challenges awaiting them in Europe. "War is a brutal business," he confides to the priest. "These kids of mine are going up against veterans, schooled in three years of war." Such sentiments pervaded the service films of the 1930s, but they assume a greater significance here. Donovan's troops are preparing for war, not maneuvers, a target competition, or a football game. To be unready is to die.

Duffy and Donovan face another challenge when the 4th Alabama joins the 69th's division. Old scars rip open as soon as the regiments come together. New Yorkers mock southerners as cornpone-eating rednecks and taunt them for losing the Civil War. Alabamians fire back; their unit decimated the 69th at Fredericksburg in 1862. Their verbal sparring swiftly devolves into a brawl that Duffy and Donovan resolve with a nationalistic plea for sectional reconciliation. "Those men on both sides were Americans," Donovan shouts. "They fought, and then rose above their hatreds to become one people again. And that's the way it should be!" North and South now belong to the same division, a Rainbow Division. "There's no room in this rainbow for sectional feuds," Donovan tells them, "because we're all one nation now, one team. An all-American team pulling together, and known as the United States Army."

In a pointed jab at Hitler's Nazi squad, *The Fighting 69th* contends that real Americans shun anti-Semitism as well as sectionalism. The 69th's "Private Mike Murphy" is actually Mischa Moskowitz, a Yiddish-speaking New Yorker who so respected the regiment's traditions that he signed up under an assumed name. Moskowitz/Murphy (Sammy Cohen) has the prominent nose and dark complexion of a stereotyped Eastern European Jew, yet none of his comrades appear to notice, or care, that he is as Irish as the Kaiser. He even participates in Duffy's interfaith church services.

Moskowitz represents a revival of *The Jazz Singer*'s dream of assimilation. His Americanization makes him a hybrid of the Jewish Harry Warner and the Irish Joseph Breen, proof that Jews are loyal Americans willing to sacrifice for their country. A German bullet finds the soldier, who gasps for breath as Duffy ministers to him. The chaplain's prayer slips seamlessly into a Hebrew chant as Moskowitz dies. In a sense Father Duffy completes what Jack Robin began back in 1927. Al Jolson's pairing of the Kol Nidre with "Mammy" was a request for the mainstream to accept Jews. Duffy's merging of Christian and Jewish rites was America's affirmative answer. At least in Warners' world the crucible of war forged a more tolerant nation. Although the Rainbow Division's lily-white racial makeup implies that tolerance does not yet extend to African Americans, Duffy's actions hold out hope that a noble crusade can create a morally righteous United States.

Complete resolution requires that the defiant Plunkett incorporate himself into the regiment. Both the soldier and the 69th appear doomed after his court-martial. Their fates are intertwined; he languishes in prison as enemy shells pin down the unit in its camp. Duffy frees Plunkett amid the chaos, allowing him to choose between a perilous road to escape and an equally dangerous commitment to the regiment. Plunkett's first instinct is to save himself. Then he watches Donovan hopping from crater to crater, inspiring his men to keep moving, soothing the wounded by reciting the Lord's Prayer with them. Such bravery leads Plunkett to a conversion experience. He throws himself into the action, commandeering a mortar to single-handedly reverse the German offensive. He completes his redemption by diving on a grenade, sacrificing himself to save his brothers in arms. Plunkett's courage marks his true integration into the 69th's patriotic crusade. The dying soldier's humble acceptance of last rites from Father Duffy marks his return to the church he once ridiculed.

These final sequences brought home the horrors of war. Plunkett's valor occurs amid destruction that ensnares civilians and soldiers alike. Duffy's closing plea for peace rounds out the film's antiwar message. "They accepted privation, wounds, and death, that an ideal might live," he says of his fallen warriors. "Don't let it be forgotten, Father. Amid turmoil and angry passions, when all worthwhile things seem swept away, let the tired eyes of a troubled world rise up and see the shining citadel of which these young lives formed the imperishable stones. America, and the citadel of peace, peace forever more." Plunkett's ghostly image appears as Duffy speaks, snapping to attention out of respect for the chaplain's words. World War I veterans found the homily so moving that some requested copies of the text from Warners.[10]

Studio executives saw *The Fighting 69th* as another chance to make the case for a Fortress America strong enough to withstand the rising tides of conflict. After previewing the film at a second 69th reunion banquet, Jack Warner said he hoped the picture would "make this world just a little better place to live in." He expressed the same sentiment to Stephen Early, who secured a print for a White House screening. At the same time, the movie's glorification of courage under fire represented another example of Hollywood's ongoing domestication of all things martial. Although Congress had not yet imposed a draft, *The Fighting 69th* gave future inductees images of what was to come, from training camp to battlefield. When taken alongside the service films and other recent World War I dramas, it contributed to a comforting familiarity with war itself. Although brutal, war was also noble, offering glory and manly camaraderie in the cause of liberty. Unlike *The Lost Patrol* and even *The Dawn Patrol,* war was meaningful in *The Fighting 69th*. It achieved a goal. This paradox—an antiwar cycle that promoted the virtues of war—offered Hollywood a middle ground that allowed for multiple interpretations of its features. It also exposed studios to attack from multiple perspectives. Critics simultaneously decried the rise of onscreen militarism and the industry's silence on global events. Hollywood could neither ignore the war nor escape charges of warmongering.[11]

To moviegoers alert enough to note which studio made a particular film, it appeared as if Warner Bros. was the only major paying attention to the outside world. Again, such an analysis missed the important fact that it took about nine months for films to move from concept to screen. Warners had a jump on its competitors, but Hollywood's true response to the European war could not be measured until the next cycle of projects reached fruition.

✺ ✺ ✺

Release of *The Fighting 69th* coincided with sweeping changes in the European war. As a result, the issues on Hollywood's mind—what to do about the war, how to be patriotic without appearing overly aggressive—increasingly entered the public mind. Hitler hastened his drive to unite Europe as Hollywood wobbled under the weight of domestic and international uncertainties. The Phony War lulled some into believing the combatants might reach a settlement. Hitler actually used the winter of 1939 to consolidate his hold on Poland while stepping up training and construction programs. He stalled for time by dangling the possibility of negotiations before the French and British even as he secretly refined his plan to crush western Europe, a necessary prerequisite to gaining *lebensraum* from the Soviets. His tactics convinced some Americans of his peaceful intentions; the House Appropriations Committee voted in April 1940 to cut the military budget by almost 10 percent.[12]

The dam collapsed with the spring thaws. German forces assaulted Norway and Denmark just as the House of Representatives considered economizing U.S. armed forces. Hitler's twin strikes caught the Norwegians and Danes unprepared and hit complacent Americans like thunderbolts. Britain's and France's ineffectual response suggested that no one could halt the Nazi juggernaut. The move left Greenland and Iceland, two strategically located islands with ties to Denmark, vulnerable. If the Germans picked them off, Hitler's minions would be only a hop away from American shores. "Old dreams of universal empire are again rampant," President Roosevelt observed. "We know that what happens in the Old World directly and powerfully affects the peace and well-being of the New."[13]

Germany's offensive was just beginning. Dawn broke on May 10, 1940, to find Nazi troops pouring through Luxembourg into Belgium and Holland. The Benelux nations' failure to coordinate their defenses with the powers to the west dashed whatever faint hope the Allies had of stalling the offensive before it crossed into France. Holland capitulated on May 15, Belgium less than two weeks later. By that time the Nazis had dashed through the Ardennes and plunged deep into France. French troops sat behind the Maginot Line as the Germans flew past their left flank on the way to Paris. The British Expeditionary Force found itself trapped between the ocean and the German steamroller. It took a motley fleet of naval, merchant, and private ships to rescue the soldiers, along with some of their French comrades, in the final days of May and first days of June. The new prime minister, Winston Churchill, saw the Dunkirk evacuation as miraculous. He also suspected that those who escaped might soon be defending the home islands against a German invasion.[14]

The "miracle" at Dunkirk did nothing to slow the German advance toward the French capital, but it did give Americans hope that the British could hold out. More immediately, the shift from "sitzkrieg" to blitzkrieg exposed glaring shortcomings in the United States' defense efforts. Germany had some 2 million troops in the western theater alone. The United States could muster only around eighty thousand in mid-May.

Roosevelt asked for $1.18 billion in supplemental defense appropriations to enlarge the army and air force. Congress gave him $1.5 billion and then another $5 billion a few months later. In all, the War Department's budget more than quintupled from 1939 to 1940.[15]

Germany's invasion of France spurred American interventionists into action. May 1940 saw the creation of the Committee to Defend America by Aiding the Allies. William Allen White, the well-respected editor of the *Emporia Gazette,* headed the group. The committee saw a British victory over the Axis as essential to the United States' long-term security. It stopped short of advocating direct involvement, instead urging the government to deliver more financial and military aid to Hitler's opponents. White's committee also served as a clearinghouse for interventionist propaganda, published flyers and pamphlets, put on radio shows, and staged public rallies. Although not purely a Roosevelt front, it maintained frequent contact and a relative unity of purpose with the administration.[16]

Hitler's actions also infused isolationists with new resolve. Charles Lindbergh informed a national radio audience that the Nazis posed no threat to the United States even as the Germans rolled through France. Lindbergh proposed that because the oceans made a properly secured America invulnerable to European hostilities, the country should focus on building up its air defenses rather than ship valuable materiel overseas. Lindbergh's speech left Roosevelt sputtering. "It could not have been better put if it had been written by Goebbels himself," he told reporters.[17]

Jack and Harry Warner had their own response to Lindbergh's talk. They wired the president the day after the broadcast to encourage him to take a stronger stand against his critics and to contact them should he have any story ideas that might help promote his policies. Warners cherished democracy and Americanism, they explained, and the brothers stood ready demonstrate "the worthiness of the causes for which the free peoples of Europe are making such tremendous sacrifices." Although Jack was an especially gifted composer of brown-nosing missives, this offer was more than mere Warner bluster. Their desire to help was sincere, their desire to serve palpable.[18]

Roosevelt remained mum on the Warners' proposal, but his address to Congress a few days later suggested that the president shared their sense of immediacy. He spoke in vivid terms of a "Fifth Column that betrays a nation unprepared for treachery," an enemy seemingly torn from the script of *Confessions of a Nazi Spy* or *Espionage Agent*. America's new foe used unconventional tactics that defied traditional methods of maintaining domestic tranquility. "Spies, saboteurs and traitors are the actors in this new strategy," Roosevelt warned. These treacherous forces used "false slogans and emotional appeals" to sow dissention, leaving nations unable to unite when totalitarian armies marched against them. The battle for American minds had begun in earnest. While not naming names, Roosevelt's oration branded isolationists like Lindbergh as either naive or disloyal while casting his own internationalism as the preferred course of any right-minded patriot.[19]

The president's speech motivated *Variety* to challenge Hollywood to lead the counterattack against internal foes. Such a charge suited the industry's material as well as its ideological purposes. "The screens of the nation cry for the right messages," the paper claimed. Millions of theatergoers yearned for movies offering "truth and high-minded leadership." Hesitation would enable saboteurs to spread confusion, weaken defense programs, and sap the nation's strength.[20]

Variety's fusillade reeked of me-tooism. Its reference to the "restrictive and annoying" antitrust suit gave its militant rhetoric the feel of a quid pro quo. Behind the scenes, however, studios had already mobilized against subversives. Universal sponsored the "Univets," a group of 174 employees, all veterans, who patrolled the studio for anything "smacking of Fifth Columnism." "The Univets are against every kind of an 'ism' except one: Americanism," studio chief Cliff Work bragged. Although Univets had "quiet and definite ways of handling situations," Work noted, they were not the paramilitary goon squad they appeared to be, as they were "careful not to be unfair or persecute anyone who is merely suspected without good evidence."[21]

Harry Warner saw Hollywood and Washington moving in his direction. He approved of the Univets and saw the president's tough talk as a call to arms worth repeating. He saw himself as the man to do it. On June 5 some six thousand people—mostly Warners workers and their families, along with a sizable contingent from other studios—gathered in Burbank. After singing "The Star-Spangled Banner," the assembly heard Warner deliver a ninety-minute lecture from a soundstage. The pugnacious executive described his travels in Europe the previous fall, his voice rising with emotion as he recounted conversations with Danes, Norwegians, and Frenchmen who scoffed at the idea of internal enemies rendering their countries vulnerable to attack. Warner implored the audience to report disloyal citizens, suspicious characters, and potential spies to the Justice Department, noting with horror that he had even found Nazi propaganda stuck to cars in his studio's parking lot. He also encouraged employees to improve their marksmanship at the Warners Rifle and Pistol Club in case the Germans invaded California.[22]

Warner asserted that his company's Americanism grew from unselfish motives. He claimed that *Juarez* convinced Mexicans to shun radical ideologies, reaffirmed his commitment to money-losing patriotic shorts, and announced a $25,000 donation to buy twenty ambulances for France and Britain. But now, he continued, was not the time to rest on past achievements. As part of Warner's Americanization campaign, his company would no longer hire members of the German-American Bund, the Communist Party, or any other outfit he deemed un-American. "If any person likes those reprehensible foreign doctrines so well let him go back there," he thundered in ungrammatical anger.

Warner closed his address with an exploration of the role of faith in the United States. He saw religion as both the nation's greatest common denominator and its greatest potential divider. "It is time that we drop racial and religious prejudices and unite for the well-being and security of all true Americans," he declared. To do otherwise was to embrace Nazi ideology. Taking the first step toward reconciliation, he told the crowd he was proud to be a Jew but saw "no finer faith in the world than Christianity." From this point forward, Warner Bros. would ask all job applicants whether they had a religious faith. His secular brother might struggle to answer the question truthfully. What specific church one favored was unimportant. To have no church, however, was unforgivable.

Here was Jack Robin again, peeking out from over the mogul's shoulder. The Jew desired acceptance into a Christian country; the newcomer sought the approval of those who arrived before him. A later generation might call Warner's sermon McCarthyesque. Its visions of foreign agents and radical ideologies boring into America anticipated arguments that would be made ten years later. Its simultaneous call for religious tolerance (we accept all faiths) and religious discrimination (except agnostics and atheists) mirrored the logic of a nation gripped by cold war hysteria. Warner would have dismissed these complaints. In his mind too much was at stake—"our very lives and those of our children and of their children"—to worry about such niceties. This was Hollywood's great chance to positively influence global affairs, its golden opportunity to win America's respect.

Warner wanted his June 5 address to resonate long after the final echoes of "God Bless America" died down. He distributed copies of the speech to every Warner Bros. employee in the world, from Burbank-based executives to ticket takers in Schenectady to stagehands in Teddington. Roosevelt received one, as did Martin Dies, other members of Congress, and American Legionnaires. Newspapers and the trade press ran front-page stories about the talk. Approving letters poured in from around the country. Warner had taken a risk in making such bold statements. His wife worried that Nazi sympathizers might kill him for expressing them. On a broader level, and more realistically, his actions invited charges of propagandizing or warmongering that might financially wound his beloved studio.[23]

Warner's audacity brought no such consequences. Talk of personal peril reflected Harry's sense of martyrdom more than any actual danger. Although bluntly stated, his sentiments were within the mainstream of public opinion. Calls for national unity upheld traditional conceptions of America's responsibilities ending at the nation's shorelines. Warner's speech accomplished exactly what he had hoped—it reaffirmed the industry's pro-Roosevelt stance and got the country thinking about dangers from within. It also confirmed him as Hollywood's number-one patriot and transformed Warner Bros. into a West Coast version of Boston's Old North Church. Its warning beacons had illuminated dark movie theaters for a year, summoning cinematic Minute Men to arms in defense of the republic. Now, before it was too late, was the time for more concrete actions to preserve democracy and Americanism.

Reinforcements were on the way. Nine months had passed since the fall of Poland. Armies were on the move in Europe. The Roosevelt administration wanted partners in its defense campaign. June 1940 was going to be an interesting month.

CHAPTER TWELVE

The Pivotal Month

❧ ❧ ❧

HARRY WARNER'S ORATION of June 5, 1940, came amid a brief spate of optimism that Great Britain might survive its showdown with Hitler. Americans' sagging hopes for the British revived with the "miracle" at Dunkirk. Prime Minister Winston Churchill celebrated his army's escape with a rousing, soon-to-be-famous speech to the House of Commons that appeared in American newspapers the same day Warner spoke. "We shall fight in France," Churchill growled. "We shall fight on the seas and oceans, we shall fight . . . in the air, we shall defend our Island, whatever the cost may be, we shall fight on the beaches, we shall fight on the landing grounds, we shall fight in the fields and in the streets, we shall fight in the hills; we shall never surrender."[1]

Churchill's brave talk lifted flagging spirits at home and abroad, but words could not reverse the German divisions pushing closer to Paris every day. Norway collapsed on June 10, the same day Italy declared war on Britain and France. Mussolini's step incensed President Roosevelt. "The hand that held the dagger has stuck it into the back of its neighbor," he said during a commencement address at the University of Virginia. Italy's action finally ended Hollywood's efforts to sneak back into the market by negotiating an alternative to the ENIC monopoly.[2]

France's collapse less than two weeks later caused a panic in the United States. "We must now face the unpalatable fact that we are no longer an isolated continent," wrote Edward Mead Earle in the *Ladies' Home Journal*. Despite Churchill's bravura, Roosevelt gave Britain a "one in three" chance of carrying on alone. Americans heard talk of instituting a draft and whispered rumors that the Nazis were preparing to cross the Atlantic Ocean. The president fielded reports of German-backed coups brewing throughout South and Central America. Such threats exaggerated reality but were dire enough that Roosevelt bulked up the United

States' naval presence in the region. Congress approved massive new expenditures in July that doubled the navy's tonnage. Just as Harry Warner hoped, the country was preparing its defenses.[3]

The Third Republic's demise wiped the continent nearly clean of Hollywood fare. Paris's movie houses fell under Germany's restrictive censorship system. Unoccupied France's collaborationist Vichy government also excluded American pictures. This latest blow left the moguls despondent. While France had only a slight financial impact on Hollywood before June 1940, the country's defeat served as an additional reminder of the industry's desperate economic situation. "Only an early peace, with England retaining control of the British Isles would help remedy a dismal outlook for overseas distribution," *Variety* said. From Hollywood's perspective, the sole scrap of good news was that the Nazi invasion left French theaters virtually untouched. American studios could easily return to the market should the Germans be expelled. A bombed-out Europe, on the other hand, meant years of rebuilding and poor grosses.[4]

Film Daily Year Book claimed there was "not a foreign department executive who does not look upon the immediate future with pessimism." Overseas income was off by half and total revenues down 20 percent. There was little hope of reversing the trend in the foreseeable future, and no one knew what to do about it. Will Hays meekly suggested that the answer to Hollywood's woes was "good entertainment."[5]

With the continent lost, Hollywood needed Great Britain more than ever. Hitler also had the island nation in his sights but with far more aggressive intentions. His *Luftwaffe* initiated the Battle of Britain on July 10 when it struck at ports along the English Channel. Churchill insisted that the Anglo people were about to have "their finest hour." Most Americans believed the Anglo people had entered their final hours. The prime minister privately feared the same, telling Roosevelt his country was doomed unless the United States provided more aid, particularly destroyers. American military assistance was "a matter of life or death," Churchill insisted.[6]

Hollywood did what little it could to help. Warners relocated two thousand children of its British employees to the United States. Bundles for Britain, a rummage shop on Sunset Boulevard that donated its profits to British charities, stepped up efforts to collect money, clothes, and other useful items. The British War Relief Association, comprising such transplants as Ronald Colman, Cedric Hardwicke, Alfred Hitchcock, Laurence Olivier, Basil Rathbone, and C. Aubrey Smith, also launched a donation drive.[7]

Calls for closer collaboration between Hollywood and Washington bore fruit with the creation of the Motion Picture Committee Cooperating for the National Defense (MPCC) on June 5, just hours before Harry Warner bared his patriotism for the world to see. The outfit became major studios' primary liaison with the military, an official connection that supplanted the informal feelers of the previous two years. Its creation marked the moment when preparedness became a sanctioned, industry-wide concern rather than the ad hoc fixation of Hollywood progressives. The MPCC's high-powered membership indicated its importance to executives eager to assist the defense effort but unsure of how much they could do before triggering a public backlash. Harry Warner joined, as did Paramount's Barney Balaban and Y. Frank Freeman, Columbia's Harry Cohn, MGM's Eddie Mannix and Nicholas Schenck, Fox's Darryl F. Zanuck and Sidney Kent, RKO's George Schaefer, Universal's Nate Blumberg, Screen Actors Guild president Edward Arnold, Screen Directors Guild president Frank Capra, Academy of Motion Picture Arts and Sciences president Walter Wanger, and Will Hays.[8]

The MPCC evolved from Hollywood's long-standing association with the Army Signal Corps. The corps initiated the relationship in 1930 as a way to professionalize its Motion Picture Division. Every year it assigned one soldier to Hollywood for training in the fundamentals of moviemaking. Warner Bros. sound engineer Nathan Levinson acted as the industry's main contact with the army. Levinson knew the corps well, having served as a major in its Photographic Division during World War I. Besides working for Warners, he also served as vice chairman of the Motion Picture Academy's little-known Research Council, which oversaw the Signal Corps program. Levinson set the recruit's schedule, arranging for him to perform various tasks with a number of major studios.[9]

Anticipating an increased workload in the event of war, the Signal Corps sought to expand its filmmaking abilities. In the fall of 1939 it began assembling a Hollywood-based unit it could quickly mobilize in an emergency. Colonel Richard Schlosberg, a 1933 graduate of the Hollywood training program who headed the corps' Motion Picture Division, led the effort. With Levinson's help he started signing up movie folk as second lieutenants or enlisted men in the 164th and 165th Photographic Companies. Warner Bros. executives winked as Levinson spent his working hours interviewing candidates instead of doing his job.[10]

Understanding the delicacy of their task, Levinson and Schlosberg proceeded cautiously. Levinson tried not to enroll people with heavy accents for fear of, as he explained it, ruining morale. He faced pressure from Zanuck, MGM troubleshooter Mendel Silberberg, and others not to incite American anti-Semitism by commissioning too many Jews. Harry Warner applied a different sort of pressure. Seeing stripes on a uniform as a symbol of status rather than as a symbol of meritorious service, Warner forced Levinson, his employee, to make his son-in-law, Fox producer Milton Sperling, a second lieutenant.[11]

The military's desire for an even closer bond with Hollywood ultimately resulted in the MPCC. Colonel Schlosberg and Major W. M. Wright of the Adjutant General's Office gathered studio heads at the Paramount lot in May 1940 to discuss the industry's cooperation with national defense. Executives balked at their lack of concrete proposals but listened because they believed in the cause and coveted the government's favor. Walter Wanger described his peers as "interested in doing everything possible to preserve our national unity." The group agreed to reconvene in New York to seek ways to fuse the industry's production, distribution, and exhibition wings into a harmonized machine that disseminated "the right type of information throughout the country."[12]

Thirty of Hollywood's most important men assembled on June 5 in New York's Union League Club. Over lunch, Wanger pitched a plan to unite producers, newsreel makers, exhibitors, distributors, and the trade press into a single committee that would transform requests from the War Department into onscreen messages that fit the military's needs. Major Ward Maris of Military Intelligence told the gathering that "it is . . . important to see that nothing gets into our pictures that tears down the foundation of proper defense for our country." After finishing their meals, Wanger, Sidney Kent, and Frank Freeman huddled to select the new committee's leadership. They chose Francis Harmon, Will Hays's executive assistant, as the MPCC's point man and then composed a statement pledging the "cooperation of the industry with Government plans for national defense."[13]

Exactly what that cooperation entailed was not immediately clear, but the MPCC nevertheless forged links between Harmon and the War Department, the State Department, and the Advisory Commission to the Council of National Defense, a blue-ribbon panel with no official portfolio but a great deal of influence over Roosevelt. One of Harmon's first tangible duties was to oversee the distribution of government-made shorts and recruiting trailers to more than nine thousand theaters. "The time is now opportune for every man, woman and child in the motion picture industry to lend themselves to this patriotic duty," Motion Picture Theatre Owners of America president Ed Kuykendall observed. At the MPCC's request, the distributing company Film Carriers, Inc., transported the celluloid for free.[14]

Hollywood's nebulous partnership with Washington assumed clearer form as 1940 wore on. Besides facilitating the flow of technical support from the film industry to the government, the MPCC asked studios to make short films that advanced the administration's priorities. Shot on a nonprofit basis, these one-reelers promoted Roosevelt's defense buildup or framed New Deal programs as crucial to the United States' democratic crusade. "Power for Defense," an homage to the Tennessee Valley Authority, began screening in February 1941. "America Preferred," which pitched war bonds, followed, along with "Army in Overalls," a puff-piece on the Civilian Conservation Corps, and twenty-two others. The MPCC also convinced studios to produce twelve recruiting trailers that arrived in theaters the same month "Power for Defense" appeared.[15]

Newsreels made up a pivotal part of the MPCC's agenda. Led by Paramount's E. B. Hatrick, executives from major newsreel companies gathered in Will Hays's office soon after the Union League Club luncheon to discuss ways to more effectively portray the national defense program. Such concern was largely unnecessary, as newsreels already focused intensely on military issues, but nevertheless reflected the industry's drive for total organization. The very nature of newsreels put them far ahead of feature films in terms of addressing foreign dangers. Henry Luce's The March of Time was particularly aggressive, following up "Inside Nazi Germany" with a succession of antifascist, war-themed episodes. Twenty-seven of the thirty-three March of Time issues released between the summer of 1939 and the winter of 1941 featured military or political subjects. Under the MPCC's guidance, newsreels also promoted the Treasury Department's War Bonds and Savings Stamps programs.[16]

Isolationists saw Hollywood's new commitment as another step toward a deluge of films aimed at tricking the public into going to war. To them, cooperating for national defense sounded like code for "propaganda films." William Randolph Hearst's *New York Journal and American* anticipated a cycle of "Communist propaganda, war propaganda, and alien propaganda of all kinds." Theater owners reported customer complaints that newsreels contained too many "marching hordes, wrecked cities and pitiful queues of refugees." Francis Harmon disagreed. As "the beneficiary of freedom," he wrote, Hollywood had an obligation to defend America during this crisis.[17]

Harmon's words reiterated what Hays and studio bosses had long insisted—that entertainment companies flourished in a capitalistic, free-enterprise system and floundered in un-democratic states. This logic justified self-regulation, government nonintervention, and open markets. Now, however, Hollywood's power brokers argued that studios must coordinate their goals with Washington's controversial overseas agenda in order to preserve their freedom.

Exactly how Hollywood would defend America onscreen remained unclear. With declining overseas revenues straining budgets, studios desperately wanted to strike box-office gold. Public tastes, however, were even harder to gauge than in peacetime. For every columnist who raised the cry of propaganda, another advised moviemakers to "roll up [their] shirt sleeves and get to work for Uncle Sam." War films were "definitely taboo" if only because it was tough to produce a relevant current-events feature. By the time Universal released *Ski Patrol* (1940), for example, the Russo-Finnish War it took as its setting had ended. *New York Times* reviewer Bosley Crowther advised producers to avoid making more pictures like *Ski Patrol* and *Women in War* (1940), Republic Studio's quickie feature about an American nurse in Britain. Such flimsy efforts demeaned the war's human cost, he argued. Crowther, for one, doubted studios would make any worthwhile war pictures before the conflict ended.[18]

Hollywood's problems extended beyond the screen. Last-ditch efforts to persuade Assistant Attorney General Thurman Arnold to sign a consent decree failed when studio lawyers again refused to concede on divorcement. The antitrust suit went to trial on June 3, 1940, two days before Harry Warner's speech and the Union League meeting. Attorneys converged on the United States Court House in lower Manhattan. The case was so sprawling, encompassing 133 defendants, forty-five corporations, and fifty-seven lawyers, that participants abandoned the building's lavishly wood-paneled, air-conditioned, thirteenth-floor courtroom in favor of larger but more rudimentary quarters on the first floor.[19]

Industry attorneys achieved a breakthrough a few days into the proceedings when they finally persuaded the Justice Department to abandon divestiture as a prerequisite to a consent decree. New Dealers' growing distaste for trust-busting, a by-product of the shift toward a wartime economy, contributed to Arnold's reversal, as did growing concerns that the government might not win the case. At best, the Justice Department expected the trial to drag on for six years before a final settlement in the Supreme Court. Studio lawyers declared victory even though details of the consent decree remained hazy. Accepting the ceasefire, Judge Henry Goddard postponed the trial after its first week. Negotiations with Justice Department lawyers assumed a leisurely pace that reflected Hollywood's confidence that only trivial differences separated the sides. The moguls had dodged a bullet.[20]

The Commerce Department proved key to preserving Hollywood's oligopoly. Harry Hopkins and his men understood the importance movies would hold in the event of fighting. They had no interest in antagonizing or weakening the industry during this moment of crisis. Such benevolence would have been unthinkable had studio heads not played ball with the administration. All the meetings, the glad-handing, the promises, the public declarations, and, above all, the generous onscreen treatment of Roosevelt's foreign priorities paid off. The war was a paradoxical creature. On the one hand, by choking off Hollywood's overseas markets, it pushed studios into filming subjects that might alienate customers. At the same time, by altering the government's fiscal and foreign policy, it changed the antitrust landscape and saved Hollywood as the moguls knew it.[21]

✿ ✿ ✿

June had been an eventful month for Hollywood. It saw the demise of the French market, the apparent end of the antitrust problem, and the creation of new bonds with Washington. But these were the concerns of corporate Hollywood, a realm unfamiliar to most Americans. Ordinary people paid attention to glittering stars and splashy premieres, not foreign income streams and political horse trading. Beyond the seats of national power, it was movies that counted. In contrast to the interstudio unity the MPCC promoted, as of June 1940 no other major had joined Warners' onscreen rebellion against the Nazis. Only a handful of films had taken Germany as their subject in recent years, and none of those had escaped the sterilizing influence of official German disapproval.

German consul Georg Gyssling intimidated Universal into moderating its rendition of *The Road Back* (1937), Erich Maria Remarque's sequel to *All Quiet on the Western Front*. Remarque's virulent anti-Nazism made him persona non grata in Germany. The Nazis banned his books in 1933 and stripped his citizenship in 1938. Gyssling's vague yet ominous threat that anyone involved in *The Road Back* would suffer unfortunate consequences sent the MPPDA howling to the State Department. Washington told the consul to back off even though it accepted his argument that Hollywood should not insult Germany. Gyssling later browbeat MGM into deleting references to Nazis and Jews from its version of Remarque's *Three Comrades* (1938). After listening to Gyssling's complaints, Production Code Administration head Joseph Breen implored Louis B. Mayer to approach *Three Comrades* from the "general standpoint of industry 'good and welfare' as a whole." MGM producers agreed, after a series of meetings with the PCA, that the film would do "nothing to indicate in any way that the story is a reflection on the Nazi government" by limiting its scope to the first few years after the armistice. Such caution resulted in two mediocre features that nevertheless performed well at the box office. *Three Comrades* turned nearly a half-million dollar profit.[22]

Europe's increasing irrelevance as a movie market removed some of the issues that had hampered not only *The Road Back* and *Three Comrades* but also *Idiot's Delight* and *It Can't Happen Here*. After its previous run-ins with the Germans, MGM seemed an unlikely candidate to join Warners in making explicitly anti-Nazi films. The reactionary Mayer preferred bucolic pleasantries to sober, topical pictures. "Controversial or newsy themes," *Fortune* magazine explained, "are regarded as pure poison in the Metro front office." But Mayer, who imagined himself a paternal figure, presided over a dysfunctional family. MGM staffers frequently clashed over the war. Politically inspired shouting matches were so common that progressives and conservatives ate lunch in separate areas of the commissary.[23]

Mayer's own position on the Nazis was as unpredictable as a Ray Bolger dance routine. In a 1938 St. Patrick's Day address he said, "I am a Jew, and I try to be a good one. In some lands, an increasing number, you are persecuted if you are a Jew; you cannot own anything, may not vote; you can be driven from your home, torn from the arms of your loved ones." A number of his studio's shorts included anti-Nazi messages. Yet MGM hosted pro-Nazi groups and, more tellingly, kept distributing films in Germany after the war began. Mayer was not a Nazi sympathizer, but neither did he want to incur their wrath.[24]

In the end Mayer saw things not as good or bad but as good or bad for MGM. His studio came above all else in his insular world. After Edward VIII abdicated the British throne in 1936, for example, Mayer considered hiring him as MGM's head of European operations simply because the ex-monarch might bring attention to the company. "What's he get?" Mayer asked story editor William Fadiman. "I don't want him to do anything; don't misunderstand me. I just want him to be the Prince of Wales." Once when Mayer was angry about protests from ethnic groups tired of being portrayed as heavies in his films, he whined, "Why can't we buy some country, for God's sake, so we can make the bastards who we want them to be?"[25]

Mayer's decision to purchase *The Mortal Storm* in mid-1939 came from the same inward-looking perspective. MGM's Victor Saville, a British-born, virulently anti-Nazi director, persuaded him to buy the rights to Phyllis Bottome's blockbuster novel about Nazism's devastating effect on a German family. More than ideological fervor, the prestige and profit possibilities of adapting a well-known novel motivated Mayer. MGM's synopsis of *The Mortal Storm* called it "not a book of propaganda, but a fair picture of the situation in Nazi Germany." Never a big reader, Mayer may not have fully understood the power of Bottome's searing indictment. *The Mortal Storm* and *Escape,* which Mayer green-lighted two weeks after the war in Europe began, would be MGM's strongest statements on Hitler's Germany prior to Pearl Harbor. Released in the pivotal month of June 1940, *The Mortal Storm* had an impact that *Escape,* which appeared several months later, could not equal. An enthusiastic *Variety* reviewer called it "a film bomb . . . a ringing challenge to the dogma that the sole function of films is to entertain."[26]

Understanding its potential impact on American popular opinion, German officials discouraged MGM from making *The Mortal Storm*. At one point during shooting a representative from the Swiss consulate relayed an oral message from the German government. The Nazis would remember this film after they won the war, he said. "I don't give a goddamn about what they were going to remember," shot back Robert Stack, who had a small part in this, his second film. Other crewmembers were not so sanguine. Robert Young wandered around the set mumbling, "What about my children? What about my kids?"[27]

The Mortal Storm showed the horrors that *Confessions of a Nazi Spy* only hinted at. Discrimination, humiliation, torture, and murder fill its scenes. It is still a difficult film to watch today. Like *Saving Private Ryan* or *Schindler's List,* it is easier to appreciate than to love. It is hard to believe the same studio released *Andy Hardy Meets Debutante* the same year. This thematic disjuncture is what ultimately made *The Mortal Storm* so shocking. It was so unlike any contemporary picture, so different from MGM's typical glamour-queen-and-wholesome-families fare, so unflinching in its attacks that it could not help but surprise moviegoers.

The Mortal Storm's idyllic setting—a university town nestled among the Alpine foothills—makes the menacing music over its opening credits doubly unnerving. Ominous crashes of thunder punctuate a godlike voice-over: "The tale we are about to tell is of the mortal storm in which man finds himself today," the speaker intones. "Again he is crying, 'I must kill my fellow man!' Our story asks, 'How soon will man find wisdom in his heart and build a lasting shelter against his ignorant fears?' "

It is a bleak beginning, and the mood rarely relents as the picture traces Hitlerism's impact on one household in this once-bucolic hamlet. The Mr. Chips–like Professor Viktor Roth (Frank Morgan), his son Rudi (Gene Reynolds), and his daughter Freya (Margaret Sullavan) are Jewish. His second wife, Amelie (Irene Rich), and her sons, Otto and Erich von Rohn (Robert Stack and William T. Orr), are Christian. Their religious differences pose no barrier to family unity until the Nazi message of hate disrupts the close-knit clan. Within one hundred minutes of screen time, Otto and Erich become Nazi automatons, Professor Roth perishes in a concentration camp, and Freya dies at the hands of her former fiancé, Fritz (Robert Young). Nazi barbarities gain intensity because the audience experiences them on a personal, individual level. There is no happy ending to ease the film's relentless impact.

Reinforcing a motif established in *Confessions of a Nazi Spy* and later mimicked by dozens of World War II–era pictures, *The Mortal Storm* posits that not all Germans are evil. Its favorable portrayals include Martin Breitner (James Stewart), a good-natured peasant who eschews politics; Professor Werner (Thomas Ross), a once-revered teacher branded as "pacifist vermin" for refusing to sing Nazi marching songs; and the Roths. Professor Roth understands that Hitlerism is a passing phenomenon. "Germany will find her own virtues again," he tells Freya and Rudi, "freedom, belief in God." Low-ranking Nazis like Erich, who secretly celebrates when Martin escapes to Austria, are compassionate and humane. Only important party members and members of the SS are truly immoral. Fritz falls into this category, as does his superior, Franz (Ward Bond).

As they were in *Black Legion* and *Confessions of a Nazi Spy,* fascists in *The Mortal Storm* are weak men who thirst for domination. "It means our country will be strong and powerful again," Fritz gloats on hearing of Hitler's 1933 electoral victory, "master of Europe and the world. . . . This is Germany's crying need, a strong man in the saddle, a leader who will fight for victory!" His exaltation suggests that the Nazis harbored expansionist thoughts from their first taste of glory and, in claiming not just the continent but the planet, subtly establishes Hitlerism as a menace to the United States. True believers like Fritz embrace the totalitarian state's groupthink, bellowing marching songs in beer halls and glaring at Professor Roth when his teachings diverge from Nazi dogma. They speak like brainwashed men reading from note cards. "A man's got to take a stand," Otto recites. "If he's not for us, he's against us and against Germany!" "The individual must be sacrificed to the welfare of the state." "Women don't know anything about politics." "In the service of your country there are no human relationships." Anyone who disputes such hackneyed sentiments is a pacifist, a communist, or a non-Aryan—the film's delicate way around using the word *Jew.*

The Jewish issue loomed over the production. Phyllis Bottome urged producer Sidney Franklin to "make the Jew question utterly clear." Los Angeles rabbi Edgar Magnin argued the opposite. A proponent of a low-key, Americanized Judaism that would not provoke the ire of gentiles, Magnin advised producer Victor Saville to sidestep the controversial subject. "The American people for the most part today are against Germany because of the rotten things for which she stands," the rabbi said. "Your picture shows all of that, and let others read into it what they will." Magnin's approach won out. No one in *The Mortal Storm* ever says, "Jew." The only direct evidence of anti-Semitism in the picture is the "J" armband Professor Roth wears while in a concentration camp.[28]

Thin as it was, the subterfuge appears to have worked. Preview audiences generally ignored or failed to comprehend the picture's delicate distinction between Christian and Jew. MGM saw this as a success. In reality it suggests a staggering ignorance of Nazism that American Jews—to say nothing of American political leaders—did little to rectify. Although attacking Nazism as a brutal, undemocratic ideology became increasingly acceptable, it remained taboo to attack it as an anti-Semitic ideology.[29]

The Mortal Storm establishes clear distinctions between Americanism and Nazism without ever mentioning the United States. Even politically naive moviegoers could understand why Hitler was dangerous after watching the film. Individualism is the first victim of Nazi rule, followed closely by pacifism. Religious tolerance is not far behind. With their village firmly in Nazi hands, Martin and Freya make a desperate, cross-country dash for Austria. They know the border is near when they hear church bells tolling over the next mountain pass—the first they have heard since January 1933. Science and rationalism also bow under totalitarianism's burden. Nazi educational censors fire Professor Roth after he claims that Aryan blood is identical to non-Aryan blood. Roth watches mournfully as demonstrators hurl the works of Einstein and other intellectuals into a bonfire.

This last atrocity mirrored the argument posited in *The Life of Louis Pasteur* and *Juarez* that dictatorship cannot coexist with progress. Warner Bros. reiterated that idea with *Dr. Ehrlich's Magic Bullet* (1940), which was in theaters at the same time as *The Mortal Storm*. Ostensibly the dramatic story of the scientist who conquered syphilis, *Dr. Ehrlich's*

Magic Bullet contains an equally significant subtext. Warners producer Hal Wallis intended the picture to disprove Hitler's 1938 statement that "a scientific discovery by a Jew is worthless." Paul Ehrlich (Edward G. Robinson) is a German Jew—or rather, a subscriber to a "particular faith"—whose medical breakthrough happens only after he breaks from the late-nineteenth-century German scientific community's stifling conformism. The film's demand for "truth and justice in sciences" made it one of Robinson's favorites, a thematic sequel to *The Life of Emile Zola*. His final speech gave that credo antifascist overtones. We must continue the struggle for enlightenment, Ehrlich tells his assistants, for "in days to come there will be epidemics of greed, hate, ignorance. We must fight them in life as we fought syphilis in the laboratory. We must fight, fight, we must never stop fighting."[30]

The Mortal Storm seconded Ehrlich's plea. Its use of Jimmy Stewart lent deep emotional appeal to its condemnation of Nazism. Stewart's performance in such pictures as *Navy Blue and Gold* established his nice-guy persona. His role in *Mr. Smith Goes to Washington* confirmed him as the quintessential everyman. In *The Mortal Storm* he plays Martin Breitner without an accent, a decision that diluted the picture's realism while heightening its impact by making his every line ring with the tones of the American heartland. In watching Stewart experience Nazism, the audience experienced themselves set adrift in a wilderness infinitely more ominous than the tangled thickets of Annapolis or the Senate. He is one of them, a lost soul in need of rescue and return to the safety of middle America.

The Mortal Storm was cinematic dynamite, but MGM made it more enticing to audiences seeking entertainment rather than propaganda by downplaying its volatile themes in its promotional campaign. Studio publicity staffers distributed ten thousand bookmarks bearing a romantic image of Martin and Freya to Los Angeles–area libraries and placed four hundred advertising cards in Los Angeles store windows, each featuring Irene Rich posing alongside a very noncontroversial bottle of Welch's Grape Juice. MGM's sleight-of-hand did not fool the Germans. Nazi diplomats warned Secretary of State Cordell Hull that *The Mortal Storm* might force Germany to formally bar American pictures. Hull passed the word to MPPDA foreign manager Frederick Herron, who implausibly argued that MGM produced the film "solely for the purpose of supplying the theatres and their public throughout the world with amusement." Hitler's men rejected Herron's argument. A Ministry of Propaganda edict banned MGM pictures from areas Germany controlled in August 1940, soon after *The Mortal Storm*'s release and a few weeks after the Nazis forbid Twentieth Century–Fox's productions. Germany did the same to Paramount the next month. Fritz Hippler, director of the ministry's film division, justified Germany's prohibition of American movies as "a necessity forced on us by America and demanded by our national honor and political self-defense."[31]

Germany imported only a few dozen new American movies a year by now, so its moves were largely symbolic. Still, the departures of MGM, Twentieth Century–Fox, and Paramount signified Hollywood's final break with the Nazis. *The Mortal Storm* never showed in Germany. Governments throughout South America also banned it. A lackluster domestic performance earned it a slight profit of just over $100,000. Exit surveys showed that most American viewers believed it depicted Nazi Germany honestly and that a significant minority thought it was "propaganda." Although moved by it, audiences did not enjoy *The Mortal Storm*.[32]

Some critics hit *The Mortal Storm* from the opposite direction. It was not too much but rather too little, too late. According to their thinking, major studios should have aired the film's arguments years ago. The *New York Times* film critic Bosley Crowther castigated studios for what he saw as a limp cinematic response to totalitarianism in recent years. *The Mortal Storm* "reaches the screen so late, so unforgivably late," he wrote. Crowther believed Americans would have turned against the Nazis earlier had Hollywood only exposed them to the evils of Hitlerism. His accusation carried more weight than merit, articulating the frustration many felt with Hollywood's timid antifascism while underestimating the industry's economic needs and overestimating Americans' desire to intervene in overseas affairs.[33]

MGM wrapped *Escape* as *The Mortal Storm* blew across the United States. With the latter underperforming in theaters, Louis B. Mayer was nervous about his studio's course. Perhaps audiences did not want anti-Nazi pictures. Mayer's edginess permeated every corner of MGM's sixty-three-acre lot. "Never was back-slapping harder, cordiality louder, mistrust greater," remembered screenwriter Christopher Isherwood.

Mayer tried to break the tension with a mass rally to benefit the American Red Cross. Thousands of employees jammed a flag-draped soundstage to hear actress Jeanette MacDonald sing the national anthem. Then Mayer sucked the air from the room with one of his notoriously rambling, maudlin speeches. Isherwood cast a cynical eye on the proceedings. "Democracy's Nuremberg Rally," he huffed. Perhaps, but with *The Mortal Storm*'s June 1940 release Mayer acquired the trappings of pro-Americanism and tentatively entered the ranks of Hollywood's anti-fascists. He did so with little confidence or ideological fervor. Some of his fellow studio heads, however, exhibited more enthusiasm for the cause.[34]

Zanuck Makes His Stand

"THEY DON'T CALL THEM moving pictures because they stand still—
they move!" Darryl F. Zanuck once said. Twentieth Century–Fox's
head of production organized his life around movement. He walked fast,
talked fast, and drove fast. His hobbies—hunting, polo, swimming, boxing, sex—were physical in nature. He wrote so fast that he distributed
his voluminous screenwriting credits between himself and three pen
names. Zanuck was not a great writer, but his prose crackled with vigor.
He was a phenom of energy, the closest thing to a perpetual-motion machine in Hollywood. "That man could, *had,* read every script on the lot,"
actress Ida Lupino remembered. "He watched every wardrobe test of
every male star, every female star; he could remember—with all the people under contract!—that he didn't like a spotted tie on a man in test
number three, or he didn't like the cut of a skirt on me in test number
four." He was, explained the screenwriter Casey Robinson, "a one-man
studio."[1]

Twentieth Century–Fox films resembled Zanuck—they moved fast. "I
cannot ever remember trying to *slow down* a scene," he told his producers. He believed moviegoers wanted entertainment based on action, not
deep characterization or psychological navel-gazing. Twentieth Century–
Fox's enviable track record at the box office suggested that the executive
knew what he was talking about. Like all great movie producers, he had
an innate sense of the public's desires. "I always thought Zanuck had a
Geiger counter in his head," writer Nunnally Johnson said. "He'd read a
script and the moment it got dull, or didn't move, or went off the track,
tick-tick-tick, he said, 'It stopped. Now where did this start?' "[2]

Zanuck converted to interventionism in 1939 but was slow to harmo-
nize his personal beliefs with his business practices. Fox maintained its

German office until the Nazis closed it in 1940, and the studio lagged behind Warner Bros. in releasing antifascist pictures. Zanuck sensed audiences' disinterest in preachy movies about the evils of totalitarianism and was for the moment content to follow their lead. His fellow executives' muddled response to the war annoyed him nevertheless. "Every time I got together with Louie Mayer or Jack Cohn," he later complained, "they tried to fill me with pious crap about giving the public what they wanted in these troublous times, which was entertainment pure and simple—by which they meant Garbo's grunts and Lana Turner's tits, and nothing to worry about except was Janet Gaynor going to get to the state fair and Andy Hardy get to kiss the girl next door. And meanwhile, out there, the Nazis were on the rampage in Europe." He was not the first mogul to dive into the breach, but he charged in close after the Warner brothers. Fox's 1939 releases *Young Mr. Lincoln* and *Drums along the Mohawk* signaled his desire to pump an enervating stream of patriotism into feature films. When the European war started, he joined MGM in initiating anti-Nazi and pro-American projects that illuminated the threat to democracy. By the end of 1940, he had joined Harry Warner atop the ranks of the industry's flag-wavers.[3]

Unlike most of his peers, Zanuck did not have to balance his emerging antifascism with concerns for domestic anti-Semitism. He was the only Christian among the great studio titans, a Methodist unburdened by the cultural baggage the Jews of eastern European descent carried. As a youth he split time between Los Angeles and Wahoo, Nebraska. Like many Californians, he was an immigrant who preserved his midwestern roots even as he settled into life in the growing metropolis. Zanuck's films often brought the two together, showing that small-town values could survive in an urbanizing nation.[4]

Zanuck was a ripped-from-the-headlines kind of moviemaker, so his attention to the war fit his character. He established a reputation as an innovator while heading production at Warner Bros. in the late 1920s and early 1930s. Besides producing *The Jazz Singer* and several earlier features using the Vitaphone sound-on-disc process, Zanuck practically invented the gangster movie, shepherding such groundbreaking films as *Doorway to Hell* (1930), *Little Caesar* (1931), and *The Public Enemy* (1931) to the screen. *I Am a Fugitive from a Chain Gang* (1932) shocked audiences with a dark realism that reflected the gloomy spirit of a Depression-plagued nation. Zanuck also produced and wrote large chunks of the archetypical backstage musical *42nd Street* (1933).

Zanuck left the Warners in 1933 after fighting with Jack and Harry over a plan to slash employee salaries. Behind this dispute lay years of conflict with the brothers. Zanuck thought Harry was a sanctimonious hypocrite and saw Jack's hail-fellow-well-met demeanor as a mask concealing a ruthless, penny-pinching tyrant. He also knew the clannish Warners would never allow him to become a partner at their studio. Zanuck formed Twentieth Century Pictures with United Artists executive Joe Schenck soon after leaving Warners. Louis B. Mayer, who wanted to buy a position for his son-in-law, William Goetz, largely financed the venture. Goetz received one-third of the new firm's stock but was otherwise a nonentity. Chafing under a restrictive distribution contract with United Artists, Zanuck and Schenck sought a new partner with top-notch studio facilities and an established exhibition network. Schenck wrangled a merger deal with the once-great Fox studio in 1935. After a brief power struggle, Zanuck emerged as the unquestioned lord of Twentieth Century–Fox's three-hundred-acre manor.[5]

The producer's office resembled the refuge of a conquering hero. Its walls were green, the same green as his Cadillac. Even the color belonged to him; it was known as "Zanuck Green." A zebra-skin bench greeted visitors with a reminder of what happened to anything that got in the executive's way. Stuffed trophies stared blankly at a lion skin stretched on the floor. Such oozing machismo extended to every corner of Zanuck's life. Although only five feet, six inches tall and cursed with a gap between his front teeth that gave his face a decidedly shrewish mien, his pride in his appearance extended far beyond mere vanity. He admired his nude body whenever possible, flexing his taut muscles for the benefit of anyone who happened to be near. He boxed, performed gymnastics, and swam laps nearly every day. Exercising his prerogative as Fox's czar, he refused to enter the Zanuck Green studio pool unless the water was bone-chillingly cold. Pool crews sometimes dumped in blocks of ice to plunge the temperature to an appropriately Zanuckian level of frigidity.[6]

Twentieth Century–Fox revolved around Zanuck's schedule. Activity perked up when his car rolled through the gates at 11:00 a.m., then slowed from 4:00 to 4:30 p.m., when his daily girl joined him among the animal skins and mounted heads. Those sharing the chief's predilections also took advantage of the half-hour lull. "I honestly think that from four to four-thirty every day at Fox," screenwriter Milton Sperling remembered, "if you could have harnessed the power from all the fucking that was going on, you could have turned the tides at Malibu."[7]

Zanuck tuned his sensitive antennae to everything happening on his studio's shoots. His story conferences became the stuff of legend. Writers, directors, and producers watched from plush leather chairs as Zanuck stalked about his lair, crashing his sawed-off polo mallet on the desk whenever he wanted to emphasize a point. Words spewed out rapid-fire as he talked his way through story proposals, explored possible plot developments, streamlined scenes, and sharpened dialogue. One of his secretaries shaped his verbal fragments into coherent notes. Zanuck threw himself into these sessions with great gusto, acting out every part as if angling for the role himself. While in his early years at Warners he even simulated Rin Tin Tin's performance.

Zanuck's mouth sometimes outpaced his brain. He talked himself into a dead end during one conference with writer Kitty Scola. "And now," he exclaimed in the midst of a particularly exciting scene, "and *now* her love turns to hate." "Why, Mr. Zanuck? Why does her love turn to hate?" Scola asked. Zanuck stopped. He looked perplexed. He stormed into the bathroom connected to his office and slammed the door. Everyone in the room waited to see what inspiration would come. He emerged a few minutes later, and with the sound of the flushing toilet still resonating in the background, delivered his verdict. Pointing his mallet squarely at Scola, he decreed: "All right, her love *doesn't* turn to hate."[8]

No script was finished until Zanuck said it was finished. Some saw his meddling as a petty way of asserting his authority. Zanuck did not care what people thought, so long as his methods produced pictures that people paid to see. He left directors alone on the set but watched their rushes every night to make sure they stuck to the script. His close supervision of Fox's editors meant that he always had the last word; no film left his studio until it was cut exactly the way he wanted it. The mogul's hands-on approach inspired deep animosities. Writer John Bright thought him "an arrogant, tin-pot Mussolini." Bright also acknowledged that "everything that I subsequently found out about movies I learned from him."[9]

Despite his gift for demagoguery, Zanuck was undeniably part of the Hollywood establishment, a member of an elite cadre of powerful men whose decisions set industry policy. He generally stood with other studio heads out of a sense of industry solidarity even though he did not particularly like them. Everyone knew he hated the Warners. He also thought Mayer was "a malevolent and vindictive bastard" and ripped the Hays Office as "a bunch of goddamned bluenoses."[10]

Zanuck took the lead in plunging Hollywood into Americana during the last months of European peace. He scored hits with *Drums along the Mohawk* and *Young Mr. Lincoln,* then followed them up with a bigger smash, *The Grapes of Wrath,* in early 1940. Zanuck was also moving his studio toward features that drew from the global crisis, applying the same current-events philosophy he had used in the early 1930s, only now concentrating on stories of international rather than domestic gangsterism. Beginning in June 1940, the same month MGM issued *The Mortal Storm,* Fox started releasing A-list pictures that exposed the evils of Nazism, boosted national and hemispheric defense, promoted improved relations with Latin America, and encouraged American patriotism. Along with *The Mortal Storm,* Zanuck's features represented the first cycle of motion pictures created after the invasion of Poland. They were Hollywood's initial onscreen response to a world at war.

His B-list programmers already reflected these influences. Although conceived in August 1939, around the same time as Fox's higher-budget internationalist films, *Charlie Chan in Panama* beat them to the screen. Appearing in February 1940, it pit the famous detective against spies scheming to gain control over the Canal Zone. As was often the case with Zanuck's pictures, the story drew on current events, in this case the December 1938 espionage trial of Hans Heinrich Schackow and thirty other Germans arrested for photographing the canal's fortifications. An otherwise routine if enjoyable installment in the Chan series, the movie assumes added significance when the wise private eye (Sidney Toler) utters the fortune-cookie-style moral: "Intelligent defense of nation best guarantee for years of peace."[11]

Zanuck decided his studio's first foray into A-list anti-Nazism would be a remake of the old Fox Studio's *Four Sons* (1928). Based on I. A. R. Wylie's short story "Grandma Bernle Learns Her Letters," John Ford's stylish original centered on a Bavarian mother whose children find themselves on opposite sides of the Great War. Three of her sons join the German military, and a fourth leaves home to enlist in the United States Army. Zanuck acted out an updated plot for communist screenwriter John Howard Lawson a week before the war in Europe began, telling Lawson to relocate the picture's action to the Sudetenland on the eve of Hitler's rise to power.[12]

Lawson had to work fast lest changing overseas circumstances render his story obsolete. The veteran of *Blockade* dashed off a script over the next few weeks that modernized Ford's film while retaining its pacifist philosophy—not surprising considering that the Hitler-Stalin alliance required dedicated communists to denounce warmongering. Fox reader Aidan Roark thought the draft was "great anti-war propaganda." Zanuck, who hired Roark more for his polo skills than his cinematic instincts, had a different take. "We do not want to get the element of pacifism into our story," he insisted. He talked up Mother Bernle's role, building her into a decent commoner crushed under a dehumanizing totalitarian system, a feminized cross between Senator Jefferson Smith and Jean Valjean. Audiences would empathize with her travails, he concluded, "and behind it all we will skillfully sneak in our message."[13]

Zanuck fleshed out his intentions as he tinkered with the script during the next few months. He changed the Bernle family to the Berns, skirted the Jewish question, and avoided the long-winded political declarations that marred *Juarez* and other Warner Bros. features. His desire to "skillfully sneak in" a message caused him to renovate the quaint, sleepy town from Lawson's treatment into a modern, bustling community. Zanuck thought Lawson's musty, old-fashioned setting made the Nazis more sympathetic. "Perhaps it is just as well that the others are coming in," audiences might think. He also rejected Lawson's suggestion that the picture include Czechs who welcomed the German invaders, a real-world nuance that Zanuck believed unnecessarily muddied the picture's clear-cut morality.[14]

Rather than indulge Lawson's penchant for lengthy exposition, Zanuck used family members' diverse fates to comment on the movements they represented. This was Hollywood's time-tested way of simplifying complicated issues, the same humanizing method MGM used in *The Mortal Storm*. Mother Bern's diabolical son Karl (Alan Curtis) jumps on the Nazi bandwagon just before the Munich Conference. Her idealistic son Chris (Don Ameche) joins the Czech resistance after the Nazis assume control. The German Army drafts youngest brother Fritz (George Ernest), while artistic Joseph (Robert Lowery) escapes to the United States.

Mother Bern (Eugenie Leontovich) emerges as the focus of sympathy. She is very much the European Ma Joad, laboring to hold the family together against impossible odds. She cannot persuade Karl to shun his Nazi "social club" or reconcile him with Chris. The brothers will never mend their relationship. Chris accidentally shoots Karl soon after the Nazis march into the Sudetenland. Mother Bern hides Chris only to have the Germans kidnap and assassinate him. Fritz dies in the Poland campaign soon after. There is nothing left for her in Germany. She bundles up Karl's widow and infant son and leaves to join Joseph in America. As they board the train, Herr Kapek, a schoolteacher recently released from a concentration camp, offers an optimistic moral to the story: "Barbed wire cannot hold the spirit of man."

The completed picture pleased Zanuck. Others around the Fox lot were relieved that *Four Sons* made its anti-Nazi case without being overly inflammatory. "There's nothing racial," exclaimed writer Julian Johnson, "nothing about Nazis, or war, or propaganda." Such views underestimated the film's power. Zanuck realized what the Warners did not fully comprehend. *Four Sons* did not need pretentious history lessons and civics primers to convey its message. Story did not have to take a backseat to significance, because audiences understood what was happening in the world. The film's cautious disclaimer that its events could have happened in "almost any nation" was unnecessary. Everyone knew this was Czechoslovakia, and everyone knew Czechoslovakia no longer existed.[15]

Unfortunately for Fox, the film's focus on plot rather than ostentatious relevance could not cause a mediocre feature to suddenly perform well at the box office. For all of Zanuck's meddling, *Four Sons* was a confusing muddle with a depressing plot. It also suffered from *The Mortal Storm*'s nearly simultaneous release. Moviegoers who spent their money on one gloomy, anti-Nazi family drama were unlikely to do it again the next week. More fundamentally, Hollywood insiders remained uncertain about whether audiences wanted to see this kind of picture. Philip Hartung's review of *Four Sons* in *Commonweal* restated the old debate over Hollywood's social function. "We already hate war," he wrote. "We are already surfeited with newsreels and headlines." Movies were supposed to be both fun and enlightening—but not too enlightening. Neither Hartung nor general audiences knew how to respond to *Four Sons*. "Certainly," Hartung concluded, "it cannot be called entertainment."[16]

Zanuck looked for another anti-Nazi feature once *Four Sons* went into production. Oscar Schisgall's "Swastika" caught his eye. The producer liked the short story because Schisgall depicted the Nazis through the eyes of an American, art critic Carol Traub, a perspective Zanuck thought would make the story more immediate for domestic audiences. Carol and her German-born husband, Eric, take their son, Ricky, on vacation to Germany in 1938. Carol is ignorant of the horrors of Hitlerism. She assumes the concentration camps are "not half as bad as they say they are," but she slowly recognizes the monstrosity Germany has become. Her husband, however, is as fascinated as she is repulsed. Finding his homeland "alive, exciting," Eric falls in with the Nazis. The couple break up after Carol mocks the Führer as "Schickelgruber." Eric's infatuation turns to self-loathing when he learns he is half-Jewish. "Jude, Jude, Jude," he moans. Carol and Ricky return home alone after she dismisses her disgraced ex-husband with a terse "Heil, heel."

Zanuck liked the treatment but wanted to minimize the story's anti-Semitism angle. He brought in Oliver H. P. Garrett for a rewrite. Garrett's mission was "so far as possible, to eliminate the Jewish element from every incident in the story." Zanuck was not averse to addressing anti-Semitism, which formed a key component of *The House of Rothschild* (1934) and later took center stage in Fox's *Gentleman's Agreement* (1947). In 1940, however, he believed that Jews did not want to see themselves persecuted onscreen and that gentiles dismissed such scenes as "propaganda." The producer also changed the lead's name from Traub, which he thought sounded too Jewish, to Hoffman. As he had during the scripting of *Four Sons*, Zanuck told Garrett to minimize newsreel-type reporting that detracted from the plot, although the film did include some *Confessions*-style footage. "Show it through the characters," he urged, "and let the audience write in its own obvious interpretations." After considering *I Married a Nazi* as a title, Zanuck instead selected the less provocative *The Man I Married*.[17]

It is easy to overstate the importance of these alterations. *The Man I Married* was obviously about the Nazis, and its substitution of "Jude" for "Jew" was a thin cover. Fox's publicity department, however, obscured the most important themes of *The Man I Married*. The studio's vague ads described a picture about a woman who discovers something disagreeable about her husband. It might be an affair, it might be a troubled past, and it might be halitosis. Fox's marketing campaign suggested that exhibitors sponsor essay contests on "How I Met the Man I Married." This kind of deceptive—or at least selective—advertising indicated the widening gap between the people who made movies and the people who sold movies. Money men fought to conceal the intentions of idea men. Such campaigns opened the industry to charges of propagandizing the public because it was quite possible for a theatergoer to walk into *The Man I Married* without knowing it was a highly political film.[18]

Fox's advertising subterfuge did not fool critics, who praised *The Man I Married* when it appeared in July 1940 even as they doubted its box-office potential. "It does not pull any punches and is a strong indictment of Hitler and his regime," exclaimed *Film Daily*. "A straight jolt of anti-Nazi propaganda," *Variety* reported. It is impossible to accurately measure returns, but reviewers expected it to perform better in cities than in rural areas, particularly in the more isolationist Midwest. That the ruthlessly imitative studios did not follow *The Mortal Storm, Four Sons,* and *The Man I Married* with a stream of projects set in Germany or its occupied territories suggests their middling performances.[19]

For all their problems, these films extended the arguments offered by *Confessions of a Nazi Spy*. Open assaults on a sovereign nation defied rhetoric about pure entertainment and respecting national feelings. Using a German rather than an American setting suggested that overseas actions were as dangerous to the United States as the domestic subversion seen in *Confessions of a Nazi Spy*. These summer 1940 features reflected both Hollywood's building sense of crisis and the new freedom that losing the European market had given studios. They suggested sincere patriotism unleashed by economics. No matter how much they despised Hitler, Mayer and Zanuck would not have authorized these projects had they jeopardized revenues. What is also remarkable about these releases is that they faced no specific resistance from Breen and

Hays, whose talk of general industry policy had affected the content of so many previous productions.

The MPPDA revisited the "hate films" issue in April 1940—months after *The Mortal Storm* and *I Married a Nazi* went into production—in response to confusion over exactly what belonged in that category. After much deliberation, Will Hays's men concluded that pictures presenting "a careful distinction between different points of view within Germany" were not hate films, even if they showed concentration camps or other atrocities. Features portraying only sinister Germans, however, were "calculated to inflame the public mind" and therefore forbidden. In Hollywood's curious logic, features like *The Mortal Storm* and *The Man I Married* were anti-German yet respected the no-hate-films edict.[20]

Zanuck sought safer ground by continuing Fox's historical cycle alongside his new anti-Nazi pictures. His films represented a double-barreled response to war, attacking the Nazis and at the same time advancing a vigorous Americanism. The patriotic drama *Brigham Young* was one of the studio's most important 1940 features. Like *Young Mr. Lincoln* and *Drums along the Mohawk,* the epic tale of the Mormon Trail promoted national unity and American ideals. Conceived in the last days of European peace and filmed during the first months of war, it went farther than earlier pictures in contrasting fascism with Zanuck's understanding of Americanism.

Zanuck saw parallels between the United States' intolerance of Mormons and Hitler's persecution of Jews, at one point referring to attacks on Nauvoo and other Mormon settlements as "pogroms." The producer commissioned Lamar Trotti, who had written *Young Mr. Lincoln* and *Drums along the Mohawk,* to compose another patriotic screenplay. In contrast to Zanuck's enthusiasm, director Henry Hathaway saw little to recommend the project. Wagon trains, he told Zanuck, were almost as boring as religion. Shrugging off Hathaway's concerns, Zanuck granted *Brigham Young* a relatively large $1.5 million budget.

Trotti turned out a brilliant script that lionized early Mormons without forcing audiences to engage or even acknowledge Mormon theology. *Brigham Young* suggests that Mormonism mostly implies a belief in God's desire for the faithful to settle the West—a mission consistent with America's quasi-secular, quasi-religious belief in Manifest Destiny. Trotti ignored Joseph Smith's discovery of the golden plates and approached polygamy, potentially the story's most explosive point, with extreme caution. Mountain man Jim Bridger, who makes a brief cameo, is apparently the only person interested in the issue. "Say, how many. . . ." "Twelve," Young (Dean Jagger) snaps, ending the discussion. Even that figure seems inflated, as Young focuses almost exclusively on just one wife, Mary Ann (Mary Astor).

Brigham Young envisions Mormons as a persecuted minority steeped in the great traditions of American history. The picture opens with a raid against a Mormon clan in Carthage, Illinois. A lynch mob blackens its faces, grabs torches, and heads for the Kent farm. They find the harmless family laughing, dancing, and making doughnuts. The Kent women and children flee into the storm cellar, but their patriarch cannot escape the crowd. The rabble shoots Mr. Kent and whips the other men. This is not the first time the Kents have faced violence, Jonathan (Tyrone Power) explains to his non-Mormon neighbor, Zina Webb (Linda Darnell). "They hate us," he tells her. "Just because you're Mormons?" she asks in bewilderment.

Inflamed with intolerance, indignant community leaders charge Joseph Smith (Vincent Price) with treason. Smith's trial becomes a landmark moment in American liberty once Brigham Young leaps up to testify in his defense. Young insists that the pertinent issue in the trial is religious freedom, not whether Smith is a false prophet. "Now gentlemen," he implores the jury, "I'm not asking you to believe a single thing Joseph Smith said. But I do ask you, let him believe it, let me believe it if we want to. Your forefathers and mine came to this country in the first place for one great reason: to escape persecution for their beliefs and to build a free country where everybody might worship God as he please."

Young's entreaties prove fruitless, and the jury convicts Smith without deliberation. Shorn of their leader, the Mormons decide to move west. Zina goes with them. Initially suspicious of her traveling companions—and they of her—her love for Jonathan gradually makes her a full-fledged member of the community. Like the combination of Alabamian and New York soldiers into *The Fighting 69th*'s Rainbow Division, their marriage symbolizes a union of formerly antagonistic elements of the American social landscape. Zina's character also offered a way for non-Mormons to identify with the feature's main characters.

Zanuck and Trotti intensified the all-American message of *Brigham Young* by interpreting the Mormon Trail within the well-worn tropes of the pioneer tradition. Fox added "Frontiersman" to the title for East Coast theaters. Joseph Smith makes his first appearance chopping wood, à la Henry Fonda's depiction of *Young Mr. Lincoln* the year before. The Mormon exodus assumes biblical overtones as the refugees ford the Mississippi after townsmen burn Nauvoo. Their flight becomes another Red Sea passage, with Young assuming the Moses role. The migrants embrace familiar elements of the frontier experience. Covered wagons and cattle herds abound. Talk of the California gold rush is in the air. Their attire is pure pioneer-chic—leather fringes and dusty cowboy boots. Native Americans populate the landscape. Even the soundtrack is unadulterated Americana, from the wistful strains of "Oh, Susannah" to the anachronistic "Dixie," written several years after the Mormons trekked to Salt Lake. On arrival, settlers apply the American virtues of hard work and self-help to build a new Eden. *Brigham Young*'s final shots of present-day Salt Lake City's magnificent Mormon Temple confirm the adventurers' ability to transform wilderness into civilization.

Brigham Young was an expensive movie that needed to draw large audiences to succeed. Packaging it as "The Great American Motion Picture," Fox crafted a promotional campaign that emphasized its action and romantic subplot. The studio staged a suitably epic premiere in Salt Lake City. Led by Governor Henry Blood and Mayor Ab Jenkins, tens of thousands greeted Zanuck, Tyrone Power, Dean Jagger, Linda Darnell, and other Fox players when their chartered United Airlines DC-3 touched down on August 23, 1940. The stars climbed into convertibles for a noontime parade that circled Temple Square before rolling through the rest of town. More than two hundred thousand waving fans greeted them along the route. *Brigham Young* debuted simultaneously at seven theaters around the city before beginning its national run. After garnering mostly positive reviews, it grossed around $2.5 million.

Zanuck again proved his ability to produce exciting pictures that offered important messages without interrupting the story. War-filled European subjects remained iffy ventures. Axis victories, however, made the contrasts between American and Nazi values more immediate and marketable. Twentieth Century–Fox still produced plenty of escapist movies, releasing, for example, two films starring the pubescent Shirley

Temple in 1940. Then again, so did Warner Bros., which released *Calling All Husbands* and *Tugboat Annie Sails Again* on the same slate as *British Intelligence* and *The Fighting 69th*. The silver screen never completely gave itself over to films that commented on the global situation. No matter how political some in Hollywood might be, producers still needed to provide the thematic diversity that appealed to mass audiences and kept their businesses afloat.

Louis B. Mayer in his office at MGM (c. 1941). MGM/Photofest.

A buoyant Jack Warner (left) laughs at his own joke as older brothers Harry (center) and Albert (right) look on (c. 1930s). Photofest.

MPPDA President Will Hays escorts Sara Delano Roosevelt, FDR's mother, to a film premiere (c. 1935). Courtesy of the Margaret Herrick Library, Academy of Motion Picture Arts and Sciences.

Marco (Henry Fonda) and Luis (Leo Carrillo) look on in horror as their unnamed enemies brutalize civilians in *Blockade* (c. 1938). Courtesy of the Margaret Herrick Library, Academy of Motion Picture Arts and Sciences.

Warner Bros.' quickie remake of *Dawn Patrol* (1938) sold war as both horrific and exciting. Warner Bros. / Photofest.

A quartet of Latin stereotypes from *Viva Villa* (1934): the sharply dressed musician, the fiery female dancer, the dirty bandit, and the drunken lout. Courtesy of the Margaret Herrick Library, Academy of Motion Picture Arts and Sciences.

Benito Juarez (Paul Muni) as the Mexican Abraham Lincoln in Warner Bros.' *Juarez* (1939). Warner Bros. Pictures / Photofest.

Franz Schlager (George Sanders) and his Nazi henchmen plan to take over the world in Warner Bros.' *Confessions of a Nazi Spy* (1939). Warner Bros. / Photofest.

Anti-Semitic propaganda in Los Angeles, c. 1939. Courtesy USC Cinematic Arts Library, Jack L. Warner Collection.

Nazi thugs destroying cultural and intellectual freedom in MGM's *The Mortal Storm* (1940). MGM/Photofest.

Adenoid Hynkel (Charlie Chaplin) and Benzini Napaloni (Jack Oakie) debate the future of Osterlich in Charles Chaplin Productions' *The Great Dictator* (1940). Charles Chaplin / Photofest.

Darryl F. Zanuck (left) chats up Nathan Levinson at a 1941 industry function as Will Hays looks on. Courtesy Getty Images.

Studio publicity for Universal's *Buck Privates* (1941) stressed the military's humorous side. Universal Pictures / Photofest.

Actor and Roosevelt confidant Douglas Fairbanks Jr. after joining the navy (c. 1943). Photofest.

Nazis arrest hunter Alan Thorndike (Walter Pidgeon) before he can assassinate Adolf Hitler in Fritz Lang's *Man Hunt* (1941). Courtesy of the Margaret Herrick Library, Academy of Motion Picture Arts and Sciences.

Alvin York (Gary Cooper) ponders God and war from a Tennessee mountaintop in Warner Bros.' *Sergeant York* (1941). Warner Bros. / Photofest.

The 1941 Senate Propaganda hearings. Senator Gerald Nye (left, in dark suit) addresses (left to right) Senators Ernest McFarland, D. Worth Clark, Charles Tobey, and Wayland Brooks. Courtesy Getty Images.

Betty Grable and Tyrone Power bring star power and romance to Darryl F. Zanuck's homage to Anglo-American unity, *A Yank in the R.A.F.* (1941). Twentieth Century Fox / Photofest.

CHAPTER FOURTEEN

Searching for a Voice

❧ ❧ ❧

A LREADY INFREQUENT, ONSCREEN DEPICTIONS of anti-Nazism grew rarer in the months following *The Mortal Storm, Four Sons,* and *The Man I Married.* These blistering indictments represented Hollywood's initial response to the European war. Imbued with righteous indignation in the tumultuous first days of fighting, producers now sat back to see what would happen next. With a few notable exceptions, the projects they issued in the latter half of 1940—the second wave of wartime films—limited themselves to safer subjects, articulating Hollywood's desire for a tolerant, internationalist America that vigilantly defended its freedoms against totalitarian aggressors. These pictures certainly represented significant responses to the war, even if they shunned direct attacks on fascism. As they had the previous year, films extended prodemocratic rhetoric to encompass the entire Western Hemisphere.

Hollywood's fascination with all things Hispanic continued through late 1940, as did its gross miscalculation of what Hispanic audiences wanted. American studios still held about three-quarters of the Latin American market. Their efforts to enlarge that share furthered their association with Roosevelt's hemispheric foreign policy yet made little impact on balance sheets. Italian and German studios were making inroads into South America, as were Axis corporations in general. Theaters in Buenos Aires, Rio de Janeiro, and other cities showed Nazi newsreels alongside a growing number of German-made features. Unwilling to offend a nation that might win the war and dominate the global film trade, Hispanic exhibitors accepted Nazi censorship demands with increasing frequency. *The Man I Married, Confessions of a Nazi Spy,* and British-made anti-Nazi picture *Pastor Hall* all struggled to find outlets in Latin America.[1]

Still closely tracking Hollywood's activities, the State Department urged studios to distribute more pictures that stressed hemispheric friendship, the virtues of democracy, and the dangers of Fifth Columnists. Some producers tried, albeit clumsily, to meet these requests. Warner Bros., for example, inserted a Brazilian pilot into *Wings of the Navy*'s (1939) group of trainees. "With the advancement of aviation," one flier noted, "Brazil is practically in your backyard." Hollywood's ongoing incompetence, however, frustrated diplomats. RKO's comedy *Escape to Paradise* (1939), the story of an American tourist in South America, enraged Hispanic crowds. The American vice consul in Buenos Aires reported that characters spoke "atrocious Spanish" and that viewers mocked the picture's awkward calls for international solidarity. The film was "a bad vehicle for propaganda," the State Department concluded.[2]

Hollywood knew it needed to do better. Speaking in his capacity as Academy president, independent producer Walter Wanger told an audience at UCLA's Institute of Latin-American Affairs that movies should show that "there still exists a way of life in which the individual counts, in which hatred and regimentation do not compose the sole motive and method of existence." Wanger declared that "we must learn about the rest of the world." Major studios pursued any Hispanic actor with a trace of talent, particularly singers and dancers that producers could plug into the inexpensive musicals they believed Latin Americans wanted to see. "Virtually anyone who can swing a chassis or warble in the South American way has either been screentested [*sic*] or is about to be," *Variety* claimed.[3]

Studios still operated under the assumption that there was such a thing as "the South American way." It did much the same with Great Britain, which it consistently depicted as a nation of affable chaps who attended school in venerable institutions or drank tea in ancient family estates. These Anglo stereotypes were at least positive, which could not always be said for Hispanic typecasting. Hollywood kept releasing tributes to Latin America only to have Latin Americans reject them. "Nearly every time Uncle Sam pours a Good Neighbor toast," remarked one critic, "somebody slips a mickey finn into South America's glass."[4]

Universal's *Argentine Nights* (1940), a light farce starring the Ritz Brothers and the Andrews Sisters as musicians at a Buenos Aires resort, typified the movie capital's clumsiness. The picture's hackneyed depictions of gauchos and bizarre casting selections, including future

Superman George Reeves as Argentinean polo star Eduardo Esteban, prompted riots at its Buenos Aires opening. Argentine consul Emilio Tegui observed that Argentineans did not do the rumba, as the film suggested, and that a female dancer in one scene wore the outfit of a Cuban prostitute. "This sort of picture is not only sheer idiocy," Tegui said, "but it's going to sever these Pan-American ties before they get knotted." Word of the *Argentine Nights* flap caused recriminations in Washington, D.C. "The picture does not represent the feelings of the American Congress or of the American people toward the friendly people of Argentina," Senator John Rankin said.[5]

Twentieth Century–Fox similarly misfired with *Down Argentine Way* (1940). American reviewers, on the one hand, saw the comedy as "a neat bit of entertaining neighborliness for the Latin-American brethren." They applauded Don Ameche's performance as Ricardo Quintano and raved that newcomer Carmen Miranda gave the picture "an authentic Argentinean note." South American audiences, on the other hand, hissed *Down Argentine Way* off the screen. They found Ameche's performance insulting and pointed out that Carmen Miranda was Brazilian, not Argentinean. The movie's musical numbers fueled their anger. Fox won a Best Song Oscar for Mack Gordon's "Argentina," which offered familiar images of "rumbas and tangos to tickle your spine/Moonlight and music and orchids and wine." Thankfully, Fox cut "Have You Met My Oucho Ma Gaucho," Gordon's never-released tune about two lovers meeting under "the pampas moon." One can imagine the outrage had its chorus wafted through South American theaters:

Have you met my oucho ma gaucho
Tho he has a bit of a poucho
When it comes to love he's no sloucho
All he says is si si si si si si
I think he's a great big seesy
Oh he is so strong and so hotcha
And I am his little muchacha
He calls me his cute cucaracha
And he drinks and he drinks and he drinks and he drinks
The soused American way.

Down Argentine Way bombed in South America.[6]

Fox's *The Mark of Zorro* provided 1940's most effective use of Hispanic imagery to convey a propaganda theme while obeying Zanuck's demand that message not overwhelm plot. The time-tested story of Don Diego de Vega (Tyrone Power) and his sword-wielding alter ego was an enjoyable adventure film with enough beautiful women, swashbuckling, and skintight trousers to interest moviegoers of all stripes. It keeps its antifascist subtext unobtrusive without burying it completely.

Don Diego had a privileged childhood in Spain's New World colonies. After a sojourn in Madrid, however, he returns to California to discover that the crown has replaced his wise father as *alcalde* with the malicious Don Luis (J. Edward Bromberg), who strips the peons of their freedoms. His minions mark the death of free speech under a New World dictatorship by cutting out the tongue of a wagon driver who criticized the regime. His soldiers impose their harsh will under the leadership of Captain Pasquale (Basil Rathbone), a ruthless man whose perpetually drawn sword and menacing glare underscore his violent nature. The church, through the outspoken Padre Felipe (Eugene Pallette), is the sole force opposing Don Luis's vicious rule. Felipe urges Don Diego to stand up for his father by joining the fight against the tyrannical government only to find that the foppish aristocrat prefers to chase women and live off his fortune. "Then you believe that we should not be moved by injustice and cruelty until it touches us," Felipe exclaims. "But my dear padre, such things exist in the world and always will," Don Diego yawns in a cruel twisting of the anti-interventionist line.

Don Diego's indifference conceals his secret identity. The masked Zorro, a master swordsman, is a nineteenth-century resistance leader who repeatedly lashes out against the tyrannical regime before vanishing into Don Diego's close-fitting finery. His infuriating raids cause Pasquale and Don Luis to commit the state's repressive machinery to capturing the mysterious rebel. They finally arrest Zorro only to discover that his calls for political liberation are more powerful than their authoritarian rule. Don Diego/Zorro escapes to rally the populace against their oppressors. Caballeros unite with peons to overthrow Don Luis, reestablish just government, and celebrate human freedom.

The Mark of Zorro was a solid hit at the box office. This was the kind of message picture audiences could embrace. Eschewing the preachiness of *Juarez,* it combined the subtle relevance of *The Life of Emile Zola* with the excitement of a service picture's dogfight scenes. It was propagandistic without being propaganda, making its point without wallowing in it. Such pictures reflected Hollywood's commitment to balancing ideological and financial concerns, supporting democracy without lessening its commitment to entertainment.

❂ ❂ ❂

After the summertime barrage of *The Mortal Storm* and *Four Sons*, only a few feature pictures took direct aim at the Axis, with mixed results. The March of Time failed to win much of an audience for its first full-length movie, the antifascist *The Ramparts We Watch*. Walter Wanger produced John Ford's *The Long Voyage Home*, a terrific film about merchant marines sailing under the threat of German air attack, only to see it, too, sink at the box office. A petulant Ford argued that "people want 'pretty' pictures and 'nice' stories. . . . They don't want 'life' in the movies. They're fed up with life and it's damned unpleasant." While grossly simplifying the motion-picture market, the director's complaint had merit. Gloomy pictures set in wartime environments generally underperformed more uplifting stories.[7]

Wanger hit pay dirt with his production of Alfred Hitchcock's *Foreign Correspondent*. Originally conceived as an adaptation of journalist Vincent Sheean's memoirs, *Personal History*, the project took several twists that preserved Sheean's anti-Nazism while radically reshaping his autobiography. Joel McCrea plays Johnny Jones, an American reporter who shifts from apathy to interventionism as Europe slides into war. Set in 1939, the movie's beginning finds Jones lazily cutting paper snowflakes in his New York office, oblivious to the emerging crisis overseas. His editor transfers him to London, where the reporter stumbles into a complex web of assassinations, secret agents, and fifth columnists that awakens him to Nazism's global ambitions. By the film's end he is screaming for the United States to save the world from German aggression.[8]

Foreign Correspondent closes with Jones making a radio address to the United States in the midst of an air raid on London. Reminiscent of Henry Fonda's monologue in *Blockade*, Hitchcock's tribute to such interventionist correspondents as Edward R. Murrow could have sounded phony. McCrea's sense of urgency, however, trumps the speech's staginess. "All that noise you hear is insanity," he tells listeners as bombs crash around the station:

> It's death coming to London. . . . You can hear the bombs falling on the streets and the homes. Don't tune me out, hang on a while—this is a big story and you're part of it. It's too late to do anything here now except stand in the dark and let them come. It's as if the lights were all out everywhere, except in America. Keep those lights burning. Cover them with steel, rail them with guns, build a canopy of battleships and bombing planes around them. Hello America. Hang on to your lights, they're the only lights left in the world!

Joseph Goebbels called *Foreign Correspondent* "a masterpiece of propaganda." It works because the message supplements rather than overwhelms its intricate plot and masterful set pieces. It is a complete picture that entertains as well as informs.[9]

Released around the same time as *Foreign Correspondent,* Warners' reworking of Rafael Sabatini's novel *The Sea Hawk* lengthened the studio's list of disguised anti-Nazi pictures. Since the early 1930s the studio had considered updating the swashbuckling epic, which appeared in 1924 as a silent film, but proceeded only after the 1938 Munich Conference signaled the Chamberlain government's inability to slow Hitler's territorial ambitions. Warners executives saw *The Sea Hawk*'s story of England's 1588 victory over the Spanish Armada as a stand-in for democracy's current battle against autocracy. In the studio's cosmology the duplicitous Lord Wolfingham (Henry Daniell), who assured Queen Elizabeth that the Spanish posed no threat to England, symbolizes British appeasers. Don Alvarez (Claude Rains), who secretly conspires with Wolfingham, acts as "a sort of one-man fifth column." Evil Spanish monarch Phillip II (Montagu Love) assumes the Hitler role. Cast as Geoffrey Thorpe, a dashing privateer who saves England by bringing word of the armada's impending arrival, Errol Flynn reprises his *Adventures of Robin Hood* function as the guarantor of liberty.[10]

Warners' advertising stressed *The Sea Hawk*'s action sequences, hailing it as "The *Robin Hood* of the Sea." Flynn's star power attracted viewers uninterested in the picture's political subtext. Thanks largely to a strong showing overseas, the film became a runaway hit. Its contemporary undertones, which audiences could grasp without missing the adventure onscreen, also gained it notice. "I am sure the Ministry [of Information] must feel obliged to Warner's for this propaganda gesture," noted the *New York Evening News.* "Quite an interesting parallel," observed Bosley Crowther of the *New York Times.* "Get it?"[11]

MGM found less success with its latest service picture, *Flight Command.* Made with script input from the United States Navy, the studio hoped the tale of a reckless pilot (Robert Taylor) who joins a top-notch fighter squadron would "not only furnish interesting entertainment but will be of definite value to the Navy's air program." Although it contained some exciting flying sequences, audiences were already growing bored by the genre. "The old service story, but at its worst," decreed the *Nation.*[12]

MGM had another box-office dud with *Escape,* which it launched at the same time as *The Mortal Storm* but did not wrap until fall 1940. Like the earlier picture, *Escape* harshly criticized Nazism. Russian actress Nazimova gave a touching performance as Emmy Ritter, an elderly woman executed in a concentration camp for helping Jews escape to America. Robert Taylor is solid as Emmy's Americanized son, who travels to Germany to track down his missing mother. Conrad Veidt is delicious as the murderous General Kurt von Kolb.

Despite receiving positive notices, *Escape* suffered from a fatal flaw. *Variety* called it "intense and passionate with emotion, depressing and dolorous in pitting its frightened devotions and sacrifices against the inexorable laws of a callous, many-fingered authority." In other words, *Escape* neither entertained nor offered any new analysis of the Nazis. Audiences already knew how evil Hitler's men were. They saw no reason to spend their leisure money to be reminded. Antifascist films succeeded or failed based on what *else* they were. Audiences tolerated such messages within the context of adventure stories or exciting mysteries. Downbeat tales of Nazi oppression, no matter how brilliant or scathing, did not draw enough viewers to make them viable.[13]

Escape and other fictionalized representations of Nazi Germany resulted from Hollywood's effort to win audiences, stay in Washington's good graces, and satisfy its patriotic urges. The results did not justify the financial risk of making such films. Studios essentially abandoned the German cycle after 1940. The Production Code's moralistic ethos had conditioned viewers to anticipate beautiful settings, simple problems, and happy endings. None of these were possible once Nazis made an appearance. Patriotic films, prodemocratic films, and even military films could be successful if well done. The next year, 1941, would see the proliferation of these themes.

One movie, however, bucked the trend in 1940, combining the grim realities of totalitarianism with big box-office returns. That picture was made only because its creator had total control over his productions and was therefore immune from the studio system's financial pressures.

○ ○ ○

Charlie Chaplin used his famous tramp shoes to imprint a trail of footsteps in the concrete sidewalk workmen poured between his dressing room and the Chaplin Studios stage. Over the ensuing years he started every picture by ritualistically retracing that trail on his way to the set. Chaplin was a perfectionist capable of filming hundreds of takes before finding one to his liking. He was especially meticulous with "Production No. 6," which eventually became *The Great Dictator*. He knew, as he once again followed those steps in the concrete in January 1939, that the fluid overseas situation might make his upcoming film obsolete at any moment (a risk he accentuated by stretching the preproduction process out over the next nine months) and that audiences might shun what he assumed would be his most controversial picture. It took around 175 days of filming, spread over a thirteen-month-long period, to get "Production No. 6" in the can.[14]

With the exception of *Gone with the Wind*, no movie from this era garnered as much advance attention as Chaplin's lampooning of European tyrants. Rumors about the plot buzzed around the world for years, some true at the time but eventually rendered false by the comedian's incessant tinkering with the script. Not everyone was excited about the forthcoming feature. Hate mail poured into Hollywood even before cameras rolled, as people objected to Chaplin, a British citizen, making an openly un-neutral picture. "Regardless of how much we deplore the inhuman persecution of a minority race in foreign lands," one detractor wrote, "this man should not be permitted to use the United States as a background and sounding board . . . with the avowed purpose of stirring up further strife and recrimination between Germany and the United States Government." German consul Georg Gyssling strongly opposed the production once word of the forthcoming shoot leaked in 1938. Studio heads took a wait-and-see approach. Many believed Chaplin's attack on the dictators would further unsettle an already tense movie environment.[15]

Such carping unnerved Chaplin, who knew his film needed big domestic returns to overcome the inevitable censorship overseas. He issued a press release from his yacht, the *Panacea,* in May 1940 denying persistent gossip that he had shelved *The Great Dictator.* "At a time like this," Chaplin wrote, "laughter is a safety valve for our sanity." He pressed onward, rewriting scenes as Europe sank deeper under Nazi domination. The Roosevelt administration quietly backed him. Commerce Secretary Harry Hopkins assured the comedian of the president's support, although what that meant remained unclear. Chaplin shot some five hundred thousand feet of footage and spent around $1.5 million before he was satisfied. The final print of *The Great Dictator* checked in at 11,600 feet. As a sign of how far things had progressed since Hays declared "hate films" off limits, the Breen Office provided surprisingly little opposition. It probably helped that Breen screened the movie in September 1940, a few weeks after Germany sealed its borders to American features. The PCA chief raved that *The Great Dictator* "is superb screen entertainment and marks Mr. Chaplin, I think, as our greatest artist." His only request, and he made it sheepishly, was that Chaplin remove the word "lousy" from the final cut.[16]

Chaplin tweaked the movie through a month of previews and private showings. Harry Hopkins joined the comedian at one press screening. "It's a great picture," Hopkins told him afterward, "a very worthwhile thing to do, but it hasn't a chance. It will lose money." Chaplin worried that Hopkins was right. His nerves were frayed by October 15, when the movie opened at Broadway's Astor and Capitol Theaters. Chaplin attended both premieres with his costar and wife, Paulette Goddard. An edgy Chaplin managed a feeble "I hope you like it" as a cordon of thirty policemen fended off the thousands of fans trying to reach the couple. A host of figures from filmdom, including Joan Crawford, Douglas Fairbanks Jr., Will Hays, Harry Warner, and Adolph Zukor, also attended. Equally notable were the nonmovie people who showed up. The presence of Democratic politico James Farley, Mayor Fiorello LaGuardia, Henry Luce, CBS's William Paley, Franklin D. Roosevelt Jr., RCA's David

Sarnoff, Senator Robert Wagner, and H. G. Wells underscored the fact that this was no ordinary picture.[17]

The Great Dictator puzzled movie fans. Chaplin's films always blended pathos with comedy, but his new effort took his thematic schizophrenia to uncomfortable places. Audiences did not know whether to chuckle or cry. It "leaves one with a queer mixture of enthusiasm and disappointment," explained *Nation*'s Franz Hollering. "Neither fish nor fowl," the *Indianapolis Star* decided. Chaplin believed the best way to attack tyrants was to laugh at them. Many, however, found concentration camps too serious for levity. "Chaplin throwing platefuls of strawberries and cream and the sight of Jews being shot in the streets do not mix," *Time* observed.[18]

Chaplin split *The Great Dictator* into two interrelated parts. Its more maudlin segments focus on a ghettoized Jewish barber, a wounded veteran of the Great War, living in the fictional country of Tomania. Here Chaplin plays the classic tramp, an unassuming fellow who finds himself plunged into events beyond his control. The barber wants what Chaplin's heroes often desired—a family and a stable home. He dreams of marrying Hannah (Goddard) and revels in his modest career. His gleeful shaving of a customer to the rhythms of a Hungarian dance speaks volumes about his appreciation for life's joys. The pure-hearted barber is an utterly sympathetic character, a foreigner who nevertheless embodies the American dream of life, liberty, and the pursuit of happiness.

Ugliness surrounds this gentle soul. Storm troopers from Adenoid Hynkel's Double Cross Party smash windows and paint "Jew" on the barber's window. People dive into doorways when Hynkel's anti-Semitic screams blare from speakers strung around the city. Double Cross soldiers abuse the barber, nearly lynch him, blow up his shop, and eventually ship him to a concentration camp. Like Martin Breitner in *The Mortal Storm* and Johnny Jones in *Foreign Correspondent,* his plight gives Nazism's monstrosities a human face. "Wouldn't it be wonderful if they let us live and be happy again?" Hannah asks in one of the film's most poignant moments.

Nazi brutality had appeared in pictures before, as had Chaplin's assertion that not all Germans are bad. Chaplin never shows civilians supporting Hynkel's government, which consists entirely of uniformed officials. Commander Schultz (Reginald Gardiner) indicates that Hynkel lacks even the military's total support. An acquaintance of the barber's from the Great War, Schultz prevents marauding storm troopers from murdering the barber, then becomes a fugitive saboteur when he denounces the dictator's anti-Jewish programs. In him the audience gains hope that the Nazi regime might collapse from internal dissent, or at least gains assurance that some Germans opposed Hitler.

Chaplin's portrayal of Hynkel distinguished *The Great Dictator* from other prewar, anti-Nazi pictures. The film's Hynkel plotline is the funnier and more interesting of its two elements. Chaplin gave a dead-on parody of Americans' perceptions of Hitler. Microphones bend away in apparent terror when the dictator belts out his angry rants. His contorted face haunts the screen as he babbles in Germanic gibberish laced with "pretzels," "sauerbraten," "schnitzels," and assorted coughs and wheezes. He thrives by demeaning weaker men, particularly his bumbling flunky, Field Marshal Herring (Billy Gilbert). Herring/Göring's ineptitude at foreign policy and penchant for harebrained military schemes infuriate the dictator, who rips off the dozens of medals adorning the field marshal's chest as punishment for his stupidity.

Chaplin invests Hynkel's cold-bloodedness with a broad streak of satirical comedy that chides Hitlerism even as it exposes its perversity. Hynkel speaks of killing all brunettes because they are insufficiently Aryan. He dreams of a blond world—with a brunette dictator. He casually orders Herring to execute three thousand striking factory men because, he explains in a disarmingly gentle voice, "I don't want any of my workers dissatisfied."

Propaganda Minister Garbitsch (Henry Daniell) lurks behind Hynkel's murderous side. He is the puppet master who fuels the dictator's mania for conquest, the callous politician who proposes anti-Semitic policies as a way of diverting public attention from Tomania's sagging economy. Hynkel becomes a pathetic, almost pitiable, figure when Garbitsch/Goebbels is near. The shaker of worlds dissolves into a fragile man who lacks confidence in his decision-making abilities. He is the youthful, prewar Hitler trying to make a name for himself in Vienna, desperately hoping for someone to pay attention to him.

Hynkel's most human moment comes during Chaplin's famous dance with the globe, an eerie parallel to the barber's blissful shave. The dictator's anguished expression when his balloon finally pops signifies the futility of his dream of world domination, transforming him from a conqueror of nations into a misguided, doomed figure. He is *Black Legion*'s Frank Taylor all over again, a small man who conceals his weakness behind hyperaggressive posturing.

Chaplin is at his most brilliant when he introduces Benzini Napaloni (Jack Oakie), the ruler of Bacteria. Oakie's preening, chest-thumping performance is a remarkably accurate send-up of Mussolini's histrionics. Napaloni's and Hynkel's efforts to upstage each other provide some of *The Great Dictator*'s most biting, and hilarious, commentary. They jostle for position at a photo op, evaluate their armies like children comparing toy soldiers, and jack up barbers' seats in an immature bid to gain superiority over the other. Napaloni clearly dominates, just as many suspected that Mussolini controlled Hitler. His boisterous "Hello, Hynkie!" greeting, accompanied by a solid smack on the back, leaves Tomania's despot spluttering for a response.

The Great Dictator outlines a system run by lunatics, men who almost start a food fight to decide who will control the nation of Osterlich. Its parody gained power from scenes grounded in reality, including spoofs on the Nuremburg rallies and the dictators' 1938 meeting at a Rome train station. The film's overt linkage of Hitlerism with anti-Semitism further separated it from competitors. Only the self-financed Chaplin could have mocked Hitler so mercilessly. Considering the moguls' avoidance of the Jewish question, only a gentile like Chaplin could have made the point so forcefully. Nazi detractors mistakenly blasted it as a "Jewish production" by "the Jew Chaplin."[19]

The closing sequence became the most talked-about part of the film. Double Cross soldiers catch the barber trying to escape the concentration camp, mistake him for Hynkel, and rush him to a party rally. His address to the faithful, delivered at the camera rather than the crowd, broke all the rules of filmmaking. It was too long, too formal, never changed angles, and tore down the fourth wall separating the actor from the audience. Its disregard for convention forced viewers to pay attention. The Little Tramp was about to speak.

Unfortunately, the Tramp does not make much sense. He denounces intolerance, greed, national borders, and "the bitterness of men who fear human progress." He promises that "the hate of men will pass, and dictators die, and the power they took from the people will return to the people." He calls for "universal brotherhood" and argues that man has become a slave to machines. He urges soldiers to ignore "unnatural men, machine men with machine minds and machine hearts." Although inspiring and utopian, his speech never focuses on a clear goal or suggests a concrete response to dictatorship. While intended as a denunciation of unthinking followers of totalitarianism, its allusions to a mechanized humanity feel like a holdover from his previous picture, *Modern Times*.

The tramp continues, talking not of American intervention but of his hopes for a lasting peace. "Look up Hannah," he implores. "The clouds are lifting, the sun is breaking through. We are coming out of the darkness and into light. We are coming into a new world, a kinder world where men rise above their hate, their greed and brutality. Look up, Hannah! The soul of man has been given wings, and at last he is beginning to fly. He is flying into the rainbow, into hope, into the future. A glorious future that belongs to you, to me, and to all of us." As he speaks, Hannah, who has escaped to Osterlich, looks to the heavens, her eyes radiant with the promise of a brighter tomorrow.

Chaplin's final oration confirmed his conception of *The Great Dictator* as more than "Production No. 6." After wrestling with the ending for months, the comedian wrote his speech as France was falling and filmed it the day Hitler entered Paris. He saw the scene as the picture's heart, his last chance to save the world from insanity. Despite his noble intentions, the closing scene left many scratching their heads. Reviewers derided it as "frighteningly bad," "embarrassingly inartistic," and "dramatically and even inspirationally futile." It was mawkish even for Chaplin.[20]

The Great Dictator was nevertheless Chaplin's biggest hit, grossing more than $5 million worldwide. Mexicans flocked to see it. The British loved it too. Churchill, who attended a private screening with his cabinet in December, thought it was fantastic. It was also banned in, among other places, Argentina, Belgium, Brazil, Denmark, France, Germany, Holland, Hungary, Italy, Japan, Luxembourg, Norway, Paraguay, Peru, Poland, Romania, and Spain. Its impact stemmed largely from its star's unparalleled reputation and its thematic uniqueness. None of the majors made a similar film or pursued his outcry against Nazi anti-Semitism. Many wrongly remember it as the only picture from the era that overtly defied the Nazis.[21]

Despite Hopkins's earlier assurances, Franklin Roosevelt harbored grave doubts about *The Great Dictator*. He thought the production would encourage Axis supporters in South America to take bolder action. When Chaplin visited the White House, the president greeted him with a stern "sit down, Charlie; your picture is giving us a lot of trouble in the Argentine." A friend later joked that the comic was "received at the White House, but not embraced."[22]

CHAPTER FIFTEEN

Closing the Ring

THE AXIS EMPIRE EXPANDED even as audiences laughed at Charlie Chaplin's dictator and thrilled at Tyrone Power's Zorro. Hitler spent the fall of 1940 moving troops into Romania and gearing up to invade his ally, the Soviet Union. Japan joined the Axis that September. German bombers were still pummeling targets in Britain. Italy was also on the move, dispatching its legions to Egypt in September and to Greece in October. Outnumbered but willing to fight, Great Britain mounted a North African offensive that December in hopes of reversing Italian gains in the region.

These same months saw pivotal developments in the United States as Roosevelt and his subordinates stepped up efforts to save Great Britain from Nazi domination. The administration's actions prompted a powerful response from well-intentioned Americans who saw the president's agenda leading to bloodshed and disillusionment. Hollywood played a role in this unfolding dispute over American aid to Britain. Studio leaders' formation of the Motion Picture Committee Cooperating for the National Defense in June indicated a beginning rather than a conclusion to the Hollywood-Washington collaboration. The film capital intertwined more intensely with the nation's capital during the fall and winter of 1940. Power brokers on both coasts needed each other's help. Hollywood broadcast the Roosevelt administration's policies to a mass audience, while the Roosevelt administration looked after Hollywood's financial needs and furthered its aspirations for social legitimacy.

The mood in Washington that fall was grim but not hopeless. Congress had allocated billions in new defense spending. Great Britain's spirited fight against the *Luftwaffe* perked up the president, who nevertheless doubted the island nation could withstand the German onslaught without American assistance. Finally overcoming his political reservations, Roosevelt acceded to Churchill's requests to reinforce Britain's devastated navy. On September 3, the first anniversary of the European conflict, the president publicized his exchange of fifty decrepit American destroyers for ten British bases in Canada and the Caribbean. The trade appeared to favor the United States and certainly suited the American people's desire for hemispheric defense. Churchill, on the other hand, viewed the destroyers-for-bases pact as the end of American neutrality. From this point forward, he told the House of Commons, the two nations were "somewhat mixed up together. . . . I could not stop it if I wished; no one can stop it. Like the Mississippi, it just keeps rolling along. Let it roll. Let it roll on full flood."[1]

Some wanted to nip this budding Anglo-American unity. Yale law student R. Douglas Stuart announced the creation of America First, an organization dedicated to keeping the United States out of war, the day after the destroyers-for-bases agreement went public. Stuart had spent months laying the foundation for America First, gaining encouragement from such important Republican senators as Champ Clark, Robert La-Follette, Robert Taft, and Burton Wheeler. Stuart persuaded retired general and current Sears, Roebuck chairman Robert Wood to serve as national chairman. America First's letterhead also listed American Olympic Committee president Avery Brundage; meat tycoon Jay Hormel; Eleanor Roosevelt's cousin, Alice Roosevelt Longworth; and former *Nation* editor Oswald Garrison Villard.[2]

Most members of America First disliked Hitler but also dismissed Britain's claims to be fighting for democracy. To them the conflict represented a European struggle for power, not an epic clash of irreconcilable political systems. American involvement might escalate the fight into a total war that destroyed capitalism in Europe and cleared the way for a communist takeover. The group urged the United States to strengthen its defenses while pushing for a negotiated peace. Boasting prominent speakers including Charles Lindbergh, novelist Kathleen Norris, and silent-film actress Lillian Gish, America First became the country's most prominent anti-interventionist organization. By late 1941 it boasted around 450 chapters and more than eight hundred thousand members, with its greatest strength coming from the Midwest and Northeast.[3]

Isolationists already unnerved by the destroyers-for-bases deal received another blow when Roosevelt signed the Selective Service Act on

September 16. The law required all men between the ages of twenty-one and thirty-five to register for the draft. Comparing the call-up to colonial-era musters, the president promoted the million-man army it would produce as integral to the Western Hemisphere's security. Anti-interventionists claimed that the Axis posed no real threat to the United States and painted selective service as a step toward military dictatorship. Senator Hiram Johnson called it the "most sinister law" he had ever encountered. Senator Burton Wheeler warned that passing the bill would "slit the throat of the last democracy still living." Roosevelt got his legislative victory, but only after a tempestuous, three-month congressional debate on the bill again exposed the bitter divides tearing the country.[4]

Enemies of Roosevelt's rearmament moves had some unwanted allies in Hollywood. The movie colony's communist population had led the charge against Nazism one year earlier. Once the Nazi-Soviet pact put Hitler and Stalin on the same side, however, these same people launched a campaign to keep the United States out of the war. The Hollywood League for Democratic Action, the group that emerged from the Hollywood Anti-Nazi League's ashes, sponsored numerous peace rallies in the Los Angeles area. The league also opposed calls to fingerprint aliens, restrict immigration, and ban communists from relief rolls. Supporters boosted these bills as security measures. The League for Democratic Action saw them as assaults on civil liberties. One FBI informant referred to the league as "a 'Communist Front' of the worst type."[5]

The Hollywood League for Democratic Action was one of several like-minded associations. Its membership overlapped with the Hollywood Peace Forum, which held that Europe was fighting for imperialistic rather than ideological causes. The league also helped establish a Los Angeles branch of the American Peace Crusade, which later became the American Peace Mobilization and then, in late 1940, the American People's Mobilization (APM). These pacifist groups especially objected to the draft, which they saw as a precursor to martial law. "Everything that has happened in Germany is being prepared for us right here at home," one flyer declared.[6]

The two-thousand-member APM's message clashed with mainstream Hollywood's actions. In November 1940, for example, the group hosted a rally at the Embassy Auditorium, a fifteen-hundred-seat Beaux Arts–style facility located just east of Hollywood proper. The crowd cheered as director/screenwriter Herbert Biberman thundered against the war, Roosevelt, Ambassador Joseph Kennedy, and Great Britain. Washington closely monitored these cinematic leftists. The FBI suspected that such "thoroughly subversive" outfits as the League for Democratic Action might undermine the Allied cause. Armed with the 1940 Smith Act, which made it a crime to belong to any organization advocating the violent overthrow of the United States government, the agency circled, waiting to see whether it needed to pounce. Its moles fingered James Cagney, Al Jolson, Ginger Rogers, and Spencer Tracy as possible revolutionaries.[7]

FBI agents saw Biberman and fellow screenwriter Samuel Ornitz, who wrote the "Second World War" treatment that so intrigued David O. Selznick back in 1933, as far more dangerous than these stars. A member of the APM and a popular speaker at peace events, Ornitz hovered near the center of Hollywood's red activities. Los Angeles district attorney Buron Fitts dragged Ornitz into a grand jury hearing on communism in August 1940 that coincided with Congressman Martin Dies's own fact-finding mission to California. Biberman, who had a higher profile in peace circles than Ornitz, struck an FBI informant as "one of the most menacing figures in local revolutionary ranks today." His intelligence, charisma, sharp wit, and smooth demeanor made him a force to be reckoned with. "Herbert is a pain in the ass," fellow communists often laughed, "but he is our pain in the ass." Biberman gave his heart to the peace cause. He was "enormously self-sacrificing," screenwriter Alvah Bessie remembered, willing to "die in pieces for what he believed in." Biberman was so persuasive that the intelligence community could not decide whether he was actually a communist or a Nazi posing as a communist to win support for pacifism.[8]

Fortunately for Hollywood moguls, local peace activists never seriously damaged the Roosevelt administration's good feelings for the industry. Washington signaled its continuing favor by terminating Thurman Arnold's antitrust suit. Industry lawyers met with government attorneys throughout the summer and fall of 1940 to flesh out the consent-decree agreement struck in June. Negotiations did not proceed smoothly. Justice Department attorneys considered restarting the trial after studios repeatedly rejected their harsh terms. Hollywood itself bickered over the decree. Columbia, Universal, and United Artists—the three majors that did not own theaters—withdrew from talks. Fearing damage to their large theater chains, Fox and Paramount also threatened to scuttle negotiations. Independent theater owners wanted divorcement and a tough solution to the block-booking problem. High-ranking administration officials, including Roosevelt, urged the parties to strike a deal.[9]

Arnold now knew how Will Hays felt. "The role of pacifier of trade disputes in the motion picture industry is a most unhappy one," he told reporters. Both sides finally hammered out a pact after a marathon session at New York City's Bar Building in October, the same month Chaplin released *The Great Dictator*. The final consent decree ended blind selling and required studios to sell films in blocks of five or fewer rather than forcing exhibitors to buy a year's worth of product at one time. It allowed majors to keep their theaters but prevented them from initiating a general program of theater purchases for three years, an intentionally vague provision that put few real restrictions on theater buying. Resolution of disputes fell to the American Arbitration Association, which established offices for hearings around the country.[10]

"An industry which has been under harassment, uncertainty and pressure for more than two years is about ready to get back to work," *Variety* exclaimed. Major studios scored an enormous victory. Their distribution network faced minor tweaking, but their exhibition system remained intact. Producers' cooperation with Roosevelt, a product of economic necessity, patriotism, and the administration's desire to cement relations on the eve of war, was largely responsible for their narrow escape. Jack Warner wrote the White House to personally thank the president for intervening and for involving Harry Hopkins. He predicted the consent decree would become a "living instrument of industry peace," a document that enabled quarrelsome studio heads to work together for the defense of American democracy and freedom.[11]

✿ ✿ ✿

The successful conclusion of the antitrust matter and deteriorating overseas situation led studios to intensify their internationalist activities through late 1940. Jack Warner volunteered to film any project the administration wanted. Paramount's Barney Balaban promised his stars for shortwave radio broadcasts designed to offset Axis influence in Latin America. Will Hays suggested that MGM collaborate with the State

Department on a film about hemispheric defense. W. S. Van Dyke offered to direct. Presidential secretary Stephen Early and Assistant Secretary of State Adolph Berle gathered material for the project, which never came off. Roosevelt did ask MGM to make a prodefense short, resulting in the October 1940 ode to naval aviators, "Eyes of the Navy." The project meant "thousands of votes" for the president, Van Dyke believed. FDR thought the propaganda short was "extraordinarily good."[12]

With the War Department's assistance, Warner Bros.' patriotic shorts series assumed a more martial tone in late 1940. The studio used real servicemen—carefully selected for their "clean-cut" appearances—and facilities in San Diego for "March On, Marines!" Studio crews returned to San Diego a few weeks later to shoot "Meet the Fleet," again with input from the War Department. August 1940's "Service with the Colors" examined an army infantry unit. Warners put "Wings of Steel" into production at year's end. Released in early 1941, the Technicolor short examined training exercises for the Army Air Corps. The War Department purchased prints to use as recruiting tools—not surprising, as the corps had a hand in scripting it. With their emphasis on group unity, institutional pride, and achieving concrete objectives, these military-themed films condensed the motifs of the service-feature genre into twenty-minute nuggets of martial pride. Their documentary tone and lack of recognizable stars gave them a more authentic feel than their feature-length kin.[13]

Hollywood's support for the president's policies demanded a strong presence in his campaign for a third term. The Hollywood for Roosevelt Committee was the most visible industry-centered, pro-FDR organization. Formed by Melvyn Douglas, Philip Dunne, W. S. Van Dyke, and other Hollywood liberals, the committee saw Roosevelt's reelection as the sole hope for "the salvation of American democracy." Members canvassed the nation during the run-up to the election. Humphrey Bogart, Douglas Fairbanks Jr., Henry Fonda, James Garfield, Walter Huston, and Groucho Marx made national radio broadcasts. Edward G. Robinson hosted a reception for pro–New Deal senator Claude Pepper. Claude Rains stumped in New York, Philadelphia, and Chicago. Joan Bennett, Dorothy Lamour, and Pat O'Brien were among those on the platform when vice presidential nominee Henry Wallace spoke at the Hollywood Bowl. The committee also placed newspaper ads, bought space on billboards, and distributed hundreds of thousands of stickers and buttons.[14]

Melvyn Douglas epitomized the intensifying Hollywood-Washington connections. A guiding force behind 1938's Committee of 56 and a long-time public critic of Nazi Germany, the debonair, deftly comedic star of *Ninotchka* developed into a seasoned politico between appearances in four movies in 1940. He served as a delegate to that year's Democratic National Convention, watching from the floor as wife Helen Gahagan Douglas sang the national anthem. An avid backer of the president's foreign policy, Douglas met frequently with Roosevelt and other major politicians. The 1940 election, he declared in one of the 168 speeches he made on FDR's behalf that year, was "a referendum—and possibly a final referendum—to determine once and for all whether or not we are to continue with the American way of life—the good, democratic way we all know and love." He ripped Republican challenger Wendell Willkie as a representative of the moneyed class and championed Roosevelt's candidacy as "democracy's last stand in America."[15]

While actors and studio workers overwhelmingly backed the president, many executives quietly rooted for the Republicans. The third-term issue bothered many, as did Roosevelt's perceived hostility to big business. Will Hays backed Willkie, of course, a fellow Indiana Republican. Among other contributions, Hays arranged for the comic duo Laurel and Hardy to visit a Willkie rally. With the exception of MGM president Nick Schenck, most MGM managers leaned Republican. Hedda Hopper, Leo McCarey, Robert Montgomery, and George Stevens appeared alongside Willkie. Jack and Harry Warner played it safe by keeping silent during the campaign. Walter Wanger hoped for a Willkie victory but doubted he could unseat the incumbent. "Apparently, he is only a short subject," the producer privately said of Willkie, "and I don't think he will ever make good in a feature. I have been very disappointed with his box-office since his acceptance speech—but here's hoping."[16]

Movie moguls moved swiftly to restore good feelings after Roosevelt's November 1940 reelection. Studio-owned theaters displayed an onscreen plea for national reconciliation that almost but did not quite congratulate the victor: "Whatever the differences were among us before the election, there should remain no doubt that there are no differences among us today. We stand behind the man of the people's choice. We must not fall prey to the plan of 'divide and conquer.' The Great Liberator has given us our rule of national life—'UNITED WE STAND, DIVIDED WE FALL.'" Well-wishes poured into the Oval Office. Douglas Fairbanks Jr.'s "thousand hurrahs" were sincere. Hays's sycophantic promise to "do all I can to make certain that a united country brings you all the aid possible" did not ring so true. The always-obsequious Jack Warner sent congratulations, along with news of another Warner Bros. donation to the British Spitfire Fund. Nick Schenck rounded up celebrities to attend the inauguration, paying for MGM's Wallace Beery, Maureen O'Hara, George Raft, Mickey Rooney, Lana Turner, and others to make the trip east.[17]

Douglas Fairbanks Jr. also attended the gala. His relationship with Franklin Roosevelt stretched back to the president's days as assistant secretary of the navy. His father, the famous actor Douglas Fairbanks Sr., became fast friends with FDR after they met during a 1918 Liberty Loan tour. Their children often roller-skated together in New York City. A grown-up Fairbanks Jr. escaped his father's considerable shadow with strong performances in the original *Dawn Patrol, Little Caesar, The Prisoner of Zenda,* and *Gunga Din* before devoting himself to studying the international scene. He cultivated Walter Wanger, columnist Walter Lippmann, and other well-informed acquaintances. His famous name gave him entrée into many of England's elite families, who provided additional perspectives for the intellectually curious actor. Although perceptive, Fairbanks was not always prescient—he found Winston Churchill brilliant when they met in 1938 but considered him too old to be politically relevant.

Fairbanks made no secret of his pro-British proclivities. As chair of the Southern California branch of William Allen White's Committee to Defend America by Aiding the Allies, he frequently spoke on behalf of Anglo-American unity. Six weeks before the presidential election he appeared at a White Committee rally in heavily isolationist Chicago alongside journalist Dorothy Thompson and Senator Claude Pepper. "I am frankly pro-British," Fairbanks told the crowd of sixteen thousand and a national radio audience, "but only because I am radically pro-American." He insisted that the United States must join Great Britain's crusade to preserve democracy or else face the prospect of a world dominated by dictators.[18]

Fairbanks thought his outspoken political beliefs undermined his box-office appeal and discouraged producers from offering him roles. The actor desperately wanted to make an intensely pro-British picture about an American living in England—a more overtly propagandistic version of *A Yank at Oxford*—but found no takers. Hollywood's tepid response to Nazism stunned him. "There is great hysteria at the moment in the film industry and no little defeatism," he told presidential secretary Stephen Early in May 1940. "Most companies are wary of *any* subject likely to offend the Germans." Studios released so few antifascist pictures that Fairbanks asked whether the president had secretly asked producers to avoid "controversial subjects." Early assured his friend that the administration did not oppose his project. "The best guidance I can offer you," Early diplomatically observed, was that Roosevelt refused to "ask that every American remain neutral in thought."[19]

Although Fairbanks never made his propaganda picture, he held fast to his interventionism. He visited the White House and Hyde Park regularly, counted Harry Hopkins and Cordell Hull among his friends, and funded three RAF hospitals. Fairbanks still made an occasional movie, even as his attention drifted toward national service; he lobbied FDR for an army or navy commission through the fall of 1940. Fairbanks spent much of his time at the inaugural discussing the need to alert people to the Axis threat with Hull, Undersecretary of State Sumner Welles, and Roosevelt's son-in-law, John Boettiger. He rode home wondering how he could do more to assist national preparedness. His Washington friends also left the meeting speculating whether the handsome, well-spoken, and politically astute performer might be useful.[20]

Hollywood's ambivalence toward Roosevelt's reelection did not stop it from relying on his administration's benevolence when a new overseas crisis heated up during the campaign's last days. The movie quota the State Department negotiated with Great Britain in late 1939 expired in October, and the hard-pressed British government was eager to extract more revenue from Hollywood. Britain's Board of Trade therefore proposed slashing the cap on movie profit exports from $17.5 million to $5 million. "The industry will barely be left with the tail off its shirt," a shocked Ambassador Kennedy complained. Weary of the British and increasingly on the outs with Roosevelt because of his pro-German views, Kennedy advised the majors to jump ship before it sank. "They might just as well show some real guts and risk the whole shirt," he told Hull. Better to abandon Britain than to sign a bad deal that might become a model for future Anglo-American trade pacts.[21]

The Board of Trade's proposal horrified studio heads. Although hampered by German bombers, MGM, Paramount, and Warners were still making films in the London area. They suggested scrapping the quota system altogether in recognition of their contributions to British morale. Kennedy dug in his heels on their behalf. Knowing Great Britain needed the United States, he threatened a boycott, as he had the year before. As they had the previous year, Anglo negotiators thought the ambassador was bluffing but retreated for fear of angering Roosevelt and the British people. Hollywood provided around three-quarters of the films shown in Britain. Losing this vital source of entertainment would strike a severe blow to national morale. Whitehall assented to the ambassador's insistence on a $12 million transfer limit, later upping it to $12.9 million after some additional hardball negotiating. Kennedy also won a front-loaded payment schedule that returned 75 percent of the transfer limit to the United States during the first six months of the yearlong agreement, a clause that reflected Kennedy's opinion on the war's future course.[22]

The State Department once again saved millions of dollars for Hollywood, a triumph that momentarily brightened a bleak reality. Revenue from Britain, which now accounted for two-thirds of foreign income, was down nearly half from its prewar level. "Foreign departments admit that they cannot see how conditions can get better," *Film Daily* conceded.[23]

Kennedy seconded the trade journal's pessimism. Recalled to the United States during the British negotiations, the ambassador accepted Jack and Harry Warner's invitation to speak to movie executives. His talk during a three-hour lunch on the Warner Bros. lot left the gathering of fifty industry leaders speechless. Kennedy told them the United States should limit aid to Britain in case the Nazis won the war, an event he thought likely. More important, he asked producers to "stop making anti-Nazi pictures or using the film medium to promote or show sympathy to the cause of the 'democracies' versus the 'dictators.' " Pictures like *The Mortal Storm, Escape,* and *Arise, My Love,* an anti-Nazi comedy released by Paramount a few weeks before Kennedy's visit, did more harm than good because they highlighted Jewish control of the movies.

Many Anglos blamed the war on Jews, Kennedy warned, and anti-Semitism was on the rise in Britain. He advised producers to "get those Jewish names off the screen." After Kennedy's lecture, screenwriter Ben Hecht remembered, "all of Hollywood's top Jews went around with their grief hidden like a Jewish fox under their Gentile vests." MGM and Paramount canceled several anti-Nazi projects, including *Heil America, Heroes, I Had a Comrade,* and *Invasion.*[24]

It was probably good for Hollywood that Kennedy left London when he did. Although he still respected Hays, the moguls' constant harping exhausted his patience. He suspected the British had roped studio chiefs into a naively interventionist course. The "Jewish boys . . . are quite nervous about the conditions and they have reason to be," Kennedy told one of his staffers. "Smart British interests have already taken over the Jewish boys . . . and have sold them an idea they already had, that they must work for England, even if it means getting us into the war."[25]

✿ ✿ ✿

Although rethinking their onscreen antifascism, Hollywood's elite did not shy away from the government's defense effort. The sheer magnitude of the military buildup overwhelmed the Army Signal Corps' ability to make training films for new recruits. Major studios filled the gap. Warners bit first, proposing in September to make a series of movies for the army at no cost. Fearful of surrendering control over content, the Signal Corps balked at the suggestion. The Motion Picture Committee Cooperating for the National Defense renewed the offer soon after, suggesting that the Academy's Research Council, whose Nathan Levinson already supervised the corps' Hollywood intern project, head the program. Research Council member Captain Gordon Mitchell pushed the idea on his superior, Chief Signal Officer Major General J. O. Mauborgne, who approved the plan. Secretary of War Henry Stimson signed off on the new program in December 1940.[26]

The Research Council grew out of the early 1930s battles over sound patents. Formed in 1934, it consisted of Captain Mitchell, representatives from the majors' technical departments, and Chairman Darryl F. Zanuck. Its primary tasks were to pool patents and promote new film-making technologies. It was not the most obvious entity to implement the new training-film plan, but Gordon Mitchell was an ambitious man whose military connections paved the way for the union. In addition, his close friend Zanuck wanted to better align Hollywood with Washington by wresting control from the unwieldy MPCC, a recalibration that would, not coincidentally, boost the Fox executive's own stature. "We were supposed to be in a national emergency," Zanuck asserted, "and nothing was being accomplished." He convinced his peers to expand the council's powers.[27]

Zanuck and Mitchell ran the training-film program with little interference from other studio bosses, largely on the basis of faith and good intentions. After receiving scenario ideas from the army, Zanuck's team hired screenwriters and doled out projects to studios. Although assignments theoretically rotated, Warners and Twentieth Century–Fox made a disproportionate number of pictures, which the Signal Corps bought at cost. The process involved no contracts or bids. Zanuck personally delivered the first two training films—one on sexual hygiene, the other on personal hygiene—to the War Department in February 1941. The Signal Corps had recognized Zanuck's labors on its behalf a few weeks earlier by making him a reserve lieutenant colonel.[28]

The Research Council's contributions to the war effort helped the majors preserve their oligopolistic control of the movie business. Zanuck's demand that studios not charge for administrative costs, materials, or overhead burnished Hollywood's patriotic image while saving the War Department a few thousand dollars per picture. It also shut out independent studios that might have been better equipped to produce training films but could not match the majors' cut-rate price. "We got the definite impression," said one small-studio manager, "that the doors were shut in Washington."[29]

Anglo-American relations had taken another turn by the time Zanuck got the training-film tie-up operating. Great Britain's financial problems strengthened an already tight bond between the two nations. British ambassador Lord Lothian bluntly appraised his country's status for American reporters in late November. "Well, boys," he said, "Britain's broke." Churchill believed his country would lose the war if it did not receive more aid from the United States. Roosevelt wanted to help but had few options, as the Neutrality Acts' cash-and-carry provision made it illegal to extend credit to nations at war.[30]

Roosevelt dreamed up a way around the Neutrality Acts while spending four days fishing and watching movies on a cruise down the Potomac. He took to the airwaves on his return to announce his plan. German bombers rained destruction on London as he spoke; it was on this night that Herbert Mason snapped his famous photo of St. Paul's Cathedral wreathed in smoke and flames. "Never before since Jamestown and Plymouth Rock has our American civilization been in such danger as now," the president said. If Britain could not stop the Nazis, the United States "would be living at the point of a gun." The only way to prevent this was to go all-out in assisting Britain. His proposal, lend-lease, called for Britain to borrow rather than buy American war materiel. "We must be the great arsenal of democracy," Roosevelt declared.[31]

Lend-lease sparked new protests from anti-interventionists. Senator Robert Taft compared the lending of military equipment with the lending of chewing gum: "you don't want it back." America First launched a massive campaign to block the bill. Chairman Robert Wood said Roosevelt wanted "a blank check book with the power to write away our manpower, our laws, and our liberties." Senator Burton Wheeler claimed that "if we lend or lease war materials today, we will lend or lease American boys tomorrow." Referring to the New Deal's Agricultural Adjustment Administration, which paid farmers to let land lie fallow, he blasted lend-lease as "the New Deal's triple 'A' foreign policy—it will plow under every fourth American boy." Roosevelt called the senator's comment "the rottenest thing that has been said in public life in my generation."[32]

Still celebrating their victory in the British quota negotiations, Hollywood chieftains applauded the president's resolve in international affairs. Louis B. Mayer called FDR's "arsenal of democracy" speech "masterful and inspiring." Jack and Harry Warner cabled a promise to "fight with you to help accomplish the principles of your noble address." Zanuck talked about a movie based on the address but worried about attacks from "anyone who is so stupid and short-sighted in not being able to agree with the President's point of view." Hays sent a congratulatory telegram after the broadcast. The new trade agreement and impending passage of lend-lease prompted a wave of pro-British film proposals. Zanuck had *A Yank in the R.A.F.* ready to go in January 1941. Selznick registered "There'll Always Be an England," with the MPPDA's title office. Twentieth Century–Fox submitted "A Yank at Dunkirk." Other studios locked up the title rights to "Royal Air Force Squadron," "Bomb Shelter," "Parachute Invasion," and "Running the Blockade."[33]

As always, it is difficult to separate sincerity from flattery. Will Hays passed a riddle around his office two months before congratulating Roosevelt for his bold speech:

> I was born in New York State in a great Mansion. I never knew what work was or is, and neither did my father. However, I know more about your work or business than you do. . . . I served four years as Governor of a great State and wrecked its finances. I have served eight years as President of the greatest nation in the World and now have it in the worst mess in its history. Through the prestige of my office, my wife and children have made fortunes. I now want to continue myself and family in office forever. WHAT'S MY NAME?

Seeing lend-lease as an opportunity to wring more money from Britain, Hays threatened to stop cooperating with the State Department's pro-Anglo agenda unless the agency used the program to free up Hollywood funds. Nor had Mayer suddenly transformed into a New Dealer. A majority of Americans backed lend-lease, which passed Congress in March of 1941, so his support corresponded with the public's position. With no revenues at stake on the continent, backing aid to Britain could only help the studios financially.[34]

But at some level these men must be taken at their word. Businessmen who made careers out of pleasing everyone, who for years hid behind the mantra of pure entertainment, were speaking out. They did not need to express an opinion; nobody would have felt cheated had Mayer and the Warners kept their thoughts to themselves. Favoring lend-lease put Hollywood at odds with millions of Americans who opposed additional aid, and it opened the studios to charges of warmongering. The moguls were patriotic, red-blooded Americans who perceived a threat to the country that made them. They benefited from democracy, freedom, and limited government, and they believed the Axis menaced those ideas. Movie producers could only carry their objections so far before colliding with the limits of what audiences wanted to see onscreen and what stockholders wanted to see on the bottom line. They did, however, make their voices heard.

The lend-lease debate offered a fitting close to a tumultuous year. Hollywood's pledge of solidarity with the president was the next step down a long road of shared objectives. The majors' divisive antitrust battle was over, the government was working for the industry overseas, and movie-makers were working with the government at home. Although much changed during the war years, the rough outlines of wartime Hollywood fell into place during 1940. Studios established most of the themes seen in wartime films. Talk of global democracy, American-style liberties, and overcoming prejudices for the sake of a greater cause permeated screens. The basic parameters of the dream factory's voluntary cooperation with Washington solidified a year before Pearl Harbor. Film folk celebrating the new year hoped 1941 would prove more peaceful abroad and less difficult at home. Neither wish would come true.

CHAPTER SIXTEEN

Weapons of Inspiration

❧ ❧ ❧

L EO THE LION WAS HOLLYWOOD'S most recognizable mascot. His roar announced not only the beginning of an MGM film but also the studio's pride in that production. He was a fitting symbol for the movie community in 1940. Like Leo, some film folk were stretching, making noise, establishing their presence. They were roaring antifascism. They were roaring Americanism, pan-Americanism, and Anglo-Americanism. They were roaring to wake a slumbering nation.

Their roar received an answering bray in January 1941. While it is hard to imagine a donkey besting a lion in some hypothetical battle of hooves and claws, the outcome was less certain in this case because the donkey symbolized one of the Democratic Party's most powerful senators, Montana's Burton K. Wheeler, a savvy politician who chewed up his opponents the same way he did the cigar that seemed permanently lodged in his mouth. One of the nation's premier isolationists, Wheeler was fed up with what he saw as the media's biased presentation of the war. Roosevelt's mastery of the press enabled the president to frame the discussion over America's role in the conflict and tar dissenters as unpatriotic. Most top radio commentators, including H. V. Kaltenborn, Raymond Gram Swing, Edward R. Murrow, and Walter Winchell, advocated intervention. Isolationists struggled to get their views aired. Wheeler saw Hollywood—Jewish-run Hollywood—as among the worst offenders. He believed newsreels and feature films deliberately promoted Roosevelt's position while demeaning his.[1]

As chair of the Senate Committee on Interstate Commerce, Wheeler was in a good position to answer Hollywood's preparedness blasts. Along with fellow isolationist Senator Gerald Nye of North Dakota, he hinted in December 1940 that an investigation of activities in the movie capital was in the works. Wheeler charged Will Hays with orchestrating a "violent propaganda campaign intending to incite the American people to the point where they will become involved in this war." The senator astutely targeted one of Hollywood's greatest fears. "I believe legislation will have to be enacted regulating the industry," he told Hays, "unless the industry itself displays a more impartial attitude." Wheeler's was one of many fusillades that hit Hollywood in the winter of 1940–1941. Oklahoma congressman Lyle Boren, for example, repeated Wheeler's call for investigations on the floor of the House of Representatives. The New York State Assembly considered a bill to prohibit movies that disseminated "hatred."[2]

Hays assumed a defensive posture, blithely maintaining that Hollywood still respected his pledge to avoid hate pictures. In a patently false statement he claimed that the few protests he had heard were equally divided between people accusing studios of being too prowar and those who saw them as excessively antiwar. Hays assured Wheeler that Hollywood was neither. "Our primary service to our nation at this time," he said, "can be rendered through the provision of wholesome entertainment." He provided statistics supposedly proving that newsreels, shorts, and feature films did not focus disproportionately on the war. Hays sent Roosevelt a copy of his reply in a bid for support. The president saw no reason to get involved but assured Hays that the industry had his sympathies. "Why do you say at the end of your letter to Wheeler 'with kindest personal regards?'" the president joked.[3]

Considering the future course of the conflict, it is easy to dismiss isolationists' charges, and isolationists themselves, as wrongheaded. They certainly engaged in political grandstanding, as does any pressure group, but their concerns were on the whole sincere. Americans were accustomed to the comforts of geographical distance. A nation that had not been invaded in more than a century could not accept that it faced real danger now. How can it be, Charles Lindbergh asked, "that our frontiers lie in Europe and that our destiny will be decided by European armies fighting upon European soil?" Wheeler and Nye, who cut their political teeth in the early-twentieth-century Progressive movement, wanted to refocus attention away from foreign affairs. Domestic matters, particularly the plight of the country's impoverished, struck them as far more pressing than a war thousands of miles away. Reflecting their western constituencies' suspicion of outsiders, they denounced the "foreign slackers, European royalty, [and] princes and potentates" pushing the United States to enter the conflict.[4]

Wheeler and his allies had not done their homework. They failed to provide titles of offensive pictures or to demonstrate evidence of having watched any prowar films. Anti-interventionists nevertheless had a point. Hollywood undoubtedly tilted away from their perspective. Major-studio releases brought up the war even when it played no role in the plot. As in other popular media, in 1941 studios incorporated the war into the language of film.

Bowery Blitzkrieg, a B movie starring Leo Gorcey and the East End Kids, revolves around a Golden Gloves tournament, not blitzkrieg or the Blitz. In RKO's comedy *Look Who's Laughing,* Throckmorton P. Gildersleeve compares Fibber McGee's broken dishwasher, which wildly flings plates and bowls, to an antiaircraft gun. One of Edgar Bergen's friends later loans Charlie McCarthy a quarter "on the lend-lease plan." In Warners' tribute to bridge builders, *Steel against the Sky,* the female lead brags that she is not wearing stockings, presumably because she is boycotting Japanese silk. Construction workers willingly take extra shifts to complete the bridge on schedule because the undertaking is somehow—exactly how is not clear—related to the defense program. Edward G. Robinson interpreted Captain Wolf Larsen as a fascist dictator in Warners' adaptation of Jack London's *The Sea Wolf.* His crew of thugs garb themselves in black, and Larsen operates the vessel like a despot. "It's my will and my will alone that runs this ship," he snarls. The physically brutal Larsen is interested solely in his own aggrandizement. His cruel monomania leaves new recruit George Leach (John Garfield) and rescued shipwreck victim Ruth Brewster (Ida Lupino) desperate to escape. "To be free," Ruth gasps. "To be let alone. To live in peace."

For all this, it is hard to fathom what noninterventionists wanted Hollywood to do. They were not moviemakers, nor did they have any real understanding of the issues facing the industry. The war was part of everyday life. Americans read about it in newspapers and magazines. They heard about it on the radio. Their children were being drafted because of it. Legislators debated the nation's response to it in the halls of Congress. Motion pictures could not ignore the war without making studios appear utterly irrelevant. Turning a blind eye to the conflict would provoke defense advocates and interventionists into accusing Hollywood of neglecting its patriotic duty. Total neutrality was impossible. Wars require people to take sides, and no studio could green-light a project portraying Nazis as heroic liberators. By the noninterventionists' logic, films discussing the conflict were inflammatory even when they concluded that war was morally wrong, as had every war picture made since 1918. To them any picture about war was a propaganda picture.

World War II pervaded the cinematic landscape. None of these features were overtly propagandistic. They instead made timely references or, in the case of *The Sea Wolf,* dealt with a timeless theme like the moral corruption of powerful men. But the majors were working on projects openly intended to pull sympathies toward the British or further familiarize Americans with the idea of fighting to defend their liberties. Not surprisingly, Warner Bros. and Twentieth Century–Fox led the way in ensuring that audiences did not forget about the conflict overseas.

ø ø ø

Darryl F. Zanuck began developing a picture about the Royal Air Force the moment the first German bomb struck London. He took inspiration from Billy Fiske, an American pilot who volunteered for the RAF, then died in August 1940 of injuries sustained in a dogfight. Two months later Zanuck dictated an eleven-page treatment for "The Eagle Squadron," the story of a bull-headed American test pilot named Pete Norton who enlists in the RAF after hearing Churchill speak on the radio. Pete's commitment to Britain grows throughout the film, culminating in his doing "some terrifically spectacular thing which ends in his death." Even though the details eluded him, the producer already envisioned "The Eagle Squadron" as a big-budget vehicle for Fox's biggest male star, Tyrone Power.[5]

Zanuck fleshed out his idea over the following weeks. He wanted to show British women contributing to the war effort while contrasting the individualistic Pete with his love interest, Duchess Patricia Bowden, whose parents trained her "to play ball with the team." Zanuck instructed his screenwriters to demonstrate that the RAF was a unified, cohesive organization that succeeded because it subordinated "the individual to the common good." By integrating into this seamless collective, Pete symbolized the importance of furthering the Anglo-American bond.[6]

Zanuck gave his RAF feature more personal attention than usual, plowing through draft after draft to nail down the film's particulars. He used *A Yank at Oxford* as a model but thought the earlier picture's comedic depictions of stuffy British aristocrats inappropriate for a movie designed to humanize America's friends across the ocean. Zanuck changed the female lead from Duchess Patricia, to Lady Patricia, to just-plain Pat, and finally to Carol Brown, an American serving in the WRENs, the RAF's women's division. To establish Zanuck's internationalist message, Pete, soon renamed Tim Baker, had to learn that "England is something more than an island . . . , that England is a spirit, that they are fighting for more than personal gain; they are fighting for freedom, for liberty, for a cause that they believe in." To bring in moviegoers, Pete/Tim must come to this realization without miring the film in long-winded speeches.[7]

Zanuck renamed his production *A Yank in the R.A.F.* after Walter Wanger registered "Eagle Squadron" for himself. The Fox head opened private talks with the British government once screenwriting got under way. "We could never get any co-operation from England unless we do some of the things they want us to do," Zanuck told his men. Air Ministry representatives objected to the treatment's implication that the British lost every dogfight with the Germans and protested its lighthearted treatment of Dunkirk. British bureaucrats urged Fox to internationalize Dunkirk by including French, Dutch, and Belgian troops. Most important, the ministry fiercely opposed Tim's death, which provided a gloomy ending that might dissuade Americans from backing the war. Zanuck relented, reworking the conclusion to have Tim marrying Carol as "There'll Always Be an England" plays in the background.[8]

British fingers left prints all over the picture. Jason Joy, one of Breen's assistants in the Production Code Administration, passed the script around the British Embassy. Minister for Aircraft Production Lord Beaverbrook provided technical advisers and stock footage. British officials urged Zanuck to get *A Yank in the R.A.F.* into production as soon as possible. The producer himself was impatient. "I have a definite obligation with the British Government and Air Ministry," he huffed, "an obligation that I intend to fulfill." Zanuck got cameras rolling in spring 1941, expediting shooting by reusing sets from *Man Hunt* and *How Green Was My Valley.* He kept his instructions to Betty Grable, cast as

Carol Brown, simple. "Act your pretty ass off for Britain," he commanded. With these words, *A Yank in the R.A.F.*, the last major pro-British picture Hollywood released before Pearl Harbor, was under way.[9]

Ten miles northeast in Burbank, the Warners lot was also humming. Vincent Sherman was filming the anti-Nazi adventure *Underground*. A much larger project, entitled *Sergeant York,* had also entered production. The latter film would become Hollywood's ultimate pre–Pearl Harbor justification for the United States' involvement in an overseas conflict.

Sergeant Alvin C. York was *the* hero of the Great War. Ironically, he joined the army in 1917 only reluctantly. York was parochial and profoundly ignorant, the possessor of a third-grade education. An intensely religious man, he applied for conscientious objector status after being drafted, but draft board officials did not recognize his tiny Church of Christ in Christian Union as a legitimate sect. He would have faded into obscurity but for one remarkable day in October 1918 when he and seven other soldiers captured 132 Germans in the Meuse-Argonne region of France. The army singled out York, awarding him the Medal of Honor and promoting him as a model of Americanism and soldierly virtue.[10]

York's heroics were a natural fit for Hollywood. Movie producers circled the soldier on his return to the United States. Jesse Lasky became York's chief pursuer after he watched New York City's boisterous parade for the sergeant in May 1919. Lasky was vice president of Famous Players–Lasky, the predecessor to Paramount and early Hollywood's premier studio. Neither his money nor his influence impressed the shy backwoodsman, who refused to commit to the project. "My life is not for sale," York insisted.[11]

York returned to Tennessee's Valley of the Three Forks of the Wolf. He retained his Christian pacifism, frequently speaking out against the war that made him famous. He found, however, that his time overseas changed him. His insularity and lack of schooling bothered him. He began working to lift his Upper Cumberland community out of rural isolation by advocating an expansion of educational opportunities, a difficult cause in a society wary of new ideas. He raised enough money to create the York Institute, but money dried up as the Depression took hold in the early 1930s. York's fervent isolationism survived the rise of fascism. He was a popular speaker for the Emergency Peace Campaign in the late 1930s, capitalizing on his unassailable credibility to argue that war led only to pain, misery, and economic suffering. By now York had little left but his ideals. He was almost broke. His neighbors, who resented his public profile and battles against the local political establishment, ostracized him.[12]

Jesse Lasky was in a similar predicament. After Paramount sacked him in 1931, he spent the next several years burning through his fortune while seeking employment. He desperately needed a hit to reestablish himself. Alvin York was never far from his mind. Lasky read biographies, compiled a book of press clippings, and assembled a rough outline for a picture about him. He visited York in 1938 to again pitch his biopic. The sergeant remained uninterested, in part because he believed motion pictures were sinful, the Devil's tool. Legend has it he had only seen one movie in his life (the legend, unfortunately, does not state what that movie was). He also objected to working with Jews, whom he regarded as Christ-killing moneygrubbers. Refusing to take no for an answer, Lasky made three more trips to Tennessee between 1938 and early 1940. He hammered at York's sense of responsibility and appealed to his passion for education. "This country is in danger again," the producer said, "and the people don't yet realize it. It's your patriotic duty to let your life serve as an example and the greatest lesson to American youth that could be told." Lasky promised the picture would focus on York's spiritual conversion and his attempts to enlighten the Upper Cumberland region. Lasky simultaneously worked the Hollywood end, begging studios to back his project. Paramount, Fox, and RKO all said there was no market for war films.[13]

York finally signed a contract in March 1940. He demanded $50,000, 2 percent of the gross receipts, a female lead who did not smoke or drink, and Gary Cooper in the starring role. Although Cooper lived in a Georgian manor across the street from Lasky, his exclusive contract with Lasky's brother-in-law, Sam Goldwyn, left him miles from doing the picture. To complicate matters, Goldwyn was in the process of divorcing Lasky's sister, Blanche, at the moment the producer needed to borrow Cooper. It took a series of Byzantine negotiations to convince Goldwyn to loan out his star. York was thrilled—he gave Cooper one of his Stetsons, which Cooper wore in *Sergeant York*'s Tennessee scenes. With York onboard, Lasky sewed up a production deal with his good friend Harry Warner. The rest of 1940 went to casting, interviewing York's acquaintances, and rounding the script into shape. Lasky's proposal that Jane Russell play Alvin York's rural, clean-living wife, Gracie, demonstrated that his cinematic instincts were not always sound. "She doesn't look like the simple, backwoods country girl to me," Warners producer Hal Wallis remarked.[14]

Written during the "no hate films" period, the initial screenplay upheld Lasky's promise to minimize the war. His writers knew that "this should not be a war picture in the usual sense of the word, and should not be definitely interpretable as either propaganda for or against war." With more than a little condescension, they also downplayed York's fundamentalism, which might make him look like "a religious fanatic," and what they saw as the knee-jerk small-mindedness of "the pellagric people" he grew up around. Their goal was to turn York into another Mr. Deeds, "a universal type of American boy . . . a 20th Century Daniel Boone," an ordinary man who did great things while remaining unspoiled.[15]

The thrust of *Sergeant York* shifted by the time principal photography began in February 1941. Director Howard Hawks saw the war as the picture's key event; diminishing it left a lifeless, choppy script. He brought in John Huston and Howard Koch to punch up the screenplay. The two interventionist writers scrapped the film's message of educational uplift and made the war its emotional heart. Harry Warner and Lasky convinced York to endorse the changes, relieving the veteran of his pacifism in the process. Under their tutelage he came to see Hitler as a threat to the United States and conceded that his life story could contribute to the interventionist cause. Conceived during an age of national retreat from global affairs, *Sergeant York* was shaping up as Warners' definitive call for internationalism.[16]

✿ ✿ ✿

Other studios assembled war-themed products as *A Yank in the R.A.F.* and *Sergeant York* went into production. In contrast to those big-budget, prestige productions, a number of pictures appeared in early 1941 that sought relevance and audience approval through a lighthearted approach to America's contemporary military situation.

Humor can be a powerful means of coping with crisis. The era's most wicked comedies came during the worst years of the Depression, when

W. C. Fields, the Marx Brothers, and Mae West skewered traditional values on their way to box-office fortune. Universal appropriated the Depression's forgotten-man character for the 1936 screwball romp *My Man Godfrey.* Charlie Chaplin was the master of blending comedy with tragedy. His genius transformed war, orphans, poverty, factory work, and city life into subjects worthy of belly laughs. *The Great Dictator* proved that audiences could laugh at fascism even if they balked at embracing the picture's overwrought plea for peace.

Audiences did not like "depressing war films or horrific anti-Nazi pictures full of concentration camps and suffering," *Commonweal* declared. Indeed, such dramas had a rough time at the box office. War comedies offered a comfortable middle ground, keeping Hollywood engaged with current events while deflecting charges of propaganda. The genre generally stayed within the safe bounds of patriotism and gentle satire. Its subtle yet unmistakably promilitary appeal was hard to express in words. No isolationist senator or America Firster could keep a straight face while accusing Jimmy Durante, Bob Hope, or Laurel and Hardy of warmongering.[17]

Although the Three Stooges mocked Hitler in their two-reelers *You Nazty Spy* (1940) and *I'll Never Heil Again* (1941), feature-length service comedies focused instead on the growing number of Americans caught in the draft. Universal was the first to capitalize on the call-up. Released at the end of January, *Buck Privates,* a low-budget picture with two largely unfamiliar stars, warranted low expectations. Bud Abbott and Lou Costello were well known on the burlesque and vaudeville circuits, but their only previous movie, *One Night in the Tropics* (1940), had flopped. Their story of two small-time shysters who accidentally join the army, however, became an unlikely smash. The $200,000 cheapie took in $4.7 million at the box office, making it Universal's biggest grosser to date.

Buck Privates did not ask much of its audience. Its razor-thin plot served mostly as an excuse for set pieces that showcased the skills the duo had honed onstage. The team runs a crooked craps game, suffers through close-order drill, and participates in a farcical boxing match. When not going through their comic paces, they integrate a snobbish Yale student, Randolph Parker (Lee Bowman), into the unit, proving again that all Americans can cooperate for democracy. *Buck Privates* never mentions the Axis. In fact, it never explains why these men are training for war.

The picture's greatest achievement was its humanization of the armed forces. Other films showed ordinary men becoming military heroes, but none made serving their country seem so fun. "The American doughboy is presented as having at the hypothetical enemy and enjoying the experience," noted one reviewer. *Buck Privates* familiarized the public with the army, and what is familiar is no longer frightening. Abbott and Costello's romp partook in obvious hyperbole; no one could believe that military duty was *that* wacky. Even so, the comic romp established a reservoir of positive feelings that partially reconciled theatergoers with the possibility that they or their loved ones might be chosen to serve.[18]

Buck Privates pairs Abbott and Costello's antics with a large dose of Americanism, linking the army with patriotism and equating antimilitarism with anti-Americanism. The Andrews Sisters, who inexplicably appear at various points, provide much of the comedy's nationalistic rhetoric. "You're a Lucky Fellow, Mr. Smith" greets the new recruits with a bombastic message of democracy's glories, replete with images of "that swell Miss Liberty gal" and "Washington, Jefferson, Lincoln, and Lee." The sisters make it clear that the nation supports its boys in uniform. "We're a hundred and thirty million strong/And we're sticking with you right along," they sing.

"This is a comedy in the interests of national defense," *Motion Picture Herald* explained, as "those who are on the side of unstinted aid to Britain have here a means of making conscription pleasant." Universal's publicity program for *Buck Privates* emphasized the movie's promilitary ethos. The studio offered special screenings at army camps and published interviews with area draftees in local newspapers. It also allowed Selective Service boards to operate recruiting stations in or near theaters showing the film.[19]

The success of *Buck Privates* led to imitators. Abbott and Costello starred in two more service comedies in 1941, *In the Navy* and *Keep 'em Flying*. Bob Hope got in on the act with Paramount's *Caught in the Draft*. Hal Roach hurried *Tanks a Million* into release in September. Jimmy Durante and Phil Silvers played two vacuum-cleaner salesmen who end up in a tank corps in Warners' *You're in the Army Now*. These were relatively low-cost, high-reward ventures designed to be relevant without alienating anyone. They were of course subject to the same self-regulation all American motion pictures faced. The Breen Office did its part to ensure that Hollywood portrayed the nation's new soldiers generously. It refused to approve Republic's *Rookies on Parade* (1941), for example, until the studio excised a shot of draftees gawking at risqué posters outside a burlesque theater.[20]

These innocuous movies raised a ruckus in some quarters. The State Department received reports that service comedies hurt the United States' reputation in South America because they mocked the armed forces. German propagandists, whose pictures unfailingly cast Nazi legions in a glowing light, were supposedly exploiting images of American buffoonery to enhance their country's stature. Though diplomats likely overstated these concerns, studios affixed prologues to foreign prints of service comedies explaining that they did not realistically depict the United States military. While probably underestimating the average South American filmgoer's capacities, Secretary of State Cordell Hull's involvement in this brouhaha and Hollywood's quick adjustment indicate the importance the government and the industry placed on placating any wounded sensibilities that might harm the Good Neighbor agenda.[21]

✿ ✿ ✿

Hollywood's distance from anti-interventionists grew as the majors barreled ahead with a promilitary and internationalist agenda. As powerful public figures sharpened their anti-Hollywood rhetoric in response, the industry wanted some assurance that it, too, had important backers. Walter Wanger decided to go straight to the top. In December 1940 he invited FDR to speak at the Academy Awards ceremony. Academy members had elevated the producer of *Blockade, Foreign Correspondent,* and *The Long Voyage Home* to the presidency earlier that year. Wanger—a prominent member of the Century Group, an organization that called for immediate, wide-ranging aid to Britain—made no secret of his interventionism. His election marked the academy's endorsement of those views.

Wanger wanted the industry to denounce dictatorship and promote Americanism. He sought Roosevelt's voice as a powerful second. Presidential aide Lowell Mellett advised FDR to accept Wanger's request.

While conscious that some of Hollywood's past support stemmed from its fear of the Justice Department, Mellett also believed it was time to "pay a deserved tribute to the industry for its cooperation in defense." Roosevelt begged off, pleading a full schedule. Wanger persisted. "Just such a gesture as the gracious recognition by the President of the United States would make us realize our full obligation and spur us on to unheard of efficiency," he told Mellett. Wanger turned his attention to presidential secretary Stephen Early as the awards drew near. "The motion picture industry is anxious and ready for great public service," the producer told his friend, "and, frankly, needs a word of encouragement and guidance."[22]

Excitement rippled through Hollywood when Roosevelt finally accepted the academy's invitation. "I cannot tell you what an inspiration this will be to the industry to assume its responsibilities in this time of crisis," Wanger gushed to Early. The academy head rushed to Washington to discuss the speech with administration officials. Wanger also used his trip to update General George Marshall on Zanuck's training film program and other efforts to increase Hollywood's cooperation with the military.[23]

Hundreds of Hollywood's elite poured into the Biltmore Hotel for the Academy Awards banquet on February 27. The tension level in the room was higher than usual. For the first time in the ceremony's thirteen-year history, no one knew the winners until presenters tore open sealed envelopes. The academy hired the accounting firm of Price Waterhouse to count the ballots after someone leaked vote tallies to the *Los Angeles Times* the year before. The competition was fierce. Ten films vied for Best Picture, including *Foreign Correspondent, The Grapes of Wrath, The Great Dictator, The Philadelphia Story,* and *Rebecca.* Charlie Chaplin was up for Best Actor, as were Henry Fonda, Raymond Massey, Laurence Olivier, and James Stewart. Whiz-kid Preston Sturges had received a Best Original Screenplay nomination for his directorial debut, *The Great McGinty.*

The luminaries barely settled in their chairs before Franklin Roosevelt's unmistakable patrician voice rang out through the room's sound system. Although not a personal appearance—FDR spoke from the White House—it was the first time a president had addressed the Academy Awards. Roosevelt did not chat in soothing tones about movies as pure entertainment or Hollywood as a dream factory. He instead spoke pointedly about the motion picture's responsibilities to a world at war. Hollywood must broadcast "the aims and aspirations and ideals of a free nation and of freedom" across the hemisphere, he told the crowd. FDR acknowledged moviemakers' contributions to the imminent passage of lend-lease, giving a special thanks to newsreels for informing the public about the proposal. He then grew more serious as he closed his six-minute speech. Only Hollywood, he said, could unite Americans and the Americas into a prodemocracy, antifascist bloc. The movie capital must continue familiarizing the country with the ongoing defense buildup. "We in Washington," he concluded, "know we shall have your continued aid in support."[24]

The mood in the room was electric. Roosevelt's address was a coming-of-age moment, the real-life equivalent of Andy Hardy getting a firm handshake and a "job well done" from his father, the judge. It was an Academy Award for the entire industry, delivered by the nation's most important presenter. The buzz continued through the ceremony. Ginger Rogers and James Stewart won their first Oscars. David O. Selznick followed up his Best Picture Award the previous year for *Gone with the Wind* by taking the same trophy for *Rebecca*. Colonel Nathan Levinson garnered a special Oscar for "efficient mobilization of the motion picture industry facilities for the production of Army training films." All anyone really wanted to talk about was the president's speech. Walter Wanger, in his closing benediction, brought the proceedings full circle by reiterating the themes FDR had raised earlier and then clarifying what Wanger saw as the industry's great task. "If America is to be the arsenal of Democracy," he said, "then we in Hollywood will assume the obligation of supplying the spiritual ammunition and the weapons of inspiration that will solidify Democracy."[25]

Roosevelt's blessing was the talk of the town. A community acutely tuned to the importance of good publicity sensed that Roosevelt's words might silence critics while solidifying Hollywood's position as a cultural arbitrator. *Boxoffice* editor Red Kann called Wanger's Academy Awards triumph "the greatest exploitation stunt of them all." Appreciative telegrams poured into the White House as Hollywood pledged fealty to the president. "Please be assured that we all stand ready to cooperate with you in any way," Frank Capra wrote. "I am doing whatever I can to assist in the great defense program and deem it a privilege to do all I can to preserve the freedom of our democracy," *Blockade* actress Madeleine Carroll declared. Screenwriter Jane Murfin promised that "we are completely at your command in this all-out defense program." With such productions as *A Yank in the R.A.F.* and *Sergeant York* in the pipeline, Hollywood seemed committed to fulfilling these promises. As always, however, the industry had concerns beyond moviemaking. Roosevelt's pep talk came during a delicate moment for Hollywood's money men, who contended with uncertainties at home and abroad as 1941 got under way.[26]

CHAPTER SEVENTEEN

Three Continents—Spring 1941

❧   ❧   ❧

Hollywood executives were more than moviemakers; they were businessmen whose interests spanned the globe. Their jobs required them to focus as much on market conditions and government policies as on scripts and casting decisions. The first half of 1941 found them juggling crises on three continents. Industry leaders had to divide their attention to prevent balls in South America, Europe, and North America from dropping to the ground with a splat. Each ball, each continent, represented a pivotal component of Hollywood's financial and ideological well-being. Failure in any of those regions would devastate the business while simultaneously undercutting Hollywood's ability to encourage antifascism at home and abroad.

David O. Selznick was still celebrating *Rebecca*'s Best Picture Oscar when he dashed off a note—an unusually short one from a man known for epic memos—to the White House. "It is already apparent," he informed FDR, that Hollywood would "further efforts, both for National Defense, and in furtherance of Latin American relations" in response to the president's Academy Awards address.

Moviemakers' preoccupation with the nations to the south continued unabated through the first half of 1941. The region's economic and strategic value made it crucial to studios' financial health and prodemocracy agenda. After the debacles of *Argentine Nights* and *Down Argentine Way*, producers saw that big-budget, Latin-themed spectacles were unlikely to bring strong returns. Studios instead went for programmers, offering up such B movies as *Along the Rio Grande, Blondie Goes Latin, Charlie Chan in Rio, South of Panama*, and the Gene Autry picture *Down Mexico Way*. Zanuck put Carmen Miranda in two pictures in 1941, *That Night in Rio* and *Weekend in Havana*. None of these did spectacular business. Neither did they stir up much controversy. Studios were playing it safe.

RKO withheld the musical comedy *They Met in Argentina* from Argentina until officials there approved it.[1]

Cinematic anti-Americanism was building despite the Good Neighbor Policy's noble intentions. Argentinean and Brazilian producers wanted to challenge Hollywood's regional supremacy by enlarging their own output. Brazil banned anti-Nazi films and floated a plan to hike taxes on money exported to the United States. Cuba and Puerto Rico also considered tax and anti-block-booking measures. Chile banned movies discussing the ideology of nations at war. These measures reflected Latin Americans' irritation with Hollywood's hypocrisy. Studios preached hemispheric solidarity while caricaturing the rest of the hemisphere. "Sometimes I'm afraid your people will never understand that we are as unlike Mexicans as New Yorkers are unlike Eskimos," a Chilean newspaperman wrote *Variety*.[2]

Producers could not figure out how to overcome the lack of goodwill. *Motion Picture Herald*'s Terry Ramsaye concluded that American moviemakers should immerse themselves in Hispanic culture as a way of winning over suspicious patrons. Others were equally certain that Hollywood should stop catering to Hispanics. "There is absolutely no reason to tailor our production schedules for South America because they like the same things we do," Fox producer Sol Wurtzel concluded. The cycle of Latin-themed musicals reflected this ambivalence by dressing up the catchy tunes North Americans adored in the festive clothes and fiery language they believed Latin Americans wanted.[3]

Hollywood's Latin American travails also stemmed from factors beyond its control. The region's rampant poverty and shortage of high-quality movie theaters, especially outside the big cities, limited potential revenues. Disputes over control of resources, such as the Mexican oil crisis, bred international hostility. German infiltration into South America diminished profits while undermining hemispheric defense and the Good Neighbor program. German banks financed South American studios with the assumption that they would make pro-Nazi pictures. Siemens-Schukert and other German companies sold moviemaking equipment at bargain prices. The Nazis focused their cinematic ambitions largely on Argentina, which regularly screened Berlin-based UFA studios' propaganda pictures such as *Victory in the West*. American film insiders speculated that the German quest for control over studios in

Buenos Aires was the first phase of a "motion picture offensive" that might spread to Brazil, Chile, and other South American republics.[4]

The Nazis' cinematic tie-up with Latin America was a difficult problem for the Americans to finesse. Doing nothing was unacceptable, but lodging stern protests against Axis activities might rankle South American anti-imperialists. Roosevelt responded to Germany's cultural expansionism by launching a new public relations crusade. He issued an executive order in August 1940 naming thirty-two-year-old Nelson Rockefeller as the coordinator of Latin American Commercial and Cultural Relations, a new bureau within the State Department's Division of Cultural Relations, a diplomatic entity created in 1938 primarily to facilitate educational and cultural exchanges with Latin America. Roosevelt charged Rockefeller's group, which soon shortened its title to the Office of the Coordinator of Inter-American Affairs (CIAA), with improving the United States' image throughout the hemisphere.[5]

Rockefeller was a fine choice for the job. The Dartmouth graduate was a high-profile figure, not just because of his famous surname but also for his work as president of New York City's Museum of Modern Art. A grandson of Standard Oil tycoon John D. Rockefeller, he had appeared on the cover of *Time* magazine the year before his appointment. More important, the future vice president knew something about Latin America. One of his first jobs was with Chase National Bank's foreign division. He had business interests in Venezuela and traveled extensively throughout the region. An aficionado of Hispanic, particularly Mexican, art, Rockefeller agonized over his country's lack of cultural awareness. On friendly terms with the president and Harry Hopkins despite being a registered Republican, he often discussed Latin American economic policy with administration figures and business leaders.[6]

Rockefeller actively sought Hollywood's cooperation, tapping John Hay "Jock" Whitney to head the CIAA's Motion Picture Division soon after his own appointment. Whitney, a well-connected member of the Museum of Modern Art's board of directors, was a known quantity to industry insiders. The blue-blooded descendant of Puritans was a major investor in Technicolor and formed Pioneer Pictures with *King Kong* producer Merian C. Cooper in 1933. Whitney had recently become chairman of Selznick International Pictures, and he spent some of his considerable fortune producing the blockbuster *Gone with the Wind*.[7]

Whitney and Rockefeller exuded the respect the moguls craved. Studio executives soon came sniffing around the new office. Whitney laid the groundwork for a new collaboration with Hollywood during a series of January 1941 meetings with the MPPDA's Harold Smith. Rockefeller announced a program to use film to promote hemispheric relations that same month. "Our American screen has always attracted the greatest audiences in the world because of its freedom of expression and expression of freedom," he said. Now, "through sympathetic study of the cultural bonds existing among the American Republics," he intended to swamp the totalitarian threat in Latin America beneath a wave of prodemocratic newsreels, shorts, and feature films oriented toward Hispanic themes.[8]

Major studios had targeted Latin America for prodemocratic entertainment ever since 1939's *Juarez*. Hollywood's tie-up with the CIAA, however, surpassed earlier efforts. Many executives, especially studios' foreign representatives, doubted the program would realize Rockefeller's grandiose promises. Producers eager to stay on the government's good side threw themselves into the CIAA's agenda nevertheless. Paramount head Y. Frank Freeman chaired a team to work with Whitney that included Hollywood heavyweights Sam Goldwyn, Louis B. Mayer, RKO chief George Schaefer, David O. Selznick, Walter Wanger, Harry Warner, and Universal's Cliff Work. Subcommittees of the Freeman group focused on film facilities, newsreels, and shorts. At the CIAA's request, Will Hays named Cuban-born Addison Durland, the former head of NBC radio's Latin American department, as the MPPDA's top consultant, script reviewer, and censor of Latin American subjects.[9]

Still reveling in his public-relations coup at the Academy Awards, Walter Wanger led the cheerleading for the CIAA. The devoted internationalist thought the new alliance bolstered his goal of making more serious, topical pictures that promoted hemispheric relations. His industry proudly backed Washington's drive to spread democracy, he told a meeting of the Southern California Inter-American Conference, and rejected warnings from critics who warned of government-organized propaganda. Films endorsing "hemispheric solidarity" were not propaganda because no one compelled people to attend them. Besides, Wanger concluded, only a fascist could oppose motion pictures preaching tolerance.[10]

The CIAA's movie mission hummed along through early 1941. Whitney's division pressed studios to increase newsreel coverage of South America. Fox's Sol Wurtzel and Universal's Nate Blumberg departed on well-publicized tours of the region. Hollywood formalized its relationship with the Rockefeller organization in March when it reconstituted the hastily assembled Freeman Committee into the Motion Picture Society for the Americas (MPSA). "Dedicated to the implementation of the Good Neighbor Policy," the Wanger-led MPSA became Hollywood's primary liaison with the CIAA. The two groups met weekly to discuss Latin American issues. The MPSA's office on Wilshire Boulevard in Beverly Hills housed a library of reading material on Latin America. Whitney and MGM donated furniture for the building.[11]

The MPSA opened Hollywood's doors to a number of prominent Latin American guests. April brought a group of Peruvian aviators and Mexican general Maximino Avila Camacho. The chiefs of Latin American naval operations got a tour of the majors and a reception on an MGM soundstage the next month. Hollywood feted Mexican Tourist Bureau head Alejandro Buelna in June and did the same for a group of Mexican police officers in July. Argentinean director Luis Saslavsky visited in August.[12]

These were friendly actions but not the kinds of publicity splashes Hollywood liked to traffic in. The CIAA wanted more from the movie capital. The Rockefeller group distributed questionnaires to Latin America experts and public relations gurus to determine how best to promote goodwill. Their responses reached a clear consensus: send stars.[13]

Armed with this material, FDR's son James sold Will Hays on the idea of a star-studded junket to Mexico. Hays approached the MPSA and CIAA, which lined up actors and arranged security details with the State Department. On April 11 the "Goodwill Fiesta" loaded into three Pan-Am planes and took off in a driving rain. Thousands of fans greeted them when they touched down in Mazatlan that evening. Even more were waiting at the Mexico City airport at 7:30 the next morning. Nearly two thousand policemen restrained the crowds as Desi Arnaz, Lucille Ball, Wallace Beery, Joe E. Brown, Frank Capra, Kay Francis, Laurel and Hardy, Mickey Rooney, David O. Selznick, Norma Shearer, Johnny Weissmuller, and

Jock Whitney stepped onto the tarmac. President Manuel Avila Camacho (the general's brother) greeted his guests before officials shuttled them to a reception with the mayor, tea with American ambassador Josephus Daniels, and a string of appearances at movie houses.

The visiting good neighbors endured a jammed itinerary the next day, Easter Sunday. Many of them attended mass at Basilica Guadalupe before embarking on a full slate of radio broadcasts, luncheons, and fashion shows. After enduring such a packed schedule, they must have been about drained of goodwill by the time they flew back to Los Angeles on Monday afternoon. An excited Whitney announced plans for more visits when the Fiesta landed.[14]

Another cinematic ambassador sailed from Miami Beach a few weeks later. A source higher than Jock Whitney and Nelson Rockefeller, however, arranged Douglas Fairbanks Jr.'s journey south. The Roosevelt administration had discussed using Fairbanks as a weapon in the United States' propaganda war against the Axis ever since the actor's meeting with Secretary of State Cordell Hull and Undersecretary of State Sumner Welles during Roosevelt's inauguration the previous fall. The president responded favorably when Welles suggested sending Fairbanks on a South American tour. The administration gave the actor two tasks. Welles publicly asked him to spread pro-American sentiment while assessing South American attitudes toward Hollywood films. Welles, Hull, and Roosevelt privately assigned him to gather information on pro-Axis organizations in the region. After crash courses in Spanish and Portuguese and an official briefing, Fairbanks became a special representative of the State Department, which allocated $5,000 for his trip.[15]

Fairbanks carried a diplomatic passport as he clutched the rail of a clipper ship bound for Rio de Janeiro. He also carried a request from British ambassador Lord Halifax, the father of a former girlfriend, for a report on his country's efforts to curry favor in South America. Although the CIAA did not officially sponsor the expedition, the Rockefeller group sent a representative with Fairbanks. The actor was excited and a little overwhelmed as his ship pulled out of the harbor. "Am both grateful and proud of the confidence placed in me," he wired FDR before departing.[16]

Though yielding few tangible results, the journey marked another milestone in Hollywood's campaign to woo South America and prove its devotion to hemispheric defense. It is not clear how successful Fairbanks was in achieving his covert objectives. If nothing else, he won a great deal of public favor. Cheering crowds greeted him throughout his two-month tour of Brazil, Chile, and Argentina. He reported that South Americans revered FDR, "despite the efficient workings of German propaganda and a somewhat general mistrust of the American people as a whole." The only sour notes came from Argentina, where hostile journalists scoffed at the United States' latest emissary. One Buenos Aires magazine lampooned Fairbanks as a "party-and-night-club friend" of Franklin Roosevelt Jr. The same city's *El pampero* blasted the "ambassador and spy extraordinary of President Roosevelt, who in his relations with American countries utilizes the resources of commercial propaganda to make an impression on the foolish."[17]

Fairbanks soon got another opportunity to serve his country. In summer 1941 he received papers calling him to active duty in Naval Intelligence. After wrapping work on *The Corsican Brothers,* he reported to the USS *Mississippi,* stationed off the coast of Iceland. The United States occupied the island that July to provide refueling bases for British convoys and maintain control over the Denmark Strait, a hotbed of German naval activity. Douglas Fairbanks Jr.'s war had begun.[18]

The success of the Fairbanks expedition and the Goodwill Fiesta prompted the CIAA and MPSA to ask Walt Disney to visit South America. The Good Neighbor organizations correctly figured that South Americans, who adored Mickey Mouse and Donald Duck, would welcome the great animator. Disney was already hard at work producing government-sponsored training pictures for war-industry workers, so this latest request from the administration fit in well with his current activities. He commissioned the slew of studio writers that traveled with him to search out subjects appropriate for his company's particular brand of genius. Disney undertook no financial risk, as the CIAA guaranteed against losses he suffered from making Latin American–themed pictures. It never had to pay. Disney's men visited Argentina, Brazil, Chile, and Uruguay during the fall of 1941. Some members of "El Groupo," as they called themselves, also traveled to Bolivia and Peru.[19]

Disney returned to the United States with a sheaf of ideas that reflected both Hollywood's enthusiasm for South America and the industry's inability to overcome its stereotypes. He promised to feature Hispanic performers in at least a dozen shorts based on South American folktales, signed Argentinean comedian Molina Campos to appear as a gaucho in live-action films, and talked of introducing an animated Brazilian parrot named Parrudo. Disney also wanted to launch a series that combined a gaucho with samba music. His trip eventually produced two animated features, *Saludos Amigos* (1943) and *The Three Caballeros* (1944), and a series of shorts, including "The Grain That Built a Hemisphere" (1942), "Defense against Invasion" (1943), and "The Winged Scourge" (1943).[20]

Despite outward appearances, the CIAA-MPSA Good Neighbor program was fraying by the time Disney came home. Studio executives saw little return for their $35,000 investment in the Goodwill Fiesta. Whitney's call for each studio to send two stars to Latin America every year would cost them upwards of $500,000. It was not clear that these trips increased profits. Theater grosses in Mexico actually fell during the Goodwill Fiesta because, *Variety* speculated, Mexicans could get a better show for free. Studios' foreign departments worried that lighthearted junkets felt out of place in such serious times; South Americans might interpret them as evidence of North American frivolity. Film executives accepted Whitney's proposal to assign each studio a South American expert with the authority to veto productions that might harm hemispheric amity—their years of experience with the Production Code Administration made them experts in working around self-censorship. The goodwill tours, however, came to a quick, inglorious end.[21]

Although the CIAA reconciled with Hollywood during the war, the agency's demands bred much grumbling in the months prior to Pearl Harbor. Foreign managers complained that Whitney acted without consulting them. MPPDA executive Carl Milliken believed studios gave more than they received. Hollywood contributed "wholeheartedly to the support of our Government's declared policy of all-out aid to the Democracies and is probably the only American industry which does not get back its production costs in so doing," he noted. Studios pitched newsreels, shorts, and features to Latin America "without one cent of profit." Milliken wanted the government to acknowledge Hollywood's help in the defense program by more aggressively opening South American markets on the industry's behalf.[22]

The State Department lacked confidence in both parties. Its career diplomats resented Whitney's ability to operate independently of their bureaucracy and doubted the sincerity of the industry's commitment to the CIAA. "It is perfectly clear that, while the Hays organization is willing to give surface cooperation to the Whitney group," one official observed, "neither Hays nor his organization intends to weaken their position with the motion picture producers." Hays saw Whitney as a threat to his own power, Whitney wanted the power to guide Hollywood in his own direction, and the powerful men who ran the studios were again caught between their need to do good for their companies and their desire to do good for their country.[23]

For all Whitney and Rockefeller's talk, most of the big projects they announced either never came off or performed below expectations. Dore Schary's *The Life of Simon Bolivar* died in preproduction, as did *Rurales, The Road to Rio,* and a proposed biopic of Emiliano Zapata. *Blood and Sand* (1941) was a good vehicle for the bankable Tyrone Power. *They Met in Argentina* was a moderate performer. None of these films convinced producers that South American subjects sold tickets.

✿ ✿ ✿

Hollywood courted the British market as it treaded water in Latin America. Fluid conditions in the United Kingdom again forced American moviemakers to balance their financial needs against their desire to parallel the president's Anglophilic foreign policy. Studio executives never considered abandoning their pro-British slant. Doing so would anger domestic political leaders, outrage their most important overseas market, and undercut hopes of creating sympathy for Great Britain. At the same time, Hollywood's power brokers used every available means to extract as much money as they could from the islands.

A triumphant Franklin Roosevelt signed the lend-lease bill into law on the afternoon of March 11, 1941. With a stroke of the pen, the United States committed itself to the defense of Great Britain. He immediately asked Congress for a $7 billion appropriation to implement the program. Winston Churchill called the act a "new Magna Carta." "The words and actions of the President and people of the United States come to us like a draught of life," he told Parliament, "and they tell us by an ocean-borne trumpet call that we are no longer alone." "Thank God! The tanks are coming," exclaimed one Londoner.[24]

Will Hays also saw lend-lease as a new Magna Carta, except he believed it granted him the freedom to prize more money from the British. The course of Anglo-American film relations displeased the movie czar. A German incendiary bomb had destroyed the MPPDA's London office a month earlier. Hays hoped this explosion was not a precursor to an even larger crackup. Rumors of a new British Films Commission that might impose a harsher quota sent him scrambling to Los Angeles' Union Station to catch the eastbound Super Chief. He was in Washington when Roosevelt won his lend-lease victory. Hays initially planned to pressure the State Department to kill the Films Commission but changed his strategy after Roosevelt signed the bill. Reasoning that the new program eased Great Britain's financial woes, he asked the president to help him free some or all of the $25 million in studio revenues frozen in Churchill's dominion. Roosevelt understood Hays's thinking. He set up a meeting with Ambassador Lord Halifax and involved Secretary Hull in the talks.[25]

Hays played a crafty game of diplomatic carrot and stick. Hollywood desperately wanted to send films to Britain. Moviemakers knew their products were essential to British morale and buttressed Anglo-American ties. Studios would not, however, maintain the status quo. Hollywood earned over $40 million in Britain in 1940 and looked to do the same in 1941, yet only around one-third of that money made it into its coffers. The financial situation was "critical," Hays reported. Unless the Churchill government released those funds, Hollywood would have no choice but to abandon the market.[26]

Hays further stirred the pot by playing the Latin American card. American films made a "special contribution" to prodemocracy and antifascist efforts in South America, he told State Department officials. A shortage of working capital would seriously stunt those efforts. Impounded British funds, therefore, severely handicapped the industry's efforts to assist the defense effort. This subtle threat spooked diplomats into redoubling their bid to persuade British negotiators to give Hollywood a better deal. Hull met with Ambassador Lord Halifax several times and coordinated talks with British Treasury officials. "Nothing is being overlooked here in our efforts to be of service in this matter," the secretary informed Hays.[27]

The loss of foreign income was real even if Hays's protestations of poverty were disingenuous. The war-fueled return of prosperity in the United States more than compensated for losses overseas. With the exception of Twentieth Century–Fox, all the major studios did better in 1940 than 1939, and 1941 promised to be an even more profitable year. British negotiators may have been aware of Hays's financial fudging but were in no mood to cause trouble. "[Movies] are doing a very good job of work in our cause," Halifax wrote Chancellor Kingsley Wood. Treasury's Sir Arnold Overton concurred. "Any attempt on our part to drive a bargain with the American film industry or to curtail their resources by administrative measures was doomed to failure," he later remembered. "In the circumstances we have felt that there was nothing for it but to mark time on major issues at any rate until the Americans had come into the war."[28]

Hollywood's superior leverage forced the British to give way at every point. The proposed Films Commission died in the planning stage. The Board of Trade agreed in October to release $20 million in frozen funds and export an additional $20 million in profits from the 1941–1942 season, a significant increase from the $12.9 million permitted under the 1940–1941 deal. Recognizing that domestic producers could not shoot enough pictures to meet quota requirements, the Board of Trade slashed the quota, making it easier for Hollywood films to dominate the British market.[29]

Hollywood's quarrel with London did not slow its onscreen celebration of all things British. Merian C. Cooper was overseas gathering material for Walter Wanger's *Eagle Squadron*. Warners was working on *International Squadron,* its answer to Zanuck's forthcoming *Yank in the R.A.F.* British-made propaganda pictures peppered American screens. The success of *London Can Take It* (1940), which compiled footage from the blitz, inspired the Ministry of Information to produce several follow-ups in 1941. *Britain on Guard, This Is England,* and *Men of the Lightship* found receptive audiences in the United States. Hollywood studios distributed these propaganda films as a way to gain the upper hand in quota and currency negotiations while at the same time upholding Louis B. Mayer's late-1940 pledge to British film executive A. W. Jarratt that Churchill could "count on the producers of Hollywood [to do] everything possible to help the great cause."[30]

United Artists contributed to the pro-British cycle by distributing Alexander Korda's *That Hamilton Woman* (1941). Working primarily at Samuel Goldwyn's studio on Santa Monica Boulevard, Korda intended his epic of Admiral Lord Nelson (Laurence Olivier) and his mistress, Lady Hamilton (Vivien Leigh, in a case of art imitating life), as an even more transparent comment on current events than *The Sea Hawk* or *The Sea Wolf*. "It is a haunting thing how the times of Lord Nelson so closely parallel those of today," he told the *New York Herald-Tribune*. The admiral had headed off Napoleon's dreams of global domination in the nineteenth century. Now it was the RAF and the modern British Navy's turn to do the same. Korda wanted the great hero's courage at Trafalgar and speeches condemning Britain's appeasement of Napoleon to inspire audiences on both sides of the Atlantic. When Nelson insists that "you cannot make peace with dictators, you have to destroy them, wipe them out," he is speaking not to the nineteenth-century admiralty so much as to twentieth-century moviegoers. "The picture carries plenty of British propaganda which will be easily tabbed by audiences," *Variety* observed.[31]

That Hamilton Woman was only part of Korda's contribution to the Anglo-American relationship. The Hungarian-born Jew was probably Great Britain's most important representative in the movie capital. His first trip to Hollywood, in 1926, was a disaster. The rough isolation of Los Angeles appalled him. "My God, I feel like Kurtz in *Heart of Darkness*," he told a friend before fleeing to more civilized shores. After producing the RAF-themed propaganda picture *The Lion Has Wings* (1939) in the United Kingdom, he returned to Hollywood in 1940 with his Tasmanian-born wife, Merle Oberon, whose recent performance opposite Olivier in *Wuthering Heights* had confirmed her Hollywood stardom. Korda appears to have come at the urging of Churchill and elements of the British Secret Service. His mission was to advance the pro-British cause through his films and to assist British agents stationed in the United States.[32]

The filmmaker rented a house in Bel Air and set up an office in New York City's Rockefeller Center, the same building that housed the British Press Service, the Inter-Allied Information Committee, and the pro-British Century Group. Korda later alleged that members of British intelligence organization MI5 used his quarters and claimed to have passed messages from his government to British propagandists operating in the United States. Although his assertions have not been proven, it is worth noting that Churchill knighted him for unspecified reasons in 1942.[33]

✪ ✪ ✪

Hollywood's informal alliance with Great Britain was a natural offshoot of its more formal ties to Washington. Backing Roosevelt's war aims meant backing Great Britain. The trade's many links to the United States government lent Hollywood a decidedly militaristic tone by spring 1941. "The studio has the appearance of an army cantonment," an approving Darryl F. Zanuck told Stephen Early. The Twentieth Century–Fox head wore his lieutenant colonel uniform to a dinner honoring Chief Signal Officer J. O. Mauborgne in March, a dinner where General Mauborgne informed executives that their works were "as indispensable to national defense as the steel industry." Camps across the United States were screening army training pictures. Production of these shorts had not yet peaked, but the system was beginning to smooth itself out.[34]

Movie folk were also signing up for the state militia. Screenwriter Rupert Hughes led a motley regiment of writers, actors, directors, and craftsmen who trained with ancient Enfield rifles in preparation for an attack on Southern California. No one in the unit had bullets. "[People] considered us total idiots," Jesse Lasky Jr. recalled. Jimmy Stewart played a more serious role in the defense effort. Following days of gorging himself to clear military weight requirements, the actor enlisted in the Army Air Corps a few weeks after Mauborgne's pep talk. He eventually flew twenty combat missions over Europe; earned the Distinguished Flying Cross, the Air Medal, and the Croix de Guerre; and was promoted to colonel before the war's end.[35]

Director John Ford, a lieutenant commander in the Naval Reserve, was also hard at work. Convinced that the United States would soon be in the war, he began organizing the Naval Field Photographic Reserve in 1939. He signed up around one hundred writers, cameramen, and technical workers during the next two years. His outfit, which had no official affiliation with the military, generated little interest within naval circles. It acquired uniforms through a costume company and drilled on a Fox soundstage. When the navy called up Ford in September 1941, however, the Photographic Reserve came with him. Renamed the Eleventh Naval

District Motion Picture and Still Photographic Group, Ford's men shot memorable footage of the Battle of Midway, D-Day, and other actions around the world.[36]

Roosevelt's proclamation of an "unlimited national emergency" in May 1941 therefore reached willing ears in Hollywood, which appeared to have already declared a national emergency on its own. "My services[,] my economic wealth[,] and my life are at the disposal of your principles," director W. S. Van Dyke telegraphed the president. Zanuck's studio offered the same. Two thousand Fox employees signed a statement that read in part: "we believe in you, Mr. President, and to you we herewith give our pledge of loyalty and service, unconditionally and without reserve."[37]

The majors backed their commitment by issuing more contributions to the screen's pervasive anti-Nazism during early 1941. Paramount's *One Night in Lisbon* recycled the antifascist, romantic melodrama model the studio followed in *Arise, My Love*. Warners premiered *Underground,* the thrilling story of German dissidents who broadcast military secrets on a pirate radio station, in June. The picture was nearly two years in the making, and the studio announced its release with a flourish, snagging famed interventionist radio announcer Eric Sevareid to narrate its trailer. *Underground* impressed reviewers and drew big returns. " 'Underground,' even knowing you've had your fill of propaganda films, deserves your patronage," Buck Herzog told readers of the *Milwaukee Sentinel*. The movie also benefited from the appearance a month earlier of the British-made and Columbia-distributed *The Voice in the Night,* which dealt with a similar topic.[38]

June 1941 also saw the release of *Man Hunt*. Surely one of the most vivid examples of wish fulfillment ever portrayed onscreen, Dudley Nichols's adaptation of the Geoffrey Household novel *Rogue Male* centers on a British sportsman ensnared by the Nazis as he hunts "the biggest game on earth": Adolf Hitler. This was anti-Nazism at its audacious best. Hitler-hater Fritz Lang brought real passion to Nichols's script. Walter Pidgeon's performance as the hunter-turned-hunted-turned-hunter Alan Thorndike is spot-on.[39]

It is a measure of how far things had come at Twentieth Century–Fox that the studio's Julian Johnson did not view *Man Hunt* as an anti-Nazi film. "It is," he concluded, "the impartial and exciting chronicle of a very unique sporting event." Fox script reader Sam Hellman more clearly grasped its appeal. "The idea of shooting Hitler or even having somebody else do it must be crowding the dreams and even the waking hours of millions," he told Zanuck. Perhaps numbering himself among the millions who fantasized about shooting Hitler, Zanuck offered to lend Pidgeon a rifle to use in the film.[40]

Production Code Administration head Joseph Breen believed *Man Hunt* fell "within the category of the so-called 'hate pictures'" and asked Will Hays for support. The disagreement caught Hays just as he was heading for New York, so Breen boarded the Super Chief with him to make his case as they chugged east. Their talk ended by the time the train reached San Bernardino. With the MPPDA head's backing, Breen leaned on Zanuck to modify his screenplay but not to the extent that Breen envisioned. The entire project would have been unthinkable two years earlier. Now Breen merely asked Fox to mitigate some of the film's violence and remove suggestions that the female lead (Joan Bennett) was a prostitute. The basic structure of *Man Hunt* stood. Thorndike was free to pursue his prey without "serious worry from the policy angle."[41]

✿ ✿ ✿

The real war raged on in the world beyond the dream factory. Japan consolidated its hold on southeast Asia and threatened the oil-rich Dutch East Indies as its negotiations with the United States stagnated. Admiral Yamamoto was already planning a strike on the American naval facility at Pearl Harbor.

After the RAF's spirited resistance forced Hitler to abandon his plan to invade Britain, the Germans lashed out at an even more imposing target. The Soviet Union had always loomed large in the Nazi leader's mind. "If we speak of soil in Europe today," Hitler wrote sixteen years earlier, "we can primarily have in mind only *Russia* and her vassal border states." His armies crossed the border on June 22, 1941, and rolled east at a furious pace. Hundreds of thousands of Russians died in the battle's first few weeks.[42]

The violent dissolution of the Nazi-Soviet pact galvanized American isolationists. Missouri senator Bennett Champ Clark could not imagine "American boys being sent to their deaths singing 'Onward Christian Soldiers' under the bloody emblem of the Hammer and Sickle."

Operation Barbarossa also reshaped Hollywood's antifascism. Germany's invasion forced industry communists to flip-flop again. Talk of warmongering was out. Now communists papered over their rift with liberals who demanded that the United States adopt a more vigorous anti-Nazi line. The left again linked hands in common cause, although without the enthusiasm seen in the Hollywood Anti-Nazi League's giddy first days. "They all found themselves now on the same side," shrugged screenwriter Albert Maltz.[43]

Public opinion tilted increasingly toward Roosevelt's internationalism. Although most Americans wanted to stay out of the war, they overwhelmingly favored the president's foreign policy. Roosevelt's provocative policies alarmed isolationists. By the time Germany invaded the Soviet Union, the administration had already assumed responsibility for protecting Greenland, sent the navy patrolling halfway across the Atlantic, and authorized the fleet to notify British authorities whenever a ship spotted a German submarine. These moves dramatically increased the likelihood of a major incident with a German warship. Senator Gerald Nye charged the administration with "blitzkrieging the American people into this war." Senator Burton Wheeler denounced interventionists and "vicious" British propagandists for maneuvering the country within a shot of war. In an attack that grabbed the moguls' attention, the old-line progressive blasted the machinations of "economic royalists . . . who direct the policies of this government."[44]

The senator was putting big business on notice. Isolationists placed Hollywood squarely in their crosshairs over the coming weeks. The years of pro-British, pro-Roosevelt, and antifascist films, and all the speeches, donations, publications, and lobbying, came back to haunt the movie community in late 1941. The end of the year, however, would see Hollywood triumphant. Like any good movie hero, it endured terrific challenges. The industry overcame its enemies' jabs at its most vulnerable points—its patriotism and its Jewishness—to finally win the respectability the moguls craved and the unity needed to be an effective weapon for morale in the difficult years to come.

Count on the Warner brothers to start the year off with a big first scene.

CHAPTER EIGHTEEN

Marching to War

ु ु ु

T HE SCENE WAS FAMILIAR around a war-torn world. Powerful searchlights arced from horizon to horizon. Beneath their beams lay a sense of nervous anticipation for what was to come. Then screams and a frenzied rush of bodies. But this was not London or Shanghai, and people were screaming with glee, not terror. This was New York City. Broadway, the scene of so many premieres. Tonight, July 1, 1941, the Astor Theatre was the hub of the action. Once managed by George M. Cohan, the movie palace had seen many exciting moments in its thirty-five years. This evening's crowd was there for the world premiere of Warner Bros.' new picture, *Sergeant York*. It was the most eagerly awaited showing since *Gone with the Wind* had its New York City opening there two years earlier.

Sergeant York's gala opening brought down the curtain on Warners' lavish prerelease publicity campaign. "It is going to be the most important thing that ever happened in New York," one overwhelmed studio publicity agent exclaimed. Warners distributed thousands of posters, convinced the United States Army Recruiting Service to circulate pamphlets with stills from the film, and organized an enormous media drive. Thousands of people, including Gary Cooper and a bevy of dignitaries, greeted Alvin York's train at Penn Station on June 30. A fleet of cars escorted York down Fifth Avenue, past the cheering throngs of New Yorkers who lined his route to the 82nd division's headquarters. From there a motorcade ferried the war hero to City Hall to meet Mayor Fiorello LaGuardia.[1]

The opening-night crowd filed under the largest electric sign ever constructed on Broadway—four stories high and half a block long, with 150,000 red, white, and blue lights (ten times the number of bulbs in Alvin York's hometown of Pall Mall, Tennessee) spelling out "Sergeant York" in letters twenty-five feet high. In deference to its majesty, other

Broadway theaters blacked out for thirty seconds when the Astor first switched it on. A smiling York waved to the gathering as a color guard from his old division, the 82nd, and an American Legion band escorted him down Broadway to the Astor Theatre, where a national radio hookup awaited. The theater's two balconies filled up as York arrived, as did its elaborate side boxes. The view alone was worth the price of admission. Patrons gawked at Gary Cooper. General "Black Jack" Pershing stood nearby, hobnobbing with a gaggle of lesser-known military figures. Henry Luce, the strongly interventionist publisher of *Time, Life,* and *Fortune* magazines and the final authority over The March of Time newsreels, was also there. Some recognized Tennessee governor Prentice Cooper posing for photographers between York and Wendell Willkie, who arrived on a special train from Washington with Eleanor Roosevelt and Tennessee's congressional delegation. The diminutive governor's white jacket and prim black bow tie gave him the unfortunate appearance of a young waiter serving the larger, more rumpled men. With so many government and military representatives present, *Sergeant York*'s debut felt like an officially sanctioned event. The audience was still humming when the lights dimmed at 8:30.[2]

The massive marquee capping the Astor was a fitting tribute to the twenty-two years that producer Jesse Lasky had worked to bring *Sergeant York* to the screen. It embodied a picture that cost around $1.5 million to produce and took over twice as long to shoot as most A-list pictures. The sign's heft testified to the 123 sets studio workers constructed, the eighty-acre battlefield they wrestled out of the San Fernando Valley, and the two miles of trenches they dug in the Santa Susanna Mountains. Its size announced a picture so important that General Pershing and Secretary of State Cordell Hull, who once represented York's district in Congress, telegrammed best wishes on the first day of shooting, so significant that the War Department loaned Cooper a Medal of Honor to wear in it. It loomed over Broadway like the film loomed over America in the second half of 1941. *Sergeant York* was, a studio poster declared, "a picture for sweethearts, a picture for mothers . . . a picture for the U.S.A." It certainly was. The movie racked up more than $6 million in ticket sales, Hollywood's third-highest gross to date.[3]

Sergeant York did not succeed simply because it was a war film. Only around 20 of the picture's 134 minutes take place in France. The United

States does not even declare war until the movie is half over. People flocked to *Sergeant York* because its satisfying image of American values reconciled the nation's antipathy to war with the desire to preserve the principles it cherished. Americans needed "a movie to affirm, with dignity and honesty and profound sincerity, our faith in the way of life that is ours," Cecilia Ager wrote in her *PM* review of *Sergeant York*. The movie tapped into the patriotism blossoming around the United States. A prointervention picture, it was not a "hate film." It never criticized the enemy and abhorred the prospect of combat.[4]

After opening with the blaring fanfare of "You're in the Army Now," Max Steiner's Oscar-nominated score slides into a pastoral elegy as the camera drifts down the thickly wooded Wolf River. The scene carries audiences into a quieter, simpler time. York's time in this wilderness associates him with the great heroes of American history. Gary Cooper's screen connotations gave this connection special power. Cooper was the American everyman—Longfellow Deeds of *Mr. Deeds Goes to Town*, John Doe of *Meet John Doe*. York splits rails in one scene, an image reminding viewers, especially those who saw *Young Mr. Lincoln* and *Abe Lincoln in Illinois*, of the Great Emancipator. His prowess in a rifle-shooting contest leads one awed spectator to liken him to Daniel Boone. The connection to Boone tightens when York strides past a tree actually inscribed by the frontiersman, who "cilled a bar" there in 1760. After a brilliant display on an army target range, a spotter equates Private York with Buffalo Bill. As Michael Birdwell and others have observed, he is a twentieth-century Natty Bumppo, an ordinary American invested with the stuff of legends.[5]

York's Valley of the Three Forks of the Wolf is a community of isolationist, yeoman farmers. They live in Jeffersonian fashion, wanting only a piece of good farmland and control over their destiny. The outside world means little to them. Rather than read the war news on the front page of the newspaper, one local studies a small bit about Cordell Hull's bid for Congress—a nice nod from the filmmakers to the Roosevelt administration. Rosier Pile (Walter Brennan), the valley's shopkeeper and preacher, gives a pushy peddler of stylish clothes the cold shoulder. The townspeople's proud ignorance shocks the salesman. When he inquires about their opinions on the fighting in Europe, one frostily responds, "We ain't done much thinkin' on it."

Young hell-raiser Alvin York exists on the fringes of this cohesive society. *Sergeant York*'s opening sequence delineates the choice he faces in life. York carouses with two buddies as the rest of the town absorbs Pastor Pile's sermon. The picture counterposes York's drunken sharpshooting—he blasts his initials into a tree from twenty paces—with his pious mother's (Margaret Wycherly) disappointment at her son's waywardness. The conflict between York's wanton lifestyle and Ma's Christian respectability builds over the next forty-five minutes as he ogles a barmaid, crosses the state line to get corn liquor, and hurls himself into a barroom brawl. Ma's pleas to straighten up fall on deaf ears, as do Pastor Pile's warnings about Satan's temptations.

York changes his ways after falling in love with the beautiful Gracie Williams (Joan Leslie). Hoping to make himself a desirable marriage partner, he vows to save money to buy a plot of fertile bottomland. He works hard to earn cash only to see the real-estate deal go awry. With it goes York's interest in living a responsible life. He storms back to his favorite sleazy dive to drink himself into an alcohol-fueled rage. As a thunderstorm crashes outside, York resolves to kill the conniving landowner who ruined his dream of economic independence. It is now, at his darkest moment, that York has his conversion experience. A bolt of lightning strikes the rifle from his hand as he passes Pastor Pile's church. With this sign, he becomes another Paul the Apostle, a true convert and devoted servant of the Lord. York staggers into the church, the light from a lamp bathing his face in a warm glow that emphasizes his spiritual awakening. He gives himself over to God, joining the congregation in "Gimme That Old-Time Religion."

The reborn York personifies Americanism. *Commonweal*'s Philip T. Hartung saw "the ringing, robust voice of Walt Whitman" within the picture's protagonist. York embodies hard work, piety, modesty, and family. He symbolizes the uniquely American blend of individual effort and devotion to the community. He is a tamer of the forest, carving a farm from a wilderness. His struggles against poverty and moral depravity offer a road map for the audience to follow. In this sense he is an American icon even before his wartime heroism makes him famous.[6]

York is teaching a Sunday school class when the town hears of President Wilson's declaration of war against Germany. York's topic that morning is the Ten Commandments. He gives particular attention to

"Thou Shalt Not Kill." This confluence of events establishes the dramatic basis for the rest of the film, as York must reconcile his religious convictions with his patriotic duty to serve his country in wartime. Audiences watched York sort out issues very much on their minds. He refuses to register for the draft because he feels the war has nothing to do with him. "War is killin'," he tells Pile, "and the Book's agin' killin', so war is agin' the Book." The pastor convinces York to sign up only after promising that the military will grant him conscientious objector status and release him from fighting.

Pile is mistaken. As with the real Alvin York, the draft board orders him to report to Camp Gordon. The private's stellar performance on the rifle range reveals his military value and leads to a promotion offer. York does not want to be a corporal; he wants to go home. "Killin' other folks ain't no part of what was He intendin' for us to do here," York tells his captain. Major Buxton (Stanley Ridges) tries to cut this Gordian knot, but York parries his theological arguments in defense of war. Buxton then tries a different approach. As "The Star-Spangled Banner" wafts through the background, he hands the private a book on American history. "That's the story of a whole people's struggle for freedom," he says. And that is what this war is about: preserving the freedom to worship as one wishes, farm as one wishes, live as one wishes. We have inherited these gifts from our forefathers and, the major explains, "the cost of that heritage is high. Sometimes it takes all we have to preserve it, even our lives." He gives York ten days' furlough to consider his decision.

As in *The Fighting 69th,* the armed forces offer a means to reconcile polar opposites. This time the military unites disparate ideals, not regions or faiths. York takes the history book and his Bible back to Tennessee. Competing voices haunt him as he studies both texts on a mountaintop retreat. The major's words—"your country"—and Pastor Pile's—"your God"—play in his mind. Then he experiences a flash of divine inspiration. A gust of wind ruffles the pages of his Bible. He picks it up to see Matthew 22:21: "Render therefore unto Caesar the things which are Caesar's; and unto God the things that are God's." Another revelatory light shines upon him, "My Country 'Tis of Thee" plays, and York—or perhaps God—has made his choice.

York will stay in the army. "It's just like Pastor Pile done told me," he informs Major Buxton; "I reckon I can just be a-trustin' in something that's a heap bigger than I be." Those words dissolve the pacifist's anti-war convictions into nothingness. Using a Christian text as their guide, the Jews—Jesse Lasky, the Warner brothers—pointed the way toward an Americanism grounded in both pacifist religion and militant nationalism. They argued that the government was trustworthy, that Americans can join its noble mission without losing their individualism or ethics. The Allied Expeditionary Force becomes a legion of Christian soldiers, marching off to make the world safe for democracy.

Previous World War I pictures such as *They Gave Him a Gun* and *The Dawn Patrol* showed combat twisting men into monsters or rendering them into soulless shells. *Sergeant York* offers a more optimistic take on war's impact. York retains his humility even after he becomes a hero. He remains a pacifist, as he demonstrates when explaining to Major Buxton why he risked his life to take out a machine-gun nest and capture all those Germans:

YORK. I figgered that them guns was killin' hundreds, maybe thousands, and there weren't nothin' anybody could do but to stop them guns, and that's what I done.

BUXTON. You mean to tell me that you did it to save lives?

YORK. Yes sir, that was why.

BUXTON. Well York, what you've just told me is the most extraordinary thing of all.

Marshal Foch gives him the Croix de Guerre. General Pershing pins a Medal of Honor on him. New York throws a ticker-tape parade. Endorsement offers totaling hundreds of thousands of dollars pour in.

York turns them all down. He does not want to profit from killing. He is the consummate citizen-soldier, a latter-day Cincinnatus who wants only to return to the Valley of the Three Forks of the Wolf. His decision to hammer his sword into a plowshare provides the final proof that Americans can engage in wars for freedom without losing their basic character, further evidence that interventionism does not require a permanent commitment to global affairs. Sergeant York will live happily with Gracie on the bottomland farm grateful Tennesseans bought for them. The United States will remain aloof but vigilant, ready for future threats to its liberty.

Although it took twenty-two years to reach the screen, *Sergeant York* arrived at exactly the right moment. Alvin York's moral dilemma echoed that of millions of Americans. The picture offered a solution to their crisis without oversimplifying issues to the point of absurdity. "Instead of merely being a flag-waving salute to a martial exploit," raved one reviewer, "it is a very human document and a searching analysis of the things for which men fight." It demonstrated that men must fight for some things—freedom, liberty, democracy—and implied that the time was right to fight for them again. "This picture may actually help to save this country," Norman Vincent Peale told Jack Warner.[7]

✿ ✿ ✿

Sergeant York's bugle call rang across the hills and valleys of the United States. Many in Hollywood and beyond joined its song, creating a harmony of interventionist instruments. Equally principled detractors sounded dissident notes that aimed to overwhelm the chorus with a different tune. As *Sergeant York* prepared Americans to go to war overseas, its release forced Hollywood one step closer to fighting a war at home.

The tone of the national debate over foreign policy darkened as Roosevelt inched the country toward a war footing. Interventionist columnist Dorothy Thompson accused Charles Lindbergh of aspiring to be an American *Gauleiter*. The usually prudent Louis B. Mayer warned a St. Patrick's Day gathering at San Francisco's Civic Auditorium that the "poisoned whisper" of disloyalty was creeping across the land. "There is a war upon our soil here in America," he informed the ten thousand in attendance and those listening on NBC's national radio hookup. Sensing that the decision for war or peace was drawing near, isolationists labored to avert the disaster they saw looming. The stakes were immense. "I do not believe that our system of government in America can survive our participation or our way of life can survive our participation," Lindbergh told a packed America First rally at Madison Square Garden.[8]

Lindbergh's congressional supporters circled Hollywood. The trade's unprecedented ability to disseminate messages made its outspoken allegiance to Rooseveltian internationalism an inviting target. Some in Washington complained that Thurman Arnold's decision to settle the

Justice Department's antitrust suit preserved Hollywood's ability to dominate public discourse on the war. Oklahoma Democrat Lyle Boren called for a new monopoly inquiry. New York Republican Hamilton Fish Jr. wanted to probe warmongering accusations. Congressman Lewis Thill of Wisconsin agreed, claiming on the floor of the House that Hollywood was "seemingly reenacting the war propaganda role played by the movies prior to the last war."[9]

Senator Burton Wheeler enhanced his position as Congress's top movie-baiter during the summer of 1941. He was in a good position to keep tabs on the industry, as his son John headed America First's Los Angeles chapter. Frustrated that the press buried his arguments beneath a shower of interventionist, pro-Britain talk, the Montanan renewed his assault on Hollywood in May, spearheading a mass-mailing campaign demanding that media outlets devote "equal attention to the non-war speakers and writers." Publicizing a recent survey showing that anti-interventionists rarely appeared in newsreels, Wheeler blustered about introducing a bill to require newsreels to allot equal time to both sides of controversial issues. He knew such a bill would not pass. His real intention was to intimidate, not legislate.[10]

These attacks frightened Will Hays, who found himself disavowing stances his employers had publicly taken. His 1941 state-of-the-industry report applauded movies that built hemispheric solidarity or promoted Americanism while at the same time reiterating earlier denials that "the screen was a breeder of hate." Hays issued a press release in July, the month *Sergeant York* appeared, that sounded more relevant to 1931 than 1941. Those who "demand that the screen subordinate its wholesome function of recreation for any cause, however sincere, are sadly mistaken," he said, because "significance is not achieved at the expense of entertainment." Showing an astonishing lack of perspective, the MPPDA head referred to the loss of foreign movie markets as one of the "calamities of war." He acknowledged in the same press release that Hollywood should depict the armed forces and the nation's preparedness program. Raising these themes did not constitute prowar propagandizing, Hays insisted, because studios did not act "under the duress of dictatorship[,] which can create only propaganda." His waffling marked an effort to promote democracy, freedom, and Hollywood's relevance while keeping the industry above partisan conflict. It also left many confused. *New*

York Times critic Theodore Strauss confessed to having "only the vaguest notions of what Mr. Hays was driving at."[11]

Hays never exerted total control over producers. The developing war crisis threatened to undercut his authority altogether. His calls for pure entertainment fell on deaf ears as executives fired back at isolationists. "This recent growth of Lindberghism must be curtailed somehow," Darryl F. Zanuck informed presidential secretary Stephen Early a few weeks after Hays issued his annual report. Walter Wanger passed around a scathing bit of doggerel that read in part:

> Hail Hero Lindy, not alone this time
> You fly the clouds and cleave the trackless blue
> Not scowling and alone—but every crime
> Of treason to Man's dream, and every hue
> Of mountebank and crackpot—as you climb
> Hangs like a looney kite tail on to you.

Hollywood was spoiling for a fight, and cautious men like Hays found themselves marginalized.[12]

The town was alive with war-related activities. Bundles for Britain kept collecting donations. Samuel Goldwyn trolled for funds on behalf of Greek War Relief. Zanuck assumed the chair of the California Division of Air Youth of America. Producers, actors, and blue-collar workers alike participated in national aluminum drives. The Fight for Freedom Committee, an organization advocating "full participation by the United States in the present war," attracted prominent names to its Stage, Screen, Radio, and Arts Division. Among those contributing to or performing in the committee's "Fun to Be Free Rallies" across the United States were Humphrey Bogart, Walt Disney, Melvyn Douglas, Phillip Dunne, Douglas Fairbanks Jr., Howard Hawks, Helen Hayes, Nunnally Johnson, Burgess Meredith, Edward G. Robinson, Walter Wanger, Jack and Harry Warner, William Wyler, and Darryl F. Zanuck.[13]

Hollywood also offered more formal support for Roosevelt's foreign policy. The Motion Picture Committee Cooperating for the National Defense placed a dozen army recruitment trailers in seventy-five hundred theaters in the spring of 1941. Zanuck's training-film program had turned out around one hundred reels by the end of July. Production costs averaged around $2,850 per reel, far below what the Signal Corps spent for comparable work. Initial installments pleased military officials, who suggested more than two hundred future subjects. Naval commanders considered a similar tie-in with the Zanuck-chaired Research Council. Studios were hard at work producing defense-related shorts for commercial release. Topics for these one-reelers grew out of the industry's discussions with the Office of Government Reports and other federal agencies.[14]

Hollywood wanted more. Walter Wanger urged General George C. Marshall to extract "greater service" from Hollywood. The producer was especially keen to win government support for morale-boosting newsreels. Marshall referred the issue to Lowell Mellett, FDR's media liaison and future head of the wartime Bureau of Motion Pictures, who advised Wanger to back off lest Americans become concerned about government control of the screen. "Having in mind there is a saturation point so far as the public is concerned," Mellett said, "I do not feel this is the time for exerting pressure on producers and other elements of the industry."[15]

Not everyone in the administration shared Mellett's caution. Peter Odegard, one of many largely unknown New Dealers surrounding the president, offered MGM several proposals that advanced the administration's goals, including a film version of O. E. Rölvaag's *Giants of the Earth* intended to dramatize "the living ties between our culture and that of Europe." Odegard also suggested a picture about Civil War–era appeasers that gave Clement Vallandigham, an Ohio politician who favored the Confederacy during the war, "all the habiliments of Senator Wheeler"; an adaptation of *Winning of the West,* Teddy Roosevelt's tribute to the pioneering spirit; and a biopic of Joseph Pulitzer, who promoted the free press that dictatorships loathed. Although MGM never followed up on these ideas, the studio did give them serious consideration.[16]

They certainly were not the worst ideas floating around Hollywood. That dubious distinction probably went to Harry Warner, whose detestation of Nazism and desire to aid Britain had gone beyond the point of mere obsession. In late July 1941 he disrupted a feel-good luncheon at MGM in honor of British ambassador Lord Halifax with a convoluted speech calling on the United States to occupy Great Britain. This move, which echoed recent American actions in Iceland, would free the British

Army to liberate France. Halifax, who was trying to shake his well-deserved reputation as an appeaser, politely promised to forward the suggestion to the Ministry of War.[17]

That was not enough for Warner, who had the bit between his teeth and was determined to run. He reiterated his scheme the next day in a letter to the president. "If we consider the Atlantic Ocean our life-line," he counseled Roosevelt, "it is an assured fact that the Island of Great Britain is certainly a part of that life-line. What fault could anyone find if we undertook to man the Island to protect it from invasion, so as to allow the English Army to go wherever they may be needed?" Warner regained his modesty for a moment, adding: "This is only a suggestion."

Roosevelt asked Stephen Early to thank Warner for his note.[18]

✿ ✿ ✿

After lunching with Lord Halifax, Hollywood's elite reassembled at Twentieth Century–Fox that night to honor Wendell Willkie. The former presidential candidate was in town to speak at the Hollywood Bowl on behalf of Fight for Freedom. Movie folk, especially Zanuck, Jack and Harry Warner, and Melvyn Douglas, took the lead in organizing his visit. Mayer, Selznick, Wanger, the Warners, and others talked movies with the Indiana Republican over plates heaped with steak, herring, and liver. Zanuck tried to turn the conversation to polo without finding any takers. Willkie's charms nevertheless ensnared the Fox chief, who arranged the banquet. The producer already admired the politician's interventionism. Meeting him in person confirmed his belief in Willkie's greatness. "I now realize why and how you can inspire an entire nation," Zanuck gasped.[19]

Willkie spoke the next evening to twenty-five thousand adoring spectators and a national radio hookup. Interventionists, who saw his speech as a response to Lindbergh's talk at the Bowl in June, ensured that the reception for Willkie outstripped the one given to the isolationist. The industry turned out to support him. Zanuck closed the Fox lot early and urged (forced, some claimed) employees to attend the meeting. "It is imperative that the Hollywood Bowl be crowded to overflowing," he told them. "[Willkie] must know that the good Americans of Hollywood can turn out as strongly as the bums and other subversive elements turned out for Mr. Lindbergh." Harry Warner, still captivated by his plan to occupy Great Britain, paraded studio workers from the Hollywood American Legion Post to the Bowl behind a large standard reading: "We'd rather march to hear Willkie on National Unity than be marched to a concentration camp."[20]

Willkie employed similarly blunt rhetoric as he exhorted the crowd to take the Axis menace seriously. Rebuffing America Firsters who insisted the war was not the United States' problem, he insisted that an Axis victory would mean the permanent transformation of national institutions. "The real issue is whether we are going to live in the future as free men," Willkie concluded, "or whether the attack of the totalitarian powers is to destroy our prospect of freedom and force us, in desperation, to undertake another form of government." Willkie's appearance moved the studios to contribute $50,000 to Fight for Freedom, boosted membership in the organization's nascent Hollywood chapter, and cemented his status as a player in the film community.[21]

It was on the surface an odd marriage. Hollywood valued sizzle, and Willkie was all steak. He was a slovenly man from Elwood, Indiana, whose tie was never straight and whose clothes never fit. Ashes from the Camels he chain-smoked rarely landed in an ashtray, instead coming to rest on his clothes or the floor. His inability to read lines gave his prepared speeches an eye-glazing, monotonic quality that discouraged many potential backers. Willkie's charisma shone through, however, when he spoke off the cuff. He had "a personality to charm a bird from a tree—if he wanted to," remembered one admirer. His Hoosier twang made him the voice of middle America, the America of Darryl F. Zanuck's childhood and the America that movie moguls wanted to reach. Producers admired his straight talk, fiscal conservatism, and up-by-the-bootstraps biography. Like them, he was a businessman, a graduate of Indiana University's law school who rose to the presidency of utilities giant Commonwealth and Southern. Raised in obscurity, Willkie fought for everything he had. He could have been one of them.[22]

His pro-British, anti–big government presidential run earned Willkie many Hollywood friends. Ironically, he did not impress the industry's most important Republican. Will Hays voted for his fellow Hoosier at the Republican National Convention and worked for favorable newsreel coverage of the candidate during the general election. Hays nevertheless found Willkie too liberal and too interventionist for his tastes.

The MPPDA head offered pro-British platitudes when film revenues were at stake, but Willkie's talk of an Anglo-American alliance unnerved him. Hays suspected that, for all their idealistic rhetoric, the British really wanted a Versailles-style peace that strengthened their country while disarming the Germans. He had no desire to fight for a more powerful Great Britain.[23]

Willkie remained popular after his defeat. He refused FDR's offer of a position in a coalition government but maintained close ties with influential pressmen like the *New York Times'* Arthur Krock, Henry Luce, and Washington columnist Drew Pearson while devoting himself to Britain's cause. A vocal backer of lend-lease, he visited London to see the war firsthand. Although he returned to the law in early 1941, Willkie never gave as much time to the New York City–based firm of Willkie, Owen, Otis, and Bailly as he did to interventionist causes.[24]

Wendell Willkie was well-known, well-connected, and well-respected. He had a reputation for tenacity and a gift for working with the media. He was a good man for movie executives to know.

CHAPTER NINETEEN

Hollywood Triumphant

SENATOR BURTON WHEELER'S TALK of investigating the movie business inserted the fuse. Senator Gerald Nye struck the spark that exploded the powder keg. The North Dakota Republican's radio address from St. Louis on August 1, 1941, left Hollywood sputtering and ushered in the climactic phase of the isolationists' debate with interventionists. Much of the senator's oration, ghostwritten by John T. Flynn, head of the New York City chapter of America First, repeated the points that anti-interventionists had argued for months. Nye raised the specter of British propaganda and asked Americans to focus on their own needs instead of the outside world's.

Nye's speech then took an unexpected turn. "Who has brought us to the verge of war?" he inquired. "Who is putting up the money for all this propaganda?" In his mind the culprit was Hollywood. "The silver screen has been flooded with picture after picture designed to rouse us to a state of war hysteria," the senator declared. Such movies as *The Great Dictator, Escape,* and *Man Hunt* incited a prowar frenzy that overwhelmed the cool rationality of neutrality. And who was responsible for these movies? Eight giant corporations, run by men who came from "Russia, Hungary, Germany, and the Balkan countries." Men from nations under Nazi control. *Jews* from nations under Nazi control, people with names like Cohn, Mayer, Goldwyn, and Schenck. With their homelands overrun by the Nazis, they had a vested interest in the war. Studios issued pro-British propaganda because their financial survival depended on revenues from Great Britain. Nye further charged that, as part of the Roosevelt administration's drive to "whip up the warrior spirit in our young men," the federal government had ordered Hollywood, that "raging volcano of war fever," to churn out militaristic pictures.

"This is the worst kind of propaganda because it is the most insidi-ous," Nye argued. People went to movies for entertainment, not propa-ganda. They relaxed in theaters, making them vulnerable to messages crafted by experts and delivered by glamorous actors who rose twenty feet high before them. Prowar propaganda was everywhere, in every movie house in the country. From Florida to Maine, from Washington, D.C., to Los Angeles, it boomed out at eighty million patrons every week. "The truth is that in 20,000 theatres in the United States tonight they are holding war mass meetings," Nye thundered.[1]

Nye understood something the moguls struggled to accept—that Hol-lywood mattered. Movie executives knew their products found huge au-diences but rarely pondered the consequences of their cultural power. Even as they knowingly and proudly disseminated messages, they re-mained profoundly uncomfortable with the attention those messages drew to the medium. In these days before television no other outlet could match the influence of motion pictures. Far from pure entertainment, movies played an indelible role in creating tastes, spreading ideas, and characterizing peoples. They were an established part of most Ameri-cans' lives, a reliable friend that could be counted on for hours of enjoy-ment every week. Hollywood's interventionism—both on and off the screen—practically guaranteed that isolationists' position would not win out. Nye knew this, and he hated it.

The senator was determined to blunt Hollywood's influence. A few hours before his speech, he and fellow isolationist Senator Bennett Champ Clark introduced a resolution, also written by John T. Flynn, requesting a formal inquiry into film and radio propaganda and mo-nopoly in the motion-picture industry. The resolution went to Senator Burton K. Wheeler's Interstate Commerce Committee. Knowing the Nye-Clark motion stood no chance in the full committee, Wheeler re-ferred it to a subcommittee headed by isolationist D. Worth Clark of Idaho, who immediately scheduled hearings.[2]

The isolationists' timing bore an impeccable sense of irony, as *Ser-geant York* had debuted in Washington, D.C., the previous evening. The hoopla in the capital approached that of the New York premiere. York arrived on July 30 with Governor Prentice Cooper, Jesse Lasky, Tennes-see's two senators, and Major General George Duncan, York's com-mander in France, in tow. A marine band played as representatives from the American War Mothers, the American Legion, the Veterans of Foreign Wars, and the Boy Scouts paid homage to the hero. The troop paraded from Union Station to the White House, where York had an audience with FDR. York gave the invocation in the Senate the next morning before Warner Bros. representatives whisked him to a luncheon, a radio address, a banquet, and the Earle Theatre, where he joined scores of diplomats, congressmen, generals, and other government officials assembled for the premiere. As usual, Jack Warner found a way to quite literally steal the spotlight, which fell on him as he escorted Gracie York to the stage for a brief peroration before the show started.[3]

President Roosevelt offered a rare, public movie review, declaring himself "thrilled" with *Sergeant York*. His endorsement helped cement the film's blockbuster status. "Dear Jack we came we saw we conquered," read Lasky's celebratory telegram to Warner. Laudatory reviews poured in as the picture expanded its run around the country. Each plaudit stood as a rebuke to Clark, Flynn, Nye, and Wheeler's insistence that Americans did not want to see interventionist pictures.[4]

Nye's accusations nevertheless hit Hollywood at an inopportune moment, threatening domestic disaster on a par with the financial meltdown overseas. Studios currently generated no income from Albania, Belgium, Bulgaria, Czechoslovakia, Danzig, Estonia, Germany, Hungary, Italy, Latvia, Lithuania, Luxembourg, Norway, Poland, Romania, the Soviet Union, or Yugoslavia. It received only minimal revenues from China, Denmark, Egypt, Finland, France and French colonies, Greece, Japan, Spain, Sweden, Switzerland, Syria, and Turkey. Almost two-thirds of its earnings from the British Empire—Great Britain, Australia, Canada, New Zealand, India—were blocked. Total foreign revenue had declined by more than half since mid-1940. Twentieth Century–Fox chairman Joseph Schenck's recent conviction on perjury and tax fraud charges also sent movie bosses reeling. Schenck's woes resulted from Hollywood's association with crooked labor leaders Willie Bioff and George Browne, who used their mob ties to transform the International Alliance of Theatrical Stage Employees (IATSE) into a corrupt organization based on intimidation and extortion. Most big producers paid them bribes in return for labor peace. Bioff was scheduled to face trial in October.[5]

The publicity surrounding the Schenck case was a black mark on Hollywood's reputation. Propaganda hearings might add to the problem.

Columbia's Harry Cohn advised a spirited offensive. "This industry has fallen into the habit of attempting to take these things in their stride," he told Hays. Perhaps, he suggested, producers could distract the public with some benevolent gesture, such as adopting British war orphans.[6]

Publicity stunts would not dissuade isolationists fixed on halting the dream factory's nefarious activities. Gerald Nye was a longtime enemy of Hollywood who had long championed equal access to the media for both sides of controversial issues. He offered a bill in 1929 to create government-owned radio stations for that purpose. Nye was also the Senate's most famous opponent of war. His 1934 hearings on the World War I–era munitions industry bared that business's Machiavellian dealings and, in the process, established Nye's reputation and fortune—he commanded a hefty speaking fee. Nye was not popular among his colleagues. His anti-Semitic streak bothered some, but more disliked his tendency toward self-aggrandizement. "He is generally held to be a sniveling cheat that would stop at nothing" to publicize himself, one reporter commented.[7]

Wheeler had his own issues with Hollywood. A prominent backer of the Neely bill, he saw the movie industry as no different from the big businesses he had battled ever since taking on Montana's giant Anaconda Copper as a young lawyer. He was a smart, savvy politician whose ironic smile masked a ruthless enemy of the Roosevelt administration. His colleagues were accustomed to hearing his New England accent, the product of a childhood spent in Boston, ring out over the Senate floor as he denounced the latest wrongheaded act of a president embarked on a destructive foreign policy. Roosevelt's repeated triumphs over Wheeler's opposition saddled the embittered senator with a persecution complex that fed his ambition for power.[8]

Nye's assault and the subsequent scheduling of hearings stunned the moguls. Although trade reporters filled pages with angry denials of propagandizing and government manipulation, producers were slow to respond to these latest attacks. The senator's exploitation of the Jewish issue struck a soft spot, and new antimonopoly talk so soon after the Thurman Arnold affair closed caught them off guard. Harry Warner demanded that Hays make an aggressive defense and allowed Walter Wanger to launch an anti-isolationist fusillade on his family's radio station, KFWB. The Academy president used his airtime to blast Nye,

Wheeler, and other "self-seeking politicians" who had, Wanger claimed, fallen under Hitler's spell. Hays, recently recovered from a bad case of pneumonia, offered a milder response: he formed a committee. The attorneys Austin Keough (Paramount), Joseph Hazen (Warner Bros.), and Robert Rubin (MGM) coordinated affairs on the East Coast, while Hays and Paramount's Y. Frank Freeman took charge in California.[9]

Hays's first instinct was to rely on a "pure entertainment" defense while placating senators with friendly words. Asking executives to keep a low profile, he commissioned a study showing that 92.7 percent of feature films released since September 1939 bore no relation to the war. Such passivity allowed the Nye-Clark forces to keep the offensive. Producers "have been operating as war propaganda machines almost as if they were directed from a single central bureau," Nye told one audience, and he suspected the administration lurked behind that central bureau. Wheeler also chipped in, declaring that Hollywood was "carrying on the most gigantic campaign of propaganda for war that has ever been known in the history of the United States." Isolationists cast a wide net, inviting Hays and executives from all the majors to testify at the upcoming hearings. D. Worth Clark promised to quiz a long list of producers, directors, and actors.[10]

Hays wanted to issue a conciliatory letter, a move some California executives supported. Industry lawyers advised against it, as did B'nai B'rith director and Hollywood insider Richard Gutstadt, who recommended a more aggressive approach. Hit at Nye's anti-Semitism and appeal to Americans' sense of fair play, Gutstadt suggested. Growing numbers of studio lawyers met on an almost daily basis to map out a plan. Austin Keough soon emerged as the group's leader. He coordinated the committee with the Hays Office, updated Clark on its progress in rounding up potential witnesses, and privately talked strategy with Lowell Mellett, Roosevelt's media liaison. Keough asked Hays to stay in the background, counseling studios to engage someone else with Washington connections to serve as their voice.[11]

Keough's robust stance carried the day. After composing a tough response to the Senate subcommittee, he persuaded Clark to narrow his expansive witness list, which soon focused on such unapologetic interventionists as Wanger, Harry Warner, and Zanuck. Operating through Mellett, he convinced Roosevelt to shut Hays, who was clamoring for an interview, out of the White House. "I think it would be better not to let Hays in until after the hearings," Mellett told the president. Besides embroiling Roosevelt in a Senate investigation, granting an audience might convey a false impression that the president endorsed the MPPDA head's accommodationist approach to the hearings, thereby discouraging those who advocated a more vigorous defense.[12]

Those ranks certainly included Darryl F. Zanuck. Like Keough, he wanted an outsider to represent Hollywood before the Senate. He consulted his friend Ulric Bell, executive director of Fight for Freedom, who suggested Wendell Willkie. Although his exact role is unclear, Roosevelt's secretary, Stephen Early, played some part in bringing the president's recent adversary into the industry's defense team. Hiring Willkie made perfect sense. He knew the producers, had national stature, and was obviously not a mouthpiece for the Roosevelt administration. The former candidate, who had not taken a case since returning to the bar, did not come cheap. At Zanuck's and Keough's urging, however, studio heads paid his $100,000 fee. The mood within the industry changed almost overnight. "I am sure that this is in good shape now," the MPPDA's Frederick Herron told Hays. After settling into a suite in Washington's Carlton Hotel, Willkie received thorough briefings from industry lawyers, viewed films likely to come up in the hearing, and hashed out ground rules with Senator Clark. Clark gave every sign of wanting a fair hearing, telling Keough that the industry's counsel would be free to cross-examine witnesses and offer questions to the subcommittee.[13]

The movie business was coming together, gaining confidence against foes who had cowed it in the past. Beleaguered executives found allies in journalists who loudly opposed the approaching inquiry. Talk of propaganda and intimations of censorship struck close to newspapermen's hearts. They had watched the rise of totalitarianism with horror. Dictators' control of the press led to fears that the same thing might happen at home. "Congress has no more right to legislate on film themes nor to impose a Nazi censorship than it has to attempt similar control of the press," the *Salem Capital-Journal* declared. "If such a precedent is established, it bodes ill for our democratic way of life." The *Buffalo Courier Express* called the hearings "a frontal attack on the constitutional guarantee of freedom of expression." Support from newspapers further convinced Hollywood to mount a counteroffensive rather than turn tail. The public, it seemed, was on the film industry's side.[14]

Although studio executives could make a decent B movie like *Murder in the Air* for what they paid Wendell Willkie, the lawyer earned his hefty fee before the hearings even started. He issued a press release on September 8, the day before the inquiry opened, that seized momentum from the senators and reframed the terms of the debate in Hollywood's favor. Willkie came out on the attack, informing D. Worth Clark that there was no need to investigate whether Hollywood was anti-Nazi. "We abhor everything which Hitler represents," he wrote. He admitted that studios "gladly, and with great pride" cooperated with the government on national defense. Movies presented the armed forces to the public, sold defense bonds, and informed Americans about the military buildup, and they did so without apology.

Willkie rejected Nye's insinuation that a Jewish-dominated Hollywood toadied up to the British for fear of losing that essential market. Highlighting the anti-Semitic undertones of Nye's St. Louis speech, he insisted that moviemakers were Americans through and through, that only a traitor could doubt their patriotism. He conceded that British revenues were important but denied Nye's allegation that money drove studios to make pro-British features. If moviemakers based decisions solely on international revenues, he reasoned, they would "still be appeasing Hitler to try to keep the Continental market." Willkie's barb ignored studio heads' long appeasement of Mussolini and the fact that several studios stayed in Hitler's Germany until compelled to leave. But his missive was designed for public consumption, not for insiders well-versed in the global film business's intricate dealings.

Willkie characterized the hearings as a referendum on basic American principles, arguing that Nye's followers had embarked on a fool's mission to capture control of the movies so as to require Hollywood to make features reflecting their perspective. They sought, in other words, the power to make their own propaganda. Surrendering to such demagoguery would be the beginning of the end for American liberties. "It is just a small step to the newspapers, magazines and other periodicals," Willkie argued. "And from the freedom of the press, it is just a small step to the freedom of the individual to say what he believes."[15]

Willkie's widely reprinted statement put his clients on the side of God and country and placed their enemies at the other extreme. To oppose Hollywood was to oppose the United States. To question its motives was to embrace Nazism. Rather than investigating legitimate issues of monopoly or exploring the government's role in determining the content of motion pictures, Clark and his colleagues had to defend themselves from charges of anti-Semitism while fighting the public impression that they had launched a grab for power. The lawyer hit his mark, dooming the hearings before they began.

✿ ✿ ✿

In lieu of a gavel, D. Worth Clark banged a glass ashtray on the table to call the subcommittee of the Senate Interstate Commerce Committee to order at 10:15 in the morning on September 9, 1941. Nearly five hundred spectators jammed the Senate caucus room. Reporters jostled with congressmen and other visitors. Gawkers stood on chairs and clung to the marble columns lining the far wall in hopes of catching a better view of the action. Although constructed only thirty-two years earlier, the venue was filled with history. Senators had investigated the *Titanic* disaster and Teapot Dome scandal in this room, which later hosted the Army-McCarthy and Watergate hearings. Massive windows rose nearly twenty feet from its floor, bringing in floods of sunlight that illuminated every crack and corner within. Bringing light to dark places—that was the purpose of this place.[16]

The location implied power. The third-floor caucus room was the largest in the Senate Office Building. The dome of the United States Capitol, which stood across Constitution Avenue, loomed over the white marble and limestone structure's Doric columns. An electric subway linked the two buildings, transforming the symbolic connection between them into a literal one. Vice President Henry Wallace had offices in the building, as did Senate Majority Leader Alben Barkley, Missouri senator Harry Truman, and archsegregationist Richard Russell. Senators Nye and Clark, the centers of attention this day, also had suites there.

Clark saw both friendly and unfriendly faces as he looked around. Those closest to him were for the most part welcoming. Gerald Nye sat across the table, looking confident as he fiddled with an adhesive patch covering a shaving cut on his chin. Senator Burton Wheeler's handpicked subcommittee flanked Clark. To Clark's left sat Charles Tobey of New Hampshire, an erratic man prone to indiscreet questions but a reliable anti-interventionist. Illinois' Charles Wayland "Curly" Brooks, another anti-interventionist, sat next to Tobey. Washington senator Homer Bone was supposed to be there but begged off because of a broken hip.[17]

Clark appeared more comfortable than he really was. He worried about the men to his right. Senator Ernest McFarland of Arizona was a wild card. The burly, square-jawed former lawyer was new to the Senate, having won election in November 1940. Although he had stumped for intervention, Wheeler saw him as safe. Freshman senators were to be seen, not heard. Wheeler soon regretted his decision to put McFarland on the subcommittee. Although friendly with Nye, Clark, and other isolationists, the Arizonian despised their views on foreign policy. McFarland emerged as a Hollywood defender before the hearings opened. "There's not a damned bit of sense holding this investigation," he told one reporter. "The isolationists are just out to get a lot of publicity, build up their case wherever they can. . . . D. Worth Clark, Curly Brooks and Senator Tobey are ready to vote now. I know I am."[18]

To McFarland's right sat Wendell Willkie, who carefully positioned himself within earshot of representatives from the newspaper syndicates. Clark sensed Willkie's hostility. The lawyer was angry at the senator, who had unexpectedly reversed his earlier assurance that Willkie could cross-examine witnesses. "They're a bunch of dumb bastards," the big Hoosier said privately of Clark, Brooks, and Tobey. Willkie did not think much of McFarland's abilities either, but he liked him and knew they were on the same side. The two held nightly strategy sessions in Willkie's Carlton Hotel suite. Their plan was simple—Willkie would hijack the investigation by making himself the media's focus. He, not the isolationists, would be the voice of the hearings.[19]

Willkie had plenty of legal assistance. Austin Keough, Joseph Hazen, Robert Rubin, Maurice Benjamin, and a battery of attorneys from his office surrounded him. Zanuck was prepped and ready to go in Los Angeles. Harry Warner was on his way from Hollywood. Will Hays was somewhere in Washington, although the movie czar never showed his face at the proceedings.[20]

Willkie's prehearing antics rattled Clark, who was determined to regain control of the inquiry. He began by announcing his decision not to let Willkie question witnesses. This, he fatuously claimed, was "established procedure" for Senate hearings. McFarland made a show of protesting the chair's decision. Clark overruled him. With this bit of political theater completed, Senator Nye began reading an hour-long statement that largely reiterated his St. Louis address. After speaking of the power a small cadre of Jewish movie producers wielded, he referred to the 1915 *Mutual* decision, which opened Hollywood to censorship by ruling that the First Amendment did not apply to motion pictures. While rejecting direct government supervision, Nye argued that the "dangerous propaganda" major studios unleashed on unsuspecting theater patrons made it essential for the committee to consider dismantling Hollywood's monopoly on moviemaking.[21]

Nye tried to clarify his stance on the Jewish issue, but Willkie's combative press release had painted him into a corner. The senator could not discuss anti-Semitism without appearing anti-Semitic. His remarks ranged from apologetic to indignant to intimidating. He denied that "bigotry, race and religious prejudice" played any role in the hearings; he then repeated his veiled threat that "many people seem to assume that our Jewish citizenry would willingly have our country and its sons taken into this foreign war." Jews who exposed themselves to public scrutiny, he argued, contributed to rising anti-Semitism in the United States.[22]

Willkie had already placed isolationists on the defensive. Senator McFarland twisted the knife by deftly exposing the hearings' futility. "I should like to know what you expect to accomplish by this investigation," he asked after Nye finished his statement. Nye did not have an answer, nor could he offer ideas for legislation that might come from the hearings. The senator limply suggested revising the Sherman Antitrust Act in some way. He had not seen most of the movies he deemed propaganda, lacked a clear definition of war propaganda, and could not imagine what a noninterventionist film might look like. His morning testimony left the impression that the inquiry's sole purpose was publicity. Willkie compounded the senator's discomfort by distributing a press release halfway through Nye's testimony. Reporters scurried off to wire their papers, leaving a flustered Nye to wonder how he could get the media on his side. The lawyer jumped on the senator's demand for Hollywood to take a more balanced approach to international affairs. "This, I presume, means that since Chaplin made a laughable caricature of

Hitler, the industry should be forced to employ Charles Laughton to do the same on Winston Churchill," he joked.[23]

Nye's suffering continued during the afternoon session. His dramatic assertion that the government forced producers to make propaganda pictures crumbled under McFarland's interrogation:

MCFARLAND. By whom?
NYE. By some agent of the Government.
MCFARLAND. And who was that?
NYE. By some agent of the Government.
MCFARLAND. Well, that is rather indefinite.

McFarland's persistence irritated the North Dakotan. "Mr. Chairman," Nye objected, "it may be that I am here in the capacity of a witness intended to prove every statement [I make]. I am not here in any such capacity."[24]

Clark looked pained. Willkie smiled broadly. The audience roared, quieting once the poker-faced McFarland renewed his pursuit. He asked Nye about the films isolationists labeled propaganda. Which of those was most objectionable, McFarland asked. "Senator, you have propounded to me a question that is most difficult to answer," Nye replied. "It is a terrible weakness of mine to go to a picture tonight and not be able to state the title of it tomorrow morning." He spoke vaguely of "I Married a Nazi," a picture that turned out to be Fox's *The Man I Married*. He had not seen *Confessions of a Nazi Spy* but had watched *The Great Dictator* and judged it propaganda. The Arizonian did not relent:

MCFARLAND. Have you seen *Flight Command?*
NYE. I do not believe I did, Senator.
MCFARLAND. *That Hamilton Woman?*
NYE. I did not see that.
MCFARLAND. *Man Hunt?*
NYE. I think not.
MCFARLAND. *Sergeant York?*
NYE. I think not.

It was with great relief that Clark banged his ashtray at 4:05 to close the day's session.[25]

The isolationists' slide continued when the hearings reopened the next day. McFarland eased into his seat just before Clark gaveled the subcommittee into session. He appeared content, like a cat lolling in the sun. Clark looked like he did not want to be there, shooting worried looks to his right every time Willkie lobbed a wisecrack at the press.[26]

Today's abbreviated session—senators were needed on the floor to debate a tax bill—belonged to Missouri senator Bennett Champ Clark (no relation to D. Worth Clark). The man who cosponsored the resolution creating the hearings also appeared uneasy. He rushed through his prepared statement like a man late for a bus, essentially restating Nye's points from the previous day without elaboration. Charges of anti-Semitism still stung; the angry legislator insisted that he had spent "a lifetime fighting for tolerance in this country." Bennett Clark's frustration was obvious. He was all for freedom of speech, but Hollywood denied that freedom to its ideological opponents. It was simply not fair that a band of monopolists could shuffle anti-interventionists to the fringes while converting "17,000 theaters into 17,000 daily and nightly mass meetings for war." He painted a dark picture of a few corporate titans huddling around a table to decide what they wanted 80 million Americans to see next week.[27]

McFarland once more stole the show. He again asked that the subcommittee allow Willkie to examine the witness. Worth Clark again refused. Under McFarland's questioning, Bennett Clark acknowledged that he had not seen most of the allegedly propagandistic pictures, did not know whether they portrayed actual facts or were inflated dramatizations, and did not have any remedy in mind. The cross-examination grew testy as the witness's patience ebbed. Worth Clark sat silent, refusing to intercede. McFarland also sounded weary. "What I have been trying to find out, senator," he noted after one contentious exchange, "really is what we are here to do."[28]

Bennett Clark did not have an answer. Neither did anyone else. The isolationists' ship was sinking, and Curly Brooks wanted a lifeboat. After remaining silent all morning, the Illinois Republican grabbed the microphone as the session closed. Speaking more to reporters and his constituents in Illinois than to either of the Clarks, he pathetically declared, "I had nothing to do with the presentation nor the drawing up of the resolutions. I was not consulted about them. . . . I had no preconceived ideas as to whether or not the movies are conducting a propaganda for war. I have not seen the pictures."[29]

Anti-interventionists had taken their best shot and proved only that they rarely went to movies. The *Chicago Tribune,* America's mighty beacon of isolationism, supported the hearings. Most other papers found them ludicrous. The *New York Post* mocked the investigation as "a low-grade sideshow." *New York Times* columnist Arthur Krock called the hearings "a Kangaroo Court." The *Tallahassee Democrat* posed the question at the core of the controversy yet never put so bluntly by a senator. "What moving picture is without propaganda?" it inquired.[30]

Indeed this was the problem. Nye, Clark, and Wheeler used the term *propaganda* to refer to messages they disliked. They talked about the need for pleasant films, for pure entertainment, without recognizing that the carefree world they presented was as propagandistic as *The Mortal Storm.* Pure entertainment offered propaganda for a world that did not exist. Anti-interventionists tried to clarify their meaning, explaining that propaganda films inspired hatred for an entire nation, but their definition felt arbitrary. It gave the public the sense that isolationists wanted the right to label movies as "propaganda" or "not propaganda," a power that smacked of censorship and repression in an age with too much of both.

McFarland's jabs and Willkie's one-liners left Nye and Clark fuming. They muttered to each other between sessions about exacting revenge on the lawyer. The $100,000 man was earning his money. Willkie's repeated requests that the committee view the movies in question rankled the senators, and his offers to produce witnesses to testify that Hollywood actually showed restraint in depicting conditions under Nazi rule cast the inquiry in terms favorable to studios.

The isolationists' mood sagged further over the next two days. Brooks was absent; he left to attend an American Legion convention that, embarrassingly, voted to endorse Roosevelt's pro-British foreign policy. America First's John T. Flynn held the floor on Thursday without adding much to his side's case. Like Nye and Bennett Clark, he spoke in general terms about the majors' ability to implant war propaganda into the minds of unsuspecting patrons. He offered no remedies and denied any desire to censor movies. His testimony was puzzling at times, as when he declared that "there is a difference between hating Hitler and hating fascism."[31]

McFarland continued his prodding, professing uncertainty about why Flynn was here and what he hoped to accomplish. His suggestion that the German-American Bund backed America First enraged the isolationist. At the conclusion of Flynn's testimony, McFarland engaged him in an exchange that again exposed the absurdity of the hearings:

MCFARLAND. What is propaganda?
FLYNN. It is an attempt to propagate an idea in the minds of the people or in the minds of any group of people.
MCFARLAND. Have you not been trying to do that today?[32]

Newspaper and radio journalist Jimmie Fidler dominated the next day. The gossip columnist, a longtime foe of major studios, made several charges designed to portray Hollywood as an ideologically homogenous monopoly that ruthlessly silenced dissenters. Fidler claimed that Louis B. Mayer tried to muzzle him after he panned MGM's *Marie Antoinette*. The critic also asserted that studios pressured the *Nashville Banner* and *Los Angeles Times* to publish more favorable coverage of their films or else lose their lucrative advertising contracts. Industry lawyers neutralized these accusations over the next few days even though they had a grain of truth. Willkie smeared Fidler in the press, branding him as "one who makes his living by unsupported and unproved statements about other people."[33]

Fidler's testimony was not without its comedy, at least from Hollywood's perspective. D. Worth Clark fumbled through his questions, asking the witness about celebrity rumors not even the gossip columnist would confirm. At one point Senator Tobey mistook Charlie Chan for a real person. Hollywood power brokers had worried about Fidler's appearance. The Hays Office compiled a sizable dossier on him to use in their defense. Their preparations turned out to be unnecessary, as his accusations failed to gain traction or develop into a larger pattern of misbehavior Clark could seize on as evidence of a coordinated monopoly. By now it was difficult to find anyone defending the hearings. Even Clark was looking for a way out.[34]

The anti-interventionist cause took another hit a few hours after Flynn testified. During a speech to an America First rally in Des Moines, Charles Lindbergh cited the British, the Roosevelt administration, and American Jews as forces pushing the United States toward war. He understood why Jews wanted the United States to enter the fight but asked them to rethink their position. Because "tolerance is a virtue that depends upon peace and strength," he told the audience, "history shows that it cannot survive war and devastation." Lindbergh observed that "their greatest danger to this country lies in their large ownership and influence in our motion pictures, our press, our radio, and our government." The flier had not meant to sound anti-Semitic. In the wake of Nye's St. Louis speech, however, his talk bore the ring of Nazi-style bigotry. "Goebbels could not have done better," *New Republic* said. Stephen Early jumped into the fray, pointing out the "striking similarity" between Lindbergh's comments and the official line from Berlin.[35]

Although Lindbergh had nothing to do with the hearings, his membership in America First and that organization's involvement in the inquiry gave Clark's subcommittee an anti-Semitic feel that, in turn, gave anti-interventionism a tinge of anti-Americanism. Lindbergh's speech "has given us all a terrible kick in the pants," Flynn told Clark. The isolationists' publicity gambit was falling apart. "This just pins the anti-Semitic label on the whole isolationist fight, lays us wide open to this charge of racial persecution," Clark worried.[36]

The committee had one chance to regain the momentum. After a week's hiatus, Hollywood took its turn on the stand. If Clark could break the executives, he might yet carry the day. It was not to be. Nick Schenck was the first witness for the defense. The soft-spoken executive proved impenetrable in his day and a half of testimony. He mumbled into his microphone as Clark labored to pin him down—on anything. Schenck could not remember what company boards he sat on and knew nothing about MGM's foreign holdings. "I have trained myself to discard out of my mind anything that is finished," he explained to the frustrated senator, who was fidgeting in his seat and smoking cigarettes at a prodigious pace. Schenck did not think a picture needed access to studio-owned, first-run theaters to be successful. He did not believe the frequent intermarriage of producers' children created a climate of interstudio cooperation. The majors could not, and would not, shut out smaller competitors. "I wish you wouldn't ask me a question like that," a horrified Schenck told Clark, "because I can't for the world see that a thing like that could possibly happen." It was a lie-down-and-play-dead defense, and no amount of poking could convince the executive to budge. He referred question after question to Howard Dietz, MGM's director of publicity, who proved similarly unhelpful when the committee interrogated him.[37]

The hearings got more interesting when Harry Warner took the stand, although attendance had thinned considerably by then. With Joseph Hazen at his side, Warner read a feisty statement written in collaboration with Willkie. "I am opposed to Nazism," he declared. "I abhor and detest every principle and practice of the Nazi movement," and he would not apologize for his beliefs. The producer supported Roosevelt's foreign policy, wanted to aid Britain, thought a Hitler victory meant disaster for the United States, and did not care who knew it. Warner scorned accusations of propaganda. "*Sergeant York* is a factual portrait of the life of one of the great heroes of the last war," he declared. "If that is propaganda, we plead guilty. *Confessions of a Nazi Spy* accurately portrayed a Nazi spy ring that actually operated in New York City. If that is propaganda, we plead guilty." The mogul then launched into his life story, casting himself as the star of a Horatio Alger novel. The committee was ready for lunch by the time he finished his rags-to-riches tale.[38]

After the break, Senators Tobey and Clark quizzed Warner on various war issues for reasons not even they seemed to grasp. The mood was sometimes tense as the sparring went back and forth between the tables. Brooks wanted nothing to do with it. He applauded *Sergeant York,* announced his approval of free speech, congratulated the movie man for his rise to greatness, and shut up. Warner went on the offensive at the end of the day. When Clark asked why Warner Bros. movies showed Nazi brutalities against "subversive elements" in Germany, Warner challenged the senator to explain what kind of films he wanted the studio to make. "Do you think we should have made a picture that showed the Nazis kissing them or in love with them, or what?"[39]

The hearings were staggering toward a sad conclusion. The public was apathetic and newspapers antagonistic. "Do they want some pro-Hitler films produced?" the *Milwaukee Journal* asked. "Do they want some anti-defense films shown? Just what is it they do want?" The committee's colleagues were equally hostile. Illinois Democrat Scott Lucas, an administration ally who chaired the Senate Audit and Control Committee, effectively killed the probe by refusing to allocate money to bring in more witnesses. Even America First was ready to throw in the towel. Ruth

Sarles, the head of the organization's speakers' bureau, wrote that "certain aspects of the investigation are so unsavory that I question the advisability of publicizing it any further."[40]

Zanuck's testimony the next morning, September 26, put the final nail in the anti-interventionist coffin. Like Warner, he was unrepentant about his interventionism. Unlike Warner, he did not have to grapple with the social and cultural baggage of Judaism. He spoke as a "real" American unburdened by foreign roots. The producer took an aggressive stance. His anti-Nazi pictures faithfully depicted reality, he told the subcommittee, and were therefore not propaganda. Clark unintentionally produced some of the day's loudest applause when he pushed the Fox head on this issue. "What is your notion of propaganda pictures?" he asked.

"Well, that is a most difficult question," Zanuck replied. "I usually find that when someone produces something that you do not like, you call it propaganda."

Clark's face flared red. He wanted out. McFarland grumbled about cutting the day short so he could catch a train to South Bend for the Notre Dame–Arizona football game.[41]

The audience paid rapt attention to Zanuck's closing statement. "I am proud to be a part of the moving-picture business," he said. "I go back and think of what this little nickelodeon business has grown to and I cannot help but be proud." He recalled such great old pictures as *The Birth of a Nation, The Big Parade,* and *The Jazz Singer,* as well as more recent ones like *Gone with the Wind* and *Grapes of Wrath.* "I remember these things, and I remember the enjoyment they have given." A trained actor may have managed a tear in the corner of his eye as he delivered Zanuck's parting lines:

> This industry has stood for a lot. By that I mean it has been the American way of life, and it has been abused in other countries; but I am sure that when the whole celluloid record is put before the world—the whole world—you are going to agree with the people of America who patronize us when they wish to and who stay away when they do not wish to see the pictures; and we have grown only because the people have let us. Thank you.

The gallery broke out in applause. Clark congratulated Zanuck for being such a great American. He knew he had lost. Willkie interrupted the proceedings to pump Zanuck's hand. "Great, great, fellow," the lawyer whispered just loudly enough for reporters to hear him.[42]

Had this been a movie, Zanuck's rousing address would have been its triumphant final scene. But this was Washington, not Hollywood, and Paramount's Barney Balaban was still waiting to testify. No one knew what to do with the studio president. "I feel a bit guilty about having called you," a remorseful Clark told him. Balaban compared himself to a chaser, the closing act that drove an audience out of a theater. Although Clark talked of questioning additional witnesses, no one contradicted Balaban's characterization.[43]

The hearings were technically ongoing. Charlie Chaplin and Alexander Korda were scheduled to appear in early October. Senator Wheeler stayed on the attack, drawing a mix of cheers and boos when he branded Hollywood "a modern Benedict Arnold" at Los Angeles' Olympic auditorium. He, Nye, and Clark postured about restarting the investigation, perhaps even broadening it to include "lewd and lascivious" content. Their bluster amounted to nothing. With no money and no support, the subcommittee of the Senate Committee on Interstate Commerce faded away.[44]

Hollywood reveled in its victory, exhibiting no fear that isolationists might revive the hearings. MGM purchased the strongly anti-Nazi novel *Above Suspicion* days after Clark suspended the inquiry. Several producers bid for the rights to William Shirer's *Berlin Diary*. At least twelve anti-Nazi scripts were in production at various studios. An ad in *Life* magazine for RKO's *All That Money Can Buy* (also known as *The Devil and Daniel Webster*) read: "Dear Congress: We urge you and every American to investigate this Sensational Motion Picture! . . . It is outright pro-movie propaganda."[45]

✺ ✺ ✺

Hollywood's vocal interventionism continued unchecked after the hearings. Melvyn Douglas was still in the thick of it, this time in his capacity as chair of the West Coast branch of the stage, screen, radio, and arts division of Fight for Freedom. The actor gave a series of saber-rattling speeches and radio addresses through the fall of 1941. "The real way to defend America is to attack Nazi Germany," he said during one NBC broadcast. Douglas mocked America First members as "Hitler's agents."

Such outspoken interventionism won praise from those who agreed with his disapproval of "traitors and Roosevelt-haters" but disappointed others. "It seems a pity that any one, such as you, who has given the people of this country so many enjoyable hours of fine entertainment, could stoop to urging our youth to give their life blood for a cause that has not yet been proven ours, or necessary," one former fan complained.[46]

Negative fan letters did not stop Douglas's crusade. He regularly hosted get-togethers with military officials at his Hollywood Hills home to discuss ways to increase the movie industry's cooperation with the defense effort. Among other ideas, the group proposed screening more British films in American theaters, particularly movies showing the benefits of lend-lease. Douglas's military friends also suggested that Hollywood establish stronger ties with the Office of Civilian Defense, the Office of Production Management (later absorbed into the War Production Board), and other new agencies. "We are more than grateful for your help and are most anxious to move ahead on the movie ideas," one of Douglas's guests wrote in early December.[47]

In the industry's most tangible example of defiance against isolationists, Jack and Harry Warner purchased two Spitfires for the RAF. The brothers asked Minister for Aircraft Production Lord Beaverbrook to name them *FDR* and *Cordell Hull*.[48]

CHAPTER TWENTY

The End of Peace

H OLLYWOOD MYTHMAKERS QUICKLY TURNED the 1941 hearings into a decisive tidal shift, a moment when producers finally stood up to their critics. "The industry, for years [an] expert sprinter to cover whenever a voice was raised against it, finally is wearing its badge of courage," gloated *Boxoffice*'s Red Kann. Movie folk spoke of the incident in military terms, as a "battle" from which they emerged triumphant. Isolationists challenged the moguls' loyalty and lost. Hollywood had a revived sense of confidence, a new determination to solidify its place at the patriotic center of American culture.[1]

The industry's new resolve so impressed Zanuck, Harry Warner, Paramount's Frank Freeman, and MGM's Eddie Mannix that they created the Committee of Six, an informal alliance of the main lawyers involved in the hearings—Maurice Benjamin, Herbert Freston, Joseph Hazen, Austin Keough, Robert Rubin, and Mendel Silberberg—as a way to advance the united front. Having stared down the Senate, the Committee of Six's next mission was to iron out differences between Los Angeles studios and the New York offices. Besides protecting Hollywood from future attacks, the committee provided a means for capitalizing on the goodwill accumulated over the past weeks. Darryl F. Zanuck saw the committee as a way to weaken the Hays Office, which he regarded as a hotbed of appeasement that diminished Hollywood's pro-American, prodefense credentials. "This great industry which has actually done so much for National Defense and every known charity must have an aggressive, important and complete representation before we are going to get out of the woods," he told Stephen Early. He urged the lawyers to formulate a strong, patriotic rebuttal to isolationists that relegated Hays's weak-kneed "straddling" to the dustbin.[2]

This was still Hollywood, a city where fact mingled with legend and mortal men became gods. The hearings were never as dangerous as the celebrations over its conclusion implied. Clark's subcommittee had no clear agenda and little support in the Senate. Newspapers and Senator McFarland upheld Hollywood's interests better than many industry witnesses. Although producers showed some determination in replacing the Hays line with a stronger approach, Schenck's flaccid performance demonstrated that not everyone adopted a go-down-swinging attitude. Warner and Zanuck left with their heads held high. They exposed themselves to scrutiny, stuck to their principles, and delivered rousing pep talks to uncertain colleagues. They also appeared after Willkie's sallies and an unfriendly press had sucked the life from the hearings.

The inquiry nevertheless rounded out Hollywood's mind-set on the eve of the United States' entrance into the war. Leaders of the movie community learned that domestic audiences tolerated pictures that trumpeted Americanism or condemned the enemy. They saw that not even its harshest critics dared mention censorship of movie content; Hollywood's long-standing cooperation with the administration soothed industry fears of new legislative attacks for the moment. With Roosevelt on their side, many of the moguls felt relatively untouchable. The Senate hearings were, in a sense, Hollywood's version of the Horst Wessel incident. Nazi propagandists inflated the 1930 murder of a minor party member into an event that energized the movement. Without pushing the comparison too far, Hollywood similarly magnified a relatively minor occurrence into a parable of the benefits of courage and unity. Much the same happened in Hollywood as moviemakers translated success in Washington into an endorsement of their recent activities. "The motion picture is one of the greatest forces for good in America," *Hollywood Reporter* noted. "It took the Senate sub-committee investigation to teach this, not only to the public, but to the industry itself. Motion pictures are a vital link in our war effort."[3]

Senate hearings and anti-interventionist rallies neither cowed Hollywood activists nor slowed the United States' drift into the war. Roosevelt and Churchill signed the Atlantic Charter—a statement of common war aims—at a secret rendezvous off the coast of Newfoundland a few weeks after Nye and Wheeler announced their propaganda hearings. On the night Lindbergh spoke in Des Moines, Roosevelt announced that, following a skirmish between a German submarine and an American destroyer named the *Greer,* the Navy had his permission to fire on Nazi vessels. The United States was in an unofficial shooting war. The situation with Japan was also deteriorating. Japan refined its plan to attack Pearl Harbor as an American embargo on oil slowly starved the island nation's war machine. Diplomacy was a sham by now; the ascension of General Tojo to prime minister in mid-October signaled victory for the country's militarist wing. British bases in Singapore bulked up their defenses, as did American outposts on Guam and in the Philippines. Heavy artillery pointed out to sea from fortifications scattered thousands of miles across the Pacific Ocean. Nervous eyes from many continents scanned watery horizons. War was but a matter of time.

❂ ❂ ❂

D. Worth Clark's committee failed to staunch the slow trickle of promilitary and pro-British pictures. Warner Bros. showed its contempt for the hearings by issuing *Dive Bomber* three weeks before they opened. Studio writers shaped Frank "Spig" Wead's short story "Beyond the Blue Sky" into the epic story of flight surgeon Doug Lee's (Errol Flynn) campaign to prevent blackouts and altitude sickness in navy pilots.[4] Wead's work was a natural fit for the studio's service genre. Jack Warner thought enough of it to approve a Technicolor production, a decision that bumped *Dive Bomber*'s budget from $800,000 to over $1.2 million. The added expense was well worth it. No other pre–Pearl Harbor picture matched the quality of its flying scenes.[5]

Dive Bomber was an arduous shoot, and not just from a technical standpoint. The notoriously difficult Errol Flynn let everyone know that he disliked his part. Director Michael Curtiz harassed Warners executives for rewrites. The company's cooperation with the United States Navy added another voice to the production. Navy censors pored over the script, looking for anything that might betray defense secrets. Warners' alliance with the military enabled Curtiz's cameramen to film barracks, operations buildings, hangars, and runways at the United States Naval Air Station in San Diego and to prowl the decks of the aircraft carrier USS *Enterprise.* This access brought both opportunities and problems. Curtiz halted the production for a week because of bad weather. Noisy shooting environments ruined take after take of dialogue. The frenzied pace of activity around the base hampered efforts to move between locations. Everything had to work perfectly. Planes that buzzed overhead even slightly off cue needed to turn around and try again. The need for perfect timing left the nation's pilots working for Hollywood, at least for the few weeks Warners shot in San Diego. Senator Nye condemned Hollywood's close collaboration with the government. Warners made it a selling point. One of the studio's publicity articles noted that Curtiz shot "every foot" of *Dive Bomber* "with Navy aid and under closest Navy supervision."[6]

The crew's hard work paid off. *Dive Bomber*'s aerial sequences stand far above the rest of the picture. In contrast to Warners' typical, fast-paced features, *Dive Bomber* takes a measured, almost luxurious approach that maximized its collaboration with the military while slowing the plot to a crawl. Planes fly in precise formation, screaming through the clouds in perfect V's. Spins, rolls, and dives come off with perfect authenticity. Curtiz mounted cameras on the Navy's planes to produce amazing point-of-view shots that took viewers inside the cockpit during difficult maneuvers or, even more dramatically, under the wings of fighters roaring off the decks of the *Enterprise*. It is impossible to watch *Dive Bomber* without appreciating the skills of navy pilots and the awesome might of an aircraft carrier. "'Dive Bomber' will thrill a nation," its publicity material bellowed. "It will make this nation proud. It should make other nations pause for thought."[7]

Dive Bomber's land-bound sequences center on Dr. Doug Lee's troubled relationship with navy pilot Joe Blake (Fred MacMurray). They are arrogant men, each completely absorbed in his profession and confident of his superiority to the other. As Hollywood formula demanded, the two overcome their initial suspicions to unite behind the common cause of improving the nation's defenses. Lee and Blake grow more similar as the picture goes on. Dr. Lee's navy pilot training makes him a full-fledged flight surgeon capable of understanding men like Blake. Blake volunteers as a human guinea pig for Lee's experiments, allowing him to appreciate the doctor's hard work on medical conditions affecting his squadron. Their combined input enables them to overcome the age's most vexing aeronautical problems. One of Blake's pilots suggests the basic outline of a device Dr. Lee fashions to combat blackouts during high g-force dives. Blake himself proposes a pressure suit capable of staving off altitude sickness, then dies during a risky mission to prove that it works, a sacrifice that again demonstrates the sense of duty pervading the armed forces. Lee's and Blake's conquest of these threats to American servicemen offered yet another Hollywood depiction of the armed forces as caring, competent institutions capable of fusing antagonistic elements into a seamless whole.

Dive Bomber could not help but be promilitary. The new recruits swarming the base and massive airplane squadrons overhead clearly reflected the contemporary defense buildup. *Dive Bomber,* however, avoids long-winded speeches on freedom, liberty, and democracy—which made it rather unique among the studio's service films—and does little to overtly place Lee's and Blake's actions within the context of an impending conflict. It is nevertheless obvious that these scientists and pilots were working toward something, readying for some future fight. *Dive Bomber* is "not without its propaganda," Philip Hartung wrote in *Commonweal,* "which stresses that all this preparation is for the coming big show which will be fought in the air; and the man on top will win, so the sky's the limit." Warners' Technicolor flight drama was one of 1941's biggest hits, eventually bringing more than $2.5 million into studio coffers. A series of product tie-ins further boosted revenues. *Dive Bomber* found its way into campaigns for watches, cigarette cases, evening gowns, and other non-defense-related items.[8]

Warners capped its association with the navy by filling *Dive Bomber*'s world premiere in San Diego with representatives from the service. A navy orchestra played as Hollywood types mingled with admirals at a dinner preceding the opening. The film's public debut followed a private screening in Washington, D.C., where officials made final demands for excisions before granting their approval. The spectacle in San Diego won approval from reviewers. "The defense program steals the show," the *Los Angeles Daily News* gushed after the movie's premiere. " 'Dive Bomber' again makes us glad we are Americans and protected by a Navy as competent as ours," Louella Parsons concluded.[9]

Other pictures soon joined *Dive Bomber* in the celluloid skies. The autumn of 1941 saw the release of Warners' *International Squadron,* a Ronald Reagan picture hustled through production to capitalize on Fox's *A Yank in the R.A.F.* A reworking of the Spig Wead story "Ceiling Zero," which the studio filmed with James Cagney and Pat O'Brien in 1935, *International Squadron* follows Jimmy Grant (Reagan), an impetuous American pilot who joins a multinational outfit within the RAF. Parts of the story were already familiar to audiences, and elements of it reappeared in *Flying Tigers* (1942) and other World War II–era pictures. The arrogant Grant is contemptuous of his colleagues, an aloofness that symbolizes Americans' general unwillingness to engage foreigners in desperate need of help. He further alienates his peers when his sloppy, individualistic flying causes another pilot to perish in a crash. Grant finally redeems himself by completing a dangerous bombing mission that ultimately leads to his own death. The international squadron, comprising pilots from France and other countries under Nazi occupation, toasts their fallen comrade, bringing Grant into their circle while underscoring the brotherhood uniting formerly democratic nations of western Europe with the great arsenal of democracy across the ocean. *International Squadron* provided timely although not inspired entertainment, reiterating well-established themes while giving audiences little that was new or fresh. The *Hollywood Citizen-News*'s reviewer yawned, "I have seen it played by Errol Flynn and Jimmy Cagney before Ronald Reagan did it." The picture's most notable element is its footage from an air raid on London and scenes of Spitfires dueling Messerschmitts, real-life material that came courtesy of technicians from Warners' Teddington branch.[10]

International Squadron made its sympathies clear from the start, opening with Churchill's famous "never in the field of human conflict has so much been owed to so few" speech. As a statement of Anglo-American harmony, however, it lacked the punch of Zanuck's *A Yank in the R.A.F.* Whereas *International Squadron* was a kind of high-end B movie, a prestige programmer, Fox considered *A Yank in the R.A.F.* a significant picture, especially as Zanuck had played such an integral role in establishing its plot and main characters back in the fall of 1940. The studio's close cooperation with British air officials gave Zanuck a personal stake in the film's box-office success and propaganda value. It marked the only time Zanuck paired his two biggest stars, Tyrone Power and Betty Grable. Another box-office blockbuster, it became the last major pro-British film prior to Pearl Harbor. If not for the juggernaut of *Sergeant York*, it might have been the biggest movie of the year.

A Yank in the R.A.F. worked because it obeyed Zanuck's demand that story comes first. He believed that "out-and-out propaganda pictures are rarely accepted by the public and, therefore, defeat their own purpose." Zanuck's hatred for Hitler rivaled Harry Warner's, but Fox's pictures eschewed the heavy-handed rhetoric that marred many of Warner Bros.' anti-Nazi and prodemocracy films. *A Yank in the R.A.F.* successfully crafted an unmistakably pro-British argument, yet audiences also enjoyed it as a dramatic comedy, an exciting aerial adventure, a romantic-triangle melodrama, and a musical.[11]

Set in the months surrounding the invasion of Poland, this story of a rakish, individualistic, and arrogant pilot who strains to fit into a cohesive military unit owed much to the mid- and late-1930s service-picture genre. Its internationalist perspective, however, distinguishes it from such earlier efforts as *West Point of the Air* and *Here Comes the Navy.* It marks the merging of that cycle with films like MGM's *A Yank at Oxford,* which Zanuck took as one of his original inspirations. It establishes a pro-British tone from its first scene, which ridicules the Neutrality Act's prohibition on delivering arms. Americans fly planes to the Canadian border and then tow them across the line to uphold the letter if not the spirit of the law.

Hotshot American mail pilot Tim Baker (Tyrone Power) is uninterested in such legal niceties. He is, in fact, uninterested in everything except himself. Baker agrees to fly warplanes from Canada to Great Britain because of the $1,000 bounty for each delivery, not because he wants to support democracy or strike a blow against Nazism. On arriving in London, he joins the RAF to impress an old girlfriend, the sometime nightclub singer, sometime WREN, and full-time wearer of revealing skirts, Carol Brown (Betty Grable). Once in the service, Baker looks forward to seeing some real action. He chafes at his elementary training program, scoffs at lectures about the weak points of a German Messerschmitt, and generally makes an ass of himself in front of his British colleagues.

The American's hostility toward his colleagues stems from the Anglos' desire to separate him from Carol. Baker's friend, the good-natured Flying Officer Roger Pillby (Reginald Gardner), makes an unsuccessful first pass at Carol before settling into his role as a distant admirer. Group Commander John Morley (John Sutton) poses a greater threat, actually proposing marriage after taking Carol out several times. His love earns

Baker's enmity but not Carol's hand. She remains torn between her two lovers, her American and her Briton.

Pillby and Morley are likable men who reflected director Henry King's desire to sculpt an England that garnered sympathy in the United States. Pillby has an excellent sense of humor. Morley is polite and well-mannered. Both are warm, human characters who defy British stereotypes. They are neither stuffy lords nor effeminate creampuffs. Great Britain itself is a timeless place, as evidenced by the Norman foundations of Morley's father's estate. London, a voice-over informs us, is "a city of homes and churches, and shops and pubs, of roast beef and old school ties, and Big Ben and fog." Its residents are stout and steady, prepared for war and confident of victory. They suffer through air-raid drills with efficiency and good humor. Class antagonisms do not exist; the lower-class Corporal Baker—the identical last name links him to the American—serves comfortably alongside the wealthy Morley.

Baker slowly appreciates that this place is worth saving. He has no sudden flash of insight and gives no long-winded speeches announcing his new faith. The foreigner's love for England builds over time. He demonstrates this with actions, not words. His sadness over the deaths of Pillby and Corporal Baker, heroic crash-landing of a wounded bomber in Holland, and sterling performance at Dunkirk testify to his devotion. The Dunkirk scenes are the picture's centerpiece. As it had for *International Squadron,* the British government donated many reels of the RAF battling German fighters. Fox employee Leslie Baker contributed recordings of bombings, collapsing buildings, and antiaircraft fire from the London area. Editors integrated these materials into footage shot on Fox's back lot and in the skies above the Burbank airport. The result was a credible reenactment that earned *A Yank in the R.A.F.* an Oscar nomination for Best Special Effects.[12]

The picture's final sequence, a product of Zanuck's negotiations with the British military, resolved the international dispute over Carol and implied a bright future for Anglo-American relations. German fighters shoot down Baker over the English Channel. Carol, who finally accepts her love for him, rushes with Morley to a ship carrying the last load of survivors from the battle. He is as worried about Baker as she. After anxious moments, a bruised but living Baker appears on the gangplank. The former playboy, the representative of America, has grown up. He wants to settle down as Carol's faithful husband. Zanuck scrapped his plan to end the movie with Tim and Carol's wedding. The couple instead walks out of the frame arm in arm with Morley. Tim's and Morley's shared feelings for Carol and mutual commitment to the British cause have united them in an unbreakable bond. All resentments are forgotten, all rivalries forgiven. The trio—and the two countries—are now one indivisible unit.

The convincing war scenes of *A Yank in the R.A.F.* did not, as isolationists would have it, repel moviegoers weary of onscreen combat. If anything, the picture skimped on the exciting battle sequences audiences had come to expect. "Too much Yank, too little R.A.F.," *Time* decided. But the film made its point, acting as another thumb in the collective eye of isolationists. "[It] has a camera angle that is certainly non-Axis," *Time*'s reviewer continued. "Isolationist Senators might well call *Yank* pro-British propaganda," he wrote. "Even more obviously it is pro-box-office propaganda."[13]

❂ ❂ ❂

War was near. Hollywood could feel it. As *International Squadron* and *A Yank in the R.A.F.* began their runs and the Senate hearings faded into memory, studios stockpiled materials that would be in high demand once the United States got involved in the fight. "Like thrifty squirrels storing up supplies for stormy days," workmen stashed piles of lumber, plywood, hardware, and building materials in spare corners around studio lots.[14]

Although war-fueled prosperity lifted box-office receipts, the conflict also created new financial uncertainties for Hollywood. Sound technicians, for example, discovered that they needed to replace their libraries of sound effects for war films. World War II simply did not sound like World War I. Everything had to be rerecorded. Miles of tape containing bomb, shell, bullet, and airplane engine noises went into the trash. Twentieth Century–Fox alone spent around $100,000 to create new effects. Washington added to the pain by hiking the federal amusement tax in October. Any protest from Hollywood would undermine its patriotic credibility, especially as studios had recently reported large profits for the 1940–1941 fiscal year. The defense buildup's impact on revenues was also unclear. Some areas experienced influxes of war workers and a corresponding growth in theater admissions. Others saw local industries shutting down because of rising costs or disappearing populations. Many factories ran twenty-four hours a day, forcing theaters to attract night-shift workers with more morning and midnight shows. The growth of the military hurt movie houses, especially those around the Washington, D.C., area, that offered discounts to servicemen. Business overall was good for now. Nobody knew what would happen if war came.[15]

Hollywood showed no signs of curtailing production of war-related features. Such military-themed comedies and dramas as *Keep 'em Flying, Navy Blues, You'll Never Get Rich,* and *3 Sons o' Guns* joined *Sergeant York* and his soldierly peers onscreen. More were on the way. Warner Bros. was shooting the interventionist parable *Casablanca* and the all-American musical *Yankee Doodle Dandy.* Walter Wanger was wrapping up *Eagle Squadron.* Universal had *Paris Calling* in the can and ready to go. RKO's *Joan of Paris,* the story of a French waitress who helps stranded RAF pilots escape her occupied country, was also in postproduction.

Studio chiefs made additional commitments to Washington during these months. At the request of the Coordinator of Inter-American Affairs, producers agreed in November to film at least twenty-four shorts on pan-American topics. The CIAA's Motion Picture Division supplied ideas and story material. Division head Jock Whitney led a team to South America to solicit additional subjects. Wunderkind director Orson Welles pledged to direct a saga encompassing several Latin American republics. That project never came off, but Hollywood turned out no fewer than sixty-one pan-American shorts by 1943, including such morale boosters as *Viva Mexico, Highway to Friendship,* and *Cuba, Land of Romance and Adventure.*[16]

The Motion Picture Committee Cooperating for the National Defense also remained active. The MPCC distributed a series of one-reelers produced by the Office for Emergency Management (OEM), a federal agency created in 1940 to coordinate the national defense program, at no charge. The former RKO director and screenwriter Garson Kanin acted as the OEM's primary film consultant, a role that required him to use his connections to bring big names to the agency's projects. Carl Sandburg wrote commentary for the OEM's *Bomber.* Katharine Hepburn narrated dialogue that Eleanor Roosevelt wrote for *Women in Defense.* As with the CIAA's Latin American–shorts program, the OEM had several new preparedness projects in the pipeline by December, including such motivational pieces as *Food for Freedom, Homes for Defense, Tanks,* and *Lake Freighter.*[17]

It is important to note that most Hollywood features in theaters at the end of 1941 had little or nothing to do with the war, democracy, or national defense. Depending on the subjects of the newsreels, shorts, and trailers appearing alongside the main presentation, it was quite easy for audiences, at least those with some choice of movie venues, to avoid these subjects altogether. *Dumbo* flapped across the screen even as Tim Baker performed his aerial heroics in *A Yank in the R.A.F.* John Ford's Oscar-winning *How Green Was My Valley* appeared in November, as did Alfred Hitchcock's thriller *Suspicion.* Clark Gable teamed with Lana Turner in the Old West romantic comedy *Honky Tonk.* Bette Davis vamped it up in *The Little Foxes,* and Humphrey Bogart approached iconic status in *The Maltese Falcon.*

Contrast that balance of topics with *Life* magazine, the day's most popular periodical. Readers of its December 1 edition found a photo of an American bomber on the cover. Inside were articles on the United States Army Air Forces, the German bombing of Rotterdam, housing for American defense workers, and an extended piece on the importance of air power. Even the advertisements applied themes relevant to the war. "You <u>Bet</u> there's *National Unity* in the Gift We Want <u>This</u> Christmas," declared a notice for Parker Vacumatic pens. A two-page spread for the United States Rubber Company touted the many products it sold to the navy. The International Harvester Company featured an army truck in its ad.

Americans were clearly willing to tolerate a great deal of war and war-related coverage. It might appear that other culture makers exceeded Hollywood in raising awareness of these issues. Magazines, radio programs, and other mass-culture media responded more quickly to the war's shifting realities than studios, which had a long lag time between beginning and wrapping a film. These other media did not have as much at stake financially on one issue or story as studios did on a major motion picture. In evaluating Hollywood's significance we must remember, however, that the film capital's popularity outshone even the fantastically popular *Life* and that Hollywood's contributions to the interventionist cause extended far beyond the silver screen. Its links with the administration and the military establishment exceeded those of any other culture-making business. Although it was not the only voice in the pre–Pearl Harbor debate between isolationists and interventionists, it was perhaps the most important.

That voice was never completely unified. Dissenting voices remained up to the final day of peace. In November *Motion Picture Herald,* the most anti-interventionist of the industry's significant trade publications, printed an allegedly unbiased survey of exhibitors' attitudes toward war pictures. The results showed a clear preference for pure entertainment over timely realism. "War pictures are 'murder' with my audiences," complained one theater owner. "They stay away in droves on anything that smells of propaganda or war." "Let's keep to comedy and drama," stated another. "The world is too full of war, etc., for propaganda and pictures of that type." The owner of the Strand Theatre in Malden, Massachusetts, pleaded, "Will producers never find out that aviation pictures are poison to women?"[18]

These exhibitors may not have represented the majority opinion. The success of *Sergeant York, Dive Bomber,* and *A Yank in the R.A.F.* indicated that fans accepted well-made war pictures. An Audience Research Institute poll found that only 38 percent of respondents thought there was too much propaganda—an admittedly vague phrase—in the movies. Only 16 percent believed there was too much propaganda in feature films, as opposed to newsreels and short subjects.[19]

Despite the prevailing trend, some executives remained wary about putting too much "propaganda" on the screen. This split in opinion became clear during the filming of MGM's intensely pro-British *Mrs. Miniver,* which became one of the biggest hits of 1942. Studio executive Eddie Mannix approved the project after hearing producer Sidney Franklin's unique pitch. "It's going to be a very simple story of a little English family," Franklin told him, "and we more than likely will lose $100,000 on the picture." "Someone should salute England," Mannix replied. William Wyler, a German-born Jew, jumped at the chance to direct. "I was a warmonger," he later said. "I was concerned about Americans being isolationists. *Mrs. Miniver* obviously was a propaganda film."[20]

Louis B. Mayer was not so sure about the picture. The Senate inquiry had rattled him, and he worried that censors would attack his film. He was particularly concerned about scenes portraying a young Nazi flier as an evil brute who terrorizes the angelic Mrs. Miniver. He called Wyler into his office to reprimand the director for his outrageous treatment of the German character.

"We don't make hate pictures," Mayer shouted. "We don't hate anybody. We're not at war."[21]

It was the first week of December 1941.

Conclusion

❧ ❧ ❧

THE UNLIKELY QUARTET OF Louis B. Mayer, Jack Warner, Harpo Marx, and Al Jolson were playing a spirited game of golf. It was a beautiful Sunday morning, bright and in the low sixties, with temperatures promising to climb as the day went on. It was the kind of weather that had drawn moviemakers to Hollywood in the early twentieth century. The group wore sweaters with caps to fend off the winter sun. Harpo hooked his tee shot into the woods, then mouthed "fuck you" when Mayer started laughing. Warner approached the tee next. Then two men burst from the pro shop and interrupted his drive.

"They've just bombed Pearl Harbor!" they shouted.

"Pearl Harbor?" Warner asked. "Where the hell is that?"[1]

The Japanese attack threw Los Angeles into a panic. Residents worried that they might be the next target. Southern California produced two-thirds of the nation's aircraft and, despite the presence of Colonel Rupert Hughes's bulletless Hollywood militia, was only lightly defended. Frightened inhabitants telephoned the police to report Japanese planes overhead. The military blacked out Los Angeles harbor but lacked the authority to darken private homes. In one of those exquisite paradoxes that can only happen in California, Christmas trees shone brightly through the blackout.

Paranoia spread across the city. White residents worried that the enemy was among them, as some fifty thousand Japanese Americans lived in the area. Arrests began a few hours after the strike. FBI agents allowed Paramount's baseball team to conclude its victory over an understandably shaken all-Japanese squad before taking the losers into custody. The FBI barred studios' Japanese employees—most of them janitors, gardeners, or window washers—from entering their workplaces until they cleared a background check. Taking no chances, Paramount simply fired

Japanese employees. Other studios tightened security and scrutinized payrolls for employees who might have questionable foreign ties.[2]

Will Hays asked for calm, requesting "the unselfish cooperation of labor and industry, through the strenuous exertion of every woman and man." He got his wish. Studios loaned the army dozens of trucks and donated their firearms, except those needed for productions already under way, to civilian defense authorities. The majors organized mutual police and fire departments and agreed to pool production facilities in the event of a Japanese attack on one or more of their lots. Hollywood instituted an eight-to-five schedule to permit employees to get home without violating blackouts by using their headlights. Movie guilds adopted no-strike pledges. Producers bumped up war-related projects. Paramount cancelled *Over the Hill*, the story of an army deserter.[3]

All this action felt good. It made movie men feel they were doing something about the crisis. Most theaters in the United States remained open, although air-raid sirens interrupted some shows. Yet the future seemed hopelessly unclear. Shares in film companies tumbled. Studios expected to lose younger male stars to the military within the next few months. The community buzzed with rumors. Would there be censorship? Government control of newsreels? Would saboteurs target Hollywood? Domestic theater owners expected business to rebound once people stopped imagining follow-up attacks and unglued themselves from their radios. People would come back after Christmas, exhibitors said. Industry insiders were less certain about foreign theaters. An Axis victory meant "a closed market insofar as American pictures are concerned." An Allied win meant a long rebuilding period that promised lean years for Hollywood. In the meantime Europe was lost, Asia was crippled, and Britain hung on by a thread. For all the industry's goodwill efforts, Latin America still offered only limited returns. Hollywood tried to keep its sense of humor, with black comedy being the preferred style of the day. "In case of air raid, go directly to RKO," went one joke. "They haven't had a hit in years."[4]

As the movie community tried to put its financial house back in order, the raid at Pearl Harbor also caused it to assess the past few years. Hollywood concluded that its antifascist endeavors and recent experience with the Senate had given it an unprecedented importance in American life. "The motion picture is now the recorder and reflector of the American way about which there is no longer controversy or dispute," *Motion Picture Herald*'s Martin Quigley argued. Finally free from any danger of warmongering charges, movie folk celebrated their recent achievements. They had contributed to creating a patriotic spirit that eased the way for national acceptance of the war, informed the public about the dangers of totalitarianism, and demonstrated that the military upheld American ideals and fostered national unity. "You have served in arming America with spiritual strength and will continue to serve," Florida senator Claude Pepper told an industry gathering in Philadelphia.[5]

Hollywood basked in its relevance. "The motion picture industry has never stood higher in Government respect than it does at present," *Hollywood Reporter* boasted. Harry Warner believed that the public's esteem for Hollywood gave it an opportunity to use its bully pulpit for good. Producers had already exhibited their pride in America, he noted in a January 1942 *Variety* editorial, but the screen must keep promoting "the freedoms of thought, of peace, of speech and of worship." Warner asked studios to exceed Roosevelt's wartime goals—freedom of speech, freedom of worship, freedom from want, freedom from fear—by articulating a "Fifth Freedom": show business's right to communicate without fear of outside censorship. He concluded that "only with that right can we do our rightful part in safeguarding the other freedoms."[6]

Warner's statement reflected his fervent nationalism and conviction that movies could improve society. It also, perhaps unconsciously, restated a duality that had marked Hollywood since before the invasion of Poland. Warner interpreted the war as a crusade to promote American values while destroying systems hostile to those values. At the same time, he viewed the war as an opportunity to realize Hollywood's own goals. Freedom of the screen meant freedom from outside interference—except for government assistance in overseas markets or lenient policies that benefited studios financially. Although much had changed over the past few years, this interpretation of the industry's needs had not. Hollywood followed its president into World War II still seeking ways to balance its ideological and financial interests.

The triumphant rhetoric surrounding Hollywood's activities in the late 1930s and early 1940s suited moviemakers' desire for acceptance and furthered their claims that movies could blossom only in a climate of freedom. Hollywood promulgated a simplified vision of its recent past that ignored its patience with dictators, focus on the bottom line, quarrels with the government, and internal disputes over the proper response to fascism and war. Hollywood's sanitized history focused on its positive deeds—its public denunciations of fascism, endorsement of the defense program, and calls for Americans to accept that they might have to fight to preserve their ideals. That Hollywood focused on only one side of the ledger is not surprising, nor is it particularly blameworthy. It would, however, do a disservice to the past to blindly accept such a one-sided take on the movie industry's actions.

❂ ❂ ❂

Hollywood had changed dramatically in the immediate pre–Pearl Harbor era, both in terms of the pictures it had produced and in terms of its relationship with political power centers. Because of the film capital's cultural clout, those changes reverberated throughout the United States and the world. It is therefore worth revisiting the themes laid out at the beginning of this book—Hollywood's association with the federal government, its dealings with foreign markets, the rise of antifascist organizations in the film community, and the shifting content of motion pictures—to more clearly see how the film industry evolved during this brief yet pivotal moment.

Hollywood's bonds with the federal government intensified and formalized over these years. Washington had proven a benevolent entity in the 1920s, as conservative Republican administrations dispatched the State and Commerce Departments to smooth Hollywood's path into foreign markets while allowing major studios to consolidate their hold on the domestic market. This remained the case during Franklin Roosevelt's administration. The film community's affinity for FDR arose from the New Deal's stabilization of the sagging economy. As the 1930s went on, new concerns cemented Hollywood's ties with Washington. The threat of war, then the outbreak of war itself, pulled the coasts into a mutually beneficial union that transcended what had been primarily an economic, one-sided relationship. Members from all rungs of Hollywood's social ladder, from carpenters to studio chiefs, saw fiscal and ideological perils in the rise of totalitarianism. The two dangers were in fact inseparable. Fascism endangered vital overseas profits. Axis nations challenged Hollywood's faith in democracy, freedom, and tolerance, ideas that not only sustained filmmakers psychologically but also promoted the liberal, open markets they needed to flourish financially.

These twin concerns—gold and country—made it almost inevitable that moviemakers would reach out to the government. They supported the president's antifascism for both spiritual and pocketbook reasons. Hollywood endorsed Roosevelt's anti-Nazi, pro-Britain, prodefense rhetoric through its films, its public statements, and its personal contacts with the White House. Created in 1940 by top-level studio executives, the Motion Picture Committee Cooperating for the National Defense was one of several new avenues of contact connecting the East and West coasts. Producers, directors, and actors publicly favored the president's policies, establishing for the first time an overt connection between the instinctively conservative movie business and a controversial political agenda. The prewar era represented Hollywood's political coming-out party, establishing its credibility as a legitimate voice in contentious national debates.

Hollywood's pro-Roosevelt stance on defense issues paid big dividends. State and Commerce Department officials brokered deals with foreign governments that put much-needed money into studios' coffers. Equally important, toeing the Roosevelt line made the president, along with his top adviser, Commerce Secretary Harry Hopkins, allies in the Department of Justice's antitrust suit against major studios. Filed in 1938 by Assistant Attorney General Thurman Arnold, the suit threatened Hollywood's basic financial structure by demanding that studios sell off their theaters. Arnold may have carried the day if not for the war, which forced Roosevelt to reassess the role of big business in the economy. Studio heads had no qualms about placing the suit within a wartime context. Take away our theaters, they told Roosevelt, and we will no longer be able to effectively disseminate a proadministration message. Their gambit worked. Roosevelt helped to squash Arnold's suit, saving Hollywood's theaters—and profits—and enabling studios to act as effective propaganda institutions when the United States entered the fight.

The European and Pacific wars forced Hollywood to adjust its stance toward important overseas markets. On one level studios acted as rational economic entities that sought to maximize profits by getting their products before the largest possible number of people. Executives aggressively pursued foreign markets regardless of a nation's political philosophy. Studio heads initially viewed Nazism and Italian Fascism from an economic perspective, questioning only whether those militant, oppressive systems included a place for Hollywood. Studios generally accommodated authoritarian regimes so long as they could make profits in those countries. No longer concerned with financial retaliation once the dictators pushed American releases off the continent, moviemakers more freely indulged their dislike of the Axis. Whether money or morals motivated major studios to oppose fascism becomes a chicken-and-egg question that tries to separate two intertwined issues. Some studio workers objected to the dictatorships for primarily ideological reasons. Others disliked their financial policies. Such hostility contributed to the Axis's adoption of more stringent financial restrictions, which prompted others in Hollywood to join the antifascist bandwagon, which inspired even tighter restrictions.

The declining European market forced studios to look elsewhere for earnings. Great Britain and Latin America were the two regions most likely to generate significant income. Financial motivations again dovetailed with ideological concerns. Studios produced pro-British and pan-American features with the intention of boosting revenues from those places. At the same time, such movies as *A Yank at Oxford, A Yank in the R.A.F.,* and *Juarez* meshed with the Roosevelt administration's and studio heads' desire to build hemispheric and Anglo-American alliances capable of opposing totalitarianism. Patriotism marched hand in hand with profits, complementary rather than contradictory stimuli.

Besides rearranging Hollywood's global priorities and reshaping its relationship with Washington, the impending war also produced an explosion of organizations devoted to promoting liberal causes in an increasingly fascist world. Unhindered by the corporate, bottom-line concerns that kept most of their bosses quiet, actors, screenwriters, and craftsmen took the lead in dragging Hollywood into political controversies. The Hollywood Anti-Nazi League, Fight for Freedom, Committee of 56, and similar groups pricked the film community's conscience while publicizing international issues to a traditionally isolationist nation. Although the Hitler-Stalin pact temporarily silenced their antifascism, communists served as prime movers behind the industry's activism. Such leftists as Herbert Biberman, Samuel Ornitz, and Donald Ogden Stewart put themselves front-and-center in Hollywood's struggle against the dictators. That fact came back to haunt them and the rest of the movie capital years later, when a changed political climate discredited those who did so much to awaken the United States to Hitlerism's menace.

Finally, the rise of the dictators and first years of war resulted in enormous changes in the content of motion pictures. The same tangled web of financial and ideological concerns that influenced Hollywood's dealings with Washington and other governments also altered the subjects that studios addressed in their films. The pro-British and pan-American cycles represented early responses to the rise of totalitarianism. Beginning in the mid-1930s, Warner Bros. began exploring antifascism through metaphor, crafting such films as *The Life of Emile Zola* to comment on contemporary events without making the films into obvious political statements. Hampered by financial worries and Hollywood's internal censorship regime, other studios were slow to follow up on Warners' tentative step into relevance. *Blockade,* Walter Wanger's failed foray into the Spanish Civil War, demonstrated the hazards awaiting filmmakers who addressed sensitive international issues. Warner Bros. pushed the cinematic envelope again with *Confessions of a Nazi Spy,* but the rest of Hollywood stuck to safer genres such as service pictures and flag-waving explorations of United States history.

With very few exceptions, Hollywood embraced onscreen antifascism only after Germany's September 1939 invasion of Poland. This first wave of wartime films did not reach theaters until mid-1940, giving the film capital a do-nothing appearance it did not fully deserve. Most motion pictures released between January 1940 and December 1941 said little about the war or the United States' role in it. At the same time, studios issued many features that, collectively, articulated a liberal, internationalist take on world affairs. *The Mortal Storm* and *Four Sons* criticized life under Nazism. *The Fighting 69th* and *Sergeant York* boosted the military's image and reconciled overseas engagements with the ideals filmmakers associated with Americanism—individualism, nationalism, democracy, independence, piety. *The Mark of Zorro* and *Brigham Young* fashioned prodemocracy, protolerance arguments. Many of these films would have been unthinkable a few years earlier and not simply because the relevant context for them did not yet exist. Hollywood's self-censorship system, headed by Joseph Breen at the Production Code Administration and his boss, MPPDA president Will Hays, dissuaded productions that dealt too closely with war or condemned other nations. Their work subdued such pictures as *Idiot's Delight* and *Three Comrades* and discouraged studios from shooting *Mad Dog of Europe* and *It Can't Happen Here*. The immediate prewar era saw a partial breakdown, or at least a reinterpretation, of the Production Code. A perceived need to cooperate with the federal government, attain social significance, and combat un-American ideologies ever-so-slightly loosened the code's strictures. While the code's constraints on sex, violence, and language remained intact, it gave way on other issues. Twentieth Century–Fox's *Man Hunt* could not have cleared the code's "National Feelings" clause prior to the fall of France in 1940.

A regular moviegoer through these years would have received fairly consistent messages regarding the war and its purpose. War was always terrible, but it was also exciting. The military was a tolerant, humane organization capable of melding the United States' heterogeneous population—at least its white population—into a cohesive fighting force. Individualism and personal glory had places in modern warfare, seamlessly coexisting with the soldiers' collective commitment to a cause that transcended their own personal interests. War achieved noble ends, preserving liberty and spreading democracy. In Hollywood's eyes this was true of the French and Indian War (*Allegheny Uprising*), the Revolutionary War (*Drums along the Mohawk*), the Napoleonic Wars (*That Hamilton Woman*), the Spanish-American War (*Teddy the Rough Rider*), and World War I (*Sergeant York*). These films established an unmistakable pattern—the United States and its allies fought only when necessary for national self-preservation—and clearly implied that Americans were facing another moment when hostile forces challenged the values they held dear. Hollywood prepared the nation for World War II by acquainting Americans with the military and conflict and by proposing a rationale for engaging in a fight that did not, at least before Pearl Harbor, appear to have any direct impact on the United States. The movie capital thus anticipated the education process undertaken by the federal government's Office of War Information during the war.

Hollywood's most notable shortcoming in its domestication of combat and the military was its near-total failure to specifically associate World War II with anti-Semitism. Its use of historical subjects dictated against this, as did the moguls' sense that raising the issue would arouse domestic anti-Semitism. Although *The Fighting 69th*'s Mischa Moskow-itz character delicately considered Judaism in a time of war, the film used him to celebrate assimilation rather than decry persecution. Of the pre-war denunciations of Nazi Germany—including *Confessions of a Nazi Spy, The Mortal Storm,* and *Four Sons*—only *The Great Dictator,* made by the gentile Charlie Chaplin, highlighted the anti-Semitism at the core of Hitler's ideology. Hollywood's timidity reflected the Roosevelt admin-istration's, which never made saving Europe's doomed Jews a military or a propaganda priority.[7]

❧ ❧ ❧

Hollywood's course during and immediately following World War II was very much a product of the prewar years. To ignore or minimize the late 1930s and early 1940s is to miss the opening chapters in the next phase of the film capital's history. The issues occupying Hollywood during these years—making films that appealed to both ticket holders and gov-ernments; sustaining a stable relationship with Washington; preserving markets in Europe, especially Great Britain; and winning new audiences in Latin America—motivated the film community during the war and beyond. These years not only saw Hollywood at its peak of popularity and respectability but also witnessed the disintegration of the Holly-wood that existed in December 1941. Its mutually beneficial relationship with Washington, dominance of American theaters, and ability to con-trol the messages that appeared on the world's screens all proved fleeting. Although the movie moguls could not have known it, the studio system that had driven filmmaking since the 1920s, the relatively cohesive oli-gopoly that had made the industry's prewar achievements possible, was on the verge of collapse.

Hollywood's connections with the Roosevelt administration served both parties well after Pearl Harbor. Although their relationship was hardly perfect, the movie industry became an essential element in pro-moting Roosevelt's wartime goals and his vision of a postwar America engaged in preserving the peace. Movie folk's contributions mirrored in many ways their prewar activities. Studio workers made patriotic pictures, war-themed newsreels, and training films and raised money through War Bonds campaigns. The industry's old friend Lowell Mellett headed the Bureau of Motion Pictures (BMP), Washington's main point of contact with Hollywood and a subsidiary of the government's most important propaganda agency, the Office of War Information (OWI). Roosevelt told Mellett that the screen must remain free from censorship "insofar as national security will permit." Voluntarily adhering—to an extent—to the OWI's *Government Information Manual for the Motion Picture Industry,* major studios used features to promote democracy, tolerance, and internationalism. As has been shown here, many prewar pictures stressed the same themes.[8]

Hollywood's primary liaison with Washington also evolved from its prewar experiences. The Motion Picture Committee Cooperating for the National Defense renamed itself the War Activities Committee of the Motion Picture Industry (WAC) ten days after Pearl Harbor. George Schaefer, president of RKO, chaired the WAC. Francis Harmon, a key member of the former committee, resigned his post with the Hays Office to serve full-time as the WAC's executive vice chair. The WAC carried on the earlier body's endeavors, distributing government-made patriotic shorts, as well as a few installments of the *Why We Fight* series and other feature-length films, free of charge.[9]

Hollywood's link with Washington extended overseas, where the government continued to intervene on behalf of the movie capital's interests. Latin America remained a particular concern owing to the loss of other overseas revenues and the fear of Axis infiltration. Studios maintained their collaboration with Jock Whitney's motion picture division of the Nelson Rockefeller–led Office of the Coordinator for Inter-American Affairs (CIAA). Studios shot and distributed scores of educational shorts and documentaries throughout Latin America at the CIAA's request. As it had in earlier years, the CIAA pressed studios to insert more information on the region in newsreels, hire more Hispanic actors, and make more features with continental appeal. Hollywood accordingly continued its prewar trend toward Hispanic news and faces, but it also continued its prewar proclivity for dreadful movies that angered Latin Americans. *Brazil* (1944), *Masquerade in Mexico* (1945), and *Song of Mexico* (1945) came from the same musical-comedy mold as *They Met in Argentina.* "Good intentions and bad art, mixed up and squandered completely in the macerating mills of Hollywood," lamented Bosley Crowther in the *New York Times.*[10]

Washington backed the industry's financial interests despite such persistent clumsiness. The State Department and CIAA leveraged their wartime control over celluloid, a key component in explosives, to the Americans' political advantage. German companies had provided much of Latin America's film stock prior to Pearl Harbor. Wartime demands, however, resulted in serious production shortages that forced Hispanic studios to look to the United States to make up the shortfall. The government happily filled orders from such friendly nations as Mexico, which subsequently became a cinematic powerhouse in the region, but was less receptive to Argentina's requests. Buenos Aires was too slow in repealing its ban on anti-Nazi pictures for American tastes, and the State Department objected to the country's ongoing censorship of Hollywood-made fare. The United States' denial of raw stock essentially starved out Argentina's film industry, clearing the way for Hollywood to dominate the market more thoroughly than before.[11]

The State Department proved similarly helpful in Great Britain. As it had prior to American intervention, the Churchill government recognized that British studios could not meet public demand for entertainment. It accordingly lowered the film quota to 25 percent and, in 1943, released Hollywood's frozen dollars. Britain's Board of Trade adopted a tougher stance in 1947, seeking to moderate the postwar outflow of cash with a 75 percent tax on foreign film profits. Hollywood halted shipments of new movies and summoned the State Department to find a solution. The Truman administration pressed London to make concessions, suggesting that failure to compromise might kill support for the Marshall Plan. Unwilling to risk losing the United States' generous postwar aid package and unable to satisfy domestic demand, the British backed down after an eight-month deadlock. The March 1948 settlement allowed Hollywood to export a considerable portion of its profits and to reinvest the rest in British film production rather than lose it through taxation. As John Trumpbour argues, the deal enabled studios to consolidate their hold on the British picture market.[12]

The State Department began to sever ties with Hollywood after 1948, though the bond between them never ruptured completely. Studio executives' rapacious desire for market share led diplomats to fear an anti-American backlash that could affect the dynamics of the emerging cold war. President Eisenhower's secretary of state, John Foster Dulles, thought Hollywood's close relationship with the State Department might lead other industries to seek comparable services. "Despite the unique character of motion picture trade problems," Dulles observed in 1954, "it appears unwise to handle these problems in a special government-to-government agreement when no other products are similarly treated." The department increasingly assumed the pose of an interested observer ready to assist where it could but unwilling to involve itself in talks with foreign governments, as it regularly had before the war.[13]

This rearranged political coalition coincided with dramatic transformations in Hollywood's economic structure. World War II brought wrenching changes. Among the more tangible problems was a shortage of film stock and other raw materials that contributed to a decline in Hollywood's output. Major studios released 533 features in 1942 and 377 in 1945. B movies became less common as studios focused on more prestigious A-listers. The war also undermined Hollywood's labor practices. High federal taxes, as much as 90 percent for those making over $200,000 a year, decimated stars' paychecks. Rather than signing for a lucrative annual salary, top actors began taking advantage of the 25 percent capital gains rate by negotiating one-picture contracts that gave them a cut of a film's profits. Studios' grip on talent further loosened in 1944 when Olivia de Havilland escaped her long-term deal with Warner Bros. after successfully suing the company under California's antipeonage laws.[14]

That same year saw the beginning of the end for the majors' stranglehold on first-run movie theaters. Thurman Arnold had moved on, accepting a seat on the United States Circuit Court of Appeals, but the Justice Department was still monitoring Hollywood. Government lawyers reopened the antitrust suit against theater-owning studios just months after the de Havilland decision. There was no negotiated settlement this time. The Supreme Court ruled in 1948's *United States v. Paramount Pictures, Inc., et al.* that studios must separate production and distribution from exhibition. The studios lost their theaters. It was the beginning of the end for the majors' domination. And with television on the horizon, a few sharp observers concluded that the Golden Age of Hollywood was drawing to a close.[15]

Hollywood's relationship with Washington unraveled after the war. Never again were the two coasts so tightly bound. The red scare of the late 1940s and early 1950s contributed to the dissolution, as talk of communism in Hollywood made the movie industry a suspect partner for many politicians. Wartime monuments of cooperation such as the pro-Russian features *Mission to Moscow* (1943), *The North Star* (1943), and *Song of Russia* (1944) became embarrassments in the new political climate. Though Hollywood antagonist Martin Dies was out of Congress between 1945 and 1953, Republican congressman J. Parnell Thomas of New Jersey energetically filled the Texan's anticommunist shoes after becoming chair of the House Committee on Un-American Activities (HUAC) in May 1947. He soon turned his sights on Hollywood, initiating an anticommunist campaign that landed ten screenwriters in prison for contempt of Congress and ultimately contributed to the blacklisting of scores of Hollywood radicals.

The story of the blacklist and the Hollywood Ten has received far lengthier treatment elsewhere.[16] What is worth noting here is that the pre–Pearl Harbor battle against Hitlerism inspired many who were later ensnared by the postwar red scare. The Hollywood Ten included several of these activists. Herbert Biberman and Samuel Ornitz were at the center of communist activities in Hollywood during the Hitler-Stalin pact era. Dalton Trumbo was a prolific screenwriter whose novel *Johnny Got His Gun* (1939) articulated the communists' antiwar ideology at that moment. Ring Lardner Jr. belonged to the Hollywood Anti-Nazi League and raised money for the Spanish Loyalists. John Howard Lawson worked on *Blockade* and *Four Sons*. Many of those blacklisted, or nearly blacklisted, had been key to the film community's interventionism prior to December 1941. Donald Ogden Stewart, one of HANL's founders, fled to London in 1950 after falling afoul of anticommunists. The U.S. government revoked his passport, trapping him in Great Britain, where he died in 1980. Edward G. Robinson saved his career only by naming Hollywood reds. Melvyn Douglas found himself on an unofficial graylist after the war. He felt the anticommunists' wrath again in 1950 when his wife, three-term congresswoman Helen Gahagan Douglas, lost a brutal Senate race to Richard Nixon, who famously derided his liberal foe "pink right down to her underwear."

Studio heads who had recently participated in Hollywood's antifascist campaign did little to protect employees who lost their livelihoods, often for acts committed before Pearl Harbor. In a nerve-wracking appearance before HUAC, Jack Warner fingered alleged communists and offered to "establish such a fund to ship to Russia people who don't like our American system of government." His brother Harry, a close friend of FBI head J. Edgar Hoover, also denounced communists, though in a manner that must have made Hollywood giggle. "If my own brother were a Communist," he told a group of two thousand Warner Bros. employees in 1951, "I'd put a rope around him and drag him to the FBI." Louis B. Mayer, Walter Wanger, Columbia's Harry Cohn, and Paramount's Barney Balaban were among those present when Eric Johnston, Will Hays's replacement as MPPDA head, summoned executives to the Waldorf-Astoria Hotel in November 1947. The resulting Waldorf Statement promised a nation suffering from cold war anxiety that the film industry would not knowingly employ communists.[17]

Darryl F. Zanuck opposed the blacklist but dared not speak against it. He secretly worked with blacklisted director Jules Dassin yet conceded to Fox's board of directors' demand that he fire blacklisted screenwriter Ring Lardner Jr. Under Zanuck's leadership, Twentieth Century–Fox released several pictures, including *Crossfire* (1947), *Gentleman's Agreement* (1947), and *Pinky* (1949), critical of anti-Semitism or racism. He drew the line at movies that denounced HUAC, rejecting on economic grounds screenwriter Philip Dunne's 1953 proposal that Fox attack witch hunters by filming George Orwell's *1984*. "No matter how you treat it," he informed Dunne, "this is a 'message' picture. Can you name me one message picture in the last three years that has not lost its shirt? Surely you have read all the notes I have written you and all of the box office facts I have given you and what happens to pictures that try to preach and 'uplift.' For good or bad, this is the age of entertainment. Audiences are sick of lectures even though they are good ones."[18]

Zanuck argued much the same throughout his career. Message took a backseat to action in Fox features. He had overcome this obstacle in the late 1930s and early 1940s, producing movies that expressed antifascist sentiments without bringing the plot to a standstill. Fifteen years older and sitting atop a disintegrating studio system, he no longer felt capable or willing to seek the same balance between entertainment and education. Zanuck let the world know he hated the Nazis but kept his disapproval of the blacklist private, hidden from the forces capable of disrupting the business he loved so much.

❧ ❧ ❧

Much of Hollywood as it was in the late 1930s and early 1940s is gone. Most of the movies remain—relics of a bygone era for some people, rarely watched curiosities for others. Beyond that, it would seem there is little else that survived the creative, exciting, and terrifying first moments of World War II. The financial and organizational structure that sustained Hollywood during these years is no more. Its formal relationship with the federal government has waned. But there is one lasting legacy from this moment. Hollywood emerged as a mature cultural identity during this time, an industry that—not without some trepidation—viewed itself as an important player in contemporary policy discussions.

Film critic J. Hoberman's recent essay on Steven Spielberg interprets the famed director within Hollywood's tradition of promoting political causes through film. Hoberman opens his brief survey in 1943, when Darryl F. Zanuck exhorted the industry to "play our part in the solutions of the problems that torture the world," and then traces this noble impulse through subsequent decades. "Hollywood exercised its responsibility and maintained a public role through the Cold War," he explains. "The studios produced anti-Communist films noir, cooperated with the Pentagon to make Korean War dramas or celebrate new Air Force technology, and ministered to the nation's sense of spiritual destiny with spectacular tales from ancient Rome or the Old Testament." Sometimes conservative, sometimes liberal, Hollywood never relinquished its role as an on- and offscreen commenter on world affairs. The post-9/11 world has seen a surge in the number of superhero films, war films, revenge films, and historical films, many of which in some way or another appeal to a country frightened by its perceived loss of control over global affairs, angered by an attack on its citizens, and keen to find justification for its ideals in the near or distant past. As I write this, the most popular movie in the United States is *300,* a drama widely interpreted as justifying anti-Iranian sentiment by casting brave Spartan defenders of Thermopylae as defenders of freedom and their Persian attackers as thuggish yet effete barbarians bent on destroying those ideals.[19]

This modern conception of Hollywood as a legitimate contributor in debates only tangentially related to the film industry first appeared on a large scale during the years leading up to Pearl Harbor. Moviemakers had spoken out before. *Birth of a Nation* (1915) clearly had contemporary social relevance, as did *I Am a Fugitive from a Chain Gang* (1933), *Dead End* (1937), and any number of other pictures. But these features existed as individual entities rather than as parts of a broader campaign to influence social or political agendas. Hollywood's support for World War I represented a temporary phenomenon, not a permanent change in the film community's culture. Studios quickly renounced anti-Hun features after the war. Charlie Chaplin's and Douglas Fairbanks Sr.'s hawking of Liberty Bonds did not carry over into similar patriotic ventures in the 1920s. It was during the tumultuous late 1930s and early 1940s that Hollywood became a mature industry, comfortable, to some extent, with voicing its opinions on affairs that did not directly pertain to it. It was then that Hollywood began consciously participating in the crucial debates that defined the course of events in the United States. As it turns out, those old movies are not relics so much as portents, cinematic arrows pointing toward modern Americans' eagerness to seek enlightenment from their entertainment.

Abbreviations

AMPAS	Academy of Motion Picture Arts and Sciences, Los Angeles, California
BFDC	Records of the Bureau of Foreign and Domestic Commerce, General Records 1914–58, NARA RG151, Index File 281
Biberman Papers	Herbert Biberman Papers, Wisconsin State Historical Society, Madison, Wisconsin
Black Books	Wisconsin State Historical Society, United Artists Collection Series 1F: Black Books
Douglas Papers	Melvyn Douglas Papers, Wisconsin State Historical Society, Madison, Wisconsin
FDRL	Franklin Delano Roosevelt Presidential Library, Hyde Park, New York
Germany Files	Confidential U.S. State Department Central Files: Germany, Internal Affairs, NARA RG59
Hopkins Papers	Papers of Harry L. Hopkins, Franklin Delano Roosevelt Presidential Library, Hyde Park, New York
Hull Papers	Cordell Hull Papers [microfilm edition], Library of Congress, Washington, D.C.
Italy Files	Confidential U.S. State Department Central Files: Italy, Internal Affairs, NARA RG59
Jackson Papers	Robert H. Jackson Papers, Library of Congress, Washington, D.C.
JLW	Jack L. Warner Collection, University of Southern California Cinematic Arts Library
Justice Files	Department of Justice Central Files, Classified Subject Files, Correspondence, 60-6-0, NARA RG60
McNaughton Papers	Frank McNaughton Papers, Harry S. Truman Presidential Library, Independence, Kansas

MPAA	Motion Picture Association of America files [microfilm edition], Margaret Herrick Library, Academy of Motion Picture Arts and Sciences, Los Angeles, California
MPSA	Motion Picture Society for the Americas Collection, Margaret Herrick Library, Academy of Motion Picture Arts and Sciences, Los Angeles, California
NARA RG59	General Records of the Department of State, National Archives and Records Administration Record Group 59
OF	Official File
PCA	Production Code Administration files, Margaret Herrick Library, Academy of Motion Picture Arts and Sciences, Los Angeles, California
PPF	President's Personal File
PSF	President's Secretary's File
UA Legal	Wisconsin State Historical Society, United Artists Collection Series 3a: Producers Legal File
UCLA ASC	University of California, Los Angeles, Arts Special Collections
UCLA DSC	University of California, Los Angeles, Department of Special Collections
USC Fox	Twentieth Century–Fox Collection, University of Southern California Cinematic Arts Library
WBA	Warner Bros. Archives, Los Angeles, California
WHP	Will Hays Papers (microfilm edition)
Willkie Papers	Wendell Willkie Papers, Indiana University Lilly Library, Bloomington, Indiana
WSHS	Wisconsin State Historical Society, Madison, Wisconsin
WWP	Walter Wanger Papers, Wisconsin State Historical Society

Introduction

1. "A Letter from Samuel Ornitz" [1951], WSHS, Samuel Ornitz Papers, b. 6, f. 2; Ornitz to David O. Selznick, 14 March 1935, WSHS, Samuel Ornitz Papers, b. 6, f. 5; Selznick to Ornitz, 15 March 1935, WSHS, Samuel Ornitz Papers, b. 6, f. 5.

2. *Boxoffice,* 22 November 1941; Jesse L. Lasky Jr., *Whatever Happened to Hollywood?* (New York: Funk & Wagnalls, 1975), 224; Otto Friedrich, *City of Nets: A Portrait of Hollywood in the 1940's* (New York: Harper & Row, 1986), 103.

3. See Michael Birdwell, *Celluloid Soldiers: The Warner Bros. Campaign against Nazism* (New York: New York University Press, 1999); Christine Ann

Colgan, "Warner Brothers' Crusade against the Third Reich: A Study of Anti-Nazi Activism and Film Production, 1933–1941" (Ph.D. diss., University of Southern California, 1985).

4. See Bernard F. Dick, *The Star-Spangled Screen: The Hollywood World War II Film* (Lexington: University Press of Kentucky, 1985); Thomas Doherty, *Projections of War: Hollywood, American Culture, and World War II,* rev. ed. (New York: Columbia University Press, 1993); Clayton R. Koppes and Gregory D. Black, *Hollywood Goes to War: How Politics, Profits, and Propaganda Shaped World War II Movies* (Berkeley: University of California Press, 1990).

5. See, e.g., Tino Balio, *Grand Designs: Hollywood as a Modern Business Enterprise, 1930–1939* (New York: Scribner, 1993); Ian Jarvie, *Hollywood's Overseas Campaign: The North Atlantic Movie Trade, 1920–1950* (New York: Cambridge University Press, 1992); Giuliana Muscio, *Hollywood's New Deal* (Philadelphia: Temple University Press, 1997); Colin Shindler, *Hollywood Goes to War: Films and American Society, 1939–1952* (London: Routledge, 1979).

6. Alexander Markey, "Motion Pictures and Public Opinion," reprinted in *Vital Speeches of the Day* 2 (15 August 1936): 726; Fred Eastman, "Chances the Movies Are Missing," *Christian Century,* 12 May 1937, 617.

7. Michael Denning, *The Cultural Front: The Laboring of American Culture in the Twentieth Century* (London: Verso, 1997).

8. *The Gallup Poll: Public Opinion, 1935–1971,* vol. 1, *1935–1948* (New York: Random House, 1972), 14, 35, 175, 184.

9. Ibid., 256, 257, 311.

10. Koppes and Black, *Hollywood Goes to War,* 1–2.

11. Leo C. Rosten, *Hollywood: The Movie Colony, the Movie Makers* (1941; reprint, New York: Arno, 1970), 78.

12. The Production Code is reprinted in Frank Miller, *Censored Hollywood: Sex, Sin, and Violence on Screen* (Atlanta: Turner Publishing, 1994), 295–297. See also Thomas Doherty, *Hollywood's Censor: Joseph I. Breen and the Production Code Administration* (New York: Columbia University Press, 2007).

Chapter One: A Wonderful Place

1. "Hollywood Is a Wonderful Place," *Life,* 3 May 1937, 28.

2. Margaret Farrand Thorp, *America at the Movies* (New Haven, Conn.: Yale University Press, 1939), 86.

3. Leo C. Rosten, *Hollywood: The Movie Colony, the Movie Makers* (1941; reprint, New York: Arno, 1970), 12; Garth Jowett, *Film: The Democratic Art* (Boston: Little, Brown, 1976), 198; Edmund Hall North Oral History, UCLA DSC.

4. Scott Eyman, *Lion of Hollywood: The Life and Legend of Louis B. Mayer* (New York: Simon & Schuster, 2005), 146.

5. Rosten, *Hollywood*, 34; Jesse L. Lasky Jr., *Whatever Happened to Hollywood?* (New York: Funk & Wagnalls, 1975), 129; Richard Fine, *West of Eden: Writers in Hollywood, 1928–1940* (Washington, D.C.: Smithsonian Institution Press, 1993), 1; "Santa Fe Super Chief," *Life,* 18 April 1938, 39. It took the Super Chief forty hours to travel from Los Angeles to Chicago. At a minimum ticket price of $100, its private rooms, cocktail lounge, and barbershop were well out of reach for most travelers.

6. John Russell Taylor, *Strangers in Paradise: The Hollywood Émigrés, 1933–1950* (New York: Holt, Rinehart and Winston, 1983), 16; Ronald Brownstein, *The Power and the Glitter: The Hollywood-Washington Connection* (New York: Vintage, 1992), 50; David Niven, *Bring on the Empty Horses* (New York: Dell, 1975), 28.

7. George Arliss, "A Londoner Looks at Hollywood," *Current History* 51 (March 1940): 40; Budd Schulberg, *What Makes Sammy Run?* (New York: Random House, 1941), 111; "Hollywood Is a Wonderful Place," 28.

8. Edward G. Robinson, *All My Yesterdays: An Autobiography* (New York: Hawthorn, 1973), 109. For more on the influence of Judaism in early Hollywood, see Neal Gabler, *An Empire of Their Own: How the Jews Invented Hollywood* (New York: Anchor, 1988).

9. Brownstein, *The Power and the Glitter,* 26–35.

10. John Trumpbour, *Selling Hollywood to the World: U.S. and European Struggles for Mastery of the Global Film Industry, 1920–1950* (Cambridge, UK: Cambridge University Press, 2002), 63–73.

11. Lary May argues that the MPPDA overstated film attendance in 1929. According to his numbers, attendance actually increased from 37.6 million admissions per week in 1929 to 45.1 million in 1932. Because of lowered ticket prices, however, gross receipts declined from around $70 million in 1929 to around $50 million in 1932, although deflation more than made up for the loss in terms of real dollars. See Lary May, *The Big Tomorrow: Hollywood and the Politics of the American Way* (Chicago: University of Chicago Press, 2000), 121–122, 289–290.

12. *1934 Film Daily Year Book,* 888–889; *1939 Film Daily Year Book,* 43; *Variety,* 8 January 1941.

13. Brownstein, *The Power and the Glitter,* 38–39; Harry Warner to Franklin Roosevelt, 30 June 1932, 8 August 1932, FDRL PPF 1050, Warner Brothers Motion Picture Company; Jack L. Warner, *My First Hundred Years in Hollywood* (New York: Random House, 1965), 207–216.

14. Leonard Mosley, *Zanuck: The Rise and Fall of Hollywood's Last Tycoon* (Boston: Little, Brown, 1984), 187; Warner, *My First Hundred Years in Hollywood,* 222–224; Carl Laemmle to Franklin Roosevelt, 6 March 1933, FDRL OF 73, Motion Pictures; Will Hays to Stephen T. Early, [March 1933], FDRL OF 73, Motion Pictures; Franklin Roosevelt to William Randolph Hearst, 1 April 1933, FDRL PPF 62, Hearst, William Randolph; Roberta Barrows to Lillian Dennison, 28 August 1941, FDRL OF 73, Motion Pictures.

15. *1934 Film Daily Year Book of Motion Pictures,* 3; *Variety,* 8 January 1941.

16. J. F. T. O'Connor to Marvin McIntyre, 15 May 1936, FDRL OF 73, Motion Pictures.

17. *Variety,* 24 April 1934; Adolph Zukor, *The Public Is Never Wrong* (New York: G. P. Putnam's Sons, 1953), 233–234; "Franklin D. Roosevelt," *Life,* 20 January 1941, 66. *Variety* estimated that FDR watched four times as many movies during his first two years in office as Herbert Hoover and five times as many as Calvin Coolidge.

18. Giuliana Muscio, *Hollywood's New Deal* (Philadelphia: Temple University Press, 1997), 36–38, 56–60; Brownstein, *The Power and the Glitter,* 26, 77; James Farley to Will Hays, 22 May 1937, WHP, reel 18.

19. Charles Higham, *Merchant of Dreams: Louis B. Mayer, M.G.M., and the Secret Hollywood* (New York: Donald I. Fine, 1993), 273; Eyman, *Lion of Hollywood,* 5.

20. Bob Thomas, *King Cohn: The Life and Times of Harry Cohn* (New York: G. P. Putnam's Sons, 1967); *Variety,* 14 March 1933, 7 March 1933.

21. David F. Schmitz, *The United States and Fascist Italy, 1922–1940* (Chapel Hill: University of North Carolina Press, 1988), 53–62, 89–92, 200–211; William Phillips, *Ventures in Diplomacy* (Boston: Beacon, 1952), 325.

22. James Hay, *Popular Film Culture in Fascist Italy: The Passing of the Rex* (Bloomington: Indiana University Press, 1987), 70; Frederick Herron to Paul Culbertson, 20 September 1933, Italy Files; Breckinridge Long to Cordell Hull, 6 October 1933, Italy Files.

23. Frederick Herron to Pierrepont Moffat, 24 October 1934, 24 January 1935, Italy Files.

24. Trumpbour, *Selling Hollywood to the World,* 5, 65; *Variety,* 31 January 1933, 6 June 1933, 5 September 1933; *New York Times,* 25 October 1933, 13 July 1935; William Phillips to Pierrepont Moffat, 23 November 1933, NARA RG59. In 1935 the German Board of Censors informed MGM that the name of Herman J. Mankiewicz, the screenwriter who had led the charge to film *Mad Dog of Europe,* could no longer appear on prints destined for Germany.

25. "Hitler at the Helm," *Commonweal* 17 (15 February 1933): 423; Kenneth Moss, "The United States, the Open Door, and Nazi Germany, 1933–1938," *South Atlantic Quarterly* 78 (autumn 1979): 489–506.

26. Pierrepont Moffat memorandum, 15 June 1934, NARA RG59; *Variety,* 18 April 1933, 21 February 1933; *New York Times,* 2 April 1933, 3 July 1933; R. R. Plant, "Films in Nazi Germany," *Nation,* 19 November 1938, 539; Larry Ceplair and Steven Englund, *The Inquisition in Hollywood: Politics in the Film Community, 1930–1960* (Garden City, N.Y.: Anchor, 1980), 96; Taylor, *Strangers in Paradise,* 46–62.

27. *Variety,* 18 April 1933, 2 May 1933, 9 May 1933, 27 June 1933.

28. *New York Times,* 9 April 1933; Ralf Georg Reuth, *Goebbels* (New York: Harcourt Brace, 1993), 184, 172, 194; George Canty to Fritz Keller, 12 November 1934, BFDC; William Phillips to John Campbell White, 18 May 1934, NARA RG59; Michael E. Birdwell, *Celluloid Soldiers: The Warner Bros. Campaign against Nazism* (New York: New York University Press, 1999), 18; *New York Times,* 30 March 1934.

29. *Variety,* 17 July 1934. Jack Warner claimed in his autobiography that he and his brother Harry decided to pull out of Germany after the Nazis murdered their German representative, Joe Kauffman. If such a crime happened, neither the newspapers nor the trade press reported it. The story is most likely one of Warner's self-aggrandizing lies.

30. "The State: Fascist and Total," *Fortune,* July 1934, 47; John P. Diggins, *Mussolini and Fascism: The View from America* (Princeton, N.J.: Princeton University Press, 1972), 162–168.

31. Diggins, *Mussolini and Fascism,* 287; *Motion Picture Herald,* 5 December 1936; Breckinridge Long to Cordell Hull, 15 April 1935, Italy Files.

32. *Variety,* 20 November 1935; Diggins, *Mussolini and Fascism,* 288; Robert Dallek, *Franklin D. Roosevelt and American Foreign Policy, 1932–1945* (New York: Oxford University Press, 1979), 114.

33. Mario Luporini to A. H. Giannini, 25 June 1936, WWP, b. 48, f. 20; *Motion Picture Herald,* 29 August 1936.

34. Mario Luporini to A. H. Giannini, 25 June 1936; Mario Luporini to Walter Wanger, 9 June 1936, 23 July 1936; Walter Wanger to Francine Fitch, 21 May 1964, WWP, b. 48, f. 20; Walter Wanger, typescript, "The Wherefore of Movie Ills," 17 November 1938, WWP, b. 36, f. 8.

35. Mario Luporini to A. H. Giannini, 25 June 1936, WWP, b. 48, f. 20; Walter Wanger to Loyd Wright, 24 June 1936; Mario Luporini to Walter Wanger, 9 June 1936, WWP, b. 48, f. 20; unknown correspondent to Walter Wanger, 17 May [1936], WWP, b. 48, f. 1.

36. Walter Wanger to Loyd Wright, 24 June 1936, UA Legal, b. 37, f. 1; "Articles of Association," 24 June 1936, UA Legal, b. 37, f. 1; *New Theatre,* August 1936, 23; Walter Wanger to Mario Luporini, 11 July 1936, 18 July 1936, 22 July 1936, 23 July 1936, WWP, b. 48, f. 20.

37. Diggins, *Mussolini and Fascism,* 107, 164–168, 259.

38. Douglas Miller to Ferdinand Mayer, 14 May 1936, BFDC; *Variety,* 1 July 1936, 22 July 1936.

39. Miller to Mayer, 14 May 1936, 10 June 1936, BFDC; Mayer to Cordell Hull, 28 May 1936, Germany Files.

40. Gabler, *An Empire of Their Own,* 11–265; Eyman, *Lion of Hollywood,* 8. In another irony, according to biographer Scott Eyman, the opening feature at Mayer's first movie theater was a film version of the notoriously anti-Semitic *Passion Play.*

41. Gabler, *An Empire of Their Own,* 140–145.

42. *Variety,* 25 April 1933; William J. Fadiman Oral History, UCLA DSC; William Orbach, "Shattering the Shackles of Powerlessness: The Debate Surrounding the Anti-Nazi Boycott of 1933–41," *Modern Judaism* 2 (1982): 151–158; Moshe Gottlieb, "The American Controversy over the Olympic Games," *American Jewish Historical Quarterly* 61 (March 1972): 181–213.

43. Gabler, *An Empire of Their Own,* 296–297, 340–342.

44. Stefan Kanfer, *Groucho: The Life and Times of Julius Henry Marx* (New York: Knopf, 2000), 5.

45. Joseph Breen to Will Hays, 18 December 1935, PCA file, *It Can't Happen Here.*

46. Ibid.; Breen to Louis B. Mayer, 31 January 1936, PCA file, *It Can't Happen Here;* Memorandum, 17 February 1936, PCA file, *It Can't Happen Here; New York Times,* 16 February 1936, 23 February 1936 (emphasis in original).

47. *New York Times,* 16 February 1936, 17 February 1936.

48. *New York Times,* 22 May 1935, 15 January 1937.

49. *New York Times,* 31 March 1936.

50. Robert A. Divine, *The Reluctant Belligerent: American Entry into World War II,* 2nd ed. (New York: Wiley, 1979), 21–29.

Chapter Two: Fires at Home, Fires Abroad

1. Herbert Biberman to unknown recipient, 22 February 1935, Biberman Papers, b. 3, f. 6; Morrie Ryskind, "No Soap-Boxes in Hollywood," *Nation,* 4 March 1936, 278.

2. Ronald Brownstein, *The Power and the Glitter: The Hollywood-Washington Connection* (New York: Vintage, 1992), 40–45; Colin Shindler, *Hollywood Goes to War: Films and American Society, 1939–1952* (London: Routledge, 1979), 63–66.

3. Edmund North Oral History, UCLA DSC; Dave Davis and Neal Goldberg, "Organizing the Screen Writers Guild: An Interview with John Howard Lawson," *Cineaste* 8 (1982): 6; Dore Schary, outline of "Hollywood as I Knew It" [1970?], WSHS, Dore Schary Papers, b. 181a, f. 14; Philip Dunne, *Take Two: A Life in Movies and Politics* (New York: Limelight, 1992), 105.

4. Herbert Biberman to Gale Sondergaard [1936], Biberman Papers, b. 3, f. 6; Brownstein, *The Power and the Glitter,* 52–53; Albert Maltz Oral History, UCLA DSC; William J. Fadiman Oral History, UCLA DSC; Larry Ceplair and Steven Englund, *The Inquisition in Hollywood: Politics in the Film Community, 1930–1960* (Garden City, N.Y.: Anchor, 1980), 54–56, 65–71, 76–77.

5. Brownstein, *The Power and the Glitter,* 59; Herbert Kline, "Hollywood Fights Back," *Nation,* 13 May 1936, 612; Donald Ogden Stewart, *By a Stroke of Luck! An Autobiography* (New York: Paddington, 1975), 223–225; Saverio Giovacchini, *Hollywood Modernism: Film and Politics in the Age of the New Deal* (Philadelphia: Temple University Press, 2001), 82.

6. Stewart, *By a Stroke of Luck!* 225.

7. Pat McGilligan, ed., *Backstory: Interviews with Screenwriters of Hollywood's Golden Age* (Berkeley: University of California Press, 1986), 345; Brownstein, *The Power and the Glitter,* 57–59; Stewart, *By a Stroke of Luck!* 213–232.

8. Ceplair and Englund, *The Inquisition in Hollywood,* 104; *Hollywood Anti-Nazi News,* 20 October 1936; *News of the World,* 10 April 1937.

9. Ceplair and Englund, *The Inquisition in Hollywood,* 104–107, 139; Brownstein, *The Power and the Glitter,* 59; Ella Winter, "Hollywood Wakes Up," *New Republic,* 12 January 1938, 277.

10. Giovacchini, *Hollywood Modernism,* 78–79, 84–86; Richard Goldstone Oral History, AMPAS.

11. *Hollywood Anti-Nazi News,* 5 November 1936.

12. *Hollywood Anti-Nazi News,* 5 February 1937, 20 February 1937, 10 April 1937.

13. *News of the World,* 7 August 1937.

14. *Hollywood Anti-Nazi News,* 20 November 1936; *News of the World,* 10 July 1937.

15. *Roosevelt's Foreign Policy, 1933–1941: Franklin D. Roosevelt's Unedited Speeches and Messages* (New York: Fred Funk, 1942), 102.

16. Brownstein, *The Power and the Glitter,* 60; Ceplair and Englund, *The Inquisition in Hollywood,* 112–114; *Motion Picture Herald,* 20 August 1938.

17. Ceplair and Englund, *The Inquisition in Hollywood,* 115–117; Bob Ford to John Ford, 30 September 1937, John Ford Papers, Indiana University Lilly Library, b. 1; *Motion Picture Herald,* 20 August 1938; Herbert Biberman to Gale Sondergaard [1936], Biberman Papers, b. 3, f. 6; John Russell Taylor, *Strangers in Paradise: The Hollywood Émigrés, 1933–1950* (New York: Holt, Rinehart and Winston, 1983), 118–119.

18. *Life,* 4 June 1937, 9; Bernard F. Dick, *The Star-Spangled Screen: The Hollywood World War II Film* (Lexington: University Press of Kentucky, 1985), 10–17.

19. "Spain in Flames," *Nation,* 27 March 1937, 340–341.

20. Joseph Breen to Walter Wanger, 3 February 1937, PCA file, *Blockade.*

21. Dore Schary, "Hollywood as I Knew It," WSHS, Dore Schary Papers, b. 182, f. 4.

22. Michael E. Birdwell, *Celluloid Soldiers: The Warner Bros. Campaign against Nazism* (New York: New York University Press, 1999), 5–7; "Warner Brothers," *Fortune,* December 1937, 208; McGilligan, *Backstory,* 75.

23. Neal Gabler, *An Empire of Their Own: How the Jews Invented Hollywood* (New York: Anchor, 1988), 124–128; "Warner Brothers," 111.

24. Gabler, *An Empire of Their Own,* 129–131; Birdwell, *Celluloid Soldiers,* 6; John Davis, "Notes on Warner Brothers Foreign Policy, 1918–1948," *Velvet Light Trap* 4 (spring 1972): 23–24.

25. Gabler, *An Empire of Their Own,* 120–131.

26. Ibid., 120–132; John Huston, *An Open Book* (New York: Knopf, 1980), 72; Cass Warner Sperling and Cork Millner, *Hollywood Be Thy Name: The Warner Brothers Story* (Rocklin, CA: Prima, 1994), 165; Birdwell, *Celluloid Soldiers,* 7; "Warner Brothers," 215.

27. Birdwell, *Celluloid Soldiers,* 6; Ceplair and Englund, *The Inquisition in Hollywood,* 10; Albert Maltz Oral History, UCLA DSC; "Warner Brothers," 215; David Niven, *Bring on the Empty Horses* (New York: Dell, 1975), 97.

28. Sperling and Millner, *Hollywood Be Thy Name,* 80–81; Gabler, *An Empire of Their Own,* 188.

29. "Warner Brothers," 111, 220; Sperling and Millner, *Hollywood Be Thy Name,* 284. Jack's dispute with Harry ended only with their deaths. Jack skipped Harry's 1958 funeral. When Jack died in 1978, he asked that his plot in Los Angeles' Home of Peace Cemetery be as far as possible from Harry's stone.

30. Birdwell, *Celluloid Soldiers,* 13; *Variety,* 28 March 1933.

31. Birdwell, *Celluloid Soldiers,* 24–31; Pandro Berman interview, 3 February 1972, WSHS, Pandro Berman Papers, b. 1, f. 1.

32. Hal Wallis and Charles Higham, *Starmaker: The Autobiography of Hal Wallis* (New York: Macmillan, 1980), 58.

33. Birdwell, *Celluloid Soldiers,* 44–47; Colin Shindler, *Hollywood in Crisis: Cinema and American Society, 1929–1939* (London: Routledge, 1996), 162–164.

34. James P. Cunningham, "The Black Legion," *Commonweal* 25 (22 January 1937): 360.

35. Mervyn LeRoy, *Mervyn LeRoy: Take One* (New York: Hawthorn, 1974), 132; Wallis and Higham, *Starmaker,* 58. For more on the Leo Frank case see Steve Oney, *And the Dead Shall Rise: The Murder of Mary Phagan and the Lynching of Leo Frank* (New York: Pantheon, 2003).

36. Giovacchini, *Hollywood Modernism,* 87, 89.

37. Warners tinkered with chronology to enhance the film's drama. Dreyfus actually left Devil's Island three years before Zola died.

38. Unpublished Gale Sondergaard autobiography, WSHS, Gale Sondergaard Papers, b. 11, f. 7; interview with Gale Sondergaard, 12 June 1979, WSHS, Gale Sondergaard Papers, b. 1, f. 6; Bernard C. Clausen, "A Moment in the Conscience of Man," *Christian Century,* 1 December 1937, 1485; Breen to Jack Warner, 17 May 1937, PCA file, *Life of Emile Zola;* Shindler, *Hollywood in Crisis,* 204.

39. Mark Van Doren, "The Novelist as Hero," *Nation,* 4 September 1937, 246; Breen to Jack Warner, 2 February 1937, PCA file, *Life of Emile Zola;* Memorandum for Files, 5 February 1937, PCA file, *Life of Emile Zola;* MPPDA Censorship Reports, PCA file, *Life of Emile Zola.*

40. RTP, "Memorandum," 24 August 1936, Italy Files; A. W. Pentland to unknown recipient, Black Books, b. 8, f. 8.

41. Will Hays to Cordell Hull, 14 October 1936, BFDC; Cordell Hull to American Embassy (Rome), 9 October 1936, BFDC; Charles A. Livengood to William Phillips, 13 October 1936, BFDC; *Variety,* 21 October 1936, 28 October 1936.

42. Mario Luporini to Walter Wanger, 15 September 1936; Walter Wanger to Mario Luporini, 9 October 1936; Walter Wanger to Carlo Roncoroni, 25 November 1936; Walter Wanger to Dino Alfieri, 17 October 1936, WWP, b. 48, f. 21; *Variety,* 26 August 1936; Ray Moseley, *Mussolini's Shadow: The Double Life of Count Galeazzo Ciano* (New Haven, Conn.: Yale University Press, 1999), 57–60.

43. Amanda Smith, ed., *Hostage to Fortune: The Letters of Joseph P. Kennedy* (New York: Viking, 2001), 135; William Phillips to Cordell Hull, 18 November 1936, 22 November 1936; James Dunn to Frederick Herron, 27 November 1936, Italy Files; Will Hays, *The Memoirs of Will H. Hays* (Garden City, N.Y.: Doubleday, 1955), 513–514, 520–522, 514–515.

44. "Quotations," 26 November 1936, WHP, reel 17; Dunn to Herron, 27 November 1936, Italy Files; Hays, *The Memoirs of Will Hays*, 515–519.

45. Dunn to Herron, 27 November 1936; William Phillips to Cordell Hull, 23 December 1936, Italy Files; Meeting notes, 27 November 1936, WHP, reel 17; "Details of Accord," 24 December 1936, Black Books, b. 8, f. 8; *Variety*, 9 December 1936, 16 December 1936; *1938 Film Daily Year Book*, 1142.

46. Enrico Galeazzi to Harold Smith, 18 April 1937, WHP, reel 18; Charles A. Livengood to William Phillips, 10 February 1937, BFDC; Lacy Kastner to Harold Smith, 25 February 1937, WHP, reel 17.

47. *Variety*, 5 May 1937; Will Hays to Enrico Galeazzi, 24 April 1937; Harold Smith to Will Hays, 27 June 1937, WHP, reel 18; "U.S. Movie Exports Set Record," *Business Week*, 26 June 1937, 50.

48. Colin Shindler, *Hollywood Goes to War: Films and American Society, 1939–1952* (London: Routledge, 1979), 2; *1939 Film Daily Year Book*, 1190; *Variety*, 6 January 1937; James Hay, *Popular Film Culture in Fascist Italy: The Passing of the Rex* (Bloomington: Indiana University Press, 1987), 87; *New York Times*, 14 June 1937; "No Particular Taste," *Time*, 9 December 1935, 26; Harold Butcher, "Japan Goes to the Movies," *Travel* 64 (April 1935): 52.

49. Memorandum, 25 March 1936; Joseph Breen to Frederick L. Herron, 11 April 1936, PCA file, *Idiot's Delight*.

50. Frederick Herron to Joseph Breen, 7 May 1937, PCA file, *Idiot's Delight*; Memorandum, 12 May 1937, PCA file, *Idiot's Delight*.

51. Hunt Stromberg to Joseph Breen, 23 June 1937, 9 July 1937, PCA file, *Idiot's Delight*.

52. *Variety*, 7 April 1937; William Dodd to Cordell Hull, 8 February 1937, Germany Files.

53. Ralf Georg Reuth, *Goebbels* (New York: Harcourt Brace, 1993), 194, 225; *Variety*, 5 January 1938; *Motion Picture Herald*, 27 March 1937, 20 March 1937; "German Film Notes," 17 December 1936, Black Books, b. 8, f. 4.

54. "Mussolini's Roach," *Time*, 4 October 1937, 21; Charles Higham, *Merchant of Dreams: Louis B. Mayer, M.G.M., and the Secret Hollywood* (New York: Donald I. Fine, 1993), 264; *Daily Variety*, 7 October 1937; "Duce's Son into Films," *Business Week*, 25 September 1937, 14.

55. Charles C. Pettijohn to John Boettiger, 24 September 1937, FDRL Boettiger Papers, b. 25, f. Pettijohn, Charles C.; *Motion Picture Herald*, 2 October 1937; "Mussolini's Roach," 21.

56. *News of the World*, 2 October 1937; *Variety*, 29 September 1937, 6 October 1937; *Daily Variety*, 7 October 1937; "Life on the American Newsfront," *Life*, 11 October 1937, 31; Higham, *Merchant of Dreams*, 270.

57. *Variety,* 13 October 1937, 16 February 1938; *Motion Picture Herald,* 2 October 1937.

58. Walter Wanger to Mario Luporini, 6 April 1937, 13 May 1938, 17 May 1938; Walter Wanger to Carlo Roncoroni, 30 April 1937; Joseph Breen to Peter Rathvon, 28 January 1938, WWP, b. 48, f. 21.

59. *1939 Film Daily Year Book,* 1195; *Variety,* 4 August 1937.

60. *Motion Picture Herald,* 20 November 1937, 30 October 1937; *1938 Film Daily Year Book,* 1143.

61. The agreement allowed the United States to send 2 million linear feet of film into Japan, the equivalent of approximately 250 feature–length pictures.

62. *1939 Film Daily Year Book,* 65, 1192; *Variety,* 9 November 1938; "The Motion Picture Industry in Japan," 24 February 1939, BFDC.

63. Birdwell, *Celluloid Soldiers,* 24; B. D. Zevin, ed., *Nothing to Fear: The Selected Addresses of Franklin Delano Roosevelt, 1932–1945* (Freeport, N.Y.: Books for Libraries Press, 1946), 110–115.

Chapter Three: Fingers in the Dike

1. *Motion Picture Herald,* 5 February 1938; Raymond Fielding, *The March of Time, 1935–1951* (New York: Oxford University Press, 1978), 186–188.

2. Fielding, *The March of Time,* 188–194.

3. *Motion Picture Herald,* 29 January 1938, 5 February 1938; *New York Times,* 21 January 1938; Otis Ferguson, "Time Steals a March," *New Republic,* 9 February 1938, 19.

4. Michael Birdwell, *Celluloid Soldiers: The Warner Bros. Campaign against Nazism* (New York: New York University Press, 1999), 29–30; Harold Rodner to Harry Warner, 22 March 1938, 15 July 1938, JLW, Nazi Data, f. 5.

5. Harry Warner to Harold Rodner, 24 March 1938, JLW, Nazi Data, f. 5.

6. *Motion Picture Herald,* 5 February 1938.

7. Ben Ray Redman, "Pictures and Censorship," *Saturday Review of Literature,* 31 December 1938, 14; Mitzi Cummings, "War on the Screen: Can It Foster Peace?" *Delineator,* July 1936, 10.

8. Redman, "Pictures and Censorship," 13.

9. Margaret Farrand Thorp, *America at the Movies* (New Haven, Conn.: Yale University Press, 1939), 64.

10. Steven Mintz and Randy Roberts, *Hollywood's America: United States History through Its Films* (St. James, N.Y.: Brandywine Press, 1993), 81; Robert Sklar, *Movie-Made America: A Cultural History of American Movies,* 2nd ed. (New York: Vintage, 1994), 127–128.

11. "The President and the Movie Code," *Christian Century,* 25 October 1933, 1327; Norman Hapgood, "Will Hays: And What the Pictures Do to Us," *Atlantic Monthly,* January 1933, 79–80; "A New Attack on Block-Booking," *Christian Century,* 30 May 1934, 715; "Block Booking and Blind Selling," *Journal of Home Economics* 28 (March 1936): 177; "A Fateful Hour for the Movies," *Christian Century,* 27 May 1936, 757; *Variety,* 8 April 1936, 16 February 1938.

12. *Manhattan (KS) Mercury,* 27 July 1938.

13. Giuliana Muscio, *Hollywood's New Deal* (Philadelphia: Temple University Press, 1997), 67–74; Will H. Hays, "Enlarging Scope of the Screen: Annual Report to the Motion Picture Producers and Distributors of America, Inc., 27 March 1939," 20; Edward G. Robinson, *All My Yesterdays: An Autobiography* (New York: Hawthorn, 1973), 190.

14. "Jug-eared" appears in, among other places, Charles Higham, *Merchant of Dreams: Louis B. Mayer, M.G.M., and the Secret Hollywood* (New York: Donald I. Fine, 1993), 53; A. Scott Berg, *Goldwyn: A Biography* (New York: Knopf, 1989), 107.

15. Jesse L. Lasky Jr., *Whatever Happened to Hollywood?* (New York: Funk & Wagnalls, 1975), 60; Will Hays, *The Memoirs of Will H. Hays* (Garden City, N.Y.: Doubleday, 1955), 3–38, 65; Hapgood, "Will Hays," 75–76.

16. Hays, *The Memoirs of Will H. Hays,* 40–65; Frank Miller, *Censored Hollywood: Sex, Sin, and Violence on Screen* (Atlanta: Turner Publishing, 1994), 28.

17. Hays, *The Memoirs of Will H. Hays,* 74–105; Hapgood, "Will Hays," 76.

18. Hays, *The Memoirs of Will H. Hays,* 108–137, 265–287; Hapgood, "Will Hays," 76; Miller, *Censored Hollywood,* 28–29.

19. Miller, *Censored Hollywood,* 28.

20. Hays, *The Memoirs of Will H. Hays,* 323–328; "The Hays Office," *Fortune,* December 1938, 139–140; Miller, *Censored Hollywood,* 29.

21. Hays, *The Memoirs of Will H. Hays,* 333; Fred Eastman, "The Movies in Politics," *Christian Century,* 15 June 1932, 764; Miller, *Censored Hollywood,* 31–34.

22. Hays, *The Memoirs of Will H. Hays,* 431; "The Hays Office," 144; Mendel Silberberg to Will Hays, 30 March 1937, WHP, reel 18.

23. Hays, *The Memoirs of Will H. Hays,* 226, 283; J. K. to E. E. Bright, 18 January 1939, WHP, reel 22; Memo from Will H. Hays, 22 January 1937, WHP, reel 17; Roy Howard to Alec G. Budge, 23 February 1938, WHP, reel 20; Enrico Galeazzi to Will Hays, 31 March 1937, WHP, reel 18; P.D.T.'s Report no. 4, 18 October 1937, WHP, reel 19. Count Galeazzi also arranged a private audience with the pope during Breen's 1938 vacation in Italy.

24. Will Hays to Daniel Schuyler, 13 June 1938, WHP, reel 21; Hays, *The Memoirs of Will H. Hays,* 448; Will Hays to Franklin Roosevelt, 14 June 1936, FDRL PPF 1944, Hays, Will H.; *Seattle Post-Intelligencer,* 29 October 1937.

25. Will Hays to Joseph Shea, 9 March 1937, WHP, reel 18; *Daily Film Renter* [London], 1 December 1936; Hays, *The Memoirs of Will H. Hays,* 477; *Film Daily,* 26 October 1938; Ian Jarvie, "Dollars and Ideology: Will Hays' Economic Foreign Policy, 1922–1945," *Film History* 2 (1988): 216; Hays, "Enlarging Scope of the Screen," 4.

26. Hays, "Enlarging Scope of the Screen," 2–4.

27. Paul Williams to Robert Jackson, 27 October 1937, Justice Files.

28. "*United States of America v. Paramount Pictures, Inc., et al.,* District Court of the United States for the Southern District of New York, 20 July 1938," 83, 101–107, 112.

29. *Variety,* 16 November 1938.

30. "The Motion Picture Industry and the Anti-Trust Laws," *Columbia Law Review* 36 (April 1936): 636; Scott Eyman, *Lion of Hollywood: The Life and Legend of Louis B. Mayer* (New York: Simon & Schuster, 2005), 262.

31. *Variety,* 15 January 1935; Will Hays to John Dickinson, 30 May 1936, and Memorandum for the Attorney General, 8 June 1936, Jackson Papers, b. 78, f. Motion Picture Industry.

32. Alan Brinkley, *The End of Reform: New Deal Liberalism in Recession* (New York: Vintage, 1996), 106–132.

33. Gene M. Gressley, *Voltaire and the Cowboy: The Letters of Thurman Arnold* (Boulder, CO: Associated University Press, 1977), 13–40.

34. Robert Jackson to Thurman Arnold, 31 December 1937, Jackson Papers, b. 77, f. Arnold, Thurman; Thurman Arnold to Robert Jackson, 6 January 1938, Jackson Papers, b. 77, f. Arnold, Thurman.

35. Gressley, *Voltaire and the Cowboy,* 46–47.

36. *New York Times,* 26 June 1938, 29 June 1938; *Variety,* 29 June 1938; Sidney Kent to Marvin McIntyre, 29 June 1938, FDRL OF 73, Motion Pictures.

37. *New York Times,* 26 June 1938; Statement by Will H. Hays, 25 June 1938, WHP, reel 21.

38. Department of Justice memorandum [summer 1938], FDRL PSF 56 Departmental File, Justice: Cummings, Homer, 1938–1939; *Variety,* 27 July 1938.

39. *Variety,* 27 July 1938; Hays, *The Memoirs of Will H. Hays,* 492.

40. *Variety,* 5 October 1938.

Chapter Four: Misfires

1. F. Scott Fitzgerald, "A Patriotic Short," in *The Pat Hobby Stories* (New York: Charles Scribner's Sons, 1970), 117.

2. Matthew Bernstein, *Walter Wanger: Hollywood Independent* (Berkeley: University of California Press, 1994), 129–130.

3. Ibid., xi, 44, 3–13.

4. Ibid., 17–35.

5. Ibid., 36–68.

6. Ibid., xvi, 116–120.

7. Ibid., 70, 118–119, 156; Walter Wanger, "Films as Foreign Offices," 10 December 1921, WWP, b. 36, f. 6.

8. Larry S. Ceplair, "The Politics of Compromise in Hollywood: A Case Study," *Cineaste* 8 (fall 1980): 5.

9. Joseph Breen to Walter Wanger, 22 February 1937, PCA file, *Blockade*.

10. Dave Davis and Neal Goldberg, "Organizing the Screen Writers Guild: An Interview with John Howard Lawson," *Cineaste* 8 (1982): 9–10; Bernstein, *Hollywood Independent*, 131; Bernard F. Dick, *The Star-Spangled Screen: The Hollywood World War II Film* (Lexington: University Press of Kentucky, 1985), 19.

11. Joseph Breen to Walter Wanger, 4 January 1938, PCA file, *Blockade*; MPPDA to Walter Wanger, 5 May 1938, PCA file, *Blockade*.

12. Davis and Goldberg, "Organizing the Screen Writers Guild," 10; Joseph Breen to Charles J. Turck, 4 August 1938, PCA file, *Blockade*; *Foreign News Flashes*, 23 May 1938, WSHS, UA Records, Samuel Cohen Papers, b. 8.

13. Dick, *The Star-Spangled Screen*, 18–20.

14. *Behind the Screen*, 13 May 1938, WSHS, UA Records, Samuel Cohen Papers, b. 5; *Motion Picture Herald*, 21 May 1938; *Around the World* [June 1938], WSHS, Samuel Cohen Papers, b. 2; Typescript, "Don Forbes' Hollywood Scrapbook," 6 January 1939, WWP, b. 36, f. 10; *London Daily Mail*, 6 June 1938.

15. Bernstein, *Hollywood Independent*, 132.

16. *Motion Picture Herald*, 11 June 1938.

17. Bernstein, *Hollywood Independent*, 134; "Blockade," *Nation,* 18 June 1938, 688; Walter Wanger to Cordell Hull, 17 May 1938, NARA RG59; Pierrepont Moffat to Walter Wanger, 19 May 1938, NARA RG59; Walter Wanger to Pierrepont Moffat, 8 June 1938, NARA RG59.

18. Knights of Columbus Hollywood Council Bulletin, 1938, PCA file, *Blockade*; Margaret Farrand Thorp, *America at the Movies* (New Haven: Yale, 1939), 211; Winchell Taylor, "Secret Movie Censors," *Nation*, 9 July 1938, 38; *Variety*, 6 July 1938, 13 July 1938; *Motion Picture Herald*, 9 July 1938, 23 July 1938.

19. National Peace Conference memorandum, 17 June 1938, WSHS, UA Collection Series 2A, O'Brien Legal File, b. 18, f. 8; *Oakland Tribune*, 28 July 1938; *Time*, 20 June 1938, 37; Walter Wanger to Associated Film Audiences [fall 1938], WWP, b. 36, f. 7.

20. Walter Wanger to Franklin Roosevelt, 28 June 1938, NARA RG59.

21. Otis Ferguson, "Spanish Omelette, with Ham," *New Republic,* 29 June 1938, 217; *Hollywood Now,* 25 June 1938.

22. *New York Times,* 17 June 1938; "Boy Meets Spy," *Time,* 20 June 1938, 37; *Variety,* 22 June 1938; "Costs/Receipts Schedule," 30 September 1939, UA Legal, b. 37, f. 3; MPPDA Censorship Reports, PCA file, *Blockade.*

23. *Boxoffice,* 30 July 1938.

24. Walter Wanger to Associated Film Audiences, fall 1938, WWP, b. 36, f. 7; Walter Wanger typescript, "The Wherefore of Movie Ills," 17 November 1938, WWP, b. 36, f. 8.

25. Walter Wanger to Mario Luporini, 6 April 1937, 13 May 1938, 17 May 1938; Walter Wanger to Carlo Roncoroni, 30 April 1937; Joseph Breen to Peter Rathvon, 28 January 1938; Hooper Pitts to Lamar Fleming, 25 February 1938; Mario Luporini to Walter Wanger, 1 September 1938, WWP, b. 48, f. 21; *Variety,* 14 July 1937; Charles Schwartz to Walter Wanger, 23 February 1938, WWP, b. 20, f. 20; Wanger, "The Wherefore of Movie Ills."

26. Joseph Breen to Louis B. Mayer, 13 May 1938, 26 August 1938, PCA file, *Idiot's Delight;* Joseph Breen to Roberto Caracciolo, 14 May 1938; Roberto Caracciolo to Joseph Breen, 20 June 1938, PCA file, *Idiot's Delight.*

27. " 'Idiot's Delight': The Film Doesn't Name Names, but It Still Carries Anti-War Punch," *Newsweek,* 6 February 1939, 24; "Idiot's Delight," *Time,* 13 February 1939, 29.

28. *Motion Picture Herald,* 9 July 1938; *1938 Film Daily Year Book,* 1122; *Variety,* 23 March 1938, 17 August 1938; Harold Smith to Enrico Galeazzi, 7 September 1938, WHP, reel 21; John P. Diggins, *Mussolini and Fascism: The View from America* (Princeton, N.J.: Princeton University Press, 1972), 319–321.

29. *1938 Film Daily Year Book,* 1122; *1939 Film Daily Year Book,* 1190; Arthur Kelly to Will Hays, 22 September 1938; Enrico Galeazzi to Harold Smith, 10 September 1938, 13 October 1938, WHP, reel 21; *Motion Picture Herald,* 24 September 1938; *Variety,* 28 September 1938, 12 October 1938.

30. *Observatore Romano,* 15 October 1938, WHP, reel 21; *1939 Film Daily Year Book,* 1190; *Variety,* 12 October 1938.

31. "Meeting of the Continental Managers," 25 October 1938, Black Books, b. 8, f. 8.

32. *Variety,* 9 November 1938; Press release, 2 February 1939, WHP, reel 22; *New York Times,* 27 November 1938, 26 February 1939. Concerned that Fascists would sue if they failed to honor existing contracts, Universal and United Artists sold a handful of films in Italy after the boycott began.

33. *Variety,* 8 November 1939; *Motion Picture Herald,* 5 August 1939; Will Hays to Cordell Hull, 18 December 1939, Italy Files; Will Hays to Enrico Galeazzi, 13 November 1939, WHP, reel 23; "Statement" [1940], WHP, reel 26; David F. Schmitz, *The United States and Fascist Italy, 1922–1940* (Chapel Hill: University of North Carolina Press, 1988), 191–198. Columbia Studios sent fifteen films in May of 1940 after Italy offered the cash-strapped company $130,000 for them. Other studios offered $100,000 for Columbia to reject the Italians. Hays urged the State Department not to interpret Columbia's move as a breakdown in unity. The films, he explained, were lousy, and the studio "needed the money very badly" ("American Motion Picture Interests in Italy," 28 May 1940, Italy Files).

Chapter Five: New Directions

1. Nicholas John Cull, *Selling War: The British Propaganda Campaign against American "Neutrality" in World War II* (New York: Oxford University Press, 1995), 7–10.

2. Ian Jarvie, "Dollars and Ideology: Will Hays' Economic Foreign Policy, 1922–1945," *Film History* 2 (1988): 211; Norman Hapgood, "Will Hays: And What the Pictures Do to Us," *Atlantic Monthly,* January 1933, 83, Ian Jarvie, *Hollywood's Overseas Campaign: The North Atlantic Movie Trade, 1920–1950* (New York: Cambridge University Press, 1992), 124.

3. Jarvie, *Hollywood's Overseas Campaign,* 114–126.

4. Ibid., 111, 135–137, 144; *Motion Picture Herald,* 30 January 1937, 6 March 1937; F. L. Harley to Will Hays, 4 December 1936, WHP, reel 17.

5. Ruth Vasey, "Foreign Parts: Hollywood's Global Distribution and the Representation of Ethnicity," *American Quarterly* 44 (December 1992): 627.

6. Ibid., 627–629.

7. Laura Elston, "The Cinema Toasts the Empire," *Canadian Magazine,* March 1935, 40.

8. David Niven, *Bring on the Empty Horses* (New York: Dell, 1975), 115–118; Hal Wallis to Sam Bischoff, 8 January 1936, in Rudy Behlmer, *Inside Warner Bros. (1935–1951)* (New York: Simon & Schuster, 1985), 28; Rowland Leigh to Hal Wallis, 28 March 1936, in Behlmer, *Inside Warner Bros.,* 30.

9. Michael Todd Bennett, "Anglophilia on Film: Creating an Atmosphere for Alliance, 1935–1941," *Film & History* 27 (1997): 5–6; *Time,* 2 November 1936, 21.

10. Jarvie, *Hollywood's Overseas Campaign,* 158, 151–155; "Summary of Recommendations of Moyne Committee" [1936], WHP, reel 19.

11. Will Hays to John Boettiger, 5 May 1937, FDRL Boettiger Papers, b. 20, f. Hays, Will H.; F. W. Allport to Will Hays, 20 April 1937, WHP, reel 18; *Variety,* 21 July 1937, 25 August 1937, 22 September 1937; Robert W. Bingham to F. W. Allport, 23 March 1937, WHP, reel 18; Joseph Kennedy to Will Hays, 29 January 1938, WHP, reel 20; Will Hays to Arthur Houghton, 19 March 1938, WHP, reel 20; Will Hays to J. P. Mitchell, 12 November 1941, WHP, reel 29.

12. *Motion Picture Herald,* 27 November 1937; Frederick Herron to Will Hays, 17 January 1938, WHP, reel 19; "Memorandum of MPPDA, Inc.," 15 February 1938, WHP, reel 20; Cordell Hull to American Embassy, 15 February, 1938, WHP, reel 20.

13. Cull, *Selling War,* 13–21; Thomas E. Hachey, "Winning Friends and Influencing Policy: British Strategy to Woo America in 1937," *Wisconsin Magazine of History* 55 (1971–72): 120, 126, 124.

14. "England—Quota," 24 June 1938, Black Books, b. 7, f. 2; H. Mark Glancy, "Hollywood and Britain: MGM and the British 'Quota' Legislation," in Jeffrey Richards, ed., *The Unknown 1930s: An Alternative History of the British Cinema, 1929–1939* (London: I. B. Tauris, 1998), 64–66.

15. *London Daily Mirror,* 17 February 1939; Rose Kennedy Diary, 4 May 1939, in Amanda Smith, ed., *Hostage to Fortune: The Letters of Joseph P. Kennedy* (New York: Viking, 2000), 332.

16. Behlmer, *Inside Warner Bros.,* 83; Michael Birdwell, *Celluloid Soldiers: The Warner Bros. Campaign against Nazism* (New York: New York University Press, 1999), 68.

17. "Conversation over Telephone," 22 September 1938, WHP, reel 21; *Hollywood Now,* 7 October 1938; Arthur Houghton to Will Hays, 27 September 1938, WHP, reel 21.

18. Harold Smith to Will Hays, 19 October 1938, WHP, reel 21.

19. For more on World War I–era films see Leslie Midkiff DeBauche, *Reel Patriotism: The Movies and World War I* (Madison: University of Wisconsin Press, 1997).

20. Todd McCarthy, *Howard Hawks: The Grey Fox of Hollywood* (New York: Grove, 1997), 102–117.

21. "Arms and the Men," *Fortune,* March 1934, 52–55, 113–120; Robert Divine, *The Reluctant Belligerent: American Entry into World War II,* 2nd ed. (New York: Wiley, 1979), 10.

22. Hal Wallis to Jack Warner, 30 April 1938, WBA, *Dawn Patrol.*

23. "Vital Statistics, Dawn Patrol" [1938], WBA, *Dawn Patrol;* "Budget," 14 July 1938, WBA, *Dawn Patrol;* Warner Bros. press release [1938], WBA, *Dawn*

Patrol; revised final script, 4 August 1938, WBA, *Dawn Patrol;* Seton I. Miller to Hal Wallis, 21 September 1938, WBA, *Dawn Patrol.*

24. "Dawn Patrol—Foreword" [1938], WBA, *Dawn Patrol;* Press book, WBA, *Dawn Patrol.*

25. *Minneapolis Tribune,* 5 January 1939.

26. *Richmond Times-Dispatch,* 26 December 1938.

Chapter Six: Good Neighbors

1. David F. Schmitz, *Thank God They're on Our Side: The United States and Right-Wing Dictatorships, 1921–1965* (Chapel Hill: University of North Carolina Press, 1999), 47, 73; Frank Freidel, *Franklin D. Roosevelt: A Rendezvous with History* (Boston: Little, Brown, 1990), 211.

2. Schmitz, *Thank God They're on Our Side,* 115; Cordell Hull to Sumner Welles, 17 December 1938, Hull Papers, reel 17; Freidel, *Franklin D. Roosevelt,* 214–215.

3. Freidel, *Franklin D. Roosevelt,* 215–220.

4. Gaizka S. de Usabel, *The High Noon of American Films in Latin America* (Ann Arbor, MI: UMI Research Press, 1982), 84; *Motion Picture Herald,* 3 October 1936; "Brazil—General," 15 March 1937, Black Books, b. 1, f. 5; "Argentine—Quota," August 1937, Black Books, b. 1, f. 1; "Argentine—Quota," 5 October 1936, Black Books, b. 1, f. 1.

5. De Usabel, *The High Noon of American Films in Latin America,* 95–96, 104; *1939 Film Daily Year Book,* 1125–1126; *Around the World* 5, no. 6 [1937], WSHS, UA Records, Samuel Cohen Papers, b. 2; *Around the World* 5, no. 2 [1937], WSHS, UA Records, Samuel Cohen Papers, b. 2; *Variety,* 29 September 1937.

6. *Variety,* 6 November 1940; "Argentine—Local Production," 15 June 1936, Black Books, b. 1, f. 4; *Motion Picture Herald,* 12 November 1938.

7. *1939 Film Daily Year Book,* 41; de Usabel, *The High Noon of American Films in Latin America,* 136, 125–126; *1938 Film Daily Year Book,* 1143; *Motion Picture Herald,* 25 March 1939; *1939 Film Daily Year Book,* 1123; *1940 Film Daily Year Book,* 39.

8. Cordell Hull to Will Hays, 15 October 1934, NARA RG59; *History of the Office of the Coordinator of Inter-American Affairs* (Washington, D.C.: Government Printing Office, 1947), 74.

9. De Usabel, *The High Noon of American Films in Latin America,* 136; *Motion Picture Herald,* 3 December 1938; *Variety,* 7 December 1938.

10. State Department memorandum, 17 December 1938, NARA RG59; Sumner Welles to American Diplomatic and Consular Officers in the American Republics, 21 December 1938, Hull Papers, reel 17.

11. Cordell Hull to Sumner Welles, 25 December 1938, Hull Papers, reel 17; Will Hays to Franklin Roosevelt, 3 April 1939, FDRL PPF 1944, Hays, Will H., 1934–1941; Memorandum in re: South American Newsreel Expedition [January 1939], FDRL PPF 1944, Hays, Will H., 1934–1941.

12. Franklin Roosevelt to Will Hays, 13 March 1939, FDRL PPF 1944, Hays, Will H., 1934–1941; Will Hays to Franklin Roosevelt, 3 April 1939, FDRL PPF 1944, Hays, Will H., 1934–1941; Memorandum in re: South American Newsreel Expedition [January 1939], FDRL PPF 1944, Hays, Will H., 1934–1941; *Variety*, 19 April 1939; C. C. Pettijohn and Gaylord R. Hawkins, "Memorandum on the Constitutionality of the Censorship of News Reels, et al.," 3 January 1939, WHP, reel 22.

13. *New York Times*, 18 December 1938.

14. Walter MacEwen to Hal Wallis, 26 August 1937, WBA, *Juarez;* Reader's Report on "The Phantom Crown" [1937], PCA file, *Juarez.*

15. John Huston, *An Open Book* (New York: Knopf, 1980), 72–73; Temporary Script for "The Phantom Crown," 6 June 1938, WBA, *Juarez;* "Explanatory Note" [1937], WBA, *Juarez;* Walter MacEwen to Henry Blanke, 11 May 1938, WBA, *Juarez;* Henry Blanke to Robert Taplinger, 9 June 1938, WBA, *Juarez.*

16. Ligon Johnson to Morris Ebenstein, 19 October 1938, WBA, *Juarez;* Morris Ebenstein to R. J. Obringer [1938], WBA, *Juarez;* Edward G. Robinson, *All My Yesterdays: An Autobiography* (New York: Hawthorn, 1973), 91; Morris Ebenstein to Henry Blanke, 28 October 1938, WBA, *Juarez.*

17. S. Frankel to Gene Werner, 21 December 1938, WBA, *Juarez;* Jack Warner to Robert Perkins, 24 December 1938, WBA, *Juarez;* Morris Ebenstein to Warren Munsell, 25 January 1939, WBA, *Juarez;* Morris Ebenstein to Harry Warner, 28 December 1938, WBA, *Juarez.*

18. Henry Blanke to Morris Ebenstein, 8 September 1938, WBA, *Juarez;* Henry Blanke to Robert Taplinger, 9 June 1938, WBA, *Juarez;* Joseph Breen to Jose Conseco, 10 November 1938, PCA file, *Juarez;* Blanke to J. G. Mullen, 21 June 1938, WBA, *Juarez;* Vincente L. Beneitez to Blanke, 6 September 1938, WBA, *Juarez.*

19. Daniel Yergin, *The Prize: The Epic Quest for Oil, Money, and Power* (New York: Simon & Schuster, 1991), 272–277.

20. Henry Blanke to Hal Wallis, 20 July 1938, WBA, *Juarez;* Steve Trilling to Hal Wallis, 19 September 1938, WBA, *Juarez.*

21. "Prestige Picture," *Time,* 16 August 1937, 35; "Biography Projects Living Portrait of Novelist," *News-Week,* 14 August 1937, 19; Thomas Elsaesser,

"Film History as Social History: The Dieterle/Warner Brothers Bio-Pic," *Wide Angle* 8 (1986): 22; Larry Ceplair and Steven Englund, *The Inquisition in Hollywood: Politics in the Film Community, 1930–1960* (Garden City, N.Y.: Anchor, 1980), 114.

22. Hal Wallis and Charles Higham, *Starmaker: The Autobiography of Hal Wallis* (New York: Macmillan, 1980), 62, 55; Henry Blanke to Hal Wallis, 19 November 1938, WBA, *Juarez;* Henry Blanke to Morris Ebenstein, 20 December 1938, WBA, *Juarez;* Henry Blanke Oral History, UCLA DSC; "Budget," 14 April 1939, WBA, *Juarez;* Jack Warner to Henry Blanke, 3 June 1939, in Rudy Behlmer, *Inside Warner Bros. (1935–1951)* (New York: Simon & Schuster, 1985), 90; "Juarez—Souvenir Program," WSHS, Gale Sondergaard Papers, b. 10, f. 7.

23. J. G. Mullen to Karl G. MacDonald, 11 June 1938, WBA, *Juarez;* Morris Ebenstein to Henry Blanke, 27 December 1938, WBA, *Juarez.*

24. Henry Blanke to Morris Ebenstein, 9 February 1939, WBA, *Juarez;* Wallis and Higham, *Starmaker,* 62; "Synopsis, Juarez" [1939], WBA, *Juarez;* Warner Bros. press release [1939], WBA, *Juarez.*

25. Robert Taplinger to Charles Einfeld, 18 April 1939, WBA, *Confessions of a Nazi Spy;* "Latin American Diplomats Crowd Opening of *Juarez,*" *Life,* 8 May 1939, 74–75; *Brooklyn Eagle,* 26 April 1939; *Chicago Tribune,* 28 April 1939; Franz Hoellering, "Juarez," *Nation,* 6 May 1939, 539.

26. Franklin Roosevelt to James W. Gerard, 11 May 1939, FDRL PPF 977, Gerard, James W.; Sumner Welles to Harry Warner, 12 May 1939, NARA RG59; Harry Warner to Sumner Welles, 16 May 1939, NARA RG59; State Department memorandum, 11 May 1939, NARA RG59.

27. Sumner Welles to American Diplomatic and Consular Officers in the American Republics, 8 June 1939, NARA RG59; Dudley G. Dwyre to Cordell Hull, 28 July 1939, NARA RG59; Winthrop R. Scott to Cordell Hull, 1 August 1939, NARA RG59; Robert Frayer to Cordell Hull, 18 September 1939, NARA RG59; William H. Hornibrook to Cordell Hull, 19 September 1939, NARA RG59.

28. Josephus Daniels to Cordell Hull, 27 June 1939, NARA RG59; William P. Blocker to Cordell Hull, 1 July 1939, NARA RG59; Myron H. Schraud to Cordell Hull, 14 July 1939, NARA RG59; Doyle C. McDonough to Cordell Hull, 3 July 1939, NARA RG59; *Acción* [San Luis Potosí], 7 July 1939.

29. Colin Shindler, *Hollywood Goes to War: Films and American Society, 1939–1952* (London: Routledge, 1979), 204–205; *Variety,* 25 October 1939, 8 November 1939.

1. Jack L. Warner, *My First Hundred Years in Hollywood* (New York: Random House, 1965), 261–262.

2. *Hollywood Reporter,* 28 April 1939.

3. Bernard F. Dick, *The Star-Spangled Screen: The Hollywood World War II Film* (Lexington: University Press of Kentucky, 1985), 51; Michael Birdwell, *Celluloid Soldiers: The Warner Bros. Campaign against Nazism* (New York: New York University Press, 1999), 70; Hal Wallis and Charles Higham, *Starmaker: The Autobiography of Hal Wallis* (New York: Macmillan, 1980), 70.

4. Walter MacEwen to Ed DePatie, 21 November 1938, WBA, *Confessions of a Nazi Spy;* Wallis and Higham, *Starmaker,* 70–71.

5. Dick, *The Star-Spangled Screen,* 52–53; Steven J. Ross, "*Confessions of a Nazi Spy:* Warner Bros., Anti-Fascism and the Politicization of Hollywood," in Martin Kaplan and Johanna Blakley, eds., *Warners' War: Politics, Pop Culture & Propaganda in Wartime Hollywood* (Los Angeles: Norman Lear Center Press, 2004), 52–54.

6. Edward G. Robinson to Hal Wallis, 20 October 1938, in Rudy Behlmer, *Inside Warner Bros. (1935–1951)* (New York: Simon & Schuster, 1985), 82; Bob Lord to Anatole Litvak, 31 October 1938, WBA, *Confessions of a Nazi Spy; Hollywood Reporter,* 27 October 1938; Georg Gyssling to Joseph Breen, 23 November 1938, PCA file, *Confessions of a Nazi Spy;* Joseph Breen to Jack Warner, 26 November 1938, PCA file, *Confessions of a Nazi Spy.*

7. Luigi Luraschi to Joseph Breen, 10 December 1938, PCA file, *Confessions of a Nazi Spy;* George Skouras to George C. Vournas, 5 May 1939, FDRL Gardner Jackson Papers, Personal Correspondence, b. 76, f. Warner Brothers.

8. *New York Times,* 15 January 1939.

9. Jacob Wilk to Jack Warner, 8 December 1938, WBA, *Confessions of a Nazi Spy;* Hal Wallis to Robert Lord, 22 December 1938, WBA, *Confessions of a Nazi Spy;* Ian Hamilton, *Writers in Hollywood, 1915–1951* (New York: Carroll & Graf, 1990), 213; Ross, "*Confessions of a Nazi Spy,*" 54; Eric J. Sandeen, "*Confessions of a Nazi Spy* and the German-American Bund," *American Studies* 20 (1979): 73. The Roosevelt administration's role in the film remains murky. Breen told Will Hays on 30 December 1938 that "indirect, if not direct, aid, assistance, and cooperation has been promised to Warner Brothers by certain important government officials," but he never elaborated on this tantalizing hint.

10. Irving Deakin to Herman Lissauer, 29 December 1938, WBA, *Confessions of a Nazi Spy;* Herman Lissauer to Jacob Wilk, 10 December 1938, WBA, *Confessions of a Nazi Spy;* Robert Lord to Joseph Breen, 24 December 1938, PCA file, *Confessions of a Nazi Spy.*

11. Dick, *The Star-Spangled* Screen, 53–54.

12. Joseph Breen to Jack Warner, 30 December 1938, PCA file, *Confessions of a Nazi Spy;* Joseph Breen to Will Hays, 30 December 1938, PCA file, *Confessions of a Nazi Spy.*

13. Morris Ebenstein to Hal Wallis, 4 January 1939, WBA, *Confessions of a Nazi Spy.*

14. In the film Dr. Kassell's business card identifies him as "Karl Kassel." The credits, however, list him as "Karl Kassell," one of several spelling discrepancies between the movie and the credits.

15. Steve Trilling to R. J. Obringer, 23 January 1939, WBA, *Confessions of a Nazi Spy;* K[arl] L[ischka], "RE: Storm over America," 22 January 1939, PCA file, *Confessions of a Nazi Spy; New York Times,* 31 January 1939.

16. Memo to Dr. Pattee, 24 January 1939, NARA RG59; Thomas Burke to Mr. DeWolf, 26 January 1939, NARA RG59.

17. "Budget—Confessions of a Nazi Spy," 2 February 1939, WBA, *Confessions of a Nazi Spy.*

18. *Variety,* 15 February 1939; Will Hays to J. H., 30 March 1939, WHP, reel 22.

19. Joseph Hazen to Jack Warner, 10 January 1939; JLW, b. 58, f. 17; Jack Warner to Joseph Hazen, 25 January 1939, JLW, b. 58, f. 17. Harry Warner's anti-Nazi paraphernalia can be found in JLW, Harry Warner Anti-Nazi Material.

20. R. J. Obringer to Charles Einfeld, 3 January 1939, WBA, *Confessions of a Nazi Spy;* Birdwell, *Celluloid Soldiers,* 71; V. F. Calverton, "Cultural Barometer," *Current History* 50 (March 1939): 47; Joseph Breen to Jack Warner, 6 April 1939, PCA file, *Confessions of a Nazi Spy.*

21. "Remarks of H. M. Warner at St. Patrick's Day Dinner at Royal Palms Hotel," 17 March 1939, JLW, Harry Warner Speeches and Interviews File, b. 56, f. 1.

22. Ross, "*Confessions of a Nazi Spy,*" 54; Jack L. Warner to All Departments, 21 April 1939, WBA, *Confessions of a Nazi Spy;* Lou Edelman to Hal Wallis, 28 April 1939, WBA, *Confessions of a Nazi Spy;* Lou Edelman to Jack Warner, 28 April 1939, WBA, *Confessions of a Nazi Spy;* Jack Warner to Franklin Roosevelt, 28 April 1939, FDRL OF 73, Motion Pictures.

23. Ross, "*Confessions of a Nazi Spy,*" 54.

24. Sander A. Diamond, *The Nazi Movement in the United States, 1924–1941* (Ithaca, N.Y.: Cornell University Press, 1974), 128–135, 252–259; Sandeen, "*Confessions of a Nazi Spy* and the German-American Bund," 77.

25. Sandeen, "*Confessions of a Nazi Spy* and the German-American Bund," 78; Diamond, *The Nazi Movement in the United States,* 324–328.

26. *Variety,* 28 April 1939; "Totem and Taboo," *Time,* 15 May 1939, 58; *Motion Picture Daily,* 28 April 1939; Otis Ferguson, "They're Down! They're Up!" *New Republic,* 10 May 1939, 20.

27. *Variety,* 21 June 1939; Birdwell, *Celluloid Soldiers,* 76; *Deutscher Weckruf und Beobachter* quoted in Sandeen, "*Confessions of a Nazi Spy* and the German-American Bund," 74; Hans Thomsen to Cordell Hull, 8 May 1939, NARA RG59; George Messersmith to Frederick Herron, 13 May 1939, NARA RG59; State Department memorandum, 26 May 1939, Germany Files.

28. Joseph Steiner to WB Pictures, Inc., 4 May 1939, WBA, *Confessions of a Nazi Spy;* J. P. Thompson to Warner Bros., 28 June 1939, WBA, *Confessions of a Nazi Spy; Hollywood Now,* 19 May 1939.

29. Sandeen, "*Confessions of a Nazi Spy* and the German-American Bund," 74; MPPDA Censorship Reports, PCA file, *Confessions of a Nazi Spy; Hollywood Now,* 28 July 1939. The best source for grosses for Warner Bros. films (as of 31 August 1944) is given in n. 6 of chap. 11 (see p. 372, below).

30. Calverton, "Cultural Barometer," 46; *New York Times,* 24 January 1939.

31. *1939 Film Daily Year Book,* 65, 1123, 1182–1183; *Motion Picture Herald,* 19 November 1938; *Variety,* 29 March 1939.

Chapter Eight: The Widening Campaign

1. "H. Warner Address to American Legion," 19 September 1938, FDRL OF 73, Motion Pictures.

2. Ibid.; Harry Warner to Franklin Roosevelt, 27 September 1938, FDRL OF 73, Motion Pictures.

3. Charles Chaplin, *My Autobiography* (New York: Simon & Schuster, 1964), 391; Charles J. Maland, *Chaplin and American Culture: The Evolution of a Star Image* (Princeton, N.J.: Princeton University Press, 1989), 165–166.

4. Georg Gyssling to Joseph Breen, 31 October 1938, PCA file, *The Great Dictator;* Joseph Breen to Georg Gyssling, 2 November 1938, PCA file, *The Great Dictator.*

5. James Brooke-Wilkinson to Joseph Breen, 3 February 1939, PCA file, *The Great Dictator;* Joseph Breen to James Brooke-Wilkinson, 13 March 1939, PCA file, *The Great Dictator.*

6. Thomas Doherty, *Projections of War: Hollywood, American Culture, and World War II,* rev. ed. (New York: Columbia University Press, 1993), 18–35; Leni Riefenstahl, *Leni Riefenstahl: A Memoir* (New York: St. Martin's, 1992), 236.

7. Doherty, *Projections of War,* 21; *New York Times,* 5 November 1938; Riefenstahl, *Leni Riefenstahl,* 236–237.

8. Riefenstahl, *Leni Riefenstahl,* 238–239.

9. Ibid.; *New York Times,* 30 November 1938.

10. *Variety,* 7 December 1938; *New York Times,* 30 November 1938; Riefenstahl, *Leni Riefenstahl,* 238–240.

11. *Hollywood Now,* 2 December 1938; Anthony Slide, "Hollywood's Fascist Follies," *Film Comment* 27 (July/August 1991): 65; Fred Taylor, ed., *The Goebbels Diaries, 1939–1941* (New York: G. P. Putnam's Sons, 1983), 9.

12. Maurice Murphy to Marvin McIntyre, 1 December 1938, FDRL OF 300, Democratic National Committee, California, "M," 1938–1939.

13. Ibid.; Dan Ford, *Pappy: The Life of John Ford* (Englewood Cliffs, N.J.: Prentice-Hall, 1979), 78.

14. Ronald Brownstein, *The Power and the Glitter: The Hollywood-Washington Connection* (New York: Vintage, 1992), 61–63.

15. Ibid., 63; Larry Ceplair and Steven Englund, *The Inquisition in Hollywood: Politics in the Film Community, 1930–1960* (Garden City, N.Y.: Doubleday, 1980), 120–121.

16. Melvyn Douglas speech, 3 December 1938, Douglas Papers, b. 10, f. 4; Melvyn Douglas speech, 23 April 1939, Douglas Papers, b. 10, f. 4; Melvyn Douglas to Jack Warner, 21 June 1939, Douglas Papers, b. 11, f. 1; Harry Warner to Melvyn Douglas, 23 June 1939, Douglas Papers, b. 11, f. 1; Beatrice Buchman to Melvyn Douglas, 29 January 1939, Douglas Papers, b. 11, f. 1.

17. Untitled newspaper clipping, 6 January 1939, Douglas Papers, b. 11, f. 1; *Variety,* 14 December 1938; Beatrice Buchman to Melvyn Douglas, 29 January 1939, Douglas Papers, b. 11, f. 1.

18. R. C. Stauder to Mrs. Melvyn Douglas, Douglas Papers, b. 11, f. 1; anonymous to Melvyn Douglas, 10 December 1938, Douglas Papers, b. 10, f. 8; "Twelve Ex-Fans" to Melvyn Douglas, 3 January 1938, Douglas Papers, b. 10, f. 8.

19. *Hollywood Now,* 23 December 1938; Memo to Will Hays, 23 February 1939, WHP, reel 22; "Declaration of Democratic Independence," WHP, reel 22.

20. "Declaration of Democratic Independence," WHP, reel 22.

21. Neal Gabler, *An Empire of Their Own: How the Jews Invented Hollywood* (New York: Anchor, 1988), 351–352.

22. August Raymond Ogden, *The Dies Committee: A Study of the Special House Committee for the Investigation of Un-American Activities, 1938–1944* (1945; reprint, Westport, Conn.: Greenwood Press, 1984), 56, 63–65; *Los Angeles Examiner,* 5 August 1938; *Variety,* 24 August 1938; Ceplair and Englund, *The Inquisition in Hollywood,* 109; *New York Times,* 23 August 1938.

23. J. F. T. O'Connor to Marvin McIntyre, 16 August 1938, FDRL OF 73, Motion Pictures; *New York Times,* 16 August 1938.

24. *Variety*, 24 August 1938; *Investigation of Un-American Activities and Propaganda Report of the Special Committee on Un-American Activities Pursuant to H. Res. 282* (Washington, D.C.: Government Printing Office, 1939), 67.

25. Jesse L. Lasky Jr., *Whatever Happened to Hollywood?* (New York: Funk & Wagnalls, 1975), 148–149; Brownstein, *The Power and the Glitter*, 64–68; Edward G. Robinson, *All My Yesterdays: An Autobiography* (New York: Hawthorn, 1973), 194.

26. Harry Warner to Harry Hopkins, 6 March 1939, Hopkins Papers, b. 117, f. Motion Pictures.

27. Stephen Early to Jack Warner, 24 March 1939, FDRL OF 73, Motion Pictures; Will Hays to Franklin Roosevelt, 20 April 1939, FDRL PSF b. 137, f. Hays, Will.

28. Joseph Hazen to Jack Warner, 20 April 1939, JLW, b. 58, f. 17; Joseph Hazen to Jack Warner, 1 May 1939, JLW, b. 58, f. 17.

29. Harry Hopkins appointment book, FDRL; *Variety*, 7 June 1939; *Niagara Falls (NY) Gazette*, 6 June 1939.

30. Unpublished Gale Sondergaard autobiography, WSHS, Gale Sondergaard Papers, b. 11, f. 7.

31. Harry Warner to Al Lichtman, 27 June 1939, JLW, Nazi Data.

32. A. Scott Berg, *Goldwyn* (New York: Knopf, 1989), 345; Affidavit [1939], WWP, b. 27, f. 2; Walter Wanger to Guaranty Trust Company, 28 January 1939, WWP, b. 27, f. 4; Joseph Breen to Al Rosen, 15 April 1939, WHP, reel 22; Joseph Breen to Louis B. Mayer, 22 March 1939, PCA file, *It Can't Happen Here;* memo to Stephen Early, 3 April 1939, FDRL OF 73, Motion Pictures; White House memorandum, 22 May 1939, FDRL OF 73, Motion Pictures; Joseph Breen to Louis B. Mayer, 2 June 1939, PCA file, *It Can't Happen Here.*

33. *Hollywood Now,* 23 June 1939.

34. Will Hays, "Motion Pictures and Business" [April 1939], WHP, reel 23; *Norfolk Virginian-Pilot,* 8 April 1939.

35. Conference on Temporary Script of 11 March 1939 (5 April 1939), in Rudy Behlmer, *Memo from Darryl F. Zanuck: The Golden Years at Twentieth Century—Fox* (New York: Grove, 1993), 22.

36. Temporary script of "Drums along the Mohawk," 11 March 1939, USC Fox, *Drums along the Mohawk* file; Conference on Temporary Script of 11 March 1939 (5 April 1939), in Behlmer, *Memo from Darryl F. Zanuck,* 22; Conference Notes with DFZ, 5 April 1939, USC Fox, *Drums along the Mohawk* file.

37. *Motion Picture Herald,* 1 February 1941, 6 December 1941; Press release, 24 November 1941, WHP, reel 29.

38. "Dodge City," *Life,* 17 April 1939, 68.

39. *Albany (NY) Knickerbocker News,* 4 April 1939; *New York World-Telegram,* 15 April 1939; Frank S. Nugent, "Hollywood Waves the Flag," *Nation,* 8 April 1939, 398–399.

40. "Cinema," *Time,* 8 May 1939, 66; Abram F. Myers to Franklin Roosevelt, 23 January 1939, FDRL OF 73, Motion Pictures.

41. Elizabeth Dalton, "Old Glory: Notes on Warners Shorts," *Velvet Light Trap* 8 (1973): 7–8.

42. Ibid., 8; WBA, *The Monroe Doctrine;* Birdwell, *Celluloid Soldiers,* 24–25.

43. Jack Warner to Stephen Early, 13 September 1939, FDRL OF 73, Motion Pictures; Jack Warner to Marvin McIntyre, 23 December 1938, FDRL OF 73, Motion Pictures; State Department memorandum, 2 October 1939, NARA RG59; Adolph Berle to Joseph Hazen, 7 October 1939, NARA RG59; Joseph Hazen to Adolph Berle, 19 October 1939, NARA RG59.

44. Richard Goldstone Oral History, AMPAS; Dalton, "Old Glory," 7–8.

45. Elizabeth Dalton, "Bugs and Daffy Go to War: Some Warners Cartoons of WWII," *Velvet Light Trap* 5 (spring 1972): 44; Birdwell, *Celluloid Soldiers,* 25.

Chapter Nine: A Fine Pickle

1. Frank Freidel, *Franklin D. Roosevelt: A Rendezvous with Destiny* (Boston: Little, Brown, 1990), 321–322; Robert A. Divine, *The Reluctant Belligerent: American Entry into World War II,* 2nd ed. (New York: Wiley, 1979), 69–75.

2. Herbert Hoover, "War in Europe: We Must Keep Out," 1 September 1939, reprinted in *Vital Speeches of the Day* 5 (15 September 1939): 736; William E. Borah, "Retain the Arms Embargo: It Helps Keep Us Out of War," 14 September 1939, reprinted in *Vital Speeches of the Day* 5 (1 October 1939): 741–743.

3. A. Scott Berg, *Lindbergh* (New York: G. P. Putnam's Sons, 1998), 384–408.

4. Wayne S. Cole, *America First: The Battle against Intervention, 1940–1941* (1953; reprint, New York: Octagon, 1971), 8; Justus D. Doenecke and John Wilz, *From Isolation to War: 1931–1941,* 2nd ed. (Arlington Heights, Ill.: Harlan Davidson, 1991), 4–10; John C. Fitzpatrick, ed., *The Writings of George Washington* (Washington, D.C.: Government Printing Office, 1940), 35:233–234.

5. A. Scott Berg, *Goldwyn: A Biography* (New York: Knopf, 1989), 337; Charles Higham, *Merchant of Dreams: Louis B. Mayer, M.G.M., and the Secret Hollywood* (New York: Donald I. Fine, 1993), 294; *New York Times,* 2 June 1940; *Hollywood Now,* 8 September 1939.

6. Douglas Fairbanks Jr., *The Salad Days* (New York: Doubleday, 1988), 342–343.

7. John Bright Oral History, UCLA DSC; Philip Dunne, *Take Two: A Life in Movies and Politics* (New York: Limelight, 1992), 111–112.

8. Larry Ceplair and Steven Englund, *The Inquisition in Hollywood: Politics in the Film Community, 1930–1960* (Garden City, N.Y.: Anchor, 1980), 155; August Raymond Ogden, *The Dies Committee: A Study of the Special House Committee for the Investigation of Un-American Activities, 1938–1944* (1945; reprint, Westport, Conn.: Greenwood Press, 1984), 125–127, 173–174; "Synopsis of Facts," 17 December 1940, FBI Hollywood Anti-Nazi League File, http://foia.fbi.gov/foiaindex/hollywoodleague.htm (accessed 9 October 2006); *Hollywood Now,* 11 August 1939.

9. Dunne, *Take Two,* 127; MPDC Bulletin, 22 February 1940, in Lib. of Cong., Thomas G. Corcoran Papers, b. 246, f. Motion Picture Democratic Committee, 1938–1940; *Hollywood Now,* 5 January 1940; Sauverio Giovacchini, *Hollywood Modernism: Film and Politics in the Age of the New Deal* (Philadelphia: Temple University Press, 2001), 120; Ronald Brownstein, *The Power and the Glitter: The Hollywood-Washington Connection* (New York: Vintage, 1992), 72.

10. Pandro Berman Oral History, WSHS, Pandro Berman Papers, b. 1, f. 3; *New York Times,* 18 January 1939; "War Hits Hollywood," *Business Week,* 3 February 1940, 49; *Variety,* 13 September 1939, 29 May 1940, 15 November 1939.

11. *Milwaukee Sentinel,* 14 September 1938; John Russell Taylor, *Strangers in Paradise: The Hollywood Émigrés, 1933–1950* (New York: Holt, Rinehart and Winston, 1983), 131; David Niven, *Bring on the Empty Horses* (New York: Dell, 1975), 137.

12. Taylor, *Strangers in Paradise,* 133.

13. Frank Daugherty, "Hollywood's Foreign Colony," *Christian Science Monitor,* 3 June 1936, 5; Niven, *Bring on the Empty Horses,* 184, 196–197; Dunne, *Take Two,* 18; Taylor, *Strangers in Paradise,* 132; John Selfridge, "Hollywood Crown Colony," *Scribner's Commentator* 9 (January 1941): 46. Selfridge estimated that British émigrés in Hollywood raised about $5 million between the invasion of Poland and the beginning of 1941.

14. 1940 *Film Daily Year Book,* 65, 1085–1087; *Around the World* 7, no. 3 [1939], WSHS, UA Records, Samuel Cohen Papers, b. 2; "War Hits Hollywood," *Business Week,* 3 February 1940, 49; Higham, *Merchant of Dreams,* 301; *New York Times,* 12 September 1939; *Variety,* 27 September 1939; Cordell Hull to Will Hays, 11 October 1939, WHP, reel 23.

15. Harry Warner to Franklin Roosevelt, 5 September 1939, FDRL OF 73, Motion Pictures; Memorandum, 6 September 1939, WHP, reel 23; Stephen Early to Edwin M. Watson, 6 September 1939, FDRL OF 73, Motion Pictures; Frank Murphy to Edwin M. Watson, 14 September 1939, FDRL OF 73, Motion Pic-

tures; Edwin M. Watson to Jack Warner, 19 September 1939, FDRL OF 73, Motion Pictures.

16. *Hollywood Citizen,* 5 September 1939; Will Hays to Harry Cohn, et al., 15 September 1939, MPAA, reel 5.

17. *Indianapolis Star,* 25 September 1939; "What America Thinks about the War . . . ," *Life,* 25 September 1939, 27.

18. United Artists press release, 15 September 1939, WSHS, UA Collection, Series 10D: News Releases and Bulletins, b. 2, f. 2; Gordon Sager, "Hollywood Carries On for Neville," *TAC: A Magazine of Theatre, Film, Radio, Music, Dance,* October 1939, 14; Bernard F. Dick, *The Star-Spangled Screen: The Hollywood World War II Film* (Lexington: University Press of Kentucky, 1985), 65.

19. PCA Analysis Chart, *Mr. Smith Goes to Washington,* 18 September 1939, PCA file, *Mr. Smith Goes to Washington.*

20. David Robinson, *Chaplin: His Life and Art* (New York: Da Capo, 1985), 496; Richard Rowland to Joseph Breen, 14 April 1939, PCA file, *The Man I Married;* "Synopsis of 'I Married a Nazi,'" 3 January 1939, UCLA ASC; Robert Lord to Joseph Breen, 11 August 1939, PCA file, *Underground;* Joseph Breen to Will Hays, 22 August 1939, PCA file, *Underground;* Joseph Breen to Jack Warner, 22 August 1939, PCA file, *Underground.*

21. *Variety,* 6 September 1939, 4 October 1939; "A Review of the Development and a Statement of the Industry Policy Relative to Propaganda and 'Hate Pictures,'" 22 April 1940, MPAA, reel 5.

22. *Nashville Banner,* 13 September 1939; Joseph Breen to Jason S. Joy, 26 April 1940, PCA file, *The Man I Married.*

Chapter Ten: A Winter of Discontent

1. Margaret Farrand Thorp, *America at the Movies* (New Haven, Conn.: Yale University Press, 1939), 16; *Variety,* 17 April 1940; John Steinbeck, *The Grapes of Wrath* (New York: Viking, 1939), 29.

2. Notes of Telephone Talk with Joseph Hazen, 14 July 1939, WHP, reel 23; Thurman Arnold to Austin Keough, et al., 16 August 1939, WHP, reel 23.

3. *Variety,* 14 June 1939, 16 August 1939, 30 August 1939, 4 October 1939; Paul Williams, "Memorandum for the Files re: Proposed Trade Practice Code," 17 August 1939, Justice Files; Memorandum, 6 September 1939, WHP, reel 23.

4. *Variety,* 30 August 1939, 6 September 1939; Frank Murphy to Harry Hopkins, 13 November 1939, Justice Files.

5. Will Hays to Franklin Roosevelt [October 1939], FDRL PPF 1944, Hays, Will H., 1934–1941; Franklin Roosevelt to Will Hays, 20 November 1939, Justice Files.

6. Al Block to Joseph Breen, 15 January 1938, PCA file, *Mr. Smith Goes to Washington;* Joseph Breen to John Hammell, 19 January 1938, PCA file, *Mr. Smith Goes to Washington;* Joseph Breen to Louis B. Mayer, 19 January 1938, PCA file, *Mr. Smith Goes to Washington;* Joseph Breen to Will Hays, 31 January 1939, PCA file, *Mr. Smith Goes to Washington.*

7. Joseph McBride, *Frank Capra: The Catastrophe of Success* (New York: Simon & Schuster, 1992), 419–420.

8. Ibid., 421.

9. *Indianapolis Star,* 31 October 1939; C. C. Pettijohn, "What Price Neely Bill," 14 December 1939, WHP, reel 24; D. P. to Will Hays, 22 March 1940, WHP, reel 24; *Variety,* 24 April 1940.

10. J. Holbrook Chapman to Cordell Hull, 29 July 1940, NARA RG59; Thomas Burke to Breckinridge Long, et al., 21 March 1940, NARA RG59; McBride, *Frank Capra,* 423; Joseph P. Kennedy to Will Hays, 12 November 1939, in Amanda Smith, ed., *Hostage to Fortune: The Letters of Joseph P. Kennedy* (New York: Viking, 2000), 400; Joseph P. Kennedy to Harry Cohn, 17 November 1939, in Smith, *Hostage to Fortune,* 400.

11. McBride, *Frank Capra,* 424; James B. Stewart to Cordell Hull, 30 January 1941, NARA RG59.

12. *Boston American,* 24 February 1940; "Synopsis of Facts," 17 December 1940, FBI Hollywood Anti-Nazi League File, http://foia.fbi.gov/foiaindex/holly woodleague.htm (accessed 9 October 2006).

13. Will Hays, memorandum, 10 November 1939, WHP, reel 23; Martin Dies, "The Reds in Hollywood," *Liberty,* 17 February 1940, 48; *Variety,* 14 February 1940.

14. *Memphis Press-Scimitar,* 16 February 1940; *Rushville (IL) Schuyler News,* 27 December 1939; *Boxoffice,* 24 February 1940; Otto Friedrich, *City of Nets: A Portrait of Hollywood in the 1940's* (New York: Harper & Row, 1986), 52.

15. *Variety,* 28 February 1940; *Springfield (MA) Evening Union,* 9 March 1940; Friedrich, *City of Nets,* 53; Dies, "The Reds in Hollywood," 48. Also see Martin Dies, "Is Communism Invading the Movies?" *Liberty,* 24 February 1940, 57–60.

16. *New York Times,* 18 July 1940, 15 August 1940, 21 August 1940, 25 August 1940, 28 August 1940.

17. *Variety,* 3 January 1940, 7 February 1940, 20 December 1939, 15 May 1940; Ian Jarvie, *Hollywood's Overseas Campaign: The North Atlantic Movie Trade, 1920–1950* (New York: Cambridge University Press, 1992), 183, 179.

18. Jarvie, *Hollywood's Overseas Campaign,* 186–189; Cordell Hull to Lord Lothian, memorandum of conversation, 22 January 1940, Hull Papers, reel 29.

19. *Variety,* 13 December 1939; "Text of Agreement," 21 November 1939, WHP, reel 23; Will Hays to Joseph Martin Jr., 19 February 1940, WHP, reel 24. Universal concluded a separate deal with the British, so only seven of the majors shared the $17.5 million distribution.

20. Joseph P. Kennedy Diary, 11 June 1940, in Smith, *Hostage to Fortune,* 438; Joseph P. Kennedy to Rose Kennedy, 2 October 1939, in Smith, *Hostage to Fortune,* 391; "Profit and Loss from Production and Distribution of American Made Pictures" [25 July 1941], MPAA, reel 6; "Study of Production and Distribution of American Made Pictures" [August 1941], MPAA, reel 6. In 1938 the major studios (excluding United Artists) took in $250,128,000 from worldwide rentals of features, shorts, and newsreels, against production and distribution expenses of $236,599,000. In 1940 they earned $238,889,000 against $241,300,000 in expenses. Net profits from Continental Europe fell from $10,039,000 in 1938 to $3,992,000 in 1940, while net profits from Great Britain and Ireland sank from $34,371,000 to $16,920,000.

21. *Variety,* 5 June 1940, 3 July 1940, 2 April 1941; *New York Times,* 2 June 1940, 26 May 1940.

22. *1940 Film Daily Year Book,* 1109; *Variety,* 30 July 1940.

23. Justus D. Doenecke and John E. Wilz, *From Isolation to War, 1931–1941,* 2nd ed. (Arlington Heights, Ill.: Harlan Davidson, 1991), 120–121; *Variety,* 2 August 1939.

24. *Variety,* 31 January 1940, 7 February 1940; "Mexico—Quota," 16 October 1939, Black Books, b. 3, f. 2.

25. *Variety,* 20 March 1940.

26. Although the movie never says who is responsible for this conspiracy and never shows or names its non-Hispanic perpetrators, one publicity poster for *South of the Border* read, "Skulking Japanese Murderers Plan a Sneak Invasion of Mexico!"

27. Joseph Breen to M. J. Siegel, 18 October 1939, PCA file, *South of the Border.*

28. "Synopsis of 'Bolivar'" [1940], WSHS, Dore Schary Papers, b. 126, f. 3.

29. "'Simon Bolivar' (Conference Notes)," 10 April 1940, 12 April 1940, WSHS, Dore Schary Papers, b. 126, f. 3; State Department memorandum, 12 April 1940, NARA RG59.

30. "'Simon Bolivar' (Conference Notes)," 9 April 1940, WSHS, Dore Schary Papers, b. 126, f. 3; Henry Blanke Oral History, UCLA DSC.

31. *New York Times,* 26 May 1940.

32. *Variety,* 10 January 1940, 17 January 1940, 13 December 1939; Department of Justice memorandum, 13 January 1940, Justice Files; Department of

Commerce, memorandum on the motion picture industry [4 January 1940], Justice Files; Will H. Hays, "The Motion Picture in a Changing World: Annual Report to the Motion Picture Producers and Distributors of America, Inc, March 25, 1940," WHP, reel 24; Department of Justice memorandum, 15 January 1940, Justice Files; "Commerce Department Proposal for a Consent Decree," 9 March 1940, Hopkins Papers, b. 117, f. Motion Pictures.

33. E. A. Tupper to Harry Hopkins, 4 April 1940, Hopkins Papers, b. 117, f. Motion Pictures; Alan Brinkley, *The End of Reform: New Deal Liberalism in Recession and War* (New York: Vintage, 1995), 117–136.

34. Copy of Neely bill, 9 April 1940, Hopkins Papers, b. 117, f. Motion Pictures; "Telephone Conversation with Russell Hardy from Washington," 20 April 1940, WHP, reel 24; *Variety,* 24 April 1940.

35. Jack Bryson to Will Hays, 23 May 1940, WHP, reel 25; Will Hays to E. C. Pulliam, 21 May 1940, WHP, reel 25; Jack Bryson to Will Hays, 18 May 1940, WHP, reel 25.

36. "Developments" [May 1940?], WHP, reel 25.

Chapter Eleven: Leading the Way

1. Darryl F. Zanuck to All Producers, 11 April 1940, in Rudy Behlmer, *Memo from Darryl F. Zanuck: The Golden Years at Twentieth Century–Fox* (New York: Grove, 1993), 39.

2. Robert Divine, *The Reluctant Belligerent: American Entry into World War II,* 2nd ed. (New York: Wiley, 1979), 80.

3. Franz Hoellering, "Films," *Nation,* 14 October 1939, 422; Otis Ferguson, "Three for the Show," *New Republic,* 18 October 1939, 301.

4. Hal Wallis to All Departments, 12 September 1939, WBA, *Murder in the Air.*

5. Erich von Stroheim played the Karloff role in a 1930 version of *British Intelligence* entitled *Three Faces East,* itself a remake of a 1926 silent film of the same title. Clive Brook played the Karloff/von Stroheim part in that picture.

6. "Warner Bros. Pictures, Inc./Comparison of Negative Costs and Gross Income on Productions (Gross Income to August 31, 1944)," William Schaefer Collection, USC Cinematic Arts Library.

7. "Vital Statistics—'The Fighting 69th'" [1940], WBA, *The Fighting 69th;* Jack Warner to Joseph Schenck, 20 September 1939, WBA, *The Fighting 69th.*

8. R. J. Obringer to Gradwell Sears, 15 August 1939, WBA, *The Fighting 69th;* Norman Reilly Paine to Hal Wallis, 30 August 1939, WBA, *The Fighting 69th;* John Hurley to Twentieth Century–Fox Film Corp. [August 1939], WBA,

The Fighting 69th; Will Hays to Jack Warner, 11 August 1939, WBA, The Fighting 69th; "Assignment" [7 November 1940], WBA, The Fighting 69th.

9. Norman Reilly Raine, "Outline of Father Duffy of the Fighting Sixty-Ninth," 27 July 1939, WBA, The Fighting 69th.

10. R. G. Mensing to Warner Bros. Studios, 28 May 1940, WBA, The Fighting 69th.

11. Jack Warner to Bryan Foy, 25 January 1940, WBA, The Fighting 69th; Jack Warner to Stephen Early, 4 January 1940, FDRL OF 73, Motion Pictures; Robert Sklar, City Boys: Cagney, Bogart, Garfield (Princeton, N.J.: Princeton University Press, 1992), 99.

12. Gerhard L. Weinberg, A World at Arms: A Global History of World War II (New York: Cambridge University Press, 1994), 154, 68–112.

13. Ibid., 113–121; Robert Dallek, Franklin D. Roosevelt and American Foreign Policy, 1932–1945 (New York: Oxford University Press, 1979), 219.

14. Weinberg, A World at Arms, 122–131; Winston Churchill, The Second World War: Their Finest Hour (Boston: Houghton Mifflin, 1949), 242–243.

15. Dallek, Franklin D. Roosevelt and American Foreign Policy, 221–223; Divine, The Reluctant Belligerent, 90.

16. Wayne S. Cole, America First: The Battle against Intervention, 1940–1941 (1953; reprint; New York: Octagon, 1971), 6–7.

17. Dallek, Franklin D. Roosevelt and American Foreign Policy, 226.

18. Jack and Harry Warner to Franklin Roosevelt, 20 May 1940, FDRL PPF 1050, Warner Brothers Motion Picture Company.

19. "Speech Given by President Roosevelt to Congress on May 26, 1940," JLW, Harry Warner Material, f. Franklin D. Roosevelt.

20. Variety, 29 May 1940.

21. Cliff Work to Harry Warner, 28 May 1940, JLW, Harry Warner Material, f. June 5th Meeting.

22. Quotes in this paragraph and the following three are taken from the Los Angeles Examiner, 6 June 1940, Variety, 12 June 1940; and Motion Picture Daily, 6 June 1940.

23. Michael Birdwell, Celluloid Soldiers: The Warner Bros. Campaign against Nazism (New York: New York University Press, 1999), 83.

Chapter Twelve: The Pivotal Month

1. Robert Rhodes James, ed., Winston S. Churchill: His Complete Speeches, 1897–1963 (New York: Bowker, 1974), 6:6231.

2. Robert Dallek, *Franklin D. Roosevelt and American Foreign Policy, 1932–1945* (New York: Oxford University Press, 1979), 228; Frederick Herron to Will Hays, 26 February 1940, WHP, reel 24; Enrico Galeazzi to James Dusmet, 1 May 1940, WHP, reel 25. David O. Selznick broke Hollywood's blockade on Italy in early 1941 when he sold distribution rights for *Rebecca* and *Intermezzo* for $30,000. Italy took the symbolic step of banning the importation of American films in April 1941. See *New York Times,* 9 February 1941, 5 April 1941.

3. Justus D. Doenecke and John E. Wilz, *From Isolation to War, 1931–1941,* 2nd ed. (Arlington Heights, Ill.: Harlan Davidson, 1991), 90; Dallek, *Franklin D. Roosevelt and American Foreign Policy,* 233–235, 243; Edward Mead Earle, "Hitler and Our Future," *Ladies' Home Journal,* September 1940, 46.

4. Jens Ulff-Møller, *Hollywood's Film Wars with France: Film-Trade Diplomacy and the Emergence of the French Film Quota Policy* (Rochester, N.Y.: University of Rochester Press, 2001), 135; *Variety,* 19 June 1940, 5 June 1940.

5. *The 1941 Film Daily Year Book,* 57; Will H. Hays, "The Motion Picture in a Changing World: Annual Report to the Motion Picture Producers and Distributors of America, Inc., March 25, 1940," 3.

6. Robert Divine, *The Reluctant Belligerent: American Entry into World War II,* 2nd ed. (New York: Wiley, 1979), 92–93; Dallek, *Franklin D. Roosevelt and American Foreign Policy,* 243.

7. *Variety,* 17 July 1940; John Selfridge, "Hollywood Crown Colony," *Scribner's Commentator* 9 (January 1941): 46.

8. *1941 Film Daily Yearbook,* 704.

9. Nathan Levinson Testimony, 1 December 1942, in David Culbert, ed., *Film and Propaganda in America: A Documentary History,* vol. 2, *World War II* (Westport, Conn.: Greenwood Press, 1990), 223–240.

10. Milton Sperling Testimony, 18 December 1942, in Culbert, *Film and Propaganda in America,* 2:252–253.

11. Nathan Levinson Testimony, 1 December 1942, in Culbert, *Film and Propaganda in America,* 2:223, 232–233, 237.

12. Walter Wanger to E. S. Adams, 29 May 1940, WWP, b. 31, f. 3.

13. Sidney Kent to Walter Wanger, 3 June 1940, 5 June 1940, WWP, b. 31, f. 3; *Variety,* 12 June 1940.

14. *1941 Film Daily Year Book,* 703; *Variety,* 12 June 1940.

15. Richard W. Steele, "The Great Debate: Roosevelt, the Media, and the Coming of the War, 1940–1941," *Journal of American History* 71 (June 1984): 74; Thomas Doherty, *Projections of War: Hollywood, American Culture, and*

World War II, rev. ed. (New York: Columbia University Press, 1993), 39, 322.

16. *Variety,* 12 June 1940; Raymond Fielding, *The March of Time, 1935–1951* (New York: Oxford University Press, 1978), 252; State Department, "Memorandum Summarizing Cooperation of American Motion Picture Industry with U.S. Treasury Department in War Activities, April 1941–May 1942" [1942], NARA RG59.

17. *New York Journal and American,* 9 August 1940; *Variety,* 19 June 1940; *The 1941 Film Daily Year Book,* 703.

18. *Pittsburgh Press,* 11 August 1940; *Variety,* 22 May 1940, 5 June 1940, 3 July 1940; *New York Times,* 2 June 1940.

19. *Variety,* 5 June 1940.

20. "Notes on Telephone Call," 7 June 1940, WHP, reel 25; *Film Daily,* 14 June 1940; *San Francisco News,* 18 June 1940.

21. The *Paramount* case was later renewed, resulting in the studios' losing their theaters in 1948.

22. Georg Gyssling to Joseph Breen, 25 March 1937, PCA file, *The Road Back;* Hollywood Anti-Nazi League to Cordell Hull, 8 April 1937, NARA RG59; James Clement Dunn to Frederick Herron, 12 June 1937, NARA RG59; Joseph Breen to Louis B. Mayer, 22 January 1938, 27 January 1938, PCA file, *Three Comrades; Variety,* 29 June 1937; *New York Times,* 18 June 1937; Scott Eyman, *Lion of Hollywood: The Life and Legend of Louis B. Mayer* (New York: Simon & Schuster, 2005), 277.

23. Edward G. Robinson, *All My Yesterdays: An Autobiography* (New York: Hawthorn, 1973), 193; Pandro Berman Oral History, 4 August 1972, WSHS, Pandro Berman Papers, b. 1, f. 3; Anita Loos, *Kiss Hollywood Good-By* (New York: Viking, 1974), 117; "Loew's Inc.," *Fortune,* August 1939, 105; Charles Higham, *Merchant of Dreams: Louis B. Mayer, M.G.M., and the Secret Hollywood* (New York: Donald I. Fine, 1993), 298.

24. Eyman, *Lion of Hollywood,* 277–278.

25. William J. Fadiman Oral History, UCLA DSC.

26. Synopsis of *The Mortal Storm,* 17 February 1939, MGM Collection, USC Cinematic Arts Library, b. 128; *Variety,* 12 June 1940.

27. Eyman, *Lion of Hollywood,* 277–279.

28. Phyllis Bottome to Sidney Franklin, 7 February 1940, USC MGM Collection, b. 128; Dr. Edgar Magnin to Victor Saville, 29 May 1940, USC MGM Collection, b. 128.

29. Howard Strickling to Victor Saville, 5 June 1940, USC MGM Collection, b. 128.

30. Hal Wallis and Charles Higham, *Starmaker: The Autobiography of Hal Wallis* (New York: Macmillan, 1980), 65; Robinson, *All My Yesterdays,* 210–211.

31. Frank Whitbeck to Howard Dietz, 22 July 1940, USC MGM Collection, b. 128; Hans Thomsen to Cordell Hull, 16 July 1940, NARA RG59; Frederick Herron to Henry F. Grady, 29 July 1940, NARA RG59; Thomas Decker, "Movies to Sell the Reich," *Nation,* 5 July 1941, 14; *New York Times,* 8 September 1940.

32. MPPDA Censorship Files, PCA file, *The Mortal Storm;* Howard Strickling to Victor Saville, 5 June 1940, USC MGM Collection, b. 128.

33. *New York Times,* 23 June 1940.

34. Eyman, *Lion of Hollywood,* 279.

Chapter Thirteen: Zanuck Makes His Stand

1. Leonard Mosley, *Zanuck: The Rise and Fall of Hollywood's Last Tycoon* (Boston: Little, Brown, 1984), 169; Pat McGilligan, ed., *Backstory: Interviews with Screenwriters of Hollywood's Golden Age* (Berkeley: University of California Press, 1986), 309; George F. Custen, *Twentieth Century's Fox: Darryl F. Zanuck and the Culture of Hollywood* (New York: Basic Books, 1997), 16, 75.

2. Darryl F. Zanuck to All "A" Directors and Producers, 4 June 1941, in Rudy Behlmer, *Memo from Darryl F. Zanuck: The Golden Years at Twentieth Century–Fox* (New York: Grove, 1993), 55; Nunnally Johnson Oral History, UCLA DSC.

3. Mosley, *Zanuck,* 195, 188.

4. Custen, *Twentieth Century's Fox,* 14, 25–38.

5. Ibid., 172–177, 193–196.

6. "Darryl Zanuck," *Life,* 14 April 1941, 97, 99; Mosley, *Zanuck,* 172–173.

7. Mosley, *Zanuck,* 176.

8. "Darryl Zanuck," 103; Custen, *Twentieth Century's Fox,* 245–246.

9. Mosley, *Zanuck,* 177–178; John Bright Oral History, UCLA DSC.

10. Mosley, *Zanuck,* 187, 189.

11. Bernard F. Dick, *The Star-Spangled Screen: The Hollywood World War II Film* (Lexington: University Press of Kentucky, 1985), 75.

12. Conference Notes with DFZ, 24 October 1939, USC Fox, *Four Sons.*

13. Aidan Roark to Darryl F. Zanuck, 14 November 1939, USC Fox, *Four Sons;* Mosley, *Zanuck,* 184; Conference Notes with DFZ, 16 November 1939, USC Fox, *Four Sons.*

14. Conference Notes with DFZ, 19 February 1940, USC Fox, *Four Sons.*

15. Julian Johnson to Darryl F. Zanuck, 19 February 1940, USC Fox, *Four Sons*.

16. Philip T. Hartung, "And All the Men and Women Merely Players," *Commonweal* 32 (21 June 1940): 92.

17. Oliver H. P. Garrett to Raymond Griffith, 17 February 1940, USC Fox, *The Man I Married*; Conference Notes with Darryl F. Zanuck, 17 April 1940, USC Fox, *The Man I Married*.

18. Allen Rostron, "No War, No Hate, No Propaganda: Promoting Films about European War and Fascism during the Period of American Isolationism," *Journal of Popular Film and Television* 30 (summer 2002): 93.

19. *Film Daily*, 16 July 1940; *Variety*, 17 July 1940; *Hollywood Reporter*, 15 July 1940.

20. "A Review of the Development and a Statement of the Industry Policy Relative to Propaganda and 'Hate Pictures,' " 22 April 1940, MPAA, reel 5.

Chapter Fourteen: Searching for a Voice

1. *Motion Picture Herald*, 27 July 1940; *Variety*, 11 September 1940, 18 September 1940, 1 January 1941.

2. *Variety*, 31 July 1940; Robert Wilson to Norman Armour, 15 July 1940, Confidential State Department Central Files: Argentina, Internal Affairs, 1940–44, NARA RG59; Norman Armour to Cordell Hull, 17 July 1940, Confidential State Department Central Files: Argentina.

3. Walter Wanger, "The Role of the Motion Picture in Inter-American Understanding," WWP, b. 36, f. 20; *Variety*, 6 November 1940.

4. *Camden (NJ) Evening Courier*, 6 May 1941.

5. *Motion Picture Herald*, 10 May 1941, 28 September 1941.

6. *Variety*, 2 October 1940; *Hollywood Reporter*, 2 October 1940; *Los Angeles Examiner*, 17 July 1941; Jason Joy to Joseph Breen, 31 May 1940, PCA file, *Down Argentine Way*.

7. Raymond Fielding, *The March of Time, 1935–1951* (New York: Oxford University Press, 1978), 244–250; John Ford to Dudley Nichols, 17 December 1940, John Ford Papers, Indiana University, b. 1, Lilly Library.

8. In a neat piece of visual imagery Jones accidentally breaks part of a neon sign outside of the Hotel Europe. The sign now reads "Hot Europe."

9. Nicholas John Cull, *Selling War: The British Propaganda Campaign against American "Neutrality" in World War II* (New York: Oxford University Press, 1995), 111–112.

10. "The Sea Hawk, Suggested Story Treatment," WSHS, Howard Koch Papers, b. 3, f. 4; *New York Mirror*, 10 August 1940.

11. *The Sea Hawk* Publicity File, WBA, *The Sea Hawk; New York Evening News,* 2 August 1940; *New York Times,* 10 August 1940.

12. H. S. Haislip to Commander Joseph B. Lynch, 14 February 1940, USC MGM Collection, *Flight Command,* b. 268; H. S. Haislip to Commander L. P. Lovette, 14 February 1940, USC MGM Collection, *Flight Command,* b. 268; Otis Ferguson, "Two-on-the-Same-Screen Department," *New Republic,* 3 March 1941, 307.

13. *Variety,* 31 October 1940.

14. "Foreign News Flashes," 14 September 1940, WSHS, UA Records, Samuel Cohen Papers, b. 8.

15. Walter W. McKenna to Robert R. Reynolds, 17 February 1939, PCA file, *The Great Dictator; New York Times,* 26 May 1940.

16. "Foreign News Flashes," 29 August 1940, WSHS, UA Records, Samuel Cohen Records, b. 8; Joseph Breen to Al Reeves, 6 September 1940, PCA file, *The Great Dictator.*

17. David Robinson, *Chaplin: His Life and Art* (New York: Da Capo, 1985), 505–507; Charles Chaplin, *My Autobiography* (New York: Simon & Schuster, 1964), 398; *New York Times,* 16 October 1940; "Foreign News Flashes," 15 October 1940, WSHS, UA Records, Samuel Cohen Papers, b. 8; Charles J. Maland, *Chaplin and American Culture* (Princeton, N.J.: Princeton University Press, 1989), 169.

18. "Films," *Nation,* 26 October 1940, 401; *Indianapolis Star,* 1 November 1940; "New Picture," *Time,* 4 November 1940, 76.

19. "The Great Dictator Overseas," *Living Age,* March 1941, 53.

20. John O'Hara, "Charlie, Charley," *Newsweek,* 28 October 1940, 60; Philip T. Hartung, "That Funny Little Man Again," *Commonweal* 33 (8 November 1940): 80; Otis Ferguson, "Less Time for Comedy," *New Republic,* 4 November 1940, 629.

21. Maland, *Chaplin and American Culture,* 178; "The Great Dictator Overseas," *Living Age,* March 1941, 53; MPPDA Censorship Reports, PCA file, *The Great Dictator; Around the World* 8, no. 4 [1940], WSHS, UA Records, Samuel Cohen Papers, b. 2.

22. Chaplin, *My Autobiography,* 405.

Chapter Fifteen: Closing the Ring

1. Robert Dallek, *Franklin D. Roosevelt and American Foreign Policy, 1932–1945* (New York: Oxford University Press, 1979), 243–247; Robert Rhodes James, ed., *Winston S. Churchill: His Complete Speeches, 1899–1963* (New York: Bowker, 1974), 6:6268.

2. Wayne S. Cole, *America First: The Battle against Intervention, 1940–1941* (1953; reprint, New York: Octagon, 1971), 10–17.

3. Ibid., 14–37.

4. Dallek, *Franklin D. Roosevelt and American Foreign Policy*, 248–249; Justus D. Doenecke and John E. Wilz, *From Isolation to War, 1931–1941,* 2nd ed. (Arlington Heights, Ill.: Harlan Davidson, 1991), 90–91.

5. "Synopsis of Facts," 17 December 1940, FBI Hollywood Anti-Nazi League file, http://foia.fbi.gov/foiaindex/hollywoodleague.htm (accessed 9 October 2006).

6. Ibid.

7. Ibid.

8. Ibid.; Patrick McGilligan and Paul Buhle, eds., *Tender Comrades: A Backstory of the Hollywood Blacklist* (New York: St. Martin's, 1997), 108.

9. *Variety,* 26 June 1940, 17 July 1940, 7 August 1940, 14 August 1940; R. E. Martin to Robert Jackson, 19 August 1940, Justice Files, b. 89.

10. *Variety,* 4 September 1940, 23 October 1940; William F. Whitman, "The Consent Decree in the Moving Picture Industry," *Fordham Law Review* 10 (January 1941): 67–71.

11. *Variety,* 30 October 1940; Jack Warner to Franklin Roosevelt, 25 November 1940, FDRL OF 73, Motion Pictures.

12. Richard W. Steele, "The Great Debate: Roosevelt, the Media, and the Coming of the War, 1940–1941," *Journal of American History* 71 (June 1984): 74–75; Diary of Adolph Berle, 27 August 1940, FDRL; Adolph Berle to Franklin Roosevelt, 28 August 1940, FDRL OF 73, Motion Pictures; W. S. Van Dyke to Stephen Early, 17 October 1940, FDRL OF 73, Motion Pictures; Missy LeHand to W. S. Van Dyke, 9 November 1940, FDRL OF 73, Motion Pictures.

13. "March On, Marines" script, 23 July 1940, WBA, "March On, Marines"; "Daily Production and Progress Report" [September 1940], WBA, "Anchors Aweigh"; May Ronsaville to William L. Guthrie, 25 July 1940, WBA, "Meet the Fleet"; Jack Warner to Brigadier General W. V. Carter, 21 April 1941, WBA, "Wings of Steel."

14. Hollywood for Roosevelt Committee circular letter [summer 1940], Douglas Papers, b. 11, f. 3; Hollywood for Roosevelt memorandum, [December 1940], FDRL PPF 7024, Hollywood for Roosevelt Committee; *Los Angeles Times,* 25 September 1940.

15. Melvyn Douglas, "Report to the Executive Board of the Motion Picture Democratic Committee," 18 December 1939, Douglas Papers, b. 15, f. 3; Melvyn Douglas to Franklin Roosevelt, 5 August 1940, Douglas Papers, b. 11, f. 3; Ronald Brownstein, *The Power and the Glitter: The Hollywood-Washington Connection*

(New York: Vintage, 1992), 83; Melvyn Douglas Speech [1940], Douglas Papers, b. 10, f. 5.

16. Watterson Rothacker to Will Hays, 1 October 1940, WHP, reel 26; Will Hays, memorandum, 30 October 1940, WHP, reel 26; *Los Angeles Times*, 30 October 1940; Walter Wanger to Mendel Silberberg, 9 September 1940, WWP, b. 22, f. 3.

17. *Film Daily*, 6 November 1940; Douglas Fairbanks Jr. to Franklin Roosevelt, FDRL PPF 7130, Fairbanks, Jr., Douglas; Will Hays to Franklin Roosevelt [November 1940], FDRL PPF 1944, Hays, Will H., 1934–1941; Jack Warner to Franklin Roosevelt, 22 January 1941, FDRL PPF 1050, Warner Brothers Motion Picture Company; *Variety*, 5 February 1941.

18. Douglas Fairbanks Jr., *The Salad Days* (New York: Doubleday, 1988), 367–368; Transcript of speech, 18 September 1940, FDRL OF 4269, Fairbanks, Jr., Douglas, 1940–1944.

19. Fairbanks, *The Salad Days*, 366; Douglas Fairbanks Jr. to Stephen Early, 27 May 1940, FDRL OF 73, Motion Pictures; Stephen Early to Douglas Fairbanks Jr., 1 June 1940, FDRL OF 73, Motion Pictures.

20. Fairbanks, *The Salad Days*, 53, 292–300, 363–366, 371; Douglas Fairbanks Jr. to Franklin Roosevelt, 11 October 1940, FDRL OF 4269, Fairbanks, Jr., Douglas, 1940–1944; Douglas Fairbanks Jr. to Franklin Roosevelt, 31 January 1941, FDRL PPF 7130, Fairbanks, Jr., Douglas.

21. Joseph Kennedy to Cordell Hull, 8 October 1940, NARA RG59.

22. Will Hays to Cordell Hull, 10 October 1940, NARA RG59; *Variety*, 9 October 1940; Will H. Hays, "Motion Pictures and Total Defense, MPPDA Annual Report, 31 March 1941," 19; Ian Jarvie, "Dollars and Ideology: Will Hays' Economic Foreign Policy, 1922–1945," *Film History* 2 (1988): 189–190; *Variety*, 9 October 1940, 1 January 1941; *1941 Film Daily Year Book*, 989; Memorandum, 9 January 1941, WHP, reel 27.

23. *Variety*, 15 January 1941; *1941 Film Daily Year Book*, 57.

24. Joseph Kennedy to Harry Warner, 7 November 1940, WHP, reel 27; A. Scott Berg, *Goldwyn: A Biography* (New York: Knopf, 1989), 346; Michael Birdwell, *Celluloid Soldiers: The Warner Bros. Campaign against Nazism* (New York: New York University Press, 1999), 86.

25. Joseph P. Kennedy to Arthur Houghton, 21 December 1940, in Amanda Smith, ed., *Hostage to Fortune: The Letters of Joseph P. Kennedy* (New York: Viking, 2001), 507.

26. M. E. Gillette, Verbatim Testimony, 19–20 January 1943, in David Culbert, ed., *Film and Propaganda in America: A Documentary History*, vol. 2, *World War II* (Westport, Conn.: Greenwood Press, 1990), 385, 393; "Hearings

before a Special Committee Investigating the National Defense Program," in Culbert, *Film and Propaganda in America*, 2:106; "Final Report, John H. Amen and Thomas S. Hinkel to the Inspector General," in Culbert, *Film and Propaganda in America*, 2:125.

27. *1942 Film Daily Year Book*, 45; "Final Report," 125; Nathan Levinson Testimony, 1 December 1942, in Culbert, *Film and Propaganda in America*, 2:225; Verbatim Testimony, Darryl F. Zanuck, 4–5 January 1943, in Culbert, *Film and Propaganda in America*, 2:323, 302.

28. John Amen to Franklin Babcock, 21 December 1942, in Culbert, *Film and Propaganda in America*, 2:85; "Hearings before a Special Committee Investigating the National Defense Program," 103, 107; George F. Custen, *Twentieth Century's Fox: Darryl F. Zanuck and the Culture of Hollywood* (New York: Basic Books, 1997), 257.

29. "Final Report," 126; Verbatim Testimony, Paul A. Bray, 18 January 1943, in Culbert, *Film and Propaganda in America*, 2:179.

30. Dallek, *Franklin D. Roosevelt and American Foreign Policy*, 252–255.

31. Ibid., 256–257.

32. Doenecke and Wilz, *From Isolation to War*, 103; Cole, *America First*, 42–49; Burton S. Wheeler, "Don't Surrender Our Independence to War-Mongers and Interventionists," reprinted in *Vital Speeches of the Day* 7 (15 January 1941): 204.

33. Louis B. Mayer to Franklin Roosevelt [January 1941], FDRL PPF 5202, Mayer, Louis B.; Harry and Jack Warner to Franklin Roosevelt, 6 January 1941, FDRL PPF 1050, Warner Brothers Motion Picture Company; Darryl Zanuck to Stephen Early, 18 January 1941, FDRL, Papers of Stephen T. Early, b. 22, f. Z—Miscellaneous; *Variety*, 12 February 1941; *1941 Film Daily Year Book*, 57.

34. "What's My Name?" 26 October 1940, WHP, reel 26; State Department memorandum, 26 March 1941, NARA RG59; Ian Jarvie, *Hollywood's Overseas Campaign: The North Atlantic Movie Trade, 1920–1950* (New York: Cambridge University Press, 1992), 356.

Chapter Sixteen: Weapons of Inspiration

1. Clayton R. Koppes and Gregory D. Black, *Hollywood Goes to War: How Politics, Profits, and Propaganda Shaped World War II Movies* (Berkeley: University of California Press, 1990), 20; Richard W. Steele, "The Great Debate: Roosevelt, the Media, and the Coming of the War, 1940–1941," *Journal of American History* 71 (June 1984): 69–92.

2. Burton Wheeler to Will Hays, 13 January 1941, FDRL PPF 1944, Hays, Will H., 1934–1941; *Motion Picture Herald,* 25 January 1941; *Variety,* 26 February 1941.

3. Will Hays to Burton Wheeler, 14 January 1941, FDRL PPF 1944, Hays, Will H., 1934–1941; Franklin Roosevelt to Will Hays, 22 January 1941, FDRL PPF 1944, Hays, Will H., 1934–1941.

4. Charles Lindbergh, "Strength and Peace," reprinted in *Vital Speeches of the Day* 7 (1 November 1940): 42; Burton K. Wheeler, "America's Present Emergency," reprinted in *Vital Speeches of the Day* 7 (15 January 1941): 203–205.

5. "The Eagle Squadron, Story Outline Dictated by Mr. Zanuck," 25 October 1940, UCLA ASC, *A Yank in the R.A.F.*

6. Robert Bassler to Darryl F. Zanuck, 28 October 1940, USC Fox, *A Yank in the R.A.F.;* Treatment for "The Eagle Flies Again," 5 November 1940, USC Fox, *A Yank in the R.A.F.*

7. Conference notes with Darryl F. Zanuck, 13–14 January 1941, USC Fox, *A Yank in the R.A.F.;* Conference notes with Darryl F. Zanuck, 25 November 1940, USC Fox, *A Yank in the R.A.F.*

8. Conference notes with Darryl F. Zanuck, 13–14 January 1941, UCLA ASC, *A Yank in the R.A.F.;* Conference notes with Darryl F. Zanuck, 31 January 1941, UCLA ASC, *A Yank in the R.A.F.*

9. Darryl F. Zanuck to the Air Ministry, 16 January 1941, UCLA ASC, *A Yank in the R.A.F.;* Darryl F. Zanuck to Hal Wallis, 3 March 1941, WBA, *International Squadron;* Conference notes with Darryl F. Zanuck, 22 and 24 February 1941, UCLA ASC, *A Yank in the R.A.F.;* Leonard Mosley, *Zanuck: The Rise and Fall of Hollywood's Last Tycoon* (Boston: Little, Brown, 1984), 196.

10. Michael Birdwell, *Celluloid Soldiers: The Warner Bros. Campaign against Nazism* (New York: New York University Press, 1999), 87–88.

11. Jesse L. Lasky, *I Blow My Own Horn* (Garden City, N.Y.: Doubleday, 1957), 252–253.

12. Birdwell, *Celluloid Soldiers,* 89–100.

13. Ibid., 102–105; Lasky, *I Blow My Own Horn,* 254–257.

14. Lasky, *I Blow My Own Horn,* 256; A. Scott Berg, *Goldwyn: A Biography* (New York: Knopf, 1989), 357; Birdwell, *Celluloid Soldiers,* 108; Hal Wallis to Jesse Lasky, 3 January 1941, WBA, *Sgt. York.*

15. Julien Josephson and Harry Chandlee to Jesse Lasky, 8 May 1940, WBA, *Sgt. York;* Bob Buckner to Hal Wallis, 4 June 1940, WBA, *Sgt. York.*

16. Birdwell, *Celluloid Soldiers,* 117–124.

17. "Of Mars and the Film," *Commonweal* 34 (20 June 1941): 208.

18. *Motion Picture Herald,* 1 February 1941.

19. Ibid., 8 March 1941.

20. *New York Times,* 16 March 1941.

21. *Variety,* 8 October 1941; Jefferson Caffery to Cordell Hull, 31 October 1941, Records of the State Department, Internal Affairs, Brazil, 1940–44, NARA RG59; Carl Milliken to Francis Colt deWolf, 14 November 1941, Records of the State Department, Internal Affairs, Brazil, 1940–44, NARA RG59.

22. Lowell Mellett to Franklin Roosevelt, 23 December 1940, FDRL PPF 7410, AMPAS; Lowell Mellett to Walter Wanger, 4 January 1941, WWP, b. 1, f. 10; Walter Wanger to Lowell Mellett, 8 January 1941, WWP, b. 1, f. 10; Walter Wanger to Stephen Early, 4 February 1941, FDRL PPF 7410, AMPAS.

23. Walter Wanger to Stephen Early, 4 February 1941, WWP, b. 1, f. 10; Walter Wanger to George C. Marshall, 4 February 1941, WWP, b. 12, f. 15; George C. Marshall to Lowell Mellett, 24 February 1941, WSHS, WWP, b. 12, f. 15.

24. Text of speech, 27 February 1941, FDRL PPF 210, Motion Pictures.

25. Walter Wanger speech [27 February 1941], WWP, b. 1, f. 10.

26. Red Kann to Walter Wanger, 28 February 1941, WWP, b. 11, f. 5; Frank Capra to Franklin Roosevelt, 28 February 1941, FDRL OF 73, Motion Pictures; Madeleine Carroll to Franklin Roosevelt, 1 March 1941, FDRL OF 73, Motion Pictures; Jane Murfin to Franklin Roosevelt, 1 March 1941, FDRL OF 73, Motion Pictures.

Chapter Seventeen: Three Continents—Spring 1941

1. David O. Selznick to Franklin Roosevelt, 3 March 1941, FDRL OF 73, Motion Pictures; *Variety,* 18 June 1941.

2. Anthony Bower, "Films," *Nation,* 15 February 1941, 193; "Latin Uproar," *Time,* 10 February 1941, 69; "North American Movies in Brazil," 23 December 1942, AMPAS, MPSA, Reports; *New York Times,* 12 January 1941, 8 January 1941, 6 July 1941; *Variety,* 9 April 1941, 25 June 1941.

3. *Motion Picture Herald,* 8 March 1941; *Variety,* 19 March 1941.

4. *Hollywood Reporter,* 20 February 1941, 21 February 1941, 24 February 1941.

5. Charles A. Thomson, "The Cultural Relations Program of the Department of State," *Journal of Educational Sociology* 16 (November 1942): 135; Darlene Rivas, *Missionary Capitalist: Nelson Rockefeller in Venezuela* (Chapel Hill: University of North Carolina Press, 2002), 44.

6. Rivas, *Missionary Capitalist,* 34–41.

7. Ibid., 45.

8. *Daily Variety,* 15 January 1941.

9. *Variety,* 22 January 1941, 19 February 1941, 9 April 1941; *History of the Office of the Coordinator of Inter-American Affairs* (Washington, D.C.: Government Printing Office, 1947), 72.

10. Walter Wanger, "Motion Pictures: An Avenue of Pan-American Understanding," 16 January 1941, WWP, b. 36, f. 25.

11. *Motion Picture Herald,* 29 March 1941; *Variety,* 19 February 1941; *History of the Office of the Coordinator of Inter-American Affairs,* 72; "The Story of the Motion Picture Society for the Americas," n.d., AMPAS MPSA—Reports.

12. "The Story of the Motion Picture Society for the Americas," n.d., AMPAS MPSA, Reports; *Variety,* 21 May 1941.

13. *Variety,* 19 February 1941.

14. *New York World-Telegram,* 18 April 1941; *Variety,* 5 March 1941; "The Story of the Motion Picture Society for the Americas," n.d., AMPAS MPSA, Reports; *Movie-Radio Guide,* 17 May 1941.

15. Sumner Welles to Franklin Roosevelt, 24 January 1941, FDRL OF 4269, Fairbanks, Jr., Douglas, 1940–1944; Sumner Welles to Franklin Roosevelt, 11 April 1941, FDRL OF 4269, Fairbanks, Jr., Douglas, 1940–1944; Fairbanks, *The Salad Days,* 381–383.

16. Douglas Fairbanks Jr. to Franklin Roosevelt, 22 April 1941, FDRL OF 4269, Fairbanks, Jr., Douglas, 1940–1944; *History of the Office of the Coordinator of Inter-American Affairs,* 82; Fairbanks, *The Salad Days,* 383.

17. Douglas Fairbanks Jr. to Franklin Roosevelt, 12 July 1941, FDRL OF 4269, Fairbanks, Jr., Douglas, 1940–1944; *Motion Picture Herald,* 10 May 1941; *Variety,* 14 May 1941.

18. Fairbanks, *The Salad Days,* 397–404.

19. Steven Watts, *The Magic Kingdom: Walt Disney and the American Way of Life* (Boston: Houghton Mifflin, 1997), 244–245; Walt Disney Productions memorandum, 14 March 1941, FDRL Isidor Lubin Papers, personal correspondence, 1935–1971, b. 93, f. Walt Disney Productions; "The Story of the Motion Picture Society for the Americas," n.d., AMPAS MPSA, Reports.

20. "Latin Film Fare," *Business Week,* 10 January 1942, 20; *Motion Picture Herald,* 25 October 1941; *Variety,* 22 October 1941.

21. *Variety,* 30 April 1941, 25 June 1941.

22. *Variety,* 21 May 1941; Carl Milliken to Chairman, Committee for Reciprocity Information, 10 June 1941, AMPAS MPAA, reel 6.

23. State Department memorandum, 25 June 1941, NARA RG59; Thomas Burke to Borisal, Duggan, Thomson, 3 July 1941, NARA RG59.

24. Justus D. Doenecke and John E. Wilz, *From Isolation to War, 1931–1941,* 2nd ed. (Arlington Heights, Ill.: Harlan Davidson, 1991), 104; Robert Rhodes James, ed., *Winston S. Churchill: His Complete Speeches, 1897–1963* (New York: Bowker, 1974), 6:6360; Doris Kearns Goodwin, *No Ordinary Time: Franklin & Eleanor Roosevelt: The Home Front in World War II* (New York: Touchstone, 1994), 214.

25. *Variety,* 19 February 1941, 12 March 1941; Will Hays to Joseph Kennedy, 6 March 1941, WHP, reel 28; Will Hays to Cordell Hull, 15 March 1941, NARA RG59.

26. State Department memorandum, 26 March 1941, NARA RG59; Will Hays, memorandum, 24 July 1941, FDRL PPF 1944, Hays, Will H., 1934–1941.

27. Will Hays, "Question of Obtaining Full Payment for Distribution of American Motion Pictures in Great Britain," 3 June 1941, NARA RG59; State Department memorandum, 2 April 1941, NARA RG59; *Variety,* 16 July 1941; Cordell Hull to Will Hays, 13 August 1941, AMPAS MPAA, reel 6.

28. *Variety,* 8 January 1941, 24 September 1941; Twentieth Century–Fox Annual Report, 1941, Willkie Papers, f. Twentieth Century–Fox Reports; Ian Jarvie, *Hollywood's Overseas Campaign: The North Atlantic Movie Trade, 1920–1950* (New York: Cambridge University Press, 1992), 190–192. After losing $517,336 in 1940, Twentieth Century–Fox turned a $4,921,926 profit in 1941.

29. *Variety,* 29 October 1941; John Winant to Cordell Hull, 5 December 1941, NARA RG59.

30. *Foreign News Flashes,* 12 February 1941, WSHS, UA Records, Samuel Cohen Papers, b. 8; Nicholas John Cull, *Selling War: The British Propaganda Campaign against American "Neutrality" in World War II* (New York: Oxford University Press, 1995), 107–108, 138–140.

31. *New York Herald-Tribune,* 16 September 1940; *Variety,* 26 March 1941.

32. Michael Korda, *Charmed Lives: A Family Romance* (New York: Random House, 1979), 79–83, 138–139; Cull, *Selling War,* 80–81.

33. Korda, *Charmed Lives,* 140–147; Cull, *Selling War,* 81, 119–120.

34. Darryl F. Zanuck to Stephen Early, 28 April 1941, FDRL OF 3062, Twentieth Century–Fox Film Corporation, 1937–1945; *Motion Picture Herald,* 8 March 1941.

35. Jesse L. Lasky Jr., *Whatever Happened to Hollywood?* (New York: Funk & Wagnalls, 1975), 225–230; Thomas Doherty, *Projections of War: Hollywood, American Culture, and World War II,* rev. ed. (New York: Columbia University Press, 1993), 197.

36. Scott Eyman, *Print the Legend: The Life and Times of John Ford* (New York: Simon & Schuster, 1999), 251–277; Dan Ford, *Pappy: The Life of John Ford* (Englewood Cliffs, N.J.: Prentice-Hall, 1979), 151–152, 163.

37. W. S. Van Dyke to FDR, 27 May 1941, PPF 6474, Van Dyke II, W. S.; *Variety,* 4 June 1941.

38. *Milwaukee Sentinel,* 11 July 1941.

39. "Rogue Male" treatment, 13 June 1940, UCLA ASC, *Man Hunt.*

40. Julian Johnson to Darryl F. Zanuck, 20 June 1940, USC Fox, *Man Hunt;* Sam Hellman to Darryl F. Zanuck, 26 July 1940, USC Fox, *Man Hunt;* Conference notes, 4 February 1941, USC Fox, *Man Hunt.*

41. Joseph Breen to Will Hays, 4 March 1941, 11 March 1941, PCA file, *Man Hunt;* Will Hays to Joseph Breen, 6 March 1941, PCA file, *Man Hunt.*

42. Adolf Hitler, *Mein Kampf* (1925; reprint, New York: Houghton Mifflin, 1943), 654 (italics in original).

43. Wayne S. Cole, *America First: The Battle against Intervention, 1940–1941* (1953; reprint, New York: Octagon, 1971), 85; Albert Maltz Oral History, UCLA DSC.

44. *The Gallup Poll: Public Opinion, 1935–1971,* vol. 1, *1935–1948* (New York: Random House, 1972), 288, 299; Gerald P. Nye, "This Is Our Critical Hour," reprinted in *Vital Speeches of the Day* 7 (15 May 1941): 453; Burton K. Wheeler, "America Beware!" *Scribner's Commentator* 10 (June 1941): 89–91.

Chapter Eighteen: Marching to War

1. Espinosa to Hal Wallis, 30 June 1941, WBA, *Sgt. York;* 1942 *Film Daily Year Book,* 724–725; Jesse L. Lasky, *I Blow My Own Horn* (Garden City, N.Y.: Doubleday, 1957), 260–261. For a more complete analysis of *Sergeant York* and of York's actions on behalf of interventionist causes, see Michael Birdwell, *Celluloid Soldiers: The Warner Bros. Campaign against Nazism* (New York: New York University Press, 1999), 117–153.

2. Espinosa to Hal Wallis, 30 June 1941, WBA, *Sgt. York;* 1942 *Film Daily Year Book,* 724.

3. "The Private Life of a Motion Picture," WBA, *Sgt. York;* John J. Pershing to Gary Cooper, 4 February 1941, WBA, *Sgt York;* Cordell Hull to Gary Cooper, 4 February 1941, WBA, *Sgt. York;* R. J. Obringer to Jesse Lasky, 14 February 1941, WBA, *Sgt. York;* Press book, WBA, *Sgt. York;* Todd McCarthy, *Howard Hawks: The Grey Fox of Hollywood* (New York: Grove, 1997), 316.

4. *PM,* 3 July 1941.

5. Birdwell, *Celluloid Soldiers,* 128.

6. Philip T. Hartung, "American House of York," *Commonweal* 34 (18 July 1941): 306.

7. *New York Herald-Tribune*, 3 July 1941; Norman Vincent Peale to Jack Warner, 2 July 1941, WBA, *Sgt. York.*

8. "Who Is Behind Lindbergh?" *New Republic*, 5 May 1941, 620; *Variety*, 19 March 1941; Charles Lindbergh, "Election Promises Should Be Kept," reprinted in *Vital Speeches of the Day* 7 (1 June 1941): 482–483.

9. *Variety*, 2 April 1941, 23 April 1941.

10. Burton Wheeler to "Dear Friend" [Willkie] [1941], Willkie Papers, f. Burton K. Wheeler; *Variety*, 7 May 1941, 14 May 1941.

11. Will H. Hays, "Motion Pictures and Total Defense, MPPDA Annual Report, 31 March 1941," 6; *Motion Picture Herald*, 26 July 1941; *New York Times*, 21 July 1941, 3 August 1941.

12. Darryl F. Zanuck to Stephen Early, 5 May 1941, FDRL, Papers of Stephen T. Early, b. 22, f. Z—Miscellaneous.

13. Samuel Goldwyn to Walter Wanger, 14 February 1941, WWP, b. 9, f. 5; Darryl F. Zanuck to Stephen Early, 28 April 1941, FDRL OF 3062, Twentieth Century–Fox Film Corporation, 1937–1945; Sol Lesser to Walter Wanger, 18 July 1941, WWP, b. 11, f. 16; *Motion Picture Herald*, 26 July 1941, 6 December 1941; "It's Fun to Be Free" program [1941], WSHS, Charles MacArthur Papers, b. 3, f. 5.

14. *New York Times*, 14 February 1941; Minutes of AMPAS Board of Governors Meeting, 4 April 1941, WWP, b. 1, f. 10; Darryl F. Zanuck to AMPAS Board of Governors, 28 July 1941, WWP, b. 1, f. 10; Walter Wanger to Victor Morrison, 16 June 1941, WWP, b. 31, f. 3; Arch Mercey to Walter Wanger, 29 January 1941, WWP, b. 31, f. 3.

15. George C. Marshall to Walter Wanger, 24 February 1941, WWP, b. 12, f. 15; Walter Wanger to George C. Marshall, 4 March 1941, WWP, b. 12, f. 15; Lowell Mellett to Walter Wanger, 17 March 1941, WWP, b. 12, f. 15.

16. Peter Odegard to Ferdinand Kuhn, memorandum, 14 July 1941, FDRL Peter Odegard Papers, b. 17, f. Motion Pictures.

17. Walter Wanger to Mendel Silberberg, 23 July 1941, WWP, b. 22, f. 4.

18. Harry Warner to Franklin Roosevelt, 23 July 1941, FDRL PPF 1050, Warner Brothers Motion Picture Company; Stephen Early to Harry Warner, 30 July 1941, FDRL PPF 1050, Warner Brothers Motion Picture Company.

19. Walter Wanger to Mendel Silberberg, 23 July 1941, WWP, b. 22, f. 4; Darryl Zanuck to Wendell Willkie, 7 May 1941, Willkie Papers, f. Darryl Zanuck, 1941–1942; Darryl Zanuck to Wendell Willkie, 23 July 1941, Willkie Papers, f. Darryl Zanuck, 1941–1942.

20. R. M. Griffith to Melvyn Douglas, 11 July 1941, Douglas Papers, b. 11, f. 5; Wendell Willkie to Harry Warner, 6 August 1941, Willkie Papers, f. Warn—Werq; "Senate Isolationists Run Afoul of Willkie in Movie 'Warmonger' Hearings," *Life,* 22 September 1941, 45; Harry Warner to Wendell Willkie, 29 July 1941, Willkie Papers f. Warn—Werq.

21. Nancy Snow, "Confessions of a Hollywood Propagandist: Harry Warner, FDR and Celluloid Persuasion," in Martin Kaplan and Johanna Blakley, eds., *Warners' War: Politics, Pop Culture & Propaganda in Wartime Hollywood* (Los Angeles: Norman Lear Center Press, 2004), 68; John R. Ellingston to Wendell Willkie, 9 August 1941, Willkie Papers, f. Darryl Zanuck, 1941–1942; Darryl Zanuck to Wendell Willkie, 31 July 1941, Willkie Papers, f. Darryl Zanuck, 1941–1942.

22. Steve Neal, *Dark Horse: A Biography of Wendell Willkie* (Lawrence: University Press of Kansas, 1989), 52, 174, 8–13, 27–30.

23. Ibid., 159–160, 124; Direlle Chaney to Will Hays, 5 September 1940, WHP, reel 26; Will Hays to Roy Howard, 24 May 1941, WHP, reel 28.

24. Neal, *Dark Horse,* 182–212, 210–211.

Chapter Nineteen: Hollywood Triumphant

1. Gerald P. Nye, "Our Madness Increases as Our Emergency Shrinks," reprinted in *Vital Speeches of the Day* 7 (15 September 1941): 720–723.

2. John E. Moser, " 'Gigantic Engines of Propaganda': The 1941 Senate Investigation of Hollywood," *Historian* 63 (summer 2001): 740.

3. *Motion Picture Herald,* 2 August 1941.

4. *Motion Picture Herald,* 9 August 1941; Jesse Lasky to Jack Warner, 1 August 1941, WBA, *Sgt. York.*

5. Carl Milliken to Chairman, Committee for Reciprocity Information, 10 June 1941, MPAA, reel 6; *Variety,* 16 April 1941; Otto Friedrich, *City of Nets: A Portrait of Hollywood in the 1940's* (New York: Harper & Row, 1986), 61–68.

6. Harry Cohn to Will Hays, 4 August 1941, WHP, reel 29.

7. Moser, " 'Gigantic Engines of Propaganda,' " 739; Frank McNaughton to David Hulburd, September 1941, McNaughton Papers.

8. Moser, " 'Gigantic Engines of Propaganda,' " 740; Hubert Kay, "Burton K. Wheeler," *Life,* 19 May 1941, 110, 114; Frank McNaughton to David Hulburd, September 1941, McNaughton Papers.

9. Harry Warner to Will Hays, 6 August 1941, WHP, reel 29; "An Open Letter to Franklin D. Roosevelt," 2 August 1941, WWP, b. 36, f. 20; *Variety,* 13 August 1941.

10. Moser, "'Gigantic Engines of Propaganda,'" 741; *Boxoffice,* 9 August 1941; *Chicago Tribune,* 13 August 1941; *Variety,* 20 August 1941.

11. Richard Gutstadt to Will Hays, 14 August 1941, WHP, reel 28; Will Hays, "Memorandum re: telephone conversation," 27 August 1941, WHP, reel 29.

12. Telephone message for Mr. Hays from Mr. Keough, 27 August 1941, WHP, reel 29; Lowell Mellett to FDR, 27 August 1941, FDRL OF 73, Motion Pictures. Wanger did not testify at the hearings.

13. Moser, "'Gigantic Engines of Propaganda,'" 741–742; Darryl F. Zanuck to Stephen Early, 28 November 1941, FDRL, Papers of Stephen T. Early, b. 22, f. Z—Miscellaneous; *Variety,* 3 September 1941; Will Hays, telephone conversation with Keough, 30 August 1941, WHP, reel 29; Frederick Herron to Will Hays, 3 September 1941, WHP, reel 29.

14. *Salem (OR) Capital-Journal,* 4 September 1941; *Buffalo Courier Express,* 5 September 1941.

15. Wendell Willkie to D. Worth Clark, 8 September 1941, AMPAS, 1941 War Film Hearings, f. 52, Wendell L. Willkie Statements.

16. *Variety,* 10 September 1941, 17 September 1941; "Senate Isolationists Run Afoul of Willkie in Movie 'Warmonger' Hearings," *Life,* 22 September 1941, 22.

17. "Senate Isolationists Run Afoul of Willkie in Movie 'Warmonger' Hearings," 21–22.

18. James E. McMillan, "McFarland and the Movies: The 1941 Senate Motion Picture Hearings," *Journal of Arizona History* 29 (autumn 1988): 277–279; Frank McNaughton to David Hulburd, 11 September 1941, McNaughton Papers.

19. Frank McNaughton to David Hulburd, 12 September 1941, McNaughton Papers.

20. *Variety,* 10 September 1941; Will Hays to George Keim, 13 September 1941, WHP, reel 29.

21. *Hearings before a Subcommittee of the Committee on Interstate Commerce, United States Senate, 78th Congress, 1st Session, on S. Res. 152* (Washington, D.C.: Government Printing Office, 1942), 3–5, 24.

22. Ibid., 7, 17.

23. Ibid., 6; Wendell Willkie Press Release, 10 September 1941, AMPAS, 1941 War Film Hearings, f. 52, Wendell L. Willkie Statements.

24. *Hearings,* 42–43.

25. Ibid., 59–60.

26. Frank McNaughton to David Hulburd, 12 September 1941, McNaughton Papers.

27. *Hearings,* 68, 71.

28. Ibid., 81.

29. Ibid., 87.

30. *New York Post,* 11 September 1941; *New York Times,* 10 September 1941; *Tallahassee Democrat,* 11 September 1941.

31. *Hearings,* 105.

32. Ibid., 133.

33. Wendell Willkie press release, 15 September 1941, AMPAS, 1941 War Film Hearings, f. 52, Wendell L. Willkie Statements. For the MPPDA's original response to Fidler's charges, see Walter Trumball to Will Hays, 26 September 1938, MPAA, reel 5.

34. The Fidler dossier can be found on MPAA, reel 6.

35. Lindbergh speech, reprinted in Randy Roberts and David Welky, *Charles A. Lindbergh: The Power and Peril of Celebrity, 1927–1941* (Maplecrest, N.Y.: Brandywine Press, 2003), 158–163; "Lindbergh's Nazi Pattern," *New Republic,* 22 September 1941, 360; "Lindbergh Raises a Storm," *Scholastic* 39 (6 October 1941): 5.

36. Moser, " 'Gigantic Engines of Propaganda,' " 746; Frank McNaughton to David Hulburd, 18 September 1941, McNaughton Papers.

37. *Hearings,* 221, 240; Frank McNaughton to David Hulburd, 25 September 1941, McNaughton Papers.

38. Frank McNaughton to David Hulburd, 25 September 1941, McNaughton Papers; *Hearings,* 339.

39. *Hearings,* 372.

40. *Variety,* 24 September 1941; *Milwaukee Journal,* 17 September 1941; Moser, " 'Gigantic Engines of Propaganda,' " 747.

41. *Hearings,* 421; Frank McNaughton to David Hulburd, 26 September 1941, McNaughton Papers.

42. *Hearings,* 423; Frank McNaughton to David Hulburd, 26 September 1941, McNaughton Papers.

43. *Hearings,* 429.

44. *Variety,* 17 September 1941, 8 October 1941, 22 October 1941.

45. *Variety,* 1 October 1941, 8 October 1941; *Life,* 13 October 1941, 61.

46. Melvyn Douglas speech, 14 November 1941, Douglas Papers, b. 10, f. 5; Melvyn Douglas speech, 26 October 1941, Douglas Papers, b. 10, f. 5; Harry Busey to Melvyn Douglas, Douglas Papers, b. 11, f. 6; Mrs. Howard W. Jannette to Melvyn Douglas, 15 November 1941, Douglas Papers, b. 11, f. 6.

47. Donald Robinson to Melvyn Douglas, 3 December 1941, Douglas Papers, b. 11, f. 7.

48. Jack Warner to Franklin Roosevelt, 30 September 1941, FDRL PPF 1050, Warner Brothers Motion Picture Company.

1. *Boxoffice,* 11 October 1941; Mendel Silberberg to Wendell Willkie, 15 October 1941, Willkie Papers, f. Sil.

2. *Hollywood Reporter,* 3 February 1941; Darryl F. Zanuck to Stephen Early, 5 November 1941, 28 November 1941, 10 January 1942, FDRL, Papers of Stephen T. Early, b. 22, f. Z—Miscellaneous.

3. *Hollywood Reporter,* 3 February 1942.

4. Warners paid future *Scientology* author L. Ron Hubbard $250 for the rights to the title. Hubbard had published an unrelated piece named "The Dive Bomber" in the July 1937 edition of *Five Novels Monthly* magazine.

5. Contract, 30 April 1941, WBA, *Dive Bomber;* Walter MacEwen to Jack Warner, 30 December 1940, WBA, *Dive Bomber;* T. C. Wright to Hal Wallis, 5 March 1941, WBA, *Dive Bomber.*

6. Robert Lord to Hal Wallis, 24 April 1941, WBA, *Dive Bomber;* A. J. Hepburn to Robert Lord, 8 July 1941, WBA, *Dive Bomber;* Al Alleborn to T. C. Wright, 1 April 1941, WBA, *Dive Bomber;* Production notes—"Dive Bomber" [1941], WBA, *Dive Bomber.*

7. Production notes—"Dive Bomber" [1941], WBA, *Dive Bomber.*

8. Philip T. Hartung, "Go to the Movies and See the World," *Commonweal* 34 (12 September 1941): 497; cost and income comparison (see n. 6 of chap. 11 on p. 372 above); *Dive Bomber* press book, WBA, *Dive Bomber.*

9. *Los Angeles Evening Herald and Express,* 13 August 1941; *Los Angeles Daily News,* 14 August 1941; *Los Angeles Examiner,* 13 August 1941.

10. *Hollywood Citizen-News,* 31 October 1941.

11. Darryl F. Zanuck to the Air Ministry, 16 January 1941, UCLA ASC, *A Yank in the R.A.F.*

12. *New York Times,* 8 June 1941.

13. "The New Pictures," *Time,* 13 October 1941, 94.

14. *Variety,* 27 August 1941.

15. *Variety,* 24 September 1941; *New York Times,* 8 June 1941; *Motion Picture Herald,* 25 October 1941.

16. *History of the Office of the Coordinator of Inter-American Affairs* (Washington, D.C.: Government Printing Office, 1947), 77–79.

17. *New York Times,* 14 December 1941.

18. *Motion Picture Herald,* 8 November 1941, 15 November 1941.

19. David Ogilvy to George Schaefer, 25 August 1941, WHP, reel 29.

20. Scott Eyman, *Lion of Hollywood: The Life and Legend of Louis B. Mayer* (New York: Simon & Schuster, 2005), 344; Jan Herman, *A Talent for Trouble:*

The Life of Hollywood's Most Acclaimed Director, William Wyler (New York: G. P. Putnam's Sons, 1995), 234.

21. A. Scott Berg, *Goldwyn: A Biography* (New York: Knopf, 1989), 364.

Conclusion

1. Cass Warner Sperling and Cork Millner, *Hollywood Be Thy Name: The Warner Brothers Story* (Rocklin, Calif.: Prima, 1994), 239–240.

2. Otto Friedrich, *City of Nets: A Portrait of Hollywood in the 1940's* (New York: Harper & Row, 1986), 102; *Variety,* 10 December 1941; *Motion Picture Herald,* 13 December 1941.

3. *Motion Picture Herald,* 13 December 1941, 20 December 1941; *Variety,* 10 December 1941, 17 December 1941; *1942 Film Daily Year Book,* 33, 79, 684.

4. *New York Times,* 10 December 1941; *Variety,* 17 December 1941; *1942 Film Daily Year Book,* 89; Henry Fonda, *Fonda: My Life* (New York: New American Library, 1981), 136.

5. *Motion Picture Herald,* 13 December 1941, 20 December 1941.

6. *Hollywood Reporter,* 3 February 1942; *Variety,* 7 January 1942.

7. For a good starting point on European Jews during the war see Martin Gilbert, *Auschwitz and the Allies: A Devastating Account of How the Allies Responded to the News of Hitler's Mass Murder* (New York: Owl, 1990).

8. Clayton R. Koppes and Gregory D. Black, *Hollywood Goes to War: How Politics, Profits, and Propaganda Shaped World War II Movies* (Berkeley: University of California Press, 1987), 56–70; *Variety,* 24 December 1941.

9. *New York Times,* 18 December 1941; Thomas Doherty, *Projections of War: Hollywood, American Culture, and World War II* (New York: Columbia University Press, 1993), 79–82.

10. Gaizka S. de Usabel, *The High Noon of American Films in Latin America* (Ann Arbor, Mich.: UMI Research Press, 1982), 153–164; *New York Times,* 29 November 1945.

11. De Usabel, *The High Noon of American Films in Latin America,* 154, 166–175.

12. John Trumpbour, *Selling Hollywood to the World: U.S. and European Struggles for Mastery of the Global Film Industry, 1920–1950* (Cambridge, U.K.: Cambridge University Press, 2002), 187–196. Under the terms of the 1948 agreement, American studios were allowed to export $17 million plus the total profits accumulated by British-made features in the United States.

13. Trumpbour, *Selling Hollywood to the World,* 94–114.

14. Friedrich, *City of Nets*, 111; Thomas Schatz, *The Genius of the System: Hollywood Filmmaking in the Studio Era* (New York: Henry Holt, 1988), 299–300, 318.

15. Robert Sklar, *Movie-Made America: A Cultural History of American Movies,* rev. ed. (New York: Vintage, 1994), 272–274.

16. See, for example, Larry Ceplair and Steven Englund, *The Inquisition in Hollywood: Politics and the Film Community, 1930–1960* (New York: Doubleday, 1980); Bernard F. Dick, *Radical Innocence: A Critical Study of the Hollywood Ten* (Lexington: University Press of Kentucky, 1989); Patrick McGilligan and Paul Buhle, *Tender Comrades: A Backstory of the Hollywood Blacklist* (New York: St. Martin's, 1997); Victor Navasky, *Naming Names* (New York: Viking, 1980).

17. Sperling and Millner, *Hollywood Be Thy Name,* 275, 277; Neal Gabler, *An Empire of Their Own: How the Jews Invented Hollywood* (New York: Anchor, 1988), 372–373.

18. George F. Custen, *Twentieth Century's Fox: Darryl F. Zanuck and the Culture of Hollywood* (New York: Basic, 1997), 315.

19. J. Hoberman, "Laugh, Cry, Believe: Spielbergization and Its Discontents," *Virginia Quarterly Review* 83 (winter 2007): 119–121. For a sense of the outrage caused by *300* see "U.S. Accused of Cultural Warfare," *Ottawa Citizen,* 14 March 2007.

T HE LITERATURE ON Hollywood is vast, as is the literature on the early
years of World War II. It would take more than a lifetime to exhaust
one field, much less two. My aim here, therefore, is not to provide a comprehensive survey of the available primary and secondary sources but rather to
point the reader toward those books, articles, and documents that I found
most useful and to suggest gaps in historical scholarship that remain to be
filled.

Primary Sources

Anyone interested in Hollywood during the late 1930s and early 1940s will
quickly discover an abundance of printed and archival primary sources.
Some are extraordinarily useful, others contain frustrating gaps, and still
others have been inexplicably overlooked. The best news for researchers of
this period is that the movies themselves are more accessible than at any time
since their original screenings. Turner Classic Movies shows many of the
pictures I have discussed here. Some, such as *The Great Dictator* or *Sergeant
York,* appear on the channel every few months. Various companies are also
releasing features from this era on DVDs of varying quality. A handful of
films I viewed are available only in VHS format. With a very few exceptions,
almost none of the movies considered here is more than a few clicks of the
mouse away.

Contemporary reviews provide an understanding of how audiences perceived these films in the pre–Pearl Harbor era. Many publications printed
film reviews, but the most perceptive ones often appeared in *Christian Century, Commonweal, Nation, New Republic,* and the *New York Times.*
Trade journals such as *Hollywood Reporter, Motion Picture Herald,* and
Variety also carried reviews. Along with *Film Daily Year Book,* these publications provide essential windows into Hollywood's mind-set during this

tumultuous moment. While generally reflecting the interests of industry executives, their extensive coverage of overseas and domestic developments related to the film business reveals Hollywood's concerns, perspectives, and priorities.

The industry's inner workings are more difficult to uncover than its public positions. Studio heads, actors, and technicians rarely wrote the informative, introspective letters historians love to peruse. Louis B. Mayer's wife famously ordered her husband's correspondence destroyed after he died because she thought his rudimentary writing skills undercut his image as a corporate titan. The moguls' more impersonal correspondence, in the form of studio memos, has survived. Records from motion-picture studios are highly uneven. Some are nearly comprehensive; others are nearly nonexistent. The most complete set of records resides in the Warner Bros. Archives in Los Angeles. The Wisconsin State Historical Society holds a voluminous set of material from United Artists, as well as the papers of Walter Wanger and many screenwriters, particularly those later caught up in the Hollywood blacklist. The University of Southern California's Cinematic Arts Library contains some Warner Bros. material, including Harry Warner's compilation of anti-Semitic propaganda, as well as scripts and treatments from Twentieth Century–Fox, much of which bears evidence of Darryl F. Zanuck's thorough editing. The Department of Special Collections at the University of California, Los Angeles, Charles E. Young Research Library, contains scripts and a large assortment of oral histories. The Margaret Herrick Library of the Academy of Motion Picture Arts and Sciences also holds a wealth of oral histories, along with the files of the Production Code Administration, Hollywood's self-censorship agency. The library's Motion Picture Association of America collection includes valuable records that date back to that organization's days as the Motion Picture Producers and Distributors of America.

Will Hays's extensive correspondence has been sadly underused. Indiana University's Lilly Library holds the originals, but almost all of Hays's papers are available in microfilm format through interlibrary loan. These documents offer a relatively complete picture of one of the most important figures in Golden Era Hollywood and would provide some enterprising historian with the foundation of a much-needed biography of the MPPDA head. Also underused, but for more understandable reasons, are Frank McNaughton's Papers in the Harry S. Truman presidential library. A Washington correspondent for *Time* magazine, McNaughton wrote insightful background reports on backstage affairs in the capital. Most useful for my needs, he witnessed the 1941 Senate propaganda hearings and wrote brutally honest dispatches for *Time*'s writers to dilute and condense when composing their own brief digests of the event.

The federal government's ties to Hollywood constitute an integral element of this study. A few locations are essential to anyone interested in this subject. Franklin Roosevelt's presidential library in Hyde Park, New York, includes an array of correspondence with or about Hollywood figures. Besides the president's own files, the Harry Hopkins Papers and Stephen T. Early Papers are particularly worthwhile. Hays, Zanuck, Fairbanks, and the Warner brothers frequently corresponded with the White House. The Cordell Hull Papers and Robert Jackson Papers in the Library of Congress also included a few gems. The National Archives' State Department and Commerce Department collections hold a wealth of material on Hollywood's global activities and are a must for any researcher. That facility's Justice Department collection is key to understanding the intricacies of the 1938 antitrust suit.

Several printed primary sources enhanced my understanding of this period. Rudy Behlmer's *Inside Warner Bros. (1935–1951)* (New York: Simon & Schuster, 1985) and *Memo from Darryl F. Zanuck: The Golden Years at Twentieth Century–Fox* (New York: Grove, 1993) contain reprints of internal studio correspondence. Documents in David Culbert, ed., *Film and Propaganda in America: A Documentary History*, vol. 2, *World War II* (Westport, Conn.: Greenwood, 1990) explore, among other things, Darryl F. Zanuck's training-film program. Patrick McGilligan, ed., *Backstory: Interviews with Screenwriters of Hollywood's Golden Age* (Berkeley: University of California Press, 1986); and Patrick McGilligan and Paul Buhle, eds., *Tender Comrades: A Backstory of the Hollywood Blacklist* (New York: St. Martin's, 1997) flesh out the behind-the-scenes figures who wrote the movies, with an emphasis on the industry's leading radicals. The Federal Bureau of Investigation closely monitored these figures. Its files on the Hollywood Anti-Nazi League appear on the agency's Freedom of Information Act Web site, at http://foia.fbi.gov/foiaindex/hollywoodleague.htm.

Historians should always approach Hollywood memoirs, a subgenre more laden with inaccuracies and self-serving anecdotes than typical autobiographies, cautiously. With that caveat in mind, I found that the following titles contain insights that illuminate this moment in Hollywood's history: Charles Chaplin, *My Autobiography* (New York: Simon & Schuster, 1964); Melvyn Douglas and Tom Arthur, *See You at the Movies: The Autobiography of Melvyn Douglas* (Lanham, Md.: University Press of America, 1986); Philip Dunne, *Take Two: A Life in Movies and Politics* (New York: Limelight, 1992); Douglas Fairbanks Jr., *The Salad Days* (New York: Doubleday, 1988); Will Hays, *The Memoirs of Will H. Hays* (Garden City, N.Y.: Doubleday, 1955); John Huston, *An Open Book* (New York: Knopf, 1980); Jesse L. Lasky, *I Blow My Own Horn* (Garden City, N.Y.: Doubleday, 1957); Jesse L. Lasky Jr., *Whatever Happened to Hollywood?* (New York: Funk & Wagnalls, 1975); David Niven, *Bring on the Empty Horses* (New York: Dell, 1975); Edward G. Robinson and Leonard Spigelgass, *All My Yesterdays: An Autobiography* (New York: Hawthorn, 1973); Donald Ogden Stewart, *By a Stroke of Luck! An Autobiography* (New York: Paddington, 1975); Hal Wallis and Charles Higham, *Starmaker: The Autobiography of Hal Wallis* (New York: Macmillan, 1975); and Jack L. Warner, *My First Hundred Years in Hollywood* (New York: Random House, 1975).

Secondary Sources

There is no shortage of notable writings on Hollywood in the 1930s and 1940s. A trio of books admirably covers the World War II era while offering relatively brief surveys of the crucial years preceding Pearl Harbor. Bernard F. Dick, *The Star-Spangled Screen: The Hollywood World War II Film* (Lexington: University Press of Kentucky, 1985) is strongest when dealing with the movie industry's response to the Spanish Civil War. Thomas Doherty, *Projections of War: Hollywood, American Culture, and World War II* (New York: Columbia University Press, 1993) includes interesting discussions of Leni Riefenstahl's impact on American filmmakers and of Hollywood's wartime alliance with the United States military. Clayton R. Koppes and Gregory D. Black, *Hollywood Goes to War: How Politics, Profits, and Propaganda Shaped World War II Movies* (Berkeley: University of California Press, 1990) opens with a useful overview of prewar Hollywood. A more focused volume, Michael E. Birdwell's *Celluloid Soldiers: The Warner Bros. Campaign against Nazism* (New York: New York University Press, 1999), scrutinizes a single studio's anti-Nazi activities while concentrating largely on both the real-life and fictional Sergeant Alvin York.

A number of more general works examine Hollywood during this period. The first half of Otto Friedrich's impressionistic yet enthralling *City of Nets: A Portrait of Hollywood in the 1940's* (New York: Harper & Row, 1986) contains much that is valuable to this study, particularly its thorough treatment of Willie Bioff and the Hollywood union scandal. Anyone seeking to understand the mechanics of the studio system should begin with Thomas Schatz, *The Genius of the System* (New York: Pantheon, 1989). A pair of books by Colin Shindler—*Hollywood in Crisis: Cinema and American Society, 1929–1939* (New York: Routledge, 1996); and *Hollywood Goes to War: Films and American Society, 1939–1952* (London: Routledge, 1979) focus almost entirely on movies themselves. Tino Balio, *Grand Design: Hollywood as a Modern Business Enterprise, 1930–1939* (New York: Scribner, 1993) does the opposite, viewing the film business from a primarily financial perspective. Much of Giuliana Muscio's *Hollywood's New Deal* (Philadelphia: Temple University Press, 1997) addresses issues from the early and mid-1930s, but it also contains an excellent examination of the 1938 antitrust case. Saverio Giovacchini, *Hollywood Modernism: Film and Politics in the Age of the New Deal* (Philadelphia: Temple University Press, 2001) studies the efforts of European émigrés and New York liberals to transform Hollywood into a bastion of antifascism. Although venerable, Leo Rosten, *Hollywood: The Movie Colony, the Movie Makers* (1941; reprint, New York: Arno, 1970) offers a fascinating sociological study of the dream factory. Three lengthy *Fortune* magazine profiles are well worth perusing: "Warner Brothers," *Fortune*, December 1937, 110–113+; "The Hays Office," *Fortune*, December 1938, 69–72+; and "Loew's Inc.," *Fortune*, August 1939, 25–30+. For more on the world of screenwriters see Richard Fine, *West of Eden: Writers in Hollywood, 1928–1940* (Washington: Smithsonian Institution Press, 1993). John Russell Taylor, *Strangers in Paradise: The Hollywood Émigrés, 1933–1950* (New York: Holt, Reinhart and Winston, 1983) discusses the struggles European refugees faced in the film capital.

Those seeking reliable biographical information, as opposed to gossipy tell-all books, on the Hollywood moguls will discover the genre's limits far too soon. A paucity of written sources and the rather pedestrian life of a hard-working businessman, even one surrounded by glamour, seems to have deterred most would-be biographers. The starting place for anyone interested in the movie moguls is Neal Gabler, *An Empire of Their Own: How the Jews Invented Hollywood* (New York: Crown, 1988). The revised edition of Bob Thomas, *King Cohn: The Life and Times of Harry Cohn* (Beverly Hills, Calif.: New Millennium Entertainment, 2000) updates the best study of the dictator of Columbia Pictures. A. Scott Berg, *Goldwyn: A Biography* (New York: Knopf, 1989) is another strong biography. Charles Higham's uneven *Merchant of Dreams: Louis B. Mayer, M.G.M., and the Secret Hollywood* (New York: Donald I. Fine, 1993) has been supplanted by Scott Eyman, *Lion of Hollywood: The Life and Legend of Louis B. Mayer* (New York: Simon & Schuster, 2005). Samuel Marx, *Mayer and Thalberg: The Make-Believe Saints* (New York: Random House, 1975) should also be consulted. David Thomson, *Showman: The Life of David O. Selznick* (New York: Knopf, 1992) is a must read, as is Matthew Bernstein, *Walter Wanger: Hollywood Independent* (Berkeley: University of California Press, 1994). Researchers should approach Cass Warner Sperling (Harry Warner's granddaughter) and Cork Millner, *Hollywood Be Thy Name: The Warner Brothers Story* (Rocklin, CA: Prima, 1994) with a measure of skepticism, but approach it nonetheless. Darryl F. Zanuck is the subject of George F. Custen, *Twentieth Century's Fox: Darryl F. Zanuck and the Culture of Hollywood* (New York: Basic Books, 1997); Mel Gussow, *Don't Say Yes until I Finish Talking: A Biography of Darryl F. Zanuck* (Garden City, N.Y.: Doubleday, 1971); and Leonard Mosley, *Zanuck: The Rise and Fall of Hollywood's Last Tycoon* (Boston: Little, Brown, 1984). Mosley draws heavily from Gussow's authorized study, while Custen dwells mostly on the themes Zanuck built into his productions. David Robinson, *Chaplin: His Life and Art* (New York: Da Capo, 1994) contains an excellent section on *The Great Dictator,* as does Charles J. Maland, *Chaplin and American Culture: The Evolution of a Star Image* (Princeton, N.J.: Princeton University Press, 1989). Although it contains practically no information on Wendell Willkie's relationship with Hollywood, Steve Neal's *Dark Horse: A Biography of Wendell Willkie* (Lawrence: University Press of Kansas, 1989) is a solid introduction to one of the central figures in the 1941 Senate propaganda hearings. Thomas Doherty's *Hollywood's Censor: Joseph I. Breen and the Production Code Administration* (New York: Columbia University Press, 2007) is as close to a full biography of that crucial figure as we are likely to get.

Two books heavily influenced my understanding of Hollywood's internal and external politics during these years. Ronald Brownstein, *The Power and the Glitter: The Hollywood-Washington Connection* (New York: Vintage, 1992) is easily the finest book on the subject. His well-researched, well-written work stretches into the 1960s but, for me, was most useful in its discussion of producers' relationship with the conservative administrations of the 1920s. Larry Ceplair and Steven Englund, *The Inquisition in Hollywood: Politics in the Film Community, 1930–1960* (Garden City, N.Y.: Anchor, 1980) is at its best when discussing the role leftists played in the film community and the anticommunist backlash against them.

Several authors have examined Hollywood's overseas affairs, but there is much left to do in this field. John Trumpbour, *Selling Hollywood to the World: U.S. and European Struggles for Mastery of the Global Film Industry, 1920–1950* (Cambridge, U.K.: Cambridge University Press, 2002) includes important chapters on how the State Department and MPPDA eased Hollywood's entrance into foreign markets. Ian Jarvie, *Hollywood's Overseas Campaign: The North Atlantic Movie Trade, 1920–1950* (New York: Cambridge University Press, 1992) explores Hollywood's interaction with Great Britain. Readers should also consult Jarvie's "Dollars and Ideology: Will Hays' Economic Foreign Policy, 1922–1945," *Film History* 2 (1988): 207–221. Nicholas John Cull, *Selling War: The British Propaganda Campaign against American "Neutrality" in World War II* (New York: Oxford University Press, 1995) considers the Hollywood-Britain relationship from an Anglo perspective. Jens Ulff-Møller, *Hollywood's Film Wars with France: Film-Trade Diplomacy and the Emergence of the French Film Quota Policy* (Rochester, N.Y.: University of Rochester Press, 2001) clarifies America's financial interest in Europe. Hollywood's involvement in Latin America and Japan during these years remains largely unexplored. Gaizka S. de Usabel, *The High Noon of American Films in Latin America* (Ann Arbor, MI: UMI Research Press, 1982) centers on United Artists and does not claim to offer a comprehensive treatment of the subject. Darlene Rivas, *Missionary Capitalist: Nelson Rockefeller in Venezuela* (Chapel Hill: University of North Carolina Press, 2002) briefly discusses the Office of Inter-American Affairs.

Pre–Pearl Harbor Hollywood makes little sense unless examined within the broader context of global developments. Robert Dallek, *Franklin D. Roosevelt and American Foreign Policy, 1932–1945* (New York: Oxford

University Press, 1979); and Robert A. Divine, *The Reluctant Belligerent: American Entry into World War II* (New York: Wiley, 1979) remain essential texts. Justus D. Doenecke and John E. Wilz, *From Isolation to War, 1931–1941*, 2nd ed. (Arlington Heights, Ill.: Harlan Davidson, 1991) is brief but useful. Richard W. Steele, "The Great Debate: Roosevelt, the Media, and the Coming of the War, 1940–1941," *Journal of American History* 71 (June 1984): 69–92 describes Roosevelt's mastery of the press in the early years of the European war. Steven Casey, *Cautious Crusade: Franklin D. Roosevelt, American Public Opinion, and the War against Nazi Germany* (New York: Oxford University Press, 2001) illuminates the delicate balance between activism and appeasement that the president had to maintain. Wayne S. Cole, *America First: The Battle against Intervention, 1940–1941* (1953; reprint, New York: Octagon Books, 1971) discusses the American anti-interventionist movement. Gerhard Weinberg's magisterial *A World at Arms: A Global History of World War II* (New York: Cambridge University Press, 1994) more than lives up to its ambitious title.

Biographies of Franklin Roosevelt are legion. The ones I found most useful were James MacGregor Burns, *Roosevelt: The Lion and the Fox, 1882–1940* (1956; reprint, New York: Smithmark, 1996); James MacGregor Burns, *Roosevelt, the Soldier of Freedom: 1940–1945* (1970; reprint, New York: Smithmark, 1996); Frank Freidel, *Franklin D. Roosevelt* (Boston: Little, Brown, 1990); and Jean Edward Smith, *FDR* (New York: Random House, 2007).

Several works explore the United States' relationship with Mussolini's Italy. David F. Schmitz, *The United States and Fascist Italy, 1922–1940* (Chapel Hill: University of North Carolina Press, 1988); and David F. Schmitz, *Thank God They're on Our Side: The United States and Right-Wing Dictatorships, 1921–1965* (Chapel Hill: University of North Carolina Press, 1999) emphasize America's long appeasement of the Fascists. John P. Diggins, *Mussolini and Fascism: The View from America* (Princeton, N.J.: Princeton University Press, 1972) uses popular media sources to provide a nuanced, chronological examination of Americans' varying attitudes toward Mussolini's government. James Hay, *Popular Film Culture in Fascist Italy: The Passing of the Rex* (Bloomington: Indiana University Press, 1987) considers Fascist-era movies in some detail. Ray Moseley, *Mussolini's Shadow: The Double Life of Count Galeazzo Ciano* (New Haven, Conn.:

Yale University Press, 1999) explores the life of Mussolini's son-in-law, one of the key characters in the Italian film industry. The literature on the Nazis and Nazism is far too vast to relate here, but Robert Edwin Herzstein, *The War That Hitler Won: Goebbels and the Nazi Media Campaign* (New York: Paragon House, 1987); and Ralf Georg Reuth, *Goebbels* (New York: Harcourt Brace, 1993) proved useful for my needs.